THE MUSICIAN'S GUIDE
TO AURAL SKILLS

THE MUSICIAN'S GUIDE TO AURAL SKILLS

Ear-Training

FOURTH EDITION

Joel Phillips
Westminster Choir College of Rider University

Paul Murphy
Muhlenberg College

Elizabeth West Marvin
Eastman School of Music

Jane Piper Clendinning
Florida State University College of Music

W. W. NORTON & COMPANY
Independent Publishers Since 1923

W. W. Norton & Company has been independent since its founding in 1923, when William Warder Norton and Mary D. Herter Norton first published lectures delivered at the People's Institute, the adult education division of New York City's Cooper Union. The firm soon expanded its program beyond the Institute, publishing books by celebrated academics from America and abroad. By midcentury, the two major pillars of Norton's publishing program—trade books and college texts—were firmly established. In the 1950s, the Norton family transferred control of the company to its employees, and today—with a staff of five hundred and hundreds of trade, college, and professional titles published each year—W. W. Norton & Company stands as the largest and oldest publishing house owned wholly by its employees.

Fourth Edition

Editor: Christopher Freitag
Assistant editor: Julie Kocsis
Development editor: Meg Wilhoite
Project editor: Michael Fauver
Managing editor, College: Marian Johnson
Managing editor, College Digital Media: Kim Yi
Copyeditor: Jodi Beder
Proofreader: Debra Nichols
Media editor: Steve Hoge
Media assistant editor: Eleanor Shirocky
Production manager: Stephen Sajdak
Design director: Rubina Yeh
Designer: Marisa Nakasone
Music typesetting and page composition: David Botwinik
Manufacturing: LSC Communications: Menasha

ISBN: 978-0-393-69708-7

W. W. Norton & Company, Inc., 500 Fifth Avenue, New York, NY 10110
www.wwnorton.com

W. W. Norton & Company, Ltd., 15 Carlisle Street, London W1D 3BS

3 4 5 6 7 8 9 0

Contents

Part IV The Twentieth Century and Beyond

Preface

The Musician's Guide series is the most comprehensive set of materials available for learning music theory and aural skills. Comprising a theory text, Workbook, Anthology, and two aural-skills texts, the series features coordinated resources that can be mixed and matched for any theory curriculum.

The Musician's Guide to Aural Skills consists of two volumes—*Ear-Training* and *Sight-Singing*. *Ear-Training* develops listening skills using two activities. Short ***Try it*** dictations focus on pattern recognition, and **Contextual Listening** exercises guide students to discover those patterns when taking dictation from music literature. *Sight-Singing* emphasizes the skills required for real-time performance. It includes strategic, progressive training in melodic- and rhythm-reading, improvisation, composition, and keyboard skills. Both texts feature a wide range of real musical repertoire of diverse origins, including classical, popular, and folk selections. Though the ordering and terminology of these two texts correspond to *The Musician's Guide to Theory and Analysis*, they may be used together, individually, or in conjunction with other theory texts.

The Musician's Guide to Aural Skills: Ear-Training is distinctive in three significant ways. First, no other source offers the hundreds of carefully selected works from a wide array of musical literature in a way that seamlessly corresponds to written skills, sight-singing, and rhythm reading. Second, since the inception of the *Musician's Guide* series, a primary goal has been to present literature from composers whose works are historically underrepresented. The fourth edition's literature significantly expands that gender, ethnic, racial, and geographical diversity with the addition of dozens of works, almost none of which have appeared in any pedagogical forum. Many of those works appear exclusively in *Ear-Training*. Third, our approach to skill acquisition emphasizes meticulous attention to scaffolding and sequencing.

Using This Volume

Ear-Training divides into 40 chapters that align with both *Sight-Singing* and *The Musician's Guide to Theory and Analysis*. Thus, instructors will find it easy to plan for class and to coordinate aural skills with conceptual understanding. All audio examples are available online. Students access audio for all of the examples as well as the Aural Skills InQuizitive activities by going to digital.wwnorton.com/auralskills4et and registering with the code inside their text or included as part of their Total Access.

Each chapter begins with specific learning objectives and key concepts that emphasize listening strategies. ***Try it*** exercises—short, self-led, self-evaluated dictations—reinforce chapter concepts and prepare students to succeed with longer excerpts from the literature.

Answers for all ***Try it*** exercises appear in the Teacher's Edition, and in an appendix of the Student Edition.

The fourth edition of *Ear-Training* improves Contextual Listening activities in three significant ways. First, we added numerous works by a broad range of composers from diverse geographical regions. Many of these appear for the first time in a pedagogical context. Second, each of the hundreds of exercises has been recast to make it more accessible to novice listeners. Initial exercises prepare students to tackle the specific problems presented in the work from literature and the Workspace redesign makes taking dictation much easier and more methodical. Third, the quality of the recordings has been improved, all playback levels normalized, and many new recordings appear, some debuting literature never heard by modern audiences.

Each chapter's Contextual Listening exercises progress from easiest to most challenging. The structure of every exercise guides students through listening in a step-by-step process. Annotated scores and answers to all Contextual Listening examples appear in the Teacher's Edition.

Contextual Listening exercises feature Workspaces, where students work from the outside inward in a strategic process that results in accurate notation of what they hear. Students might begin by notating meter and rhythm on a single staff, to which they then assign solfège syllables or scale-degree numbers. They then map this information onto notes on the staff to complete accurate transcriptions. Targeted analytic questions guide students through the process and deepen conceptual understanding.

Assessing and Assigning Contextual Listening

Contextual Listening assignments develop strategic thinking. The more students practice, the better their skills. To encourage regular practice, many teachers score these exercises holistically (e.g., 2–1–0; good, fair, redo). Students can focus on the main concepts without chasing perfection. Conversely, if time permits, allowing students to redo assignments until they earn the top score is a great way to encourage more practice.

- Because Contextual Listening exercises move from easy to challenging, teachers can match assignment demands to the skill level of each student.

- Consider completing the initial exercises during class to prepare students to finish the Contextual Listening on their own.

- Contextual Listening assignments can make good partner work, particularly if students have complementary skill strengths.

- Especially for longer or more complex works, consider assigning and checking one portion before continuing.

Planning Your Curriculum

The Musician's Guide covers concepts typically taught during the first two years of college instruction in music. We hope that instructors who adopt both the *Theory and Analysis* and *Aural Skills* texts will appreciate the consistent pedagogical approach, terminology, and order of presentation. Because students' aural and practical skills sometimes develop more slowly than their grasp of theoretical concepts, there is no harm done if aural and practical instruction trails slightly behind conceptual understanding. For this reason, we summarize the organization of the volumes and suggest strategies for using them.

Deployed over four or five semesters, these two models coordinate with typical music theory college curricula.

Plan 1 (four semesters, including one semester dealing with musical rudiments)

	Sight-Singing	Ear-Training
Term 1	Chapters 1–10	Chapters 1–10
Term 2	Chapters 11–21	Chapters 11–21
Term 3	Chapters 22–33	Chapters 22–33
Term 4	Chapters 34–40	Chapters 34–40

Alternatively, the following organization is one suggestion for those curricula that offer a dedicated rudiments class in addition to a four-semester core sequence.

Plan 2 (a rudiments class followed by four semesters)

	Sight-Singing	Ear-Training
Rudiments	Chapters 1–8	Chapters 1–8
Term 1	Chapters 9–14	Chapters 9–14 (with review of modes from Chapter 5)
Term 2	Chapters 15–21	Chapters 15–21
Term 3	Chapters 22–33	Chapters 22–33
Term 4	Chapters 34–40	Chapters 34–40

Applying Solfège Syllables and Scale-Degree Numbers

All singing systems have merit, and choosing *some* system is far superior to using none. To reinforce musical patterns, we recommend singing with movable-*do* solfège syllables and/or scale-degree numbers, but we provide a summary explanation of both the movable- and fixed-*do* systems in Chapter 1 to help students get started. (A quick reference for diatonic and chromatic syllables also appears at the front of this volume.) For solfège in modal contexts, we present two systems in Chapter 9, one using syllables derived from major and minor, and one using relative (rotated) syllables.

Applying a Rhythm-Counting System

Many people use some counting system to learn and perform rhythms—in effect, "rhythmic solfège." For example, a rhythm in $\frac{2}{4}$ meter might be vocalized "du de, du ta de ta" (Edwin Gordon system), or "1 and, 2 e and a" (McHose/Tibbs system), or "Ta di Ta ka di mi" (Takadimi system). We leave it to the discretion of each instructor whether to use such a system and which to require.

Our Thanks to . . .

A work of this size and scope is helped along the way by many people. We are especially grateful for the support of our families and our students. Our work together as coauthors has been incredibly rewarding, a collaboration for which we are sincerely thankful.

For subvention of the recordings, we thank James Undercofler (director and dean of the Eastman School of Music), as well as Eastman's Professional Development Committee. For audio engineering, we are grateful to recording engineers John Ebert and John Baker. For audio production work, we thank Glenn West, Christina Lenti, and Lance Peeler, who assisted in the recording sessions. We also thank our colleagues at both Westminster Choir College and the Eastman School of Music who gave of their talents to help make the recordings. The joy of their music making contributed mightily to this project.

We are grateful for the thorough and detailed work of our prepublication reviewers, whose suggestions inspired many improvements, large and small: Erin Perdue Brownfield (East Ascension High School), Tracy Carr (Eastern New Mexico University), David Davies (Texas A&M University-Commerce), Amy Engelsdorfer (Luther College), Stefanie Harger Gardner (Glendale Community College, AZ), William Heinrichs (University of Wisconsin-Milwaukee), Ronald Hemmel (Westminster Choir College), Jennifer Jessen-Foose (Cedar Grove High School), Kimberly Goddard Loeffert (Oklahoma State University), Ryan Messling (Prairie High School), David Parker (Bob Jones University), Brian Parrish (Parkway West High School), Richard Robbins (University of Minnesota Duluth), Jennifer Russell (Northern Arizona University), Janna Saslaw (Loyola University), and Heather Thayer (Henderson State University). For previous editions, reviewers have included Michael Berry (University of Washington), David Castro (St. Olaf College), Melissa Cox (Emory University), Gary Don (University of Wisconsin-Eau Claire), Jeff Donovick (St. Petersburg College), Terry Eder (Plano Senior High School), Jeffrey Gillespie (Butler University), Bruce Hammel (Virginia Commonwealth University), Melissa Hoag (Oakland University), Rebecca Jemian (University of Louisville), Charles Leinberger (University of Texas-El Paso), David Lockart (North Hunterdon High School), Robert Mills (Liberty University), Daniel Musselman (Union University), Kristen Nelson (Stephen F. Austin State University), Shaugn O'Donnell (City College, CUNY), Tim Pack (University of Oregon), Scott Perkins (DePauw University), Ruth Rendleman (Montclair State University), Sarah Sarver (Oklahoma City University), Alexander Tutunov (Southern Oregon University), and Annie Yih (University of California at Santa Barbara).

We are indebted to the staff of W. W. Norton for their commitment to this project and their painstaking care in producing these volumes. Most notable among these are Chris Freitag, who has capably guided this edition with great enthusiasm; Meg Wilhoite, who served as Development Editor; Justin Hoffman, who steered the second and third editions with a steady hand; and Maribeth Anderson Payne, whose vision helped launch the series with great aplomb. Michael Fauver was project editor of the volume, with assistance from copyeditor Jodi Beder and proofreader Debra Nichols. We appreciate the invaluable assistance of media experts Steve Hoge and Eleanor Shirocky. Julie Kocsis was assistant editor, David Botwinik was typesetter, and Stephen Sajdak was production manager.

Joel Phillips, Paul Murphy, Elizabeth West Marvin, and Jane Piper Clendinning

THE MUSICIAN'S GUIDE
TO AURAL SKILLS

PART

I

Elements of Music

CHAPTER 1

Pitch and Pitch Class

NAME _____

In this chapter you'll learn to:

- Use this book and its related materials
- Identify melodic contour and organization
- Identify whole and half steps
- Map pitches to notes, solfège syllables, scale-degree numbers, and letter names
- Use solfège syllables and scale-degree numbers to transpose a melody

Dictation and Pattern Recognition

Taking dictation is the process of listening to music and capturing one or more of its elements by memorizing, performing, analyzing, and notating what you hear. These elements—such as pitch, rhythm, harmony, and form—fall into patterns, so pattern recognition is fundamental to understanding music and improving aural skills.

Contextual Listening

Contextual Listening is dictation based on performances of musical literature.

Choosing Audio Playback Equipment

When listening to the playlist, use high-quality earbuds or headphones or connect your device's audio output to an external amplifier and speakers. The built-in speakers on computers, phones, and tablets are inadequate for the careful listening required of these activities.

Solmization

Several systems may be used to sing pitches or represent patterns. While all systems have their pluses and minuses, it is much better to pick a system and use it than to use none.

Movable Systems

Singing with *movable-do* solfège syllables reinforces musical patterns and helps produce the best vocal tone. Singing with *scale-degree numbers* is analogous to using movable *do*. With these movable systems, the tonic pitch is always called *do* ($\hat{1}$) whether the key is major or minor. All *Musician's Guide* materials emphasize the movable-*do* ($\hat{1}$) system.

Another movable system calls the major-key tonic *do* and the minor-key tonic *la*. To use the *do/la* system with this book, sing at sight with *do/la* syllables and reinforce tonal patterns using scale-degree numbers.

Fixed Systems

In the *fixed-do* system, solfège syllables are associated with specific notes, regardless of the key. The note C is always *do*, the note D is always *re*, and so on. To use fixed *do* with this book, sing at sight with fixed-*do* syllables and reinforce tonal patterns using scale-degree numbers. Singing with letter names is analogous to singing with fixed-*do*.

Mapping Pitches to Notes, Solfège Syllables, Scale Degrees, and Letters

Pitches may be represented as notes on a staff. Pitch classes may be represented as solfège syllables, scale-degree numbers, and letter names. Associating a pitch with a note, syllable, number, or letter is called "mapping." When you sing solfège syllables, sing pure vowels, like those in Spanish or Italian. When you sing numbers, use "*sev*" for scale-degree 7 ($\hat{7}$).

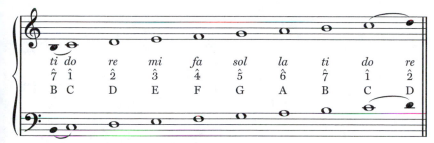

ti	*do*	*re*	*mi*	*fa*	*sol*	*la*	*ti*	*do*	*re*
$\hat{7}$	$\hat{1}$	$\hat{2}$	$\hat{3}$	$\hat{4}$	$\hat{5}$	$\hat{6}$	$\hat{7}$	$\hat{1}$	$\hat{2}$
B	C	D	E	F	G	A	B	C	D

Try it

Try it exercises let you practice skills needed to complete contextual listening.

Contour is melodic shape. Successive pitches repeat, ascend, or descend, creating the simple contours that can be represented as —, ⟋, and ⟍. Longer melodies create contours such as ⌃ or ⌄.

1. Listen to two-pitch patterns and circle the contour (—, ⟋, or ⟍).

   (a) — ⟋ ⟍ (b) — ⟋ ⟍ (c) — ⟋ ⟍

   (d) — ⟋ ⟍ (e) — ⟋ ⟍ (f) — ⟋ ⟍

2. Listen to three-pitch patterns and circle the contour (— —, ⌃, or ⌄).

   (a) — — ⌃ ⌄ (b) — — ⌃ ⌄ (c) — — ⌃ ⌄

   (d) — — ⌃ ⌄ (e) — — ⌃ ⌄ (f) — — ⌃ ⌄

3. Look at the notation and listen to hear half and whole steps (**H** and **W**).

4. Listen to two-pitch patterns. Circle the contour (—, ╱, or ╲) and **S** for same, **H** for half step, or **W** for whole step.

(a) — ╱ ╲ **S H W**   (b) — ╱ ╲ **S H W**   (c) — ╱ ╲ **S H W**

(d) — ╱ ╲ **S H W**   (e) — ╱ ╲ **S H W**   (f) — ╱ ╲ **S H W**

Contextual Listening Strategies

Use these strategies as you work through the Contextual Listening exercises.

- Memorize what you hear as quickly as possible.
- Perform the music in your imagination. Slow it down to figure it out.
- Focus on one element at a time, such as contour or pitch.

Contextual Listening 1.1

Listen to a melody consisting of two five-pitch segments. Then complete the exercises.

1. Pitches 1–3 create which contour? — ⟋ ⟍ ⋀ ⋁

2. Pitches 3–5 create which contour? — ⟋ ⟍ ⋀ ⋁

3. Pitches 6–10 create which contour? — ⟋ ⟍ ⋀ ⋁

4. Use the workspace to capture the melody and analyze its construction.

   (a) Beneath the staff in the blanks provided, begin with the given solfège syllable, scale-degree number, and letter name, and write the remaining syllables, numbers, and letters of the melody.

   (b) The starting pitch is C4. In the staff, draw an appropriate clef and notate the melodic pitches using note *heads* only; don't worry about the rhythm. For help, refer to your solfège syllables, scale-degree numbers, and letter names.

   (c) Below the pitch labels, for each pair of pitches write **S** for same pitch, **H** for half step, or **W** for whole step.

   (d) Play *do* ($\hat{1}$) and sing your answer with solfège, numbers, and letters. After singing each note, check the pitch by playing it on a keyboard.

Solfège:	*do*	__	__ __ __	__ __ __	__	__ __ __	__ __
Numbers:	$\hat{1}$	__	__ __ __	__ __ __	__	__ __ __	__ __
Letters:	C	__	__ __ __	__ __ __	__	__ __ __	__ __
Contour:		__	__	__ __	__	__ __	__ __

5. Use the workspace answers in exercise 4 to transpose the melodic pitches to begin on C3. Draw an appropriate clef and use note heads only—don't worry about the rhythm.

6. Use the workspace answers in exercise 4 to transpose the melodic pitches to begin on F4. Draw an appropriate clef and use note heads only—don't worry about the rhythm. Include any necessary accidental(s).

Contextual Listening 1.2

Listen to a melody consisting of four segments and complete the following exercises.

Segment 1, pitches 1–4

1. Pitches 1–4 create which contour? — ╱ ╲ ⋀ ⋁

2. Between pitches 1–2, which applies? **S** **H** step **W** step

3. Between pitches 2–3, which applies? **S** **H** step **W** step

Segment 2, pitches 5–8

4. Compared with pitches 1–4, pitches 5–8 are: the same   similar   different

Segment 3, pitches 9–11

5. Pitches 9–11 create which contour? — ╱ ╲ ⋀ ⋁

6. Between pitches 9–10, which applies? **S** **H** step **W** step

7. Between pitches 10–11, which applies? **S** **H** step **W** step

Segment 4, pitches 12–14

8. Compared with pitches 9–11, pitches 12–14 are: the same   similar   different

9. Use the workspace to capture the melody and analyze its construction.

   (a) Beneath the staff in the blanks provided, begin with the given solfège syllable, scale-degree number, and letter name, and write the remaining syllables, numbers, and letters of the melody.

   (b) The starting pitch is C4. In the staff, draw an appropriate clef and notate the melodic pitches using note *heads* only; don't worry about the rhythm. For help, refer to your solfège syllables, scale-degree numbers, and letter names.

   (c) Play *do* (1̂) and sing your answer with solfège, numbers, and letters. After singing each note, check the pitch by playing it on a keyboard.

Segment 1	Segment 2	Segment 3	Segment 4

Solfège: __ __ __ __   __ __ __ __   __ __ __   __ __ __

Numbers: __ __ __ __   __ __ __ __   __ __ __   __ __ __

Letters: __ __ __ __   __ __ __ __   __ __ __   __ __ __

10. Use the workspace answers from exercise 9 to transpose the melody to begin on D3. Draw an appropriate clef and notate the melody using note heads only; don't worry about the rhythm. Include any necessary accidental(s).

Segment 1	Segment 2	Segment 3	Segment 4

CHAPTER 2

Simple Meters

NAME _____

In this chapter you'll learn to:

- Identify and notate beats and beat divisions in common simple-meter signatures
- Capture accompanied melodies by mapping solfège syllables, scale-degree numbers, letter names, and pitches
- Notate melodies that begin on a pitch other than tonic
- Notate music that begins with an anacrusis or includes syncopation

Try it

1. Conduct or tap in four while performing the four-beat patterns below. Choose a system of rhythm-counting syllables and sing aloud.

   Now, listen to a four-beat count-off followed by a melody made from two of the patterns. In the blanks provided, write the rhythm-pattern numbers.

   (a) _____   (b) _____   (c) _____   (d) _____

2. Conduct or tap in two while performing the two-beat patterns below. Sing aloud with counting syllables. Note the syncopated rhythms in patterns 7–8.

   Now, listen to a two-beat count-off followed by a melody made from two of the patterns. In the blanks provided, write the rhythm-pattern numbers.

   (a) _____   (b) _____   (c) _____   (d) _____

3. Conduct or tap in three while performing the three-beat patterns below. Sing aloud with counting syllables.

   Now, listen to a three-beat count-off followed by a melody made from two of the patterns. In the blanks provided, write the rhythm-pattern numbers.

   (a) _____   (b) _____   (c) _____   (d) _____

4. Each of the following melodies is preceded by a count-off. In the staff provided, notate the rhythm, being mindful of any syncopations. Include all bar lines. Sing aloud with counting syllables to compare your notation with the original.

♩ **Beat Unit ($\frac{2}{4}$, $\frac{4}{4}$, and $\frac{3}{4}$)**

The first exercise is started for you.

♩ **Beat Unit ($\frac{2}{4}$, $\frac{4}{4}$, and $\frac{3}{4}$) with Anacrusis**

Each of the following exercises begins with an anacrusis.
The first exercise is started for you.

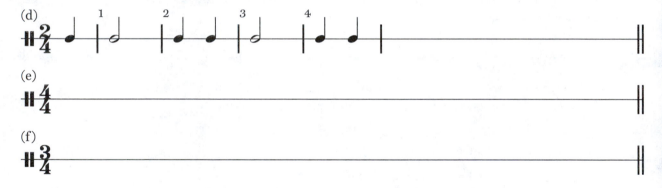

Contextual Listening 2.1

After a two-measure introduction, exercises 1–3 feature a melody that begins on *do*, *mi*, or *sol* (1̂, 3̂, or 5̂) and consists of two rhythm patterns. For each melody:

- Determine the starting pitch and circle it. Hint: Listen to the example and then sing *do* (1̂). Then sing up or down by step until you match pitch 1.

- Write the rhythm-pattern numbers in the blanks.

1. The starting pitch is: *do* (1̂)   *mi* (3̂)   *sol* (5̂)   Rhythm-pattern numbers: _____

2. The starting pitch is: *do* (1̂)   *mi* (3̂)   *sol* (5̂)   Rhythm-pattern numbers: _____

3. The starting pitch is: *do* (1̂)   *mi* (3̂)   *sol* (5̂)   Rhythm-pattern numbers: _____

Now, listen to a two-measure introduction, followed by part of a folk song, and complete the remaining exercises.

4. Use the following workspace to capture the melody.

   (a) In the single-line staff, begin with an eighth note and notate the melody's rhythm. Write an appropriate meter signature, beam notes to show beat grouping, and include all bar lines.

   (b) In the blanks provided beneath the single-line staff, begin with the given letter name and write the remaining solfège, numbers, and letters of the melody.

   (c) The starting pitch is E4. In the five-line staff, draw an appropriate clef and meter signature. Notate the melodic pitches using note heads, incorporating the rhythm from the single-line staff. For help with pitches, refer to your solfège syllables, scale-degree numbers, and letter names.

   (d) Play *do* (1̂) and sing your answer using solfège, numbers, or letters. After singing each note, check the pitch by playing it on a keyboard.

Solfège: __ __ __ __   __ __ __ __   __ __ __ __ __

Numbers: __ __ __ __   __ __ __ __   __ __ __ __ __

Letters: E4   __ __ __   __ __ __   __ __ __ __ __

Contextual Listening 2.2

After a two-measure introduction, exercises 1–3 feature a melody that begins on *do*, *mi*, or *sol* ($\hat{1}$, $\hat{3}$, or $\hat{5}$) and consists of two rhythm patterns. For each melody:

- Determine the starting pitch and circle it. Hint: Listen to the example and then sing *do* ($\hat{1}$). Then sing up or down by step until you match pitch 1.

- Write the rhythm-pattern numbers in the blanks.

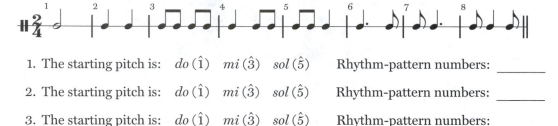

1. The starting pitch is: *do* ($\hat{1}$)   *mi* ($\hat{3}$)   *sol* ($\hat{5}$)   Rhythm-pattern numbers: _____

2. The starting pitch is: *do* ($\hat{1}$)   *mi* ($\hat{3}$)   *sol* ($\hat{5}$)   Rhythm-pattern numbers: _____

3. The starting pitch is: *do* ($\hat{1}$)   *mi* ($\hat{3}$)   *sol* ($\hat{5}$)   Rhythm-pattern numbers: _____

Now, listen to a one-measure count-off followed by a melody from a musical. Then, complete the remaining exercises.

4. Use the following workspace to capture the melody.

   (a) In the single-line staff, begin with an eighth note and notate the melody's rhythm. Write an appropriate meter signature, beam notes to show beat grouping, and include all bar lines.

   (b) In the blanks provided beneath the single-line staff, begin with the given letter name and write the remaining syllables, numbers, and letters of the melody.

   (c) The starting pitch is C3. In the five-line staff, draw an appropriate clef and meter signature. Notate the melodic pitches using note heads and incorporating the rhythm from the single-line staff. For help with pitches, refer to your solfège syllables, scale-degree numbers, and letter names.

   (d) Play *do* ($\hat{1}$) and sing your answer using solfège, numbers, or letters. After singing each note, check the pitch by playing it on a keyboard.

Solfège: __ __ __ __ __   __ __   __ __ __ __ __   __ __

Numbers: __ __ __ __ __   __ __   __ __ __ __ __   __ __

Letters: C3 __ __ __ __   __ __   __ __ __ __ __   __ __

Contextual Listening 2.3

After an introduction, a melody begins on *do*, *mi*, or *sol* ($\hat{1}$, $\hat{3}$, or $\hat{5}$). It consists of two rhythm patterns. For each melody:

- Determine the starting pitch and circle it. Hint: Listen to the example.
  Sing *do* ($\hat{1}$), then sing up or down by step until you match pitch 1.

- Write the rhythm-pattern numbers in the blanks.

1. The starting pitch is: *do* ($\hat{1}$) *mi* ($\hat{3}$) *sol* ($\hat{5}$)   Rhythm-pattern numbers: _____

2. The starting pitch is: *do* ($\hat{1}$) *mi* ($\hat{3}$) *sol* ($\hat{5}$)   Rhythm-pattern numbers: _____

3. The starting pitch is: *do* ($\hat{1}$) *mi* ($\hat{3}$) *sol* ($\hat{5}$)   Rhythm-pattern numbers: _____

Now, listen to a one-measure count-off followed by a melody from a musical.
Then, complete the remaining exercises.

4. Use the following workspace to capture the melody.

   (a) In the single-line staff, begin with an eighth note and notate the melody's rhythm, being mindful of any syncopations. Write an appropriate meter signature, beam notes to show beat grouping, and include all bar lines.

   (b) In the blanks provided beneath the single-line staff, begin with the given letter name and write the remaining syllables, numbers, and letters of the melody.

   (c) The starting pitch is C4. Draw an appropriate clef and meter signature. Notate the melodic pitches using note heads and incorporating the rhythm from the single-line staff. For help with pitches, refer to your solfège syllables, scale-degree numbers, and letter names.

   (d) Play *do* ($\hat{1}$) and sing your answer using solfège, numbers, or letters. After singing each note, check the pitch by playing it on a keyboard.

Solfège: __ __ __ __ __ __   __ __ __ __ __ __ __ __

Numbers: __ __ __ __ __ __   __ __ __ __ __ __ __ __

Letters: C4 __ __ __ __ __   __ __ __ __ __ __ __ __

Pitch Collections, Scales, and Major Keys

CHAPTER 3

NAME _____

In this chapter you'll learn to:

- Recognize common pitch collections of the major scale
- Learn to relate notes, solfège syllables, scale-degree numbers, and letters to major keys
- Notate simple-meter melodies in treble, bass, and alto clefs

Try it

A one-measure count-off precedes a melody that begins on the pitch given. The smallest note value in the melody is an eighth note.

- In the clef, key, and meter given, notate the melody's pitches and rhythm.
- Beam notes to show beat grouping.
- Notate all bar lines, including a double bar at the end.
- *Strategies*:
  - Memorize the melody and replay it in your mind. Slow it down if necessary.
  - Work quickly, writing a one-stroke "tick" for each note head. Fill it in later.
  - Sketch the rhythm beneath the staff.
  - Sing aloud as you write the solfège syllable or scale degree beneath each note in the rhythm sketch.

1. The major pentachord

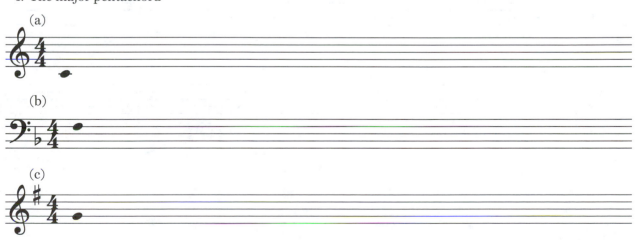

(d)

2. The major scale

(a)

(b)

(c)

(d)

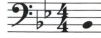

3. The major pentatonic scale

(a)

(b)

(c)

(d)

Contextual Listening 3.1

Listen to an excerpt from a traditional song and complete the exercises.

1. Tap the beat. Listen for strong and weak beats to determine beat grouping.
   Tap the beat division.
   Then, conduct while singing the melody from memory.

2. Circle the number of beats in each measure: 2   3   4

3. Circle the melody's lowest note.

   do (1̂)   *re* (2̂)   *mi* (3̂)   *fa* (4̂)   *sol* (5̂)   *la* (6̂)   *ti* (7̂)   *do* (1̂)

4. Circle the melody's highest note.

   do (1̂)   *re* (2̂)   *mi* (3̂)   *fa* (4̂)   *sol* (5̂)   *la* (6̂)   *ti* (7̂)   *do* (1̂)

5. Together, all melodic pitches complete which pattern?

   major pentachord   major pentachord scale   major scale

6. Use the workspace to capture the excerpt.

   (a) In the single-line rhythm staff, begin with two beamed eighth notes and notate the melody's rhythm. Include the meter signature and bar lines. Beam eighth notes in pairs to show beat grouping.

   (b) Below the rhythm staff and under each note, write the solfège syllables or scale-degree numbers for the melody.

   (c) In the five-line staff, write an appropriate clef, meter signature, and key signature. Begin with C4 and notate both pitches and rhythm.

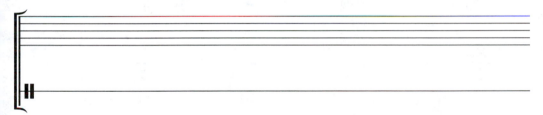

   (d) Play *do* (1̂) and sing the first melodic pitch with its syllable or number. Sing pitch 2, then check it by playing. Continue this way, always singing first, then checking by playing.

Contextual Listening 3.2

Listen to part of a holiday song and complete the exercises.

1. Tap the beat. Listen for strong and weak beats to determine beat grouping.
   Tap the beat division.
   Then, conduct while singing the melody from memory.

2. In which meter types might this melody be notated?
   duple or triple   duple or quadruple   triple or quadruple

3. Sing the last note, *do* (1̂). Then, sing up the scale until you match the first note.
   On which pitch does the melody begin?   *do* (1̂)   *mi* (3̂)   *sol* (5̂)

4. Together, all melodic pitches complete which pattern?
   major pentachord   major pentachord scale   major scale

5. Pitch 6's rhythm is best described as an/a:
   anacrusis   syncopation   dotted note

6. Use the workspace to capture the excerpt.

   (a) In the single-line rhythm staff, begin with two beamed eighth notes and notate
       the melody's rhythm. Include the meter signature and bar lines. Beam eighth
       notes in pairs.

   (b) Below the rhythm staff and under each note, write the solfège syllables or scale-
       degree numbers for the melody.

   (c) In the five-line staff, write an appropriate clef, meter signature, and key signature.
       Begin with G3 and notate both pitches and rhythm.

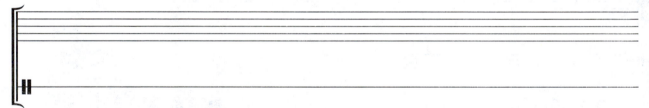

   (d) Sing the melody, then play it on a keyboard.

Contextual Listening 3.3

Listen to part of a folk song and complete the exercises.

1. Tap the beat. Listen for strong and weak beats to determine beat grouping.
   Tap the beat division.
   Then, conduct while singing the melody from memory.

2. Which is the meter type?   duple   triple   quadruple

3. The second beat is the first strong beat. This means the first beat is an/a:
   anacrusis   syncopation   dotted note

4. Circle the melody's lowest note.
   do ($\hat{1}$)   *re* ($\hat{2}$)   *mi* ($\hat{3}$)   *fa* ($\hat{4}$)   *sol* ($\hat{5}$)   *la* ($\hat{6}$)   *ti* ($\hat{7}$)   *do* ($\hat{1}$)

5. Circle the melody's highest note.
   do ($\hat{1}$)   *re* ($\hat{2}$)   *mi* ($\hat{3}$)   *fa* ($\hat{4}$)   *sol* ($\hat{5}$)   *la* ($\hat{6}$)   *ti* ($\hat{7}$)   *do* ($\hat{1}$)

6. Together, all melodic pitches complete which pattern?
   major pentachord   major scale   major pentatonic scale

7. The third-to-last pitch is an/a: anacrusis   syncopation   dotted note

8. Use the workspace to capture the excerpt.

   (a) Assume a quarter-note beat unit. In the single-line rhythm staff, begin with two
       beamed eighth notes and notate the rhythm. Include the meter signature and bar
       lines. Beam eighth notes in pairs.

   (b) Below the rhythm staff and under each note, write the solfège syllables or scale-
       degree numbers for the melody.

   (c) In the five-line staff, write an appropriate clef, meter signature, and key signature.
       Begin with C4 and notate both pitches and rhythm.

   (d) Sing the melody, then play it on a keyboard.

CHAPTER 4

Compound Meters

NAME _____

In this chapter you'll learn to:

- Hear the difference between simple and compound meters
- Identify and notate beats and beat divisions in compound meters
- Capture accompanied melodies by mapping syllables, numbers, letters, and pitches

Try it

1. Conduct or tap in two while performing the four patterns below. Choose a system of rhythm-counting syllables and sing aloud.

2. Listen to a two-beat count-off followed by a melody made from two of the patterns. In the blanks provided, write the rhythm-pattern numbers.

   (a) _____   (b) _____   (c) _____   (d) _____

3. Following a two-beat count-off, each melody begins with the given pitch(es) and rhythm. Notate the remaining rhythm and pitches. Beam three eighths to show beat grouping.

   (a)

   (b)

   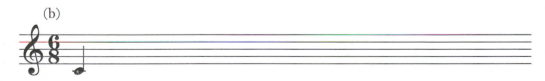

   (c)

(d)

(e)

(f)

Contextual Listening 4.1

Hearing beat divisions and beat grouping in simple and compound meters:

- As you listen to each excerpt, tap the beat with one hand and beat divisions with the other.
  - ○ If beats divide into twos and fours, circle "simple" in the table below.
  - ○ If beats divide into threes, circle "compound."
- Group beats into measures.
  - ○ For groups of two, circle "duple"; for three, "triple"; for four, "quadruple."
- Check each answer by conducting the beat grouping while tapping the beat division.

	Beat Division		Beat Grouping		
1.	simple	compound	duple	triple	quadruple
2.	simple	compound	duple	triple	quadruple
3.	simple	compound	duple	triple	quadruple
4.	simple	compound	duple	triple	quadruple
5.	simple	compound	duple	triple	quadruple
6.	simple	compound	duple	triple	quadruple
7.	simple	compound	duple	triple	quadruple

Contextual Listening 4.2

1. After an introduction, a melody begins on *do*, *mi*, or *sol* ($\hat{1}$, $\hat{3}$, or $\hat{5}$). It consists of two rhythm patterns. Circle the starting pitch and write the rhythm-pattern numbers in the blanks.

   Hint: Sing *do* ($\hat{1}$). Sing up or down by step until you match pitch 1.

   (a) The starting pitch is: *do* ($\hat{1}$)   *mi* ($\hat{3}$)   *sol* ($\hat{5}$)

   Rhythm-pattern numbers: _____

   (b) The starting pitch is: *do* ($\hat{1}$)   *mi* ($\hat{3}$)   *sol* ($\hat{5}$)

   Rhythm-pattern numbers: _____

2. After an introduction, a melody begins with an eighth-note anacrusis. Identify melodic pitches 1-2.

   Hint: Sing *do* ($\hat{1}$). Then sing up or down to match the melodic pitches.

   (a) Melodic pitches 1-2 are:

   do-mi ($\hat{1}$-$\hat{3}$)   *sol-do* ($\hat{5}$-$\hat{1}$)   *mi-sol* ($\hat{3}$-$\hat{5}$)   *sol-mi* ($\hat{5}$-$\hat{3}$)

   (b) Melodic pitches 1-2 are:

   do-mi ($\hat{1}$-$\hat{3}$)   *sol-do* ($\hat{5}$-$\hat{1}$)   *mi-sol* ($\hat{3}$-$\hat{5}$)   *sol-mi* ($\hat{5}$-$\hat{3}$)

Now, listen to a traditional song and complete the remaining exercises.

3. Use the workspace to capture the melodic rhythm and pitches.

   (a) In the single-line staff, begin with an eighth-note anacrusis and notate the melody's rhythm. Write an appropriate meter signature, beam notes to show beat grouping, and include all bar lines.

   (b) In the blanks provided beneath the single-line staff, begin with the given letter name, and write the remaining syllables, numbers, and letters of the melody.

   (c) In the treble staff, write appropriate key and meter signatures. Notate the melodic pitches using note heads. For help with pitches, refer to your solfège syllables, scale-degree numbers, and letter names.

   (d) In the treble staff, incorporate the rhythm from the single-line staff. Draw bar lines from the top of the treble staff to the bottom of the bass staff, aligned with the bar lines in the single-line staff.

   (e) Sing the melody, then play it on a keyboard.

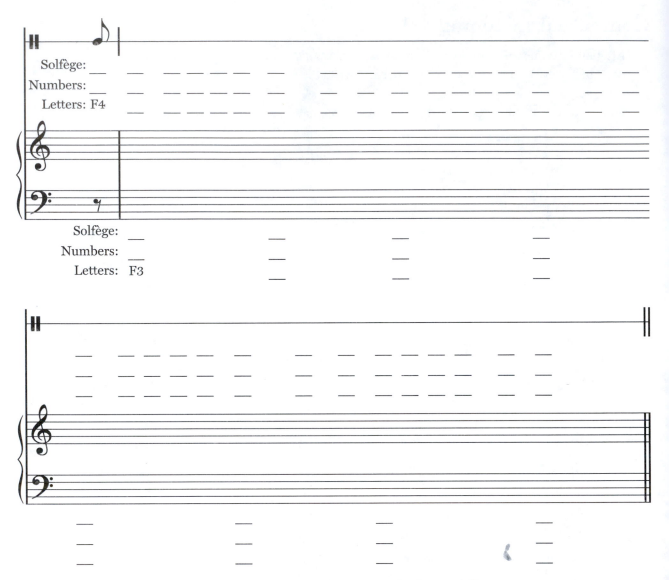

Solfège: __ __ __ __ __ __ __ __ __ __ __ __ __
Numbers: __ __ __ __ __ __ __ __ __ __ __ __ __
Letters: F4 __ __ __ __ __ __ __ __ __ __ __ __

Solfège: __   __   __   __
Numbers: __   __   __   __
Letters: F3   __   __   __

4. Use the workspace in exercise 3 to capture the first bass pitch of every full measure.

   (a) In the blanks provided beneath the bass staff, begin with the given letter name and write the remaining syllables, numbers, and letters of the bass pitches.

   (b) In the bass staff, write appropriate key and meter signatures. Notate the first bass pitch of every measure using note heads only. For help with pitches, refer to your solfège, numbers, and letters.

   (c) Sing the bass line, then play it on a keyboard.

Contextual Listening 4.3

1. After an introduction, a melody begins on *do*, *mi*, or *sol* ($\hat{1}$, $\hat{3}$, or $\hat{5}$). It consists of two rhythm patterns. Circle the starting pitch and indicate the pattern numbers.
   Hint: Sing *do* ($\hat{1}$). Sing up or down by step until you match pitch 1.

   (a) The starting pitch is: *do* ($\hat{1}$)   *mi* ($\hat{3}$)   *sol* ($\hat{5}$)
       Rhythm-pattern numbers: _____

   (b) The starting pitch is: *do* ($\hat{1}$)   *mi* ($\hat{3}$)   *sol* ($\hat{5}$)
       Rhythm-pattern numbers: _____

2. After an introduction, a melody begins with an eighth-note anacrusis. Identify melodic pitches 1–2.
   Hint: Sing *do* ($\hat{1}$). Then sing up or down to match the melodic pitches.

   (a) Melodic pitches 1–2 are:
       do-mi ($\hat{1}$–$\hat{3}$)   *sol-do* ($\hat{5}$–$\hat{1}$)   *mi-sol* ($\hat{3}$–$\hat{5}$)   *sol-mi* ($\hat{5}$–$\hat{3}$)

   (b) Melodic pitches 1–2 are:
       do-mi ($\hat{1}$–$\hat{3}$)   *sol-do* ($\hat{5}$–$\hat{1}$)   *mi-sol* ($\hat{3}$–$\hat{5}$)   *sol-mi* ($\hat{5}$–$\hat{3}$)

Now, listen to a traditional melody and complete the remaining exercises.

3. Use the workspace to capture the melodic rhythm and pitches.

   (a) In the single-line staff, notate the melody's rhythm. Write an appropriate meter signature, beam notes to show beat grouping, and include all bar lines.

   (b) In the blanks provided beneath the single-line staff, begin with the given letter name, and write the remaining syllables, numbers, and letters of the melody. Hint: To identify the pitch after a skip, sing the notes between the first and second note.

   (c) In the treble staff, write appropriate key and meter signatures. Notate the melodic pitches using note heads. For help with pitches, refer to your solfège, numbers, and letters.

   (d) In the treble staff, incorporate the rhythm from the single-line staff. Draw bar lines from the top of the treble staff to the bottom of the bass staff, aligned with the bar lines in the single-line staff.

   (e) Sing the melody, then play it on a keyboard.

Solfège: ___ ___ ___ ___ ___ ___ ___ ___ ___ ___ ___ ___ ___ ___ ___ ___ ___
Numbers: ___ ___ ___ ___ ___ ___ ___ ___ ___ ___ ___ ___ ___ ___ ___ ___ ___
Letters: C5 ___ ___ ___ ___ ___ ___ ___ ___ ___ ___ ___ ___ ___ ___ ___ ___

Solfège: ___ ___ ___ ___ ___ ___
Numbers: ___ ___ ___ ___ ___ ___
Letters: C3 ___ ___ ___ ___ ___

4. Use the workspace in exercise 3 to capture the bass pitches.

   (a) In the blanks provided beneath the bass staff, begin with the given letter name and write the remaining syllables, numbers, and letters of the bass pitches.

   (b) In the bass staff, write appropriate key and meter signatures. Notate the pitches and rhythm of the bass line. For help with pitches, refer to your solfège, numbers, and letters. For the rhythm, assume there are no rests.

   (c) Sing the bass line, then play it on a keyboard.

CHAPTER 5

Minor Keys and the Diatonic Modes

NAME _____

In this chapter you'll learn to:

- Recognize pitch collections in minor keys and the diatonic modes
- Capture accompanied melodies by mapping syllables, numbers, letters, and pitches
- Notate minor and modal melodies in simple and compound meters
- Transpose melodies to different keys and clefs

Try it

Minor Scale Forms and Aeolian Mode

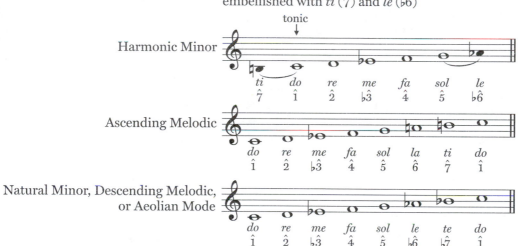

1. A tonic pitch (or modal "final") sounds, followed by silence and then a melody. In the blank, write the pitch-collection name. Then, circle the beat division: simple or compound.

(a) _____   simple   compound

(b) _____   simple   compound

(c) _____   simple   compound

(d) _____   simple   compound

(e) _____   simple   compound

(f) _____   simple   compound

Diatonic Modes

Dorian

| do | re | me | fa | sol | la | te | do |
| $\hat{1}$ | $\hat{2}$ | $\flat\hat{3}$ | $\hat{4}$ | $\hat{5}$ | $\hat{6}$ | $\flat\hat{7}$ | $\hat{1}$ |

Phrygian

| do | ra | me | fa | sol | le | te | do |
| $\hat{1}$ | $\flat\hat{2}$ | $\flat\hat{3}$ | $\hat{4}$ | $\hat{5}$ | $\flat\hat{6}$ | $\flat\hat{7}$ | $\hat{1}$ |

Lydian

| do | re | mi | fi | sol | la | ti | do |
| $\hat{1}$ | $\hat{2}$ | $\hat{3}$ | $\sharp\hat{4}$ | $\hat{5}$ | $\hat{6}$ | $\hat{7}$ | $\hat{1}$ |

Mixolydian

| do | re | mi | fa | sol | la | te | do |
| $\hat{1}$ | $\hat{2}$ | $\hat{3}$ | $\hat{4}$ | $\hat{5}$ | $\hat{6}$ | $\flat\hat{7}$ | $\hat{1}$ |

2. Now, listen to melodies in diatonic modes. Write the pitch-collection name in the blank and circle the beat division.

(a) _____   simple   compound

(b) _____   simple   compound

(c) _____   simple   compound

(d) _____   simple   compound

(e) _____   simple   compound

(f) _____   simple   compound

3. Following a count-off, a melody begins with the given pitch and rhythm. Notate the remaining rhythm and pitches. Beam divisions and subdivisions to show beat grouping and include all bar lines.

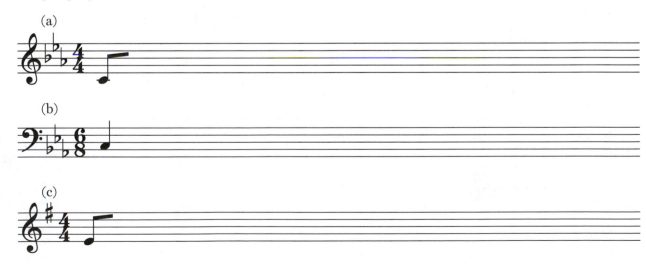

(a)

(b)

(c)

(d)

(e)

(f)

(g)

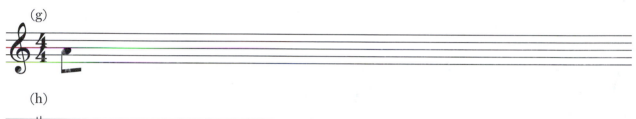

(h)

Contextual Listening 5.1

In exercises 1–4, a two-beat introduction precedes a melody that begins on *do* (1̂). For each exercise, circle the melodic pitches, the beat division, and the best choice of meter signature.

Melodic pitches		*Beat division*		*Meter signature*	

1. *do-re* (1̂-2̂)   *do-me* (1̂-♭3̂)   simple   compound $\frac{2}{4}$ $\frac{6}{8}$
    do-fa (1̂-4̂)   *do-sol* (1̂-5̂)

2. *do-re* (1̂-2̂)   *do-me* (1̂-♭3̂)   simple   compound $\frac{2}{4}$ $\frac{6}{8}$
    do-fa (1̂-4̂)   *do-sol* (1̂-5̂)

3. *do-re* (1̂-2̂)   *do-me* (1̂-♭3̂)   simple   compound $\frac{2}{4}$ $\frac{6}{8}$
    do-fa (1̂-4̂)   *do-sol* (1̂-5̂)

4. *do-re* (1̂-2̂)   *do-me* (1̂-♭3̂)   simple   compound $\frac{2}{4}$ $\frac{6}{8}$
    do-fa (1̂-4̂)   *do-sol* (1̂-5̂)

Now, focus your listening on the melody from a piano work.

5. Use the workspace to capture the melodic rhythm and pitches.

   (a) In the single-line staff, begin with an eighth note and notate the melody's rhythm in two-beat measures. Write an appropriate meter signature, beam notes to show beat grouping, and include all bar lines.

   (b) In the blanks provided beneath the single-line staff, begin with the given letter name and write the syllables, numbers, and letters of the melody.

   (c) In the treble staff, write appropriate key and meter signatures. Notate the melodic pitches using note heads. For help with pitches, refer to your solfège, numbers, and letters.

   (d) In the treble staff, incorporate the rhythm from the single-line staff, aligning the bar lines with those in the single-line staff.

   (e) Sing the melody, then play it on a keyboard.

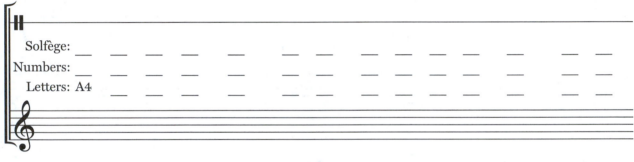

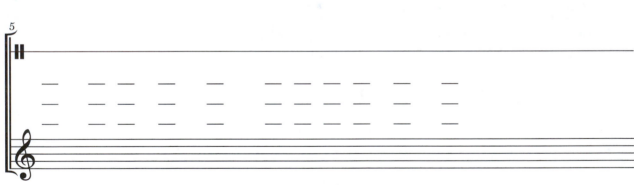

6. Which is the range (lowest pitch to highest pitch) of this melody?

   do-me (î–♭3̂)   *do-fa* (î–4̂)   *do-sol* (î–5̂)   *do-do* (î–î)

7. As a collection, the melodic pitches complete which minor-key pattern?

   pentachord   ascending melodc   natural (descending melodic)   harmonic

Contextual Listening 5.2

In exercises 1–2, a three-beat introduction precedes a melody that begins on *do* (1̂). For each exercise, circle the melodic pitches, the beat division, and the best choice of meter signature.

	Melodic Pitches			*Beat Division*		*Meter Signature*	
1.	*do-me* (1̂–♭3̂)	*do-sol* (1̂–5̂)	*do-do* (1̂–1̂)	simple	compound	¾	⁹⁄₈
2.	*do-me* (1̂–♭3̂)	*do-sol* (1̂–5̂)	*do-do* (1̂–1̂)	simple	compound	¾	⁹⁄₈

In exercises 3–4, a three-beat count-off precedes a melody that begins on *do* (1̂).

3. To which scale do all melodic pitches belong?

major   ascending melodic   natural minor   harmonic   Dorian

The melodic rhythm includes some of these numbered patterns.

In the blanks, write the pattern number that occurs on the beat indicated.

⁹⁄₈ __ __ __ | __ __ ‖

4. To which scale or mode do all melodic pitches belong?

major   ascending melodic   natural minor   harmonic   Dorian

The melodic rhythm includes some of these numbered patterns.

In the blanks, write the pattern number that occurs on the beat indicated.

¾ __ __ __ | __ __ ‖

Now, listen to a piano work that begins on *do* ($\hat{1}$).

5. Focus first on melodic pitches 1–2, the beat division, and the meter. Circle the correct answers.

Melodic Pitches 1-2			*Beat Division*		*Meter Signature*
do-me ($\hat{1}$–♭$\hat{3}$)	*do-sol* ($\hat{1}$–$\hat{5}$)	*do-do* ($\hat{1}$–$\hat{1}$)	simple	compound	$\frac{3}{4}$ $\frac{9}{8}$

6. Melodic pitches 1–5 belong to which scale or mode?

   harmonic minor   natural minor   Dorian mode   Lydian mode

7. The final three melodic pitches belong to which scale or mode?

   harmonic minor   natural minor   Dorian mode   Lydian mode

8. Use the workspace to capture the melodic rhythm and pitches.

   (a) In the single-line staff, begin with a quarter note and notate the melody's rhythm in three-beat measures. Write an appropriate meter signature, beam notes to show beat grouping, and include all bar lines.

   (b) In the blanks provided beneath the single-line staff, begin with the given letter name and write the syllables, numbers, and letters of the melody.

   (c) In the treble staff, write appropriate key and meter signatures. Notate the melodic pitches using note heads. For help with pitches, refer to your solfège, numbers, and letters.

   Hint: Minor-key music *always* requires an accidental on *ti* ($\hat{7}$).

   (d) In the treble staff, incorporate the rhythm from the single-line staff, aligning the bar lines with those in the single-line staff.

   (e) Sing the melody, then play it on a keyboard.

Solfège: __ __   __   __ __   __ ___ ___ ___ __   __ __

Numbers: __   __   __   __ __   __ ___ ___ ___ __   __ __

Letters: E3   __   __   __ __   __ ___ ___ ___ __   __ __

Contextual Listening 5.3

Listen to a folk song that ends on *do* (1̂) and complete the following exercises.

1. The melody begins with which rhythmic feature?

   syncopation   rubato (uneven tempo)   dotted-note values   anacrusis

2. Circle the beat division and best choice of meter signature.

   simple   compound $\frac{3}{4}$ $\frac{9}{8}$

3. The melody begins on which pitch?
   Hint: Sing the last pitch, *do* (1̂). Then, sing up until you match pitch 1.

   do (1̂)   *re* (2̂)   *me* (♭3̂)   *sol* (5̂)

4. Use the workspace to capture the melodic rhythm and pitches.

   (a) In the single-line staff, begin with an eighth note and notate the melody's rhythm in three-beat measures. Write an appropriate meter signature, beam notes to show beat grouping, and include all bar lines.

   (b) In the blanks provided beneath the single-line staff, begin with the given letter name and write the syllables, numbers, and letters of the melody.

   (c) In the treble staff, draw appropriate key and meter signatures. Notate the melodic pitches using note heads. For help with pitches, refer to your solfège, numbers, and letters.

   (d) In the treble staff, incorporate the rhythm from the single-line staff. Align the bar lines with those in the single-line staff.

Solfège: __ __   __ __ __ __   __ __ __   __ __ __   __ __   __ __   __
Numbers: __ __   __ __ __ __   __ __ __   __ __ __   __ __   __ __   __
Letters: G4 __   __ __ __ __   __ __ __   __ __ __   __ __   __ __   __

5. All melodic pitches belong to which scale or mode?

   major   Dorian mode   harmonic minor   ascending melodic minor

6. Which is the range (lowest pitch to highest pitch) of the melody?

   do-do (1̂–1̂)   *do-sol* (1̂–5̂)   *ti-le* (7̂–♭6̂)   *sol-sol* (5̂–5̂)

Contextual Listening 5.4

Listen to an accompanied melody for piano and complete the following exercises.

1. Listen low. *Do* (1̂), the lowest pitch, sounds on every beat of the accompaniment. Circle the beat division and best choice of meter signature.

   simple   compound $\frac{2}{4}$ $\frac{6}{8}$

2. Listen high. The melody begins with which rhythmic feature?

   syncopation   rubato (uneven tempo)   dotted-note values   anacrusis

3. The melody begins and ends on which pitch?
   Hint: Sing *do* (1̂), then sing the scale until you match the first (or last) melodic pitch.

   sol (5̂)   *me* (♭3̂)   *re* (2̂)   *do* (1̂)

4. Use the workspace to capture the melodic rhythm and pitches.

   (a) In the single-line staff, begin with an eighth note and notate the melody's rhythm. Write an appropriate meter signature, beam notes to show beat grouping, and include all bar lines. Hint: Look at the answers to exercises 1–2.

   (b) In the blanks provided beneath the single-line staff, begin with the given letter name and write the syllables, numbers, and letters of the melody.

   (c) In the treble staff, write appropriate key and meter signatures. Notate the melodic pitches using note heads. For help with pitches, refer to your solfège, numbers, and letters.

   (d) In the treble staff, incorporate the rhythm from the single-line staff. Align the bar lines with those in the single-line staff.

   (e) Sing the melody, then play it on a keyboard.

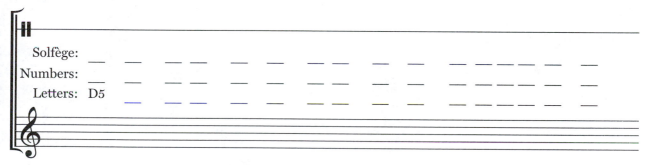

5. All melodic pitches belong to which scale or mode?

   natural minor   Dorian mode   Lydian mode   major scale

6. Which is the range (lowest pitch to highest pitch) of the melody?

   do-do (1̂–1̂)   *do-sol* (1̂–5̂)   *ti-le* (7̂–♭6̂)   *sol-sol* (5̂–5̂)

7. Begin on E5 and use the solfège or numbers from exercise 4 to transpose the melody up one whole step to create a B♭ clarinet part. In the staff below, write an appropriate clef, key signature, and meter signature.

B♭ clarinet

Contextual Listening 5.5

Translation: The sea glimmered out in the distance by the light of evening's last glow . . .

Listen to part of an art song. Focus first on the accompaniment, then the melody.

1. Listen low. At the beginning, *do* (1̂), the lowest pitch, sounds on beat 1 in each measure of the accompaniment. Circle the beat division and best choice of meter signature.

    simple   compound $\frac{2}{4}$ $\frac{6}{8}$

2. Listen high. The melody begins with which rhythmic feature?

    syncopation   tied note   duplet   anacrusis

3. Beginning with melodic pitch 3, which describes the recurring rhythmic feature?

    syncopation   tied note   duplet   anacrusis

4. Use the workspace to capture the melodic rhythm and pitches.

    (a) In the single-line staff, begin with an eighth note and notate the melody's rhythm. Write an appropriate meter signature, beam notes to show beat grouping, and include all bar lines. Hint: Look at the answers to exercises 1–2.

    (b) In the blanks provided beneath the single-line staff, begin with the given letter name, and write the syllables, numbers, and letters of the melody.

    (c) In the treble staff, write appropriate key and meter signatures. Notate the melodic pitches using note heads. For help with pitches, refer to your solfège, numbers, and letters.

    (d) In the treble staff, incorporate the rhythm from the single-line staff. Align the bar lines with those in the single-line staff.

    (e) Sing the melody, then play it on a keyboard.

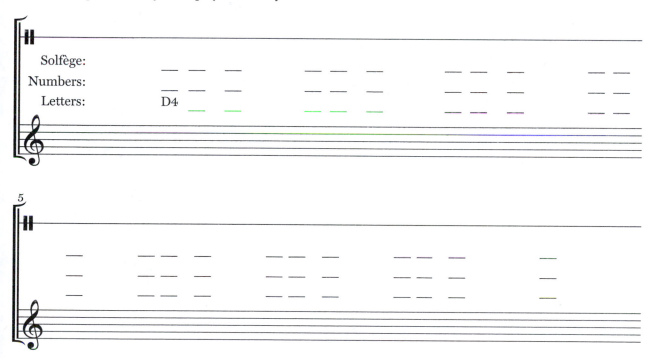

5. The melody ends with which pitch?

   do (1̂)   *re* (2̂)   *me* (♭3̂)   *sol* (5̂)

6. Listen low at the end. The accompaniment ends with which lowest pitch?

   do (1̂)   *re* (2̂)   *me* (♭3̂)   *sol* (5̂)

7. Given your answers to exercise 5, why can you tell this is *not* the end of the song?

Contextual Listening 5.6

Listen again to the work from Contextual Listening 5.1. Focus first on the left-hand accompaniment part. Then, focus on the right-hand melody plus its accompaniment.

1. Which is the rhythm of the accompaniment (the lower parts)?

2. The lowest-sounding part of the accompaniment begins on *do* (1̂). Which of these represents pitches 1-2? Hint: Sing *do* (1̂), then sing up the scale until you match pitch 2.

   do-re (1̂-2̂)   *do-me* (1̂-♭3̂)   *do-fa* (1̂-4̂)   *do-sol* (1̂-5̂)

3. The middle part begins on *sol* (5̂). Which describes the middle part's next pitch?

   S   **H** below   **W** below   **H** above   **W** above

4. The letter names below represent a scale from which all melodic and accompanying pitch classes are drawn. The first and last are given. After each letter, write the pitch class's accidental: ♮, ♭, or ♯. Write ? after the one note that *isn't* played.

   A♮ ____ ____ ____ ____ ____ ____ A♮

5. To which scale(s) could the melodic and accompanying pitch classes belong? Circle all that apply. Hint: Think of different possibilities for the missing (?) note.

   ascending melodic minor   harmonic minor   natural minor   Dorian mode

CHAPTER 6

Intervals

NAME _____

In this chapter you'll learn to:

- Identify intervals in major- and minor-key music
- Abbreviate solfège syllables
- Think letter names without writing them
- Notate music in simple and compound meters
- Transpose melodies to different keys and clefs

Try it

An introduction precedes a two-measure melody. For each one:

- Circle the beat division—simple or compound.
- Circle the interval formed by the specified melodic pitches. Hint: Map the pitches to syllables or numbers in your head.
- Circle the melody's key—major or minor.
- Refer to the appropriate patterns—compound or simple—and write the rhythm-pattern numbers.

Compound-beat rhythm patterns   *Simple-beat rhythm patterns*

1. Division: simple   compound

   Pitches 1-2 form: M3   P4   A4   P5

   do-mi ($\hat{1}$-$\hat{3}$) do-fa ($\hat{1}$-$\hat{4}$) do-fi ($\hat{1}$-$\sharp\hat{4}$) do-sol ($\hat{1}$-$\hat{5}$)

   Key: major   minor

   Patterns: ___ ___ | ___ ___ ‖

2. Division: simple   compound

   Pitches 1-2 form: M3   P4   A4   P5

   do-mi ($\hat{1}$-$\hat{3}$) do-fa ($\hat{1}$-$\hat{4}$) do-fi ($\hat{1}$-$\sharp\hat{4}$) do-sol ($\hat{1}$-$\hat{5}$)

   Key: major   minor

   Patterns: ___ ___ | ___ ___ ‖

3. Division: simple compound

   Pitches 1–2 form: M2 m3 P4 P5

                do–re ($\hat{1}$–$\hat{2}$) *do–me* ($\hat{1}$–♭$\hat{3}$) *do–fa* ($\hat{1}$–$\hat{4}$) *do–sol* ($\hat{1}$–$\hat{5}$)

   Key: major minor

   Patterns: ___ ___ | ___ ___ ‖

4. Division: simple compound

   Pitches 1–2 form: M3 P4 P5 m6

                sol–me ($\hat{5}$–♭$\hat{3}$) *sol–re* ($\hat{5}$–$\hat{2}$) *sol–do* ($\hat{5}$–$\hat{1}$) *sol–ti* ($\hat{5}$–$\hat{7}$)

   Key: major minor

   Patterns: ___ ___ | ___ ___ ‖

5. Division: simple compound

   Pitches 1–2 form: P4 m6 M6 m7

                sol–do ($\hat{5}$–$\hat{1}$) *sol–me* ($\hat{5}$–♭$\hat{3}$) *sol–mi* ($\hat{5}$–$\hat{3}$) *sol–fa* ($\hat{5}$–$\hat{4}$)

   Key: major minor

   Patterns: ___ ___ | ___ ___ ‖

6. In melody 6, focus on melodic pitches 4–5.

   Division: simple compound

   Pitches 4–5 form: m3 P4 d5 m6

                ti–re ($\hat{7}$–$\hat{2}$) *ti–mi* ($\hat{7}$–$\hat{3}$) *ti–fa* ($\hat{7}$–$\hat{4}$) *ti–sol* ($\hat{7}$–$\hat{5}$)

   Key: major minor

   Patterns: ___ ___ | ___ ___ ‖

7. Melody 7 begins with an eighth-note anacrusis, which is given.

   Division: simple compound

   Pitches 1–2 form: P4 P5 M6 m7

                sol–do ($\hat{5}$–$\hat{1}$) *sol–re* ($\hat{5}$–$\hat{2}$) *sol–mi* ($\hat{5}$–$\hat{3}$) *sol–fa* ($\hat{5}$–$\hat{4}$)

   Key: major minor

   Patterns: ♪ | ___ ___ | ___ ___ ‖

8. Melody 8 begins with an eighth-note anacrusis, which is given.

   Division: simple compound

   Pitches 1–2 form: M3 P5 M6 M7

                sol–me ($\hat{5}$–♭$\hat{3}$) *sol–do* ($\hat{5}$–$\hat{1}$) *sol–te* ($\hat{5}$–♭$\hat{7}$) *sol–le* ($\hat{5}$–♭$\hat{6}$)

   Key: major minor

   Patterns: ♪ | ___ ___ | ___ ___ ‖

Contextual Listening 6.1

Listen to two melodies. For each, circle melodic pitch 1, the beat division, and the meter signature.

Hint: Sing *do* (1̂). Sing up or down until you match the starting pitch.

	Melodic pitch 1			Beat division		Meter signature	
1.	*do* (1̂)	*mi* (3̂)	*sol* (5̂)	simple	compound	$\frac{2}{4}$	$\frac{6}{8}$
2.	*do* (1̂)	*mi* (3̂)	*sol* (5̂)	simple	compound	$\frac{2}{4}$	$\frac{6}{8}$

Listen to exercises 1–2 again. This time, identify the first and last melodic intervals.

3. First melodic interval: M2 M3 P4 P5

   Last melodic interval: M2 M3 P4 P5

4. First melodic interval: M2 M3 P4 P5

   Last melodic interval: M2 M3 P4 P5

Now, focus your listening on the melody from a piano work.

5. Use the workspace to capture the melodic rhythm and pitches.

   (a) In the single-line staff, begin with a dotted-quarter note and notate the melody's rhythm in two-beat measures. Write an appropriate meter signature, beam notes to show beat grouping, and include all bar lines.

   (b) In the blanks provided beneath the single-line staff, begin with the given letter name, and write the syllables, numbers, and letters of the melody.

   (c) In the treble staff, draw appropriate key and meter signatures. Notate the melodic pitches using note heads. For help with pitches, refer to your syllables, numbers, and letters.

   (d) In the treble staff, incorporate the rhythm from the single-line staff. Align the bar lines with those in the single-line staff.

   (e) Play *do* (1̂) and sing your answer with solfège, numbers, and letters. Sing the melody, then play it on a keyboard.

   (f) Beneath the treble staff, beginning with PU, write the interval names between each melodic pitch.

Solfège: __   __ __ __   __   __   __ __ __ __   __

Numbers: __   __ __ __   __   __   __ __ __ __   __

Letters: G♯4   __ __ __   __   __   __ __ __ __   __

Intervals: PU   __ __ __   __   __   __   __ __ __   __

6. The melody's pitches belong to which scale?

   ascending melodic minor   natural minor (descending melodic minor)

   harmonic minor   major scale

7. From the melody's lowest pitch to its highest, which is its range?

   do–sol ($\hat{1}$–$\hat{5}$)   *ti–la* ($\hat{7}$–$\hat{6}$)   *do–do* ($\hat{1}$–$\hat{1}$)   *sol–sol* ($\hat{5}$–$\hat{5}$)

8. At the beginning, listen low. The lowest pitches 1–2 form which interval?
   Hint: Sing pitch 1, *do* ($\hat{1}$), then sing down until you match pitch 2.

   m2; *do–ti* ($\hat{1}$-$\hat{7}$)   m3; *do–la* ($\hat{1}$-$\hat{6}$)   P4; *do–sol* ($\hat{1}$-$\hat{5}$)   P5; *do–fa* ($\hat{1}$-$\hat{4}$)

Contextual Listening 6.2

Listen to a melody. Then, circle melodic pitch 1, the beat division, and the meter signature.

Hint: Sing *do* (1̂). Then if necessary, sing up or down until you match the starting pitch.

	Melodic pitch 1			*Beat division*		*Meter signature*	
1.	*do* (1̂)	*mi* (3̂)	*sol* (5̂)	simple	compound	𝄴	$\frac{12}{8}$
2.	*do* (1̂)	*mi* (3̂)	*sol* (5̂)	simple	compound	𝄴	$\frac{12}{8}$

Listen to exercises 1–2 again. This time, identify the first and last melodic intervals.

3. First melodic interval: m2   M2   m3   M3

    Last melodic interval: m2   M2   m3   M3

4. First melodic interval: m2   M2   m3   M3

    Last melodic interval: m2   M2   m3   M3

Now, listen to a passage that features violin, viola, and cello. Focus first on the violin melody—the highest part.

5. Violin pitch 1 is: *do* (1̂)   *mi* (3̂)   *sol* (5̂)

6. The beat division is: simple   compound

7. The meter signature is: 𝄴 $\frac{12}{8}$

8. All violin pitches belong to which scale?

    major scale   natural minor (descending melodic minor)

    ascending melodic minor   harmonic minor

9. On pitches 1–4, the violin and viola play together.

    The interval between them is a: unison   third   sixth

    Hint: A unison sounds identical, a third sounds close, and a sixth sounds farther apart.

10. The lowest part is played by the cello. Cello pitch 1 is:

    do (1̂)   *mi* (3̂)   *sol* (5̂)

11. Cello pitches 1–2 form which interval?

    M3   P5   M6   P8

12. Use the workspace to capture the violin's melodic rhythm and pitches.

    (a) In the single-line staff, begin with a quarter note and notate the melody's rhythm in four-beat measures. Write an appropriate meter signature, beam notes to show beat grouping, and include all bar lines. Notate two measures per staff system.

    (b) In the blanks provided beneath the single-line staff, begin with the given letter name, and write the syllables and numbers of the melody.

        To save time, write only the first letter of a solfège syllable.

    (c) In the treble staff, draw appropriate key and meter signatures. Begin with the given pitch and notate all melodic pitches using note heads.

        Hints: Refer to your syllables and numbers and map them to pitches in the key. *Think* the letter names as you notate, but don't write them out.

(d) In the treble staff, incorporate the rhythm from the single-line staff, aligning the bar lines with those in the single-line staff.

(e) Sing the melody, then play it on a keyboard

Solfège:
Numbers:

B♭4

3

Contextual Listening 6.3

A melody begins on *do* (1̂) and features two rhythm patterns. The pitches belong to the top of a minor scale—from *sol* (5̂) up to *do* (1̂). Identify the pattern numbers and the scale.

Rhythm patterns	*All melodic pitches belong to this minor scale:*		
1. ___ ___	ascending melodic	natural	harmonic
2. ___ ___	ascending melodic	natural	harmonic
3. ___ ___	ascending melodic	natural	harmonic

Now, listen to part of an art song, and complete the remaining exercises.

4. Consult the pattern chart above. Write the rhythm-pattern number for each measure of the singer's rhythm.

   ___ ___ ___ ___   ___ ___ ___ ___

5. The singer's first two and last two pitches form which interval?

   m2   M2   m3   M3

6. The singer's pitch collection belongs to which scale?

   major scale   natural minor (descending melodic minor)

   ascending melodic minor   harmonic minor

7. Use the workspace to capture the singer's melodic rhythm and pitches.

   (a) In the single-line staff, write the meter signature, then notate the melody's rhythm. Hints: Refer to exercise 4. Notate four measures per staff system.

   (b) In the blanks provided beneath the single-line staff, begin with the given letter name, and write the syllables and numbers of the melody.

   Hint: To save time, write only the first letter of solfège syllables that occur in the major scale. For example, a minor-pentachord melody might look like this: *d t d r me f s le s.*

   (c) In the treble staff, draw appropriate key and meter signatures. Begin with the given pitch and notate all melodic pitches using note heads.

   Hints: Refer to your syllables and numbers and map them to pitches in the key. *Think* the letter names as you notate, but don't write them out.

   (d) In the treble staff, incorporate the rhythm from the single-line staff, aligning the bar lines with those in the single-line staff.

   (e) Sing the melody, then play it on a keyboard.

Solfège: — — — — — — — — — — —
Numbers: — — — — — — — — — — —
C5

5

— — — — — — — — — — —
— — — — — — — — — —

Translation: Oh, that you were taken away, never more to return!

Contextual Listening 6.4

Listen to a melody. Then, circle melodic pitch 1, the beat division, and the meter signature.
Hint: Sing *do* ($\hat{1}$). Sing up or down until you match the starting pitch.

Melodic pitch 1			Beat division		Meter signature	
1.	*do* ($\hat{1}$)	*me* ($\flat\hat{3}$)	*sol* ($\hat{5}$)	simple	compound	$\frac{2}{4}$ $\frac{6}{8}$
2.	*do* ($\hat{1}$)	*me* ($\flat\hat{3}$)	*sol* ($\hat{5}$)	simple	compound	$\frac{2}{4}$ $\frac{6}{8}$

Listen to exercises 1–2 again. This time, identify the first and last melodic intervals.

3. First melodic interval: m2   m3   M3   P4

    Last melodic interval: m2   m3   M3   P4

4. First melodic interval: m2   m3   M3   P4

    Last melodic interval: m2   m3   M3   P4

Now listen to a song from an opera and complete the remaining exercises.

5. Melodic pitches 1–2 form which interval?
    m3   M3   P4   P5

6. Melodic pitches 6–7 form which interval?
    m3   M3   P4   P5

7. The final melodic pitches (pitches 15–16) form which interval?
    m3   M3   P4   P5

8. Melodic pitches 1–8 belong to which pattern?
    major tetrachord   minor tetrachord   major pentachord   minor pentachord

9. The melody's pitch collection belongs to which scale?
    major scale   natural minor (descending melodic minor)
    ascending melodic minor   harmonic minor

10. Use the workspace to capture the vocal melodic rhythm and pitches.

  (a) In the single-line staff, write an appropriate meter signature. Begin with an eighth note and notate the melody's rhythm in two-beat measures. Beam notes to show beat grouping and include all bar lines. Notate three measures per staff system.

  (b) In the blanks provided beneath the single-line staff, begin with F♯4, and write the syllables and numbers of the melody. Hint: For any major-scale pitch, write only the first letter of its solfège syllable. For other notes, continue writing the entire syllable. A minor-key melody might look like this: *d t d r me f s le s.*

  (c) In the treble staff, draw appropriate key and meter signatures. Begin with the given pitch and notate all melodic pitches using note heads. Hint: Refer to your syllables and numbers and *think* the letter names as you notate, but don't write them out.

  (d) In the treble staff, incorporate the rhythm from the single-line staff, aligning the bar lines with those in the single-line staff.

  (e) Sing the melody, then play it on a keyboard.

Solfège: __ __ __ __   __ __   __   __   __

Numbers: __ __ __ __   __ __   __   __   __

F♯4

4

__   __ __   __ __   __   __

__   __ __   __ __   __   __

Translation: Black is the night, the wind howls, the spraying sea swells swiftly . . .

CHAPTER 7

Triads

NAME _____

In this chapter you'll learn to:

- Identify melodic and harmonic triads in major- and minor-key music
- Notate simple- and compound-meter music that features melodic and harmonic triads

Try it

1. The following eight melodies outline a triad. For each, identify the triad quality and the interval between the last two notes. Choose whether the meter is simple or compound. Then write the pattern numbers for each complete beat of rhythm.

Simple-meter patterns

Compound-meter patterns

(a) Triad quality:

	major	minor	diminished	augmented
Last two pitches form:	M3	P4	A4	P5
	do-mi ($\hat{1}$-$\hat{3}$)	*do-fa* ($\hat{1}$-$\hat{4}$)	*do-fi* ($\hat{1}$-$\sharp\hat{4}$)	*do-sol* ($\hat{1}$-$\hat{5}$)
simple or compound:	___	___	___	___

(b) Triad quality:

	major	minor	diminished	augmented
Last two pitches form:	m3	M3	P4	P5
	me-do ($\flat\hat{3}$-$\hat{1}$)	*mi-do* ($\hat{3}$-$\hat{1}$)	*fa-do* ($\hat{4}$-$\hat{1}$)	*sol-do* ($\hat{5}$-$\hat{1}$)
simple or compound:	___	___	___	___

(c) Triad quality:

	major	minor	diminished	augmented
Last two pitches form:	m3	M3	P4	P5
	do-me ($\hat{1}$-$\flat\hat{3}$)	*do-mi* ($\hat{1}$-$\hat{3}$)	*do-fa* ($\hat{1}$-$\hat{4}$)	*do-sol* ($\hat{1}$-$\hat{5}$)
simple or compound:	___	___	___	___

(d) Triad quality:

	major	minor	diminished	augmented
Last two pitches form:	m3	M3	P4	P5
simple or compound:	mi-sol ($\hat{3}$-$\hat{5}$)	me-sol ($\flat\hat{3}$-$\hat{5}$)	re-sol ($\hat{2}$-$\hat{5}$)	do-sol ($\hat{1}$-$\hat{5}$)
	___	___ | ___		___ ‖

(e) The melody ends on *do* ($\hat{1}$). Identify the quality of the triad outlined by pitches 5–7.

Triad quality:	major	minor	diminished	augmented
Last two pitches form:	m2	m3	M3	P4
simple or compound:	ti-do ($\hat{7}$-$\hat{1}$)	la-do ($\hat{6}$-$\hat{1}$)	le-do ($\flat\hat{6}$-$\hat{1}$)	sol-do ($\hat{5}$-$\hat{1}$)
	___	___ | ___		___ ‖

(f) Identify the quality of the triad outlined by pitches 4–6.

Triad quality:	major	minor	diminished	augmented
Last two pitches form:	M3	P4	A4	P5
simple or compound:	do-mi ($\hat{1}$-$\hat{3}$)	do-fa ($\hat{1}$-$\hat{4}$)	do-fi ($\hat{1}$-$\sharp\hat{4}$)	do-sol ($\hat{1}$-$\hat{5}$)
	___	___ | ___		___ ‖

(g) Melody 7 begins with an eighth-note anacrusis.

Triad quality:	major	minor	diminished	augmented
Last two pitches form:	M3	P4	P5	M6
simple or compound: ♪ |	do-mi ($\hat{1}$-$\hat{3}$)	do-fa ($\hat{1}$-$\hat{4}$)	do-sol ($\hat{1}$-$\hat{5}$)	do-la ($\hat{1}$-$\hat{6}$)
	___	___ | ___		___ ‖

(h) Melody 8 begins with an eighth-note anacrusis.

Triad quality:	major	minor	diminished	augmented
Last two pitches form:	m3	M3	P4	P5
simple or compound: ♪ |	me-do ($\flat\hat{3}$-$\hat{1}$)	mi-do ($\hat{3}$-$\hat{1}$)	fa-do ($\hat{4}$-$\hat{1}$)	sol-do ($\hat{5}$-$\hat{1}$)
	___	___ | ___		___ ‖

2. An introduction precedes two triads played first melodically, then harmonically. Identify each chord's quality: **M**ajor, **m**inor, **d**iminished, or **A**ugmented.

(a) Chord 1: ___ Chord 2: ___ (b) Chord 1: ___ Chord 2: ___

(c) Chord 1: ___ Chord 2: ___ (d) Chord 1: ___ Chord 2: ___

(e) Chord 1: ___ Chord 2: ___ (f) Chord 1: ___ Chord 2: ___

(g) Chord 1: ___ Chord 2: ___ (h) Chord 1: ___ Chord 2: ___

(i) Chord 1: ___ Chord 2: ___ (j) Chord 1: ___ Chord 2: ___

3. Listen to four chords played harmonically. Identify the quality of each chord.

(a) Chord 1: ____   Chord 2: ____   Chord 3: ____   Chord 4: ____

(b) Chord 1: ____   Chord 2: ____   Chord 3: ____   Chord 4: ____

(c) Chord 1: ____   Chord 2: ____   Chord 3: ____   Chord 4: ____

(d) Chord 1: ____   Chord 2: ____   Chord 3: ____   Chord 4: ____

Contextual Listening 7.1

Listen to four chords played harmonically. Identify the quality of each chord as **Major**, **minor**, **diminished**, or **Augmented**.

1. Chord 1: ____   Chord 2: ____   Chord 3: ____   Chord 4: ____

2. Chord 1: ____   Chord 2: ____   Chord 3: ____   Chord 4: ____

3. Chord 1: ____   Chord 2: ____   Chord 3: ____   Chord 4: ____

Now, listen to the beginning of a piece played on harpsichord.

4. The key is: major   minor

5. Sing *do* (1̂). Then, sing up or down from *do* (1̂) until you match pitch 1.

   Melodic pitch 1 is: *do* (1̂)   *mi* (3̂)   *me* (♭3̂)   *sol* (5̂)

6. (a) The meter is: duple   triple   quadruple

   (b) Assume a ♩ beat unit. The meter signature is: $\frac{2}{2}$ $\frac{3}{2}$ $\frac{4}{2}$

7. Use the workspace to capture the melody and the triad qualities of the accompaniment.

   (a) In the single-line staff, write the meter signature. Begin with a half note and notate the melody's rhythm. Bar lines are included.

   (b) In the blanks provided beneath the single-line staff, write the syllables and numbers of the melody.

   (c) Beneath beat 1 of any measure with a "quality" blank, indicate the chord quality by writing "M" for major or "m" for minor.

   (d) In the treble staff, draw appropriate key and meter signatures. Beginning with F4, notate the melodic pitches. Refer to your syllables and numbers.

   (e) In the treble staff, incorporate the rhythm from the single-line staff.

   (f) Sing the melody, then play it on a keyboard.

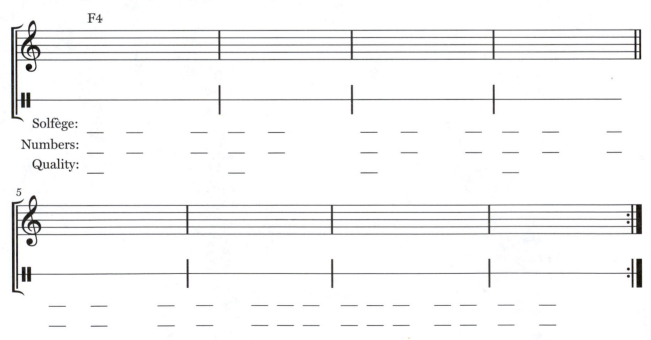

NAME _____

Contextual Listening 7.2

Listen to four chords played harmonically. Identify the quality of each chord as **M**ajor, **m**inor, **d**iminished, or **A**ugmented.

1. Chord 1: ____   Chord 2: ____   Chord 3: ____   Chord 4: ____

2. Chord 1: ____   Chord 2: ____   Chord 3: ____   Chord 4: ____

3. Chord 1: ____   Chord 2: ____   Chord 3: ____   Chord 4: ____

Now, listen to the harmonization of an early American melody and complete the following exercises.

4. The key is: major   minor

5. Sing *do* (1̂). Then, sing up or down from *do* (1̂) until you match pitch 1.

   Melodic pitch 1 is: *do* (1̂)   *mi* (3̂)   *me* (♭3̂)   *sol* (5̂)

6. Capture the melody and the triad qualities of the accompaniment.

   (a) Key and meter signatures as well as bar lines are given. In the single-line staff, begin with a half note and notate the melody's rhythm.

   (b) Beneath the single-line staff, write the syllables and numbers of the melody.

   (c) In each "quality" blank, write "M" for major triads and "m" for minor triads.

   (d) In the treble staff, begin with half-note G4 and notate the melodic rhythm and pitches. For help with pitches, refer to your syllables and numbers.

   (e) Sing the melody, then play it on a keyboard.

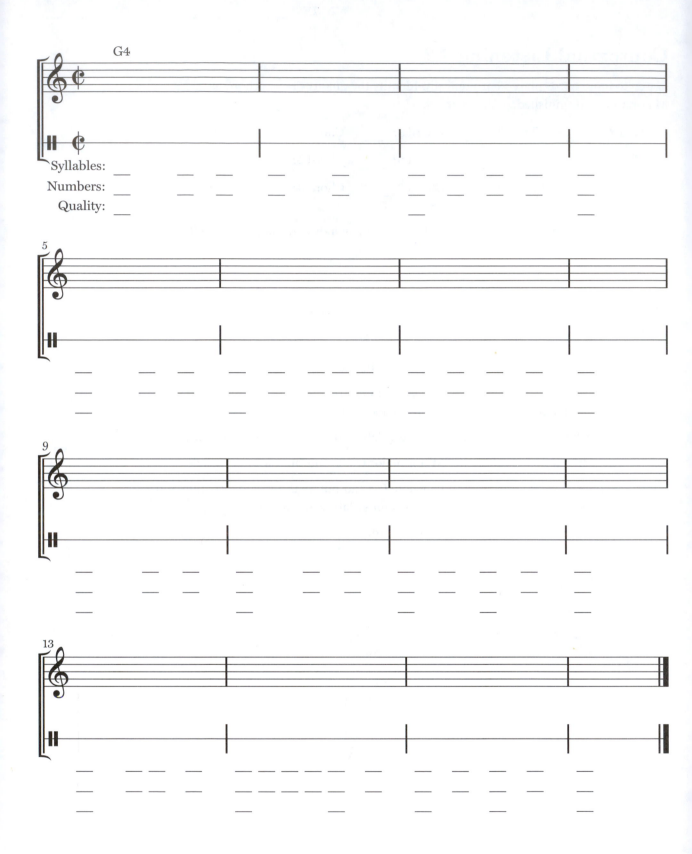

G4

Syllables:
Numbers:
Quality:

5

9

13

Contextual Listening 7.3

A two-beat introduction precedes a melodic triad and two beats of cut-time rhythm. Identify the triad quality as **M**ajor, **m**inor, **d**iminished, or **A**ugmented, and write the rhythm-pattern numbers.

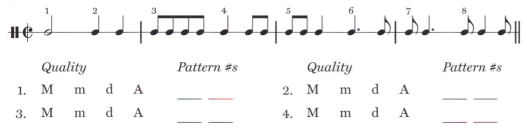

	Quality	Pattern #s		Quality	Pattern #s
1.	M m d A	___ ___	2.	M m d A	___ ___
3.	M m d A	___ ___	4.	M m d A	___ ___

Now, listen to part of a piano work and complete the following exercises.

5. The key is: major   minor

6. Sing *do* (1̂). Then, sing up or down from *do* (1̂) until you match pitch 1.

   Melodic pitch 1 is: *do* (1̂)   *mi* (3̂)   *me* (♭3̂)   *sol* (5̂)

7. Melodic pitches 1–5 belong to a triad of which quality?   M   m   d   A

8. Capture the melodic rhythm and pitches.

   (a) Key and meter signatures as well as bar lines are given. In the single-line staff above the piano score, begin with a quarter note and notate the melody's rhythm. The last measure is incomplete; write a quarter note.

   (b) Write the syllables and numbers of the melody beneath the upper single-line staff.

   (c) In the treble staff, begin with quarter-note C4 and notate the melodic rhythm and pitches. For help with pitches, refer to your syllables and numbers. Align your rhythm with that in the single-line staff.

   (d) Sing the melody, then play it on a keyboard.

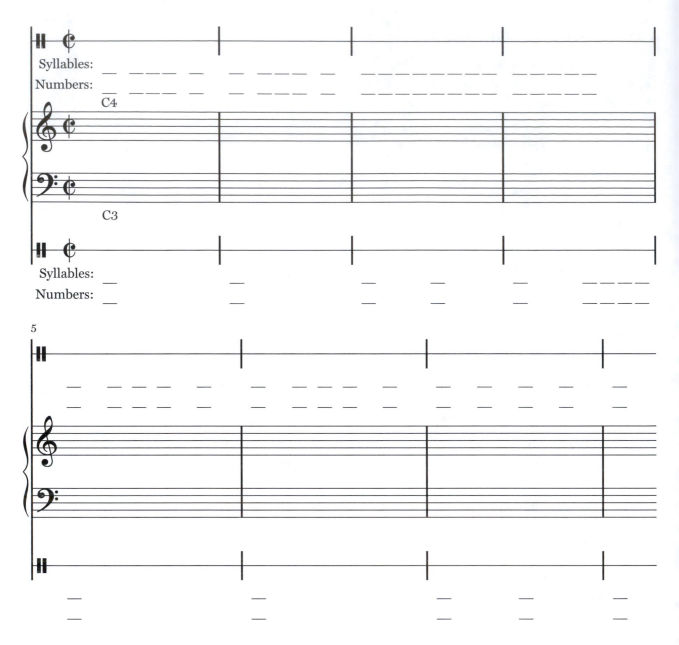

9. At the end, the last five melodic pitches complete which pattern?

   major pentatonic   major pentachord   minor pentatonic   minor pentachord

10. At the end, the melodic pitches are harmonized at which interval?   third   sixth

    Hint: Are the lower pitches close or far away?

11. Use the workspace in exercise 8 to capture the bass line's pitches and rhythm.

    (a) In the single-line staff below the piano score, begin with a quarter note and notate the bass line's rhythm. The last measure is incomplete; write a quarter note.

    (b) In the blanks provided beneath the lower single-line staff, write the syllables and numbers of the bass line.

    (c) In the bass staff, begin with quarter-note C3 and notate the bass line's rhythm and pitches. For help with pitches, refer to your syllables and numbers. Align your rhythm with that in the single-line staff.

Contextual Listening 7.4

A two-beat introduction precedes a melodic triad and two beats of compound-meter rhythm. Identify the triad quality as **M**ajor, **m**inor, **d**iminished, or **A**ugmented, and write the rhythm-pattern numbers.

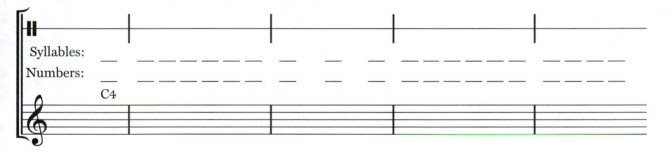

	Quality				Pattern #s			Quality				Pattern #s
1.	M	m	d	A	___ ___	2.		M	m	d	A	___ ___
3.	M	m	d	A	___ ___	4.		M	m	d	A	___ ___

Now, listen to a piano melody and complete the following exercises.

5. Pitches 1–6 belong to a triad of which quality? M   m   d   A

6. The melodic pitches are doubled at which interval?

   m3   M3   M6   P8

7. In the workspace, capture the melodic rhythm and pitches.

   (a) In the single-line staff, write the meter signature. Begin with an eighth-note anacrusis and notate the melody's rhythm.

   (b) Write the syllables and numbers of the melody beneath the single-line staff.

   (c) In the treble staff, write the key and meter signatures. Beginning with eighth-note C4, notate the melodic rhythm and pitches. For help with pitches, refer to your syllables and numbers. Align your rhythm with that in the single-line staff.

   (d) Sing the melody, then play it on a keyboard.

Syllables: __ __ __ __ __ __ __ __ __ __ __ __ __ __ __

Numbers: __ __ __ __ __ __ __ __ __ __ __ __ __ __ __

C4

8. All melodic pitches belong to which scale?

   major   ascending melodic minor   natural minor   harmonic minor

9. Between pitches 8–9, the interval is a: PU   P4   P5   P8

CHAPTER 8

Seventh Chords

NAME _____

In this chapter you'll learn to:

- Identify melodic and harmonic seventh chords in major- and minor-key music
- Label seventh-chord quality and use lead-sheet symbols
- Associate seventh-chord types with specific major- and minor-key scale degrees

Try it

1. To identify root-position seventh chords, listen first for triad quality, then the quality of the seventh.

Triad quality	7th quality	Seventh-chord type	Lead-sheet symbol
M	M	MM7	maj7
M	m	Mm7	7
m	m	mm7	min7
d	m	dm7	ø7
d	d	dd7	o7

Each seventh chord is played melodically, then harmonically. Identify its quality.

(a) MM7   Mm7   mm7   dm7   dd7   (b) MM7   Mm7   mm7   dm7   dd7

(c) MM7   Mm7   mm7   dm7   dd7   (d) MM7   Mm7   mm7   dm7   dd7

(e) MM7   Mm7   mm7   dm7   dd7   (f) MM7   Mm7   mm7   dm7   dd7

The next exercises feature equivalent symbols using lead-sheet notation.

(g) maj7   7   min7   ø7   o7   (h) maj7   7   min7   ø7   o7

(i) maj7   7   min7   ø7   o7   (j) maj7   7   min7   ø7   o7

2. Memorize the seventh chord associated with each major- and minor-key scale degree. Then, listen for the key type and scale degree to recall the chord quality.

Root scale degree	Major-key seventh chord	Minor-key seventh chord
$\hat{7}$	dm7	dd7
$\flat\hat{7}$	—	Mm7
$\hat{6}$	mm7	MM7
$\hat{5}$	Mm7	Mm7
$\hat{4}$	MM7	mm7
$\hat{3}$	mm7	MM7
$\hat{2}$	mm7	dm7
$\hat{1}$	MM7	mm7

An introduction precedes two seventh chords played first melodically, then harmonically. Identify the quality of each chord.

	Chord 1					Chord 2				
(a)	MM7	Mm7	mm7	dm7	dd7	MM7	Mm7	mm7	dm7	dd7
(b)	MM7	Mm7	mm7	dm7	dd7	MM7	Mm7	mm7	dm7	dd7
(c)	MM7	Mm7	mm7	dm7	dd7	MM7	Mm7	mm7	dm7	dd7

The next exercises feature equivalent symbols using lead-sheet notation.

	Chord 1					Chord 2				
(d)	maj7	7	min7	ø7	o7	maj7	7	min7	ø7	o7
(e)	maj7	7	min7	ø7	o7	maj7	7	min7	ø7	o7

3. Listen to a series of root-position chords and identify the quality of each.

- For triads, write M, m, d, or A.

- For seventh chords, write MM7, Mm7, mm7, dm7, or dd7.

(a) Chord: 1   2   3   4
     Quality: _____   _____   _____   _____

(b) Chord: 1   2   3   4
     Quality: _____   _____   _____   _____

(c) Chord: 1   2   3
     Quality: _____   _____   _____

(d) Chord: 1   2   3
     Quality: _____   _____   _____

(e) Chord: 1   2   3   4   5   6   7   8
     Quality: _____   _____   _____   _____   _____   _____   _____   _____

4. Listen again to exercise 3 (a)–(e). After each chord root, write the chord quality using lead-sheet symbols: maj, maj7, min, min7, dim, ∅7, or °7.

(a) Chord: 1   2   3   4
     Symbol: C   A   D   G

(b) Chord: 1   2   3   4
     Symbol: C   A♭   F   G

(c) Chord: 1   2   3
     Symbol: C♯   D   A

(d) Chord: 1   2   3
     Symbol: F♯   B   E

(e) Chord: 1   2   3   4   5   6   7   8
     Symbol: A   D   G   C   F   B   E   A

Contextual Listening 8.1

Identify the quality of each chord in a series of root-position seventh chords.

- First, label the triad and seventh quality: MM7, Mm7, mm7, dm7, or dd7.
- Then, use lead-sheet symbols. The root of each chord is given.

1. Chord: 1   2   3   4   5   6   7   8

   Quality: _____ _____ _____ _____ _____ _____ _____ _____

   Lead: 1   2   3   4   5   6   7   8

   Sheet: D   F   G   D   B♭   E   A   D

2. Chord: 1   2   3   4   5   6   7   8

   Quality: _____ _____ _____ _____ _____ _____ _____ _____

   Lead: 1   2   3   4   5   6   7   8

   Sheet: D   F♯   G   D   B   E   A   D

Now, listen to the beginning of a piano piece and complete the remaining exercises.

3. The key is: major   minor

4. The final bass pitch is *do* (1̂). Sing up or down from *do* until you match bass pitch 1.

   Bass pitch 1 is: *do* (1̂)   *mi* (3̂)   *fa* (4̂)   *sol* (5̂)

5. Sing up or down from *do* (1̂) until you match melodic pitch 1.

   Melodic pitch 1 is: *do* (1̂)   *mi* (3̂)   *fa* (4̂)   *sol* (5̂)

6. (a) The meter is: duple   triple   quadruple

   (b) Assume a ♩ beat unit. The meter signature is: 2/4   3/4   4/4

7. In the workspace, capture the chord quality, bass line, and melody. Bar lines are given.

   (a) At the beginning of both single-line staves, write the meter signature.

   - In the lower single-line staff, notate the rhythm of the bass pitch (lowest note).
   - Beneath that staff, write the syllable and number of each bass pitch.
   - Write the seventh-chord quality: MM7, Mm7, mm7, dm7, or dd7.
   - In the upper single-line staff, notate the melodic rhythm.
   - Beneath that staff, write the syllable and number of each melodic pitch.

   (b) In the grand staff, draw appropriate key and meter signatures.

   - Beginning with G2, notate the bass pitches.
   - Beginning with F♯5, notate the melodic pitches.
   - Refer to your syllables and numbers and incorporate the rhythm from the single-line staves.
   - Sing the melody while playing the bass line at a keyboard.

Syllables:

Numbers:

G2

Syllables: ___ ___ ___ ___

Numbers: ___ ___ ___ ___

Quality: _____ _____ _____ _____

5

F♯5

Contextual Listening 8.2

A melody begins with a seventh chord; choose the symbol that matches its chord quality.

1. MM7   Mm7   mm7   dm7   dd7   2. MM7   Mm7   mm7   dm7   dd7

3. MM7   Mm7   mm7   dm7   dd7   4. MM7   Mm7   mm7   dm7   dd7

Now, listen to part of a piano work and complete the remaining exercises.

5. Melodic pitch 1 is *do* (1̂). Sing up or down until you match bass pitch 1.

   Bass pitch 1 is: *do* (1̂)   *mi* (3̂)   *fa* (4̂)   *sol* (5̂)

6. Compared with bass pitches 1–3, the melody's motion is:

   contrary   oblique   similar   parallel

7. Compared with bass pitches 4–7, the melody's motion is:

   contrary   oblique   similar   parallel

8. Melodic pitches 4–7 outline which seventh chord?

   MM7   Mm7   mm7   dm7   dd7

9. In the workspace, capture the bass and melodic lines. Key and meter signatures, starting pitches, and bar lines are given.

   (a) In the single-line staves, notate the rhythm of the bass and melodic lines. Beneath each staff, write the syllables and numbers of the pitches.

   (b) Beginning with E3 and C5 respectively, notate the pitches and rhythm of the bass and melody. Refer to your syllables and numbers and incorporate the rhythm from the single-line staves.

   (c) Sing the melody while playing the bass line on a keyboard.

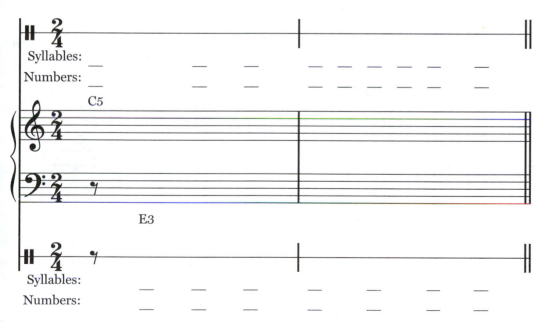

Contextual Listening 8.3

A melody begins with a seventh chord. For each exercise, choose the symbol that matches its chord quality.

1. MM7   Mm7   mm7   dm7   dd7   2. MM7   Mm7   mm7   dm7   dd7

3. MM7   Mm7   mm7   dm7   dd7   4. MM7   Mm7   mm7   dm7   dd7

Now, listen to part of a piano work and complete the remaining exercises.

5. The final *bass* pitch is *do* (1̂). Sing up or down from *do* until you match melodic pitch 1.

    Melodic pitch 1 is: *do* (1̂)   *mi* (3̂)   *fa* (4̂)   *sol* (5̂)

6. Melodic pitches 1–4 outline which seventh chord?

    MM7   Mm7   mm7   dm7   dd7

7. The opening texture is:

    monophonic   homophonic   heterophonic   polyphonic

8. The final bass pitches form which *melodic* interval?

    M3   P4   P5   M6

9. In the workspace, capture the melody's pitches and rhythms. Key and meter signatures as well as bar lines are given.

    (a) In the single-line staff, notate the rhythm of the melody. Beneath the staff, write the syllables and numbers of its pitches.

    (b) Beginning with D♭5, notate the pitches and rhythm of the melody. Refer to your syllables and numbers and incorporate the rhythm from the single-line staff.

    (c) Sing the melody, then play it on a keyboard.

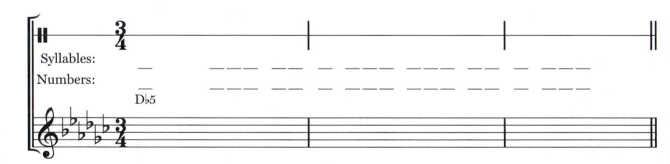

Contextual Listening 8.4

1. Listen to a series of root-position seventh chords. After each given root, write the chord quality using lead-sheet symbols: maj7, 7, min7, ⌀7, or °7.

    (a) Chord: 1   2   3   4

       Quality: __A__   __F__   __C__   __G__

    (b) Chord: 1   2   3   4

       Quality: __D__   __G__   __C__   __A__

Now listen to part of a jazz standard and complete the remaining exercises.

2. Use the workspace to capture the bass line, melody, and seventh chords. Key and meter signatures as well as the initial pitches, rhythms, syllables, and numbers are given.

    (a) In the single-line staves, finish notating the rhythm of the bass and melody.

    (b) Below each single-line staff, finish writing the syllables and numbers of the pitches.

    (c) In the grand staff, finish notating the bass line and melody. Refer to your syllables and numbers and incorporate the rhythm from the single-line staves.

    (d) Write chord symbols above the treble staff.

       • In the chord blanks, write the letter name of the chord's root (C, D, E♭, G, etc.). Hint: All chords are root-position seventh chords, so the root is the bass pitch.

       • Listen for the quality of each seventh chord. Then, write it after the letter name using lead-sheet symbols (Cmaj7, Dmin7, etc.).

    (e) Sing the melody while playing the bass line on the keyboard.

3. Melodic pitches 1–2 create which interval?

    m3   M3   P4   P5

4. The last two melodic pitches create which interval?

    P5   m6   M6   m7

5. The last two bass pitches create which interval?

    P8   M6   m6   P4

CHAPTER 9

Note-to-Note Counterpoint

NAME _____

In this chapter you'll learn to:

- Use contour to identify types of motion in note-to-note (1:1) counterpoint
- Identify harmonic intervals in a two-part contrapuntal texture
- Take dictation of two-part works

Types of Motion

In two-part music, the contours of the two parts interact to create four types of motion.

Type	How parts move	Contour diagrams
Contrary	Different directions	
Oblique	One part moves, the other stays	
Parallel	Same direction, *same* interval	
Similar	Same direction, *different* interval	

Try it

Listen to six measures of two-part music. Above and below the staff, write the solfège syllables and numbers for each part, then notate the remaining pitches, one whole note per measure. Beneath each measure, write the harmonic interval number. Between the measures, write the type of motion: *contrary, oblique, parallel,* or *similar.* If neither part moves, write *none.*

1.

Syllables: *d*   ___   ___   ___   ___   ___

Numbers: 1̂   ___   ___   ___   ___   ___

Syllables: *d*   ___   ___   ___   ___   ___

Numbers: 1̂   ___   ___   ___   ___   ___

Intervals: U   ___   ___   ___   ___   ___

Motion: contrary

2.

Syllables: *d*   ___   ___   ___   ___   ___

Numbers: $\hat{1}$ ___   ___   ___   ___   ___

Syllables: *d*   ___   ___   ___   ___   ___

Numbers: $\hat{1}$ ___   ___   ___   ___   ___

Intervals: U   ___   ___   ___   ___   ___

Motion: contrary   ___   ___   ___   ___

3.

Syllables: *d*   ___   ___   ___   ___   ___

Numbers: $\hat{1}$ ___   ___   ___   ___   ___

Syllables: *d*   ___   ___   ___   ___   ___

Numbers: $\hat{1}$ ___   ___   ___   ___   ___

Intervals: U   ___   ___   ___   ___   ___

Motion: contrary   ___   ___   ___   ___

4.

Syllables: *d*   ___   ___   ___   ___   ___

Numbers: $\hat{1}$ ___   ___   ___   ___   ___

Syllables: *d*   ___   ___   ___   ___   ___

Numbers: $\hat{1}$ ___   ___   ___   ___   ___

Intervals: U   ___   ___   ___   ___   ___

Motion: contrary   ___   ___   ___   ___

5.

Syllables: *d*   ___   ___   ___   ___   ___

Numbers: $\hat{1}$ ___   ___   ___   ___   ___

Syllables: *d*   ___   ___   ___   ___   ___

Numbers: $\hat{1}$ ___   ___   ___   ___   ___

Intervals: 8   ___   ___   ___   ___   ___

Motion: contrary   ___   ___   ___   ___

6.

| Syllables: | *d* | — | — | — | — | — |
| Numbers: | î | — | — | — | — | — |

Syllables:	*d*	—	—	—	—	—
Numbers:	î	—	—	—	—	—
Intervals:	8	—	—	—	—	—
Motion:	contrary	___	___	___	___	

Exercises 7 and 8 contain eight measures of two-part music.

7.

| Syllables: | *d* | — | — | — | — | — | — | — |
| Numbers: | î | — | — | — | — | — | — | — |

Syllables:	*d*	—	—	—	—	—	—	—
Numbers:	î	—	—	—	—	—	—	—
Intervals:	U	—	—	—	—	—	—	—
Motion:	contrary	___	___	___	___	___	___	

8.

| Syllables: | *d* | — | — | — | — | — | — | — |
| Numbers: | î | — | — | — | — | — | — | — |

Syllables:	*d*	—	—	—	—	—	—	—
Numbers:	î	—	—	—	—	—	—	—
Intervals:	8	—	—	—	—	—	—	—
Motion:	contrary	___	___	___	___	___	___	

Contextual Listening 9.1

For exercises 1–4, do the following:

- Write the syllables and numbers of each part.
- On the grand staff, notate the pitches and rhythm of both parts.
- Between the staves, write the numbers for the harmonic intervals.

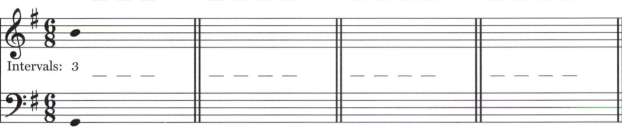

Syllables: *m* _ __ __ __   __ __ __ __   __ __ __ __   __ __ __ __

Numbers: $\hat{3}$ _ __ __ __   __ __ __ __   __ __ __ __   __ __ __ __

Intervals: 3 _ __ __   __ __ __   __ __ __   __ __ __

Syllables: *d* _ __ __ __   __ __ __ __   __ __ __ __   __ __ __ __

Numbers: $\hat{1}$ _ __ __ __   __ __ __ __   __ __ __ __   __ __ __ __

Refer to exercises 1–4, comparing the contours of the melody and the bass.

5. In exercise 1, the motion between the parts is:

    all contrary   all parallel   contrary, then parallel   parallel, then contrary

6. In exercise 2, the motion between the parts is:

    all contrary   all parallel   contrary, then parallel   parallel, then contrary

7. In exercise 3, the motion between the parts is:

    all contrary   all parallel   contrary, then parallel   parallel, then contrary

8. In exercise 4, the motion between the parts is:

    all contrary   all parallel   contrary, then parallel   parallel, then contrary

Now, listen to the beginning of a piano piece and complete the remaining exercises.

9. In the workspace, begin with the given items and capture the two parts.

   (a) In the single-line staves, notate the rhythm of each part. Beneath the staves, write the syllables and numbers.

   (b) In the grand staff, notate the pitches and rhythm of both parts. For help, refer to the single-line staves. Check your work at a keyboard.

   (c) In the blanks between the treble and bass staves, write the numbers of the harmonic intervals.

In exercises 10–15, compare the contours of the melody and the bass.

10. Between bass pitches 1–3 and the melody, the motion is:

    contrary   oblique   parallel   similar

11. Between bass pitch 3 and the melody, the motion is:

    contrary   oblique   parallel   similar

12. Between bass pitches 4–6 and the melody, the motion is:

    contrary   oblique   parallel   similar

13. Between bass pitches 7–9 and the melody, the motion is:

    contrary   oblique   parallel   similar

14. Between bass pitches 10–11 and the melody, the motion is:

    contrary   oblique   parallel   similar

15. Between the last two bass pitches and the melody, the motion is:

    contrary   oblique   parallel   similar

16. Melodic pitches 2–3 create which interval?

    M3   P4   P5   M6

17. The last two bass pitches create which melodic interval?

    m2   M2   P4   P5

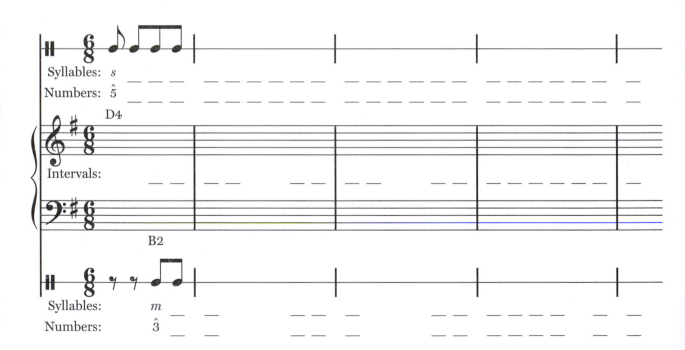

Contextual Listening 9.2

Exercises 1–3 are adaptations of a 1:1 counterpoint. For each, begin with the given items and write syllables and numbers for each part. Then, notate the remaining pitches, one whole note per measure. Beneath each measure, write the harmonic interval number. Between the measures, write the type of motion: *contrary*, *oblique*, *parallel*, or *similar*. Refer to your answers to identify the exercise's tonality/modality.

1. The tonality/modality is:

      minor   Dorian   Phrygian   Lydian   Mixolydian

Syllables: *d*   ___ ___ ___ ___ ___ ___ ___ ___
Numbers: 1̂   ___ ___ ___ ___ ___ ___ ___ ___

Syllables: *d*   ___ ___ ___ ___ ___ ___ ___ ___
Numbers: 1̂   ___ ___ ___ ___ ___ ___ ___ ___
Intervals: U   ___ ___ ___ ___ ___ ___ ___ ___
Motion: ___ ___ ___ ___ ___ ___ ___ ___

2. The tonality/modality is:

      minor   Dorian   Phrygian   Lydian   Mixolydian

Syllables: *d*   ___ ___ ___ ___ ___ ___ ___
Numbers: 1̂   ___ ___ ___ ___ ___ ___ ___

Syllables: *d*   ___ ___ ___ ___ ___ ___ ___
Numbers: 1̂   ___ ___ ___ ___ ___ ___ ___
Intervals: U   ___ ___ ___ ___ ___ ___ ___
Motion: ___ ___ ___ ___ ___ ___ ___

3. The tonality/modality is:

      major   Dorian   Phrygian   Lydian   Mixolydian

Syllables: *d*   ___ ___ ___ ___ ___ ___ ___
Numbers: 1̂   ___ ___ ___ ___ ___ ___ ___

Syllables: *d*   ___ ___ ___ ___ ___ ___ ___
Numbers: 1̂   ___ ___ ___ ___ ___ ___ ___
Intervals: U   ___ ___ ___ ___ ___ ___ ___
Motion: ___ ___ ___ ___ ___ ___ ___

Now, listen to the beginning of a string quartet. The excerpt consists of four segments, each eight pitches long.

4. In the workspace, begin with the given items and capture the two parts.

   (a) In the single-line staves, notate the rhythm of each part. Beneath these staves, write the syllables and numbers.

   (b) In the grand staff, notate the pitches and rhythm of both parts. For help, refer to the single-line staves. Check your work at a keyboard.

   (c) In the blanks between the treble and bass staves, write the harmonic interval numbers.

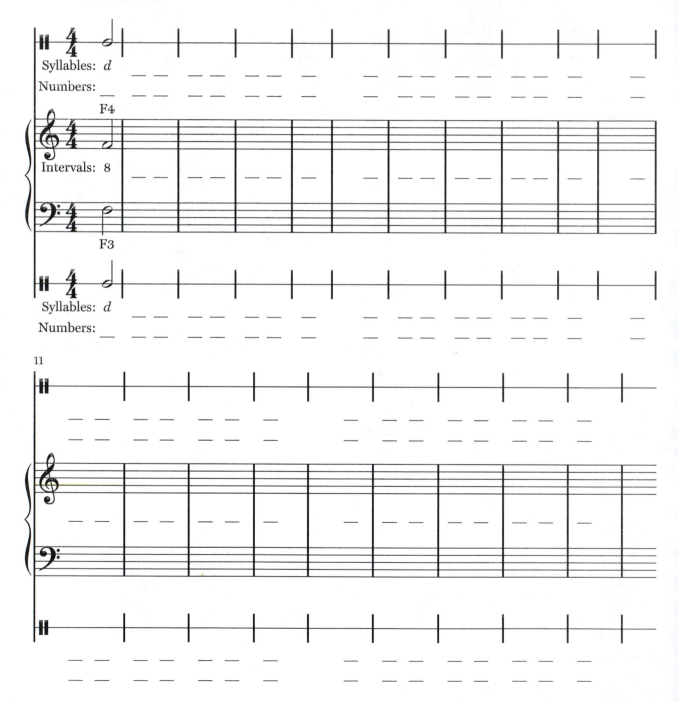

5. Bass pitches 1–3 outline which triad quality?

   major   minor   diminished   augmented

6. Which describes the types of motion in segment 2?

   parallel throughout   parallel, then contrary

   contrary, then parallel   oblique, then contrary

7. In segment 3, the first two pitches of the melody and bass create which type of motion?

   contrary   oblique   parallel   similar

8. Segment 4 includes which unusual succession of harmonic intervals?
   Hint: Focus on pitches 3–4.

   PU–PU   P4–P4   P5–P5   P8–P8

9. The melodic high point occurs at the end of which segment?

   1   2   3   4

10. The excerpt ends with which harmonic intervals?

    m3–M6   M3–m6   P5–P8   M3–P8

11. Which harmonic interval types are heard most frequently in this excerpt?

    thirds and fifths   thirds and sixths   fifths and octaves   sixths and octaves

12. On which tonality or modality is the excerpt based?

    major   minor   Dorian   Lydian

Contextual Listening 9.3

Beginning with the given items, write syllables and numbers for each part. Then, notate the remaining pitches, one whole note per measure. Beneath each measure, write the number of the harmonic interval. Between the measures, write the type of motion: *contrary*, *oblique*, *parallel*, or *similar*.

1.

Syllables: *d*   __   __   __   __   __   __
Numbers: $\hat{1}$ __   __   __   __   __   __

Syllables: *d*   __   __   __   __   __   __
Numbers: $\hat{1}$ __   __   __   __   __   __
Intervals: U   __   __   __   __   __   __
Motion: ___   ___   ___   ___   ___   ___

2.

Syllables: *s*   __   __   __   __
Numbers: $\hat{5}$ __   __   __   __

Syllables: *s*   __   __   __   __
Numbers: $\hat{5}$ __   __   __   __
Intervals: U   __   __   __   __
Motion: ___   ___   ___   ___

3.

Syllables: *d*   __   __   __   __   __
Numbers: $\hat{1}$ __   __   __   __   __

Syllables: *d*   __   __   __   __   __
Numbers: $\hat{1}$ __   __   __   __   __
Intervals: 8   __   __   __   __   __
Motion: ___   ___   ___   ___   ___

Now, listen to part of a choral work. The six segments are separated by rests. Sopranos sing the higher part and altos sing the lower.

4. In the workspace, begin with the given items and capture the two parts.

   (a) In the single-line staves, notate the rhythm of each part. Beneath these staves, write the syllables and numbers.

   (b) In the treble staves, notate the pitches and rhythm of both parts. For help, refer to the single-line staves. Check your work at a keyboard. Hint: The sopranos' seventh pitch requires an accidental.

   (c) In the blanks between the treble staves, write the numbers of the harmonic intervals.

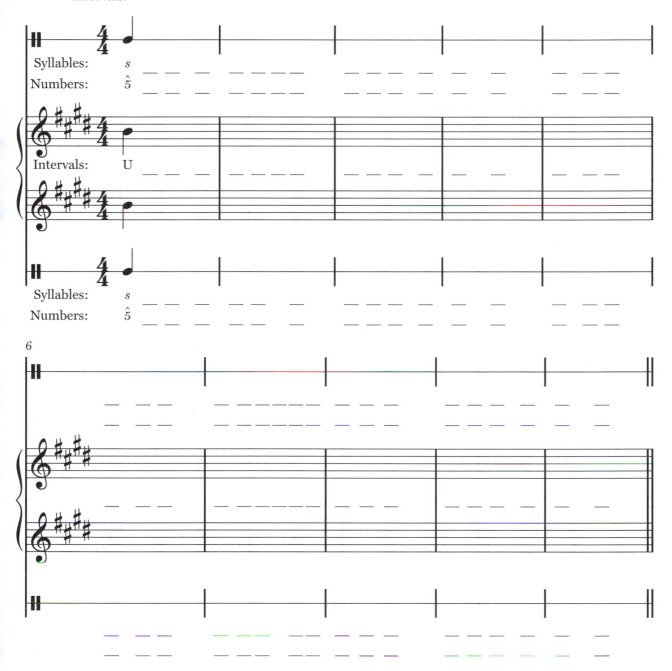

Translation: If loving Nature or Spirit gave you wings, follow in my light steps, up to the rosy hill.

5. The excerpt's tonality/modality is:

    major   minor   Dorian   Lydian

6. Segments 3 and 4 consist entirely of which type of motion?

    contrary   oblique   parallel   similar

7. Segment 5's beginning ("*folget meiner leichten Spur*") features which motion?

    contrary   oblique   parallel   similar

8. During segment 5, the higher part outlines triads of which qualities?

    minor, minor   major, minor   major, major   diminished, major

9. The last segment begins with sopranos outlining a triad of which quality?

    major   minor   augmented   diminished

10. The last segment's motion is:

    parallel throughout   contrary throughout

    parallel, then contrary   oblique, then parallel

11. The last segment ends with which harmonic intervals?

    m3–M6   M3–m6   P4–M6   A4–m6

12. The last segment concludes like which earlier segment?

    1   2   3   4   5

13. Which segments consist entirely of note-to-note counterpoint? Choose all that apply.

    1   2   3   4   5   6

14. The harmonic intervals heard most often are:

    thirds and fifths   thirds and sixths   fifths and octaves   sixths and octaves

15. Transpose the excerpt to D major, this time for men's voices. Write appropriate clefs and the key and meter signatures. Include any necessary accidental(s). Between the staves write interval numbers.

Contextual Listening 9.4

In exercises 1–2, identify the tonality/modality. Beneath the rhythm staves, write the syllables and numbers of each part. From the given items, notate the pitches and rhythm of both parts on the grand staff. Below the treble staff, write the harmonic intervals.

1. The tonality/modality is:

   major   minor   Lydian   Mixolydian

2. The tonality/modality is:

   major   minor   Lydian   Mixolydian

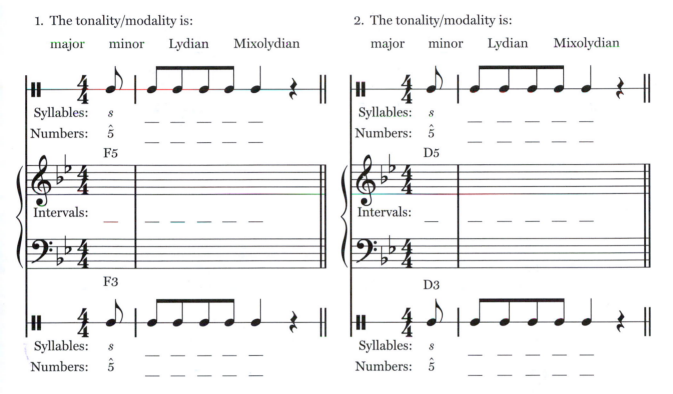

Now, listen to an excerpt from a keyboard work and complete the remaining exercises.

3. The excerpt's tonality/modality is:

   major   minor   Lydian   Mixolydian

4. In the workspace, capture the two parts.

   (a) The rhythm of each part appears in the single-line staves. Beneath each note, write the syllables and numbers.

   (b) In the grand staff, begin with the given items and notate the remaining pitches and rhythm of both parts. Notate the rhythm according to the single-line staves. Check your work at a keyboard.

   (c) Below the treble staff, write the harmonic interval numbers only where blanks appear.

5. Melodic pitches 1–2 create which type of motion against the bass?

contrary   oblique   parallel   similar

6. Melodic pitches 5–6 create which type of motion against the bass?

contrary   oblique   parallel   similar

7. Melodic pitches 7–8 create which type of motion against the bass?

contrary   oblique   parallel   similar

8. Beginning with melodic pitch 14, three triads are outlined. Which are their qualities?

M-m-d   m-M-d   d-M-m   d-m-M

Embellishment in Two-Part Counterpoint

NAME _____

In this chapter you'll learn to:

- Identify embellishments in two-voice counterpoint
- Convert simple-meter notation to compound meter

Embellishments

Prolongation occurs when embellishment sustains the effect of a pitch, interval, or chord. There are several types of embellishment.

Embellishment	Definition	Original, then embellished idea
consonant skip (CS) chordal skip (CS)	Skips/leaps within a chord or that create consonant intervals above the bass	
passing tone (P)	Pitch that fills a consonant skip	
neighbor tone (N)	The pitch above (or below) a prolonged pitch	
incomplete neighbor (IN)	Neighbor tone that omits the prolonged pitch either before or after	
suspension (S)	A strong-beat dissonance that descends by step, delaying the resolution to a consonant interval or chord tone	
retardation (S)	A "suspension" that resolves up	
voice exchange (VE)	Two voices that "trade places," moving from 3 to 6 or from 6 to 3	
anticipation (A)	Pitch that arrives earlier than expected	

Try it

Listen to two-part music and complete the exercises by circling the correct answers.

1. Listen to exercise 1.

    (a) From melodic pitch 1 to 2, the motion between parts is:

    contrary   oblique   parallel   similar

    (b) The initial harmonic intervals are:

    thirds   fifths   sixths   octaves

    (c) The final harmonic interval is a/an:

    unison   third   fifth   octave

2. Listen to exercise 1, then to exercise 2.

    (a) Compared with exercise 1, which part is embellished in exercise 2?

    higher   lower   both

    (b) The type of embellishment is:

    suspension   neighbor tone   consonant skip   passing tone

3. Listen to exercise 1, then to exercise 3.

    (a) Compared with exercise 1, which part is embellished in exercise 3?

    higher   lower   both

    (b) The type of embellishment is:

    suspension   neighbor tone   consonant skip   passing tone

4. Listen to exercise 1, then to exercise 4.

    (a) Compared with exercise 1, which part is embellished in exercise 4?

    higher   lower   both

    (b) The type of embellishment is:

    suspension   neighbor tone   consonant skip   passing tone

5. Listen to exercise 1, then to exercise 5.

    (a) Compared with exercise 1, which part is embellished in exercise 5?

    higher   lower   both

    (b) The type of embellishment is:

    suspension   neighbor tone   consonant skip   passing tone

6. Listen to exercise 1, then to exercise 6.

    (a) Compared with exercise 1, which part is embellished in exercise 6?

    higher   lower   both

    (b) The type of embellishment is:

    suspension   neighbor tone   consonant skip   passing tone

7. This time, listen first to exercise 2. Then, listen to exercise 7.

   (a) Compared with exercise 2, which part is embellished in exercise 7?

      higher   lower   both

   (b) The type of embellishment is:

      suspension   neighbor tone   consonant skip   passing tone

8. Listen to exercise 2, then to exercise 8.

   (a) Compared with exercise 2, the higher part in exercise 8 is embellished with a:

      suspension   neighbor tone   consonant skip   passing tone

   (b) Compared with exercise 2, the lower part in exercise 8 is embellished with a:

      suspension   neighbor tone   consonant skip   passing tone

9. Listen to exercise 9.

   (a) Between melodic pitches 1–2, the motion between parts is:

      contrary   oblique   parallel   similar

   (b) The initial harmonic intervals are:

      thirds   fifths   sixths   octaves

   (c) The final harmonic interval is a/an:

      unison   third   fifth   octave

10. Listen again to exercise 9, then to exercise 10.

   (a) Compared with exercise 9, which part is embellished in exercise 10?

      higher   lower   both

   (b) The type of embellishment is:

      suspension   neighbor tone   consonant skip   passing tone

11. Listen again to exercise 9, then to exercise 11.

   (a) Compared with exercise 9, which part is embellished in exercise 11?

      higher   lower   both

   (b) Initially, the type of embellishment is a/an

      suspension   incomplete neighbor   anticipation   voice exchange

   (c) The final embellishment is a/an:

      suspension   incomplete neighbor   anticipation   voice exchange

12. Listen again to exercise 9, then to exercise 12.

   (a) Compared with exercise 9, which part is embellished in exercise 12?

      higher   lower   both

   (b) The type of embellishment is a/an:

      suspension   incomplete neighbor   anticipation   voice exchange

Contextual Listening 10.1

1. Listen to a series of chords and identify their quality. For triads, write M, m, or d. For seventh chords, write MM7, Mm7, mm7, dm7, or dd7.

   Chord: 1   2   3   4   5   6   7

   Quality: _____   _____   _____   _____   _____   _____   _____

Now, listen to part of a piano work and complete the following exercises.

2. Capture the excerpt in the workspace.

   (a) In the single-line staves, begin with the given items and notate the rhythm of the outermost parts. Beneath these staves, write the syllables and numbers.

   (b) In the grand staff, begin with the given items and notate the outermost parts' remaining pitches and rhythm. Refer to the syllables and numbers. Check your work at a keyboard.

   (c) Between the staves, write the harmonic interval numbers.

   (d) Circle each dissonant interval and label its function using the abbreviations P (passing tone) or N (neighbor).

   (e) In the blanks marked "Chords," write the chord quality. For triads, write M, m, or d. For seventh chords, write the triad-plus-seventh symbol (MM7, Mm7, etc.). Circle the correct answers below. Hint: Measure 1 is the first complete measure.

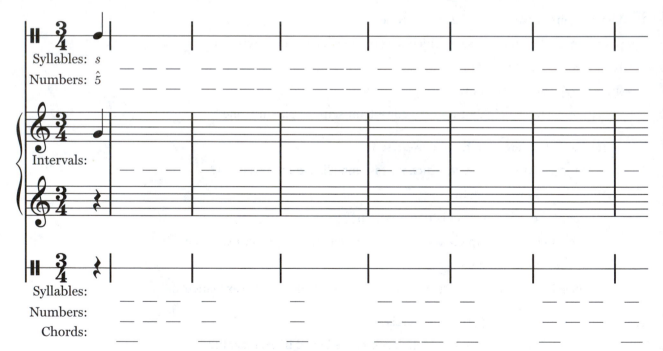

3. In measures 1–3, the motion between the outermost parts is:

   contrary   oblique   parallel   similar

4. Voice exchanges occur during which two measures?

   1 and 3   2 and 4   3 and 5   4 and 6

Contextual Listening 10.2

In each of the following, begin with the given items and notate the remaining pitches and rhythm. Then, complete the exercises.

1. Listen to exercise 1.

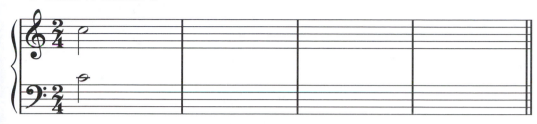

   (a) Between melodic pitches 1–2, the motion between the parts is:

      contrary   oblique   parallel   similar

   (b) Between melodic pitches 2–3, the motion between the parts is:

      contrary   oblique   parallel   similar

   (c) Between melodic pitches 3–4, the motion between the parts is:

      contrary   oblique   parallel   similar

   (d) Between melodic pitches 4–5, the motion between the parts is:

      contrary   oblique   parallel   similar

2. Listen to exercise 1, then exercise 2. In measure 3, the new embellishments are:

   suspensions   neighbor tones   consonant skips   passing tones

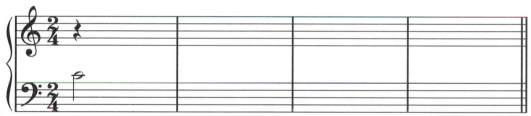

3. Listen to exercise 2, then exercise 3. In measure 2, the new embellishment is a:

   suspension   neighbor tone   consonant skip   passing tone

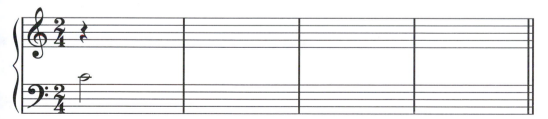

4. Listen to exercise 3, then exercise 4. In measure 3, the new embellishments are:

suspensions   neighbor tones   consonant skips   passing tones

5. Listen to exercise 4, then exercise 5. In measures 1–2, the new embellishments are:

suspensions   neighbor tones   consonant skips   passing tones

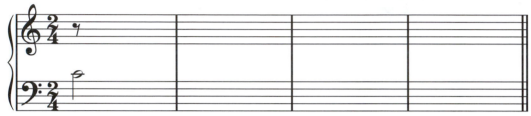

Now, listen to an excerpt from a cantata, and complete the following exercises.

6. Capture the excerpt in the workspace.

   (a) Begin with the given items and notate the remaining pitches and rhythm.

   (b) Between the staves, write the harmonic interval numbers.

   (c) Circle each dissonant interval number and label its function using the abbreviations
       N (neighbor) and P (passing tone).

Contextual Listening 10.3

Listen to part of an art song, then complete the following exercises.

Translation: Hopping and skipping, happily, whoever can.

1. In the given meter, notate the rhythm of the piano accompaniment for measure 1.

Piano R.H. $\quad$ 𝄆 4/4

Piano L.H. $\quad$ 𝄆 4/4

2. In the given meter, notate the rhythm of the piano accompaniment for measure 1.

Piano R.H. $\quad$ 𝄆 12/8

Piano L.H. $\quad$ 𝄆 12/8

3. The composer wrote her music in $\frac{4}{4}$. Are there musical reasons to select one meter signature over another? Could she have chosen $\frac{12}{8}$ instead?

Listen again to the art song excerpt, then focus on chord quality.

4. During beats 1–2, which is the chord quality?

    M triad   m triad   MM7   Mm7   mm7

5. On the downbeats of measures 2 and 3, which is the chord quality?

    M triad   m triad   MM7   Mm7   mm7

6. Which is the final chord's quality?

    M triad   m triad   MM7   Mm7   mm7

Contextual Listening 10.4

In each of the following, begin with the given items and notate the remaining pitches and rhythm. Then, complete the exercises.

1. Listen to exercise 1.

 (a) The first harmonic interval is a: M3 P4 d5 P5

 (b) The second harmonic interval is a: M3 P4 d5 P5

 (c) Between measures 2–3, the motion between the parts is:

   contrary oblique parallel similar

 (d) Between measures 3–4, the motion between the parts is:

   contrary oblique parallel similar

2. Listen to exercise 1, then exercise 2.

 (a) Compared with exercise 1, the lower part is embellished with:

   suspensions neighbor tones consonant skips passing tones

 (b) Compared with exercise 1, the higher part's embellishment is a/an:

   suspension incomplete neighbor consonant skip passing tone

3. Listen to exercise 2, then exercise 3.

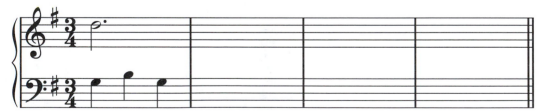

 (a) Compared with exercise 2, measures 1–2 are embellished with:

   suspensions neighbor tones consonant skips passing tones

 (b) In measure 1, all the pitches together create which chord?

   major triad minor triad MM7 Mm7

(c) In measure 2, all the pitches together create which chord?

     major triad   minor triad   MM7   Mm7

(d) Compared with exercise 2, measure 3 of the higher part is embellished with a:

     suspension   neighbor tone   consonant skip   passing tone

4. Listen to exercise 3, then exercise 4.

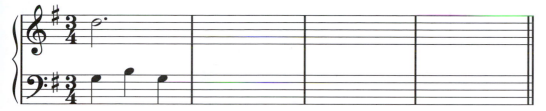

(a) Compared with exercise 3, measure 3 of the higher part is embellished with a:

     suspension   neighbor tone   consonant skip   passing tone

(b) Compared with exercise 3, measure 4 of the higher part is embellished with a:

     suspension   neighbor tone   consonant skip   passing tone

Now, listen to a string quartet excerpt that features just the violin and cello.

5. Melodic pitches 1–2 create which interval?

     P5   m6   M6   m7   M7

6. In measure 1, all the pitches together create which chord?

     major triad   minor triad   MM7   Mm7

7. In measure 2, all the pitches together create which chord?

     major triad   minor triad   MM7   Mm7

8. Begin with the given items and notate the remaining pitches and rhythm.

(a) Between the staves, write the harmonic interval numbers.

(b) Circle each dissonant interval and label its function using the abbreviations S (suspension), IN (incomplete neighbor), or P (passing tone).

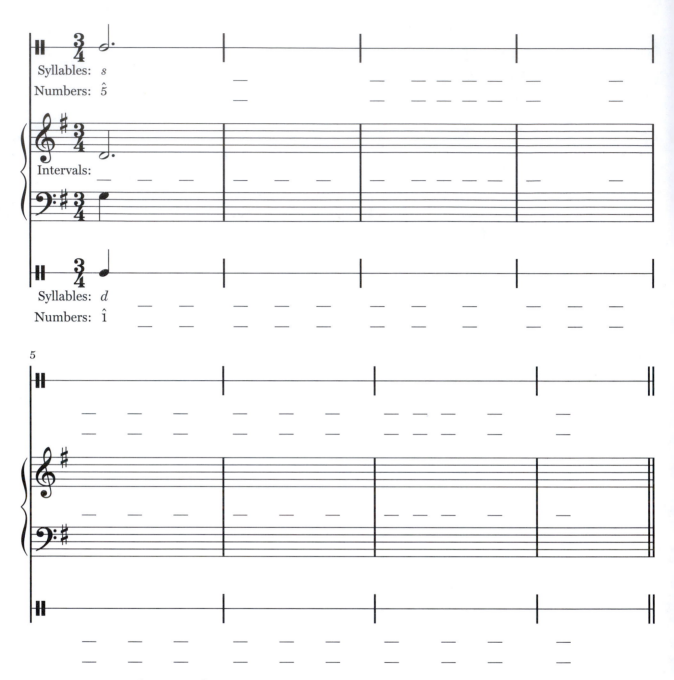

9. In measure 5, the motion between parts creates:

parallel motion   a voice exchange   rhythmic contrast

PART II

Diatonic Harmony and Tonicization

Soprano and Bass Lines in Eighteenth-Century Style

CHAPTER 11

NAME _____

In this chapter you'll learn to:

- Classify cadences as conclusive or inconclusive
- Perform and notate the outer parts of eighteenth-century chorales

Phrase and Cadence

A *phrase* is a distinct musical idea that concludes with a cadence. The cadential pitches of the bass (lowest part) and soprano (highest part) determine how conclusive the music sounds.

If the cadential bass pitches are . . .	And the cadential soprano pitch is . . .	The cadence is . . .
sol–do ($\hat{5}$–$\hat{1}$)	*do* ($\hat{1}$)	conclusive
sol–do ($\hat{5}$–$\hat{1}$)	*mi* or *sol* ($\hat{3}$ or $\hat{5}$)	less conclusive
ti–do ($\hat{7}$–$\hat{1}$)	*do* ($\hat{1}$)	less conclusive
any note to *mi* ($\hat{3}$)	*do* or *sol* ($\hat{1}$ or $\hat{5}$)	less conclusive
any note to *sol* ($\hat{5}$)	*re, ti,* or *sol* ($\hat{2}$, $\hat{7}$, or $\hat{5}$)	inconclusive

Try it

Listen to two-part music that concludes with a cadence. Focus on the final bass and soprano pitches to identify the cadence. From the given items, notate the remaining pitches and rhythm of both parts. Include any necessary accidentals and bar lines. Write harmonic interval numbers between the staves.

1. The cadence is:

   conclusive   less conclusive   inconclusive

   Interval: ___   ___   ___

2. The cadence is:

   conclusive   less conclusive   inconclusive

   Interval: ___   ___   ___

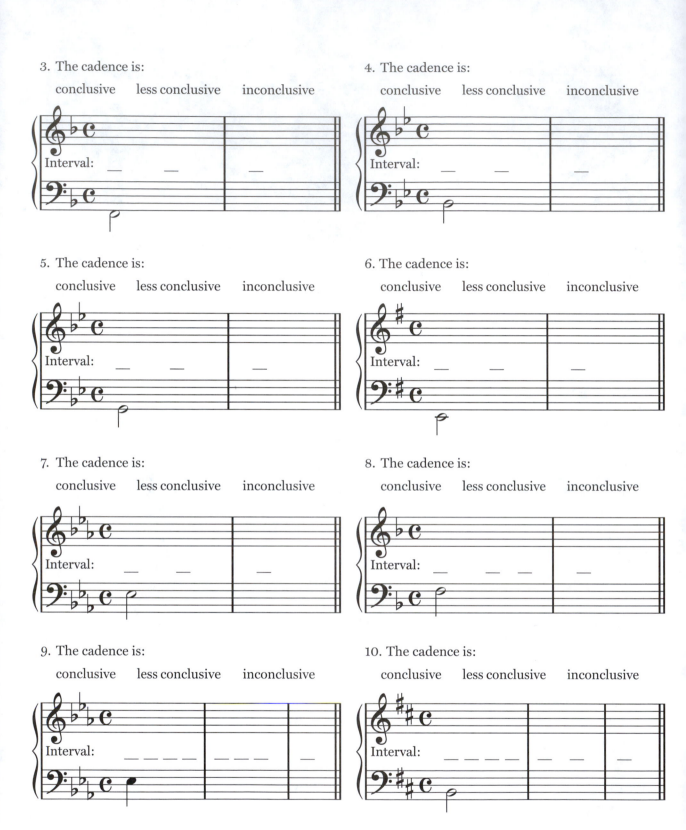

3. The cadence is:

  conclusive   less conclusive   inconclusive

  Interval: ___ ___   ___

4. The cadence is:

  conclusive   less conclusive   inconclusive

  Interval: ___ ___   ___

5. The cadence is:

  conclusive   less conclusive   inconclusive

  Interval: ___ ___   ___

6. The cadence is:

  conclusive   less conclusive   inconclusive

  Interval: ___ ___   ___

7. The cadence is:

  conclusive   less conclusive   inconclusive

  Interval: ___ ___   ___

8. The cadence is:

  conclusive   less conclusive   inconclusive

  Interval: ___ ___   ___

9. The cadence is:

  conclusive   less conclusive   inconclusive

  Interval: ___ ___ ___ ___ ___

10. The cadence is:

  conclusive   less conclusive   inconclusive

  Interval: ___ ___ ___ ___ ___

Contextual Listening 11.1

Listen to two-part music and identify the cadence. From the given items, notate the remaining pitches of both parts using whole notes. Include any necessary accidentals. Write harmonic interval numbers between the staves.

1. The cadence is:

conclusive   less conclusive   inconclusive

Interval: ___   ___   ___   ___

2. The cadence is:

conclusive   less conclusive   inconclusive

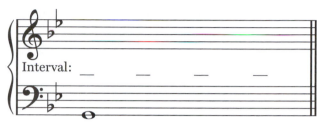

Interval: ___   ___   ___   ___

3. The cadence is:

conclusive   less conclusive   inconclusive

Interval: ___   ___   ___   ___

Now, listen to one phrase from a chorale, and complete the following exercises.

4. Beginning with the given items, capture the excerpt in the workspace.

   (a) In the single-line staves, notate the rhythm of the bass and soprano lines.

   (b) Below each note, write the syllables and numbers of the pitches.

   (c) In the grand staff, notate the pitches and rhythm of both parts. Refer to the single-line notation. Check your work at a keyboard.

   (d) Write harmonic interval numbers between the treble and bass staves.

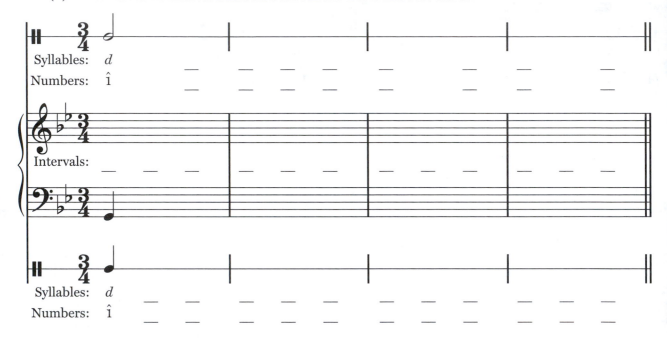

5. Bass pitches 1–2 create which melodic interval?

   P4   P5   M6   P8

6. Bass pitches 6–7 create which melodic interval?

   M3   P4   d5   P5

7. The phrase's cadence is: conclusive   less conclusive   inconclusive

8. The melody's pitch collection belongs to which pattern?

   major tetrachord   minor tetrachord   major pentachord   minor pentachord

9. The bass line's pitch collection belongs to which scale?

   major   natural minor (descending melodic)

   ascending melodic minor   harmonic minor

Contextual Listening 11.2

Listen to two-part music and identify the cadence. From the given items, notate the remaining pitches of both parts using whole notes. Include any necessary accidentals. Write harmonic interval numbers between the staves.

1. The cadence is:

   conclusive   less conclusive   inconclusive

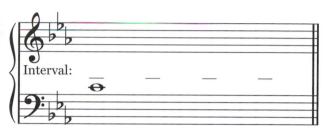

2. The cadence is:

   conclusive   less conclusive   inconclusive

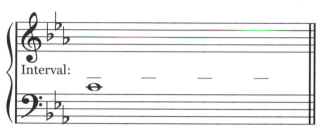

3. The cadence is:

   conclusive   less conclusive   inconclusive

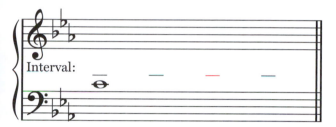

Now, listen to two phrases from a chorale and complete the following exercises.

4. Beginning with the given items, capture the excerpt in the workspace.

   (a) In the single-line staves, notate the rhythm of the bass and soprano lines.

   (b Below each note, write the syllables and numbers of the pitches.

   (c) In the grand staff, notate the pitches and rhythm of both parts. Refer to the single-line notation. Check your work at a keyboard.

   (d) Write harmonic interval numbers between the treble and bass staves.

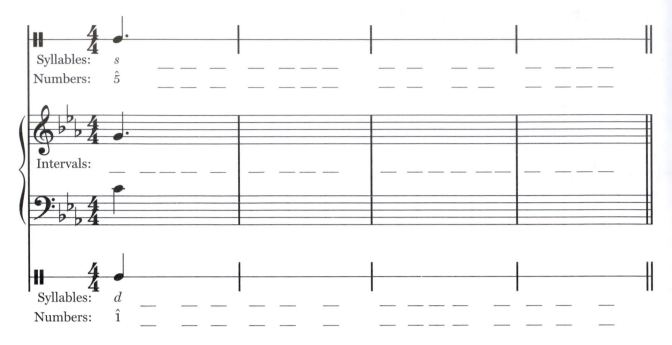

Syllables: _s_ _ _ _ _ _ _ _ _ _ _ _ _
Numbers: $\hat{5}$ _ _ _ _ _ _ _ _ _ _ _ _ _

Intervals: _ _ _ _ _ _ _ _ _ _ _ _

Syllables: _d_ _ _ _ _ _ _ _ _ _ _ _ _
Numbers: $\hat{1}$ _ _ _ _ _ _ _ _ _ _ _ _

Exercises 5–7 focus only on phrase 1.

5. Soprano pitches 1–2 create which melodic interval?

   m3   P4   P5   m6

6. Between harmonic intervals 3–5, the motion is:

   contrary   oblique   similar   parallel

7. Phrase 1's cadence is: conclusive   less conclusive   inconclusive

Bonus! From phrase 1's cadential bass pitch, read the line _backward_. Compare this to phrase 1's soprano line read _forward_. How do they relate?

Exercises 8–12 focus only on phrase 2.

8. Between harmonic pitches 1–2, the motion is:

   contrary   oblique   similar   parallel

9. Between the last two harmonic intervals, the motion is:

   contrary   oblique   similar   parallel

10. The final bass pitches create which melodic interval?

    M3   P4   d5   P5

11. Phrase 2's cadence is: conclusive   less conclusive   inconclusive

12. Phrase 2's bass-line pitch collection belongs to which scale?

    major   natural minor (descending melodic)

    ascending melodic minor   harmonic minor

Contextual Listening 11.3

Listen to two-part music and identify the cadence. From the given items, notate the remaining pitches of both parts using whole notes. Include any necessary accidentals. Write harmonic intervals between the staves.

1. The cadence is:

    conclusive   less conclusive   inconclusive

2. The cadence is:

    conclusive   less conclusive   inconclusive

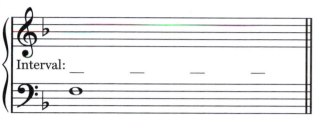

3. The cadence is:

    conclusive   less conclusive   inconclusive

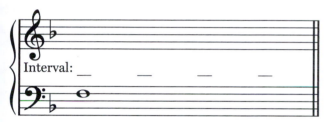

Now, listen to two phrases from a chorale and complete the following exercises.

4. Beginning with the given items, capture the excerpt in the workspace.

    (a) In the single-line staves, notate the rhythm of the bass and soprano lines.

    (b) Below each note, write the syllables and numbers of the pitches.

    (c) In the grand staff, notate the pitches and rhythm of both parts. Refer to the single-line notation. Check your work at a keyboard.

    (d) Write harmonic interval numbers between the treble and bass staves.

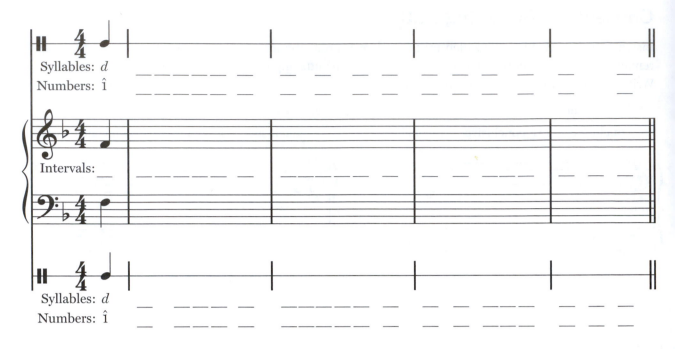

Syllables: *d*
Numbers: 1̂

Intervals: __

Syllables: *d*
Numbers: 1̂

Exercises 5–7 focus only on phrase 1.

5. Soprano pitches 1–2 create which melodic interval?

    m3   P4   P5   m6

6. Harmonic pitches 1–2 produce which type of motion?
    contrary   oblique   similar   parallel

7. Phrase 1's cadence is: conclusive   less conclusive   inconclusive

Exercises 8–12 focus only on phrase 2.

8. Harmonic pitches 1–4 produce which type of motion?
    contrary   oblique   similar   parallel

9. The last two harmonic pitches produce which type of motion?
    contrary   oblique   similar   parallel

10. The final bass pitches create which melodic interval?

    m3   P4   P5   m6

11. Phrase 2's cadence is: conclusive   less conclusive   inconclusive

12. The excerpt's pitch collection belongs to which scale?

    major   natural minor (descending melodic)

    ascending melodic minor   harmonic minor

Contextual Listening 11.4

Listen to two-part music and identify the cadence. From the given items, notate the remaining pitches of both parts using whole notes. Include any necessary accidentals. Write harmonic intervals between the staves.

1. The cadence is:

   conclusive   less conclusive   inconclusive

2. The cadence is:

   conclusive   less conclusive   inconclusive

3. The cadence is:

   conclusive   less conclusive   inconclusive

Now, listen to two phrases from a chorale and complete the following exercises.

4. Beginning with the given items, capture the excerpt in the workspace.

   (a) In the single-line staves, notate the rhythm of the bass and soprano lines.

   (b) Below each note, write the syllables and numbers of the pitches.

   (c) In the grand staff, notate the pitches and rhythm of both parts. Refer to the single-line notation. Check your work at a keyboard.

   (d) Write harmonic interval numbers between the treble and bass staves.

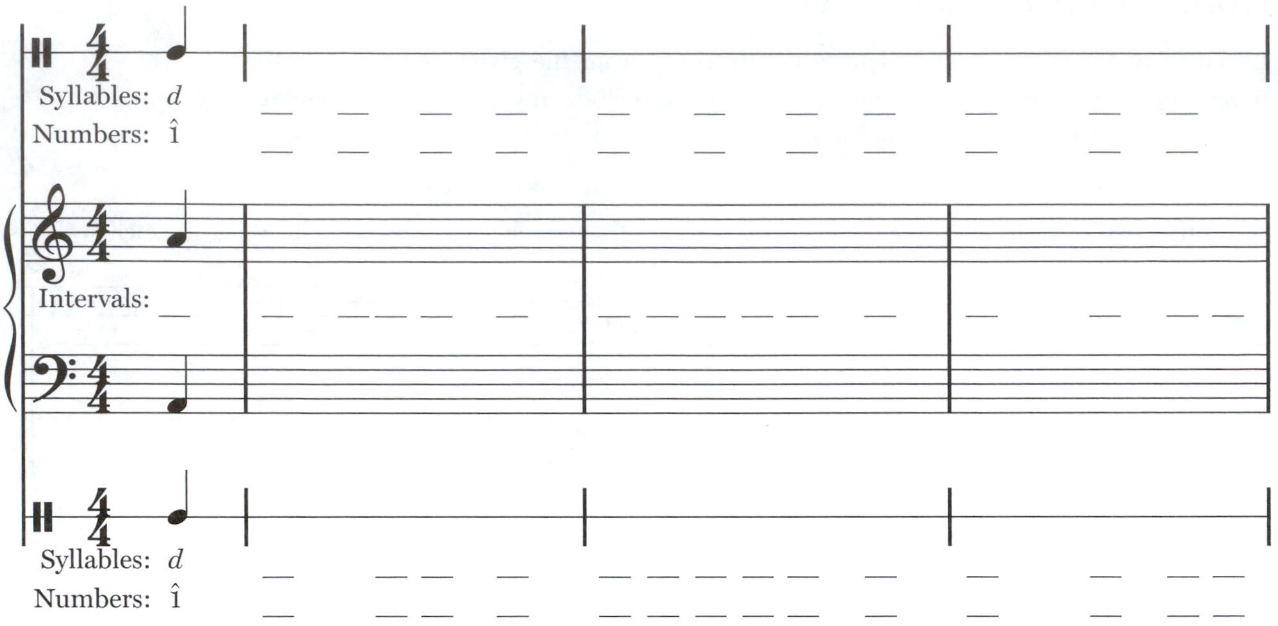

Syllables: *d*
Numbers: 1̂

Intervals: __

Syllables: *d*
Numbers: 1̂

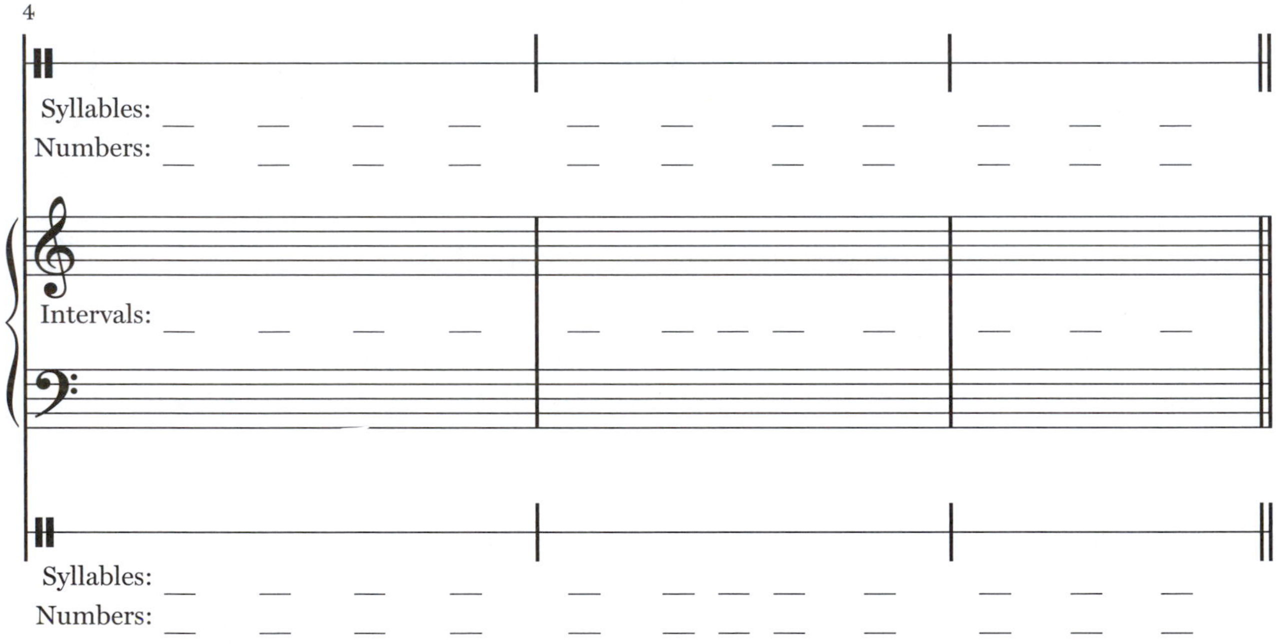

4

Syllables:
Numbers:

Intervals:

Syllables:
Numbers:

Exercises 5–6 focus only on phrase 1.

5. Soprano pitches 1–2 create which melodic interval?

   M2   m3   M3   P4

6. Phrase 1's cadence is: conclusive   less conclusive   inconclusive

Exercises 7–8 focus only on phrase 2.

7. Phrase 2's cadence is: conclusive   less conclusive   inconclusive

8. The final bass pitches create which interval?

   P4   P5   m6   M6

CHAPTER 12

The Basic Phrase in Chorale Style

NAME _____

In this chapter you'll learn to:

- Identify harmonies and notate them with Roman numerals and figures
- Identify cadences and label them by type: HC, IAC, PAC
- Transcribe a concert-pitch melody for B♭ clarinet

Tonic–Dominant–Tonic (T–D–T) Roman Numerals and Cadence Types

Focusing on bass pitches helps you determine dominant- and tonic-function chords and their Roman-numeral representations.

If the bass pitch is . . .	Write	And listen above the bass for . . .	If present, then write
sol–do ($\hat{5}$–$\hat{1}$)	V	sol–fa ($\hat{5}$–$\hat{4}$)	V$^{8–7}$
ti ($\hat{7}$)	V^6		
do ($\hat{1}$)	I or i		

Cadential bass pitches help you determine the most common cadence types: half and authentic.

If the bass is . . .	and the soprano is . . .	the ending is . . .	and the cadence type is . . .
sol–do ($\hat{5}$–$\hat{1}$)	do ($\hat{1}$)	conclusive	perfect authentic (PAC)
do ($\hat{1}$)	mi ($\hat{3}$) or sol ($\hat{5}$)	less conclusive	imperfect authentic (IAC)
sol ($\hat{5}$)	re ($\hat{2}$), ti ($\hat{7}$), or sol ($\hat{5}$)	inconclusive	half (HC)

Try it

Look at the given items, then listen to four-part progressions. Sing aloud with syllables or numbers.

- In the blank beneath the bass staff, write the key name and its quality: uppercase for major, lowercase for minor (e.g., C, F, b, g, etc.)
- In the grand staff, notate the pitches and rhythm of the bass and soprano parts.
- Beneath each bass pitch, write the Roman numeral and figure (if needed).
- Circle the cadence type: PAC (perfect authentic), IAC (imperfect authentic), HC (half)
- For an extra challenge, perform and then notate the inner voices.

1. Cadence type: PAC   IAC   HC

2. Cadence type: PAC   IAC   HC

3. Cadence type: PAC   IAC   HC

4. Cadence type: PAC   IAC   HC

5. Cadence type: PAC   IAC   HC

6. Cadence type: PAC   IAC   HC

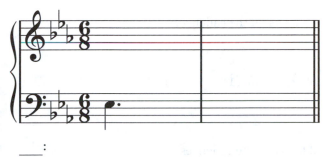

___ :

7. Cadence type: PAC   IAC   HC

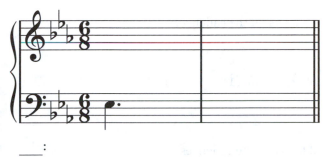

___ :

8. Cadence type: PAC   IAC   HC

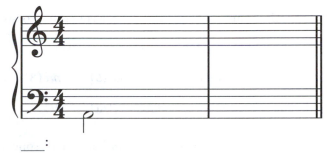

___ :

Contextual Listening 12.1

This activity features excerpts from works by three different composers.

CL 12.1A Listen to one phrase from a piano work and focus on the end—a cadence that's extended.

1. The final bass pitch is: *sol* (5̂)   *do* (1̂)

2. The final melodic pitch is: *sol* (5̂)   *mi* (3̂)   *re* (2̂)   *do* (1̂)   *ti* (7̂)

3. The cadence type is: PAC   IAC   HC

   Hints: HC melodies end on *re* (2̂), *ti* (7̂), or *sol* (5̂). PACs end on *do* (1̂) and IACs on *mi* (3̂) or *sol* (5̂).

CL 12.1B Listen to one phrase from a concerto grosso and focus on the cadence.

4. The final bass pitch is: *sol* (5̂)   *do* (1̂)

5. The final melodic pitch is: *sol* (5̂)   *mi* (3̂)   *re* (2̂)   *do* (1̂)   *ti* (7̂)

6. The cadence type is: PAC   IAC   HC

CL12.1C Listen to the introduction from an art song and focus on the cadences. Cadence 1 occurs halfway through the excerpt, just before the melody returns.

7. Cadence 1's bass pitch is: *sol* (5̂)   *do* (1̂)

8. Cadence 1's melodic pitch is: *sol* (5̂)   *mi* (3̂)   *re* (2̂)   *do* (1̂)   *ti* (7̂)

9. Cadence 1's type is: PAC   IAC   HC

Cadence 2 occurs at the end of the excerpt.

10. The final bass pitch is: *sol* (5̂)   *do* (1̂)

11. The final melodic pitch is: *sol* (5̂)   *mi* (3̂)   *re* (2̂)   *do* (1̂)   *ti* (7̂)

12. Cadence 2's type is: PAC   IAC   HC

Contextual Listening 12.2

Simple-meter patterns   *Compound-meter patterns*

In exercises 1–2, a four-beat count-off precedes four beats of rhythm. Determine whether the meter is simple or compound. Then, from the choices provided, select the pattern number of each beat.

1. (a) The meter type is: simple   compound

    (b) Write the correct rhythm-pattern numbers: ___ ___ ___ ___

2. (a) The meter type is: simple   compound

    (b) Write the correct rhythm-pattern numbers: ___ ___ ___ ___

In exercises 3–4 a clarinet plays tonic, rests, and then plays a four-beat melody.

3. (a) The meter type is: simple   compound

    (b) Write the correct rhythm-pattern numbers: ___ ___ ___ ___

    (c) The triad arpeggiated is: I   ii   IV   V

    (d) Pitches 1–2 form which pitch interval?   m3   P4   P5   M6

4. (a) The meter type is: simple   compound

    (b) Write the correct rhythm-pattern numbers: ___ ___ ___ ___

    (c) The triad arpeggiated is: tonic   supertonic   subdominant   dominant

    (d) Pitches 1–2 form which pitch interval?   m3   P4   P5   M6

Now, listen to two phrases from a twentieth-century ballet and complete the following exercises.

5. Pitches 1–2 form which interval?   m3   P4   P5   M6

6. The meter is: simple quadruple   compound quadruple

7. Beginning with the given items, capture the excerpt in the workspace.

    (a) In the single-line staff, begin with a half-note anacrusis and notate the melodic rhythm. Include the meter signature and all bar lines. Beam notes to show beat grouping.

    (b) Beginning with *sol* ($\hat{5}$), write the remaining syllables or numbers beneath each note.

    (c) In the five-line staff, begin with C4 and write the appropriate clef, key signature, and meter signature. Refer to the single-line staff and notate the pitches and rhythm of the melody.

Cadence 1 occurs halfway through the excerpt, *just before* the opening idea returns.

8. Cadence 1 features which triad arpeggiation?

   tonic   supertonic   subdominant   dominant

9. Phrase 1's cadence type is: PAC   IAC   HC

Cadence 2 occurs at the end of the excerpt.

10. The final melodic pitch is: *do* (1̂)   *re* (2̂)   *mi* (3̂)   *sol* (5̂)

11. The final pitch implies which chord?   I   ii   V   vi

12. The final cadence type is: PAC   IAC   HC

13. What is the range (lowest pitch to highest pitch) of the melody?

    do-sol (1̂-5̂)   *ti-la* (7̂-6̂)   *do-do* (1̂-1̂)   *sol-sol* (5̂-5̂)

14. On the given staves, create a part for B♭ clarinet. Notate a new key signature and transpose the concert-pitch melody up a M2. Hint: Refer to your workspace answers.

Contextual Listening 12.3

Simple-meter patterns   *Compound-meter patterns*

In exercises 1–2, a two-beat count-off precedes four beats of rhythm.

1. (a) The meter type is: simple   compound

   (b) Write the correct rhythm-pattern numbers: ___ ___ ___ ___

2. (a) The meter type is: simple   compound

   (b) Write the correct rhythm-pattern numbers: ___ ___ ___ ___

In exercises 3–4 the tonic pitch sounds. After a rest, a woodwind trio performs one phrase.

3. (a) Bass pitch 1 is: *do* (1̂)   *re* (2̂)   *mi* (3̂)   *sol* (5̂)

   (b) Soprano pitch 1 is: *do* (1̂)   *re* (2̂)   *mi* (3̂)   *sol* (5̂)

   (c) Chord 1 is: I   ii   IV   V

   (d) The final bass pitch is: *do* (1̂)   *re* (2̂)   *mi* (3̂)   *sol* (5̂)

   (e) The final chord is Roman numeral: I   ii   IV   V

   (f) The cadence type is: PAC   IAC   HC

      Hints: For HCs, the bass is *sol* (5̂). For IACs, the bass is *do* (1̂) and the soprano is
      either *mi* (3̂) or *sol* (5̂). A PAC's bass and soprano pitches are both *do* (1̂).

4. (a) The final bass pitch is: *do* (1̂)   *re* (2̂)   *mi* (3̂)   *sol* (5̂)

   (b) The final soprano pitch is: *do* (1̂)   *re* (2̂)   *mi* (3̂)   *sol* (5̂)

   (c) The final chord is Roman numeral: I   ii   IV   V

   (d) The cadence type is: PAC   IAC   HC

Now, listen to one phrase from a holiday song and complete the following exercises.

5. The meter is: compound duple   simple duple

6. The bassoon's first note is: *do* (1̂)   *re* (2̂)   *mi* (3̂)   *sol* (5̂)

7. The bassoon's first note implies which chord?   I   ii   IV   V

8. The flute melody begins on: *do* (1̂)   *re* (2̂)   *mi* (3̂)   *sol* (5̂)

9. During pitches 1–3 the flute and oboe move in which type of motion?

   contrary   parallel   similar   oblique

10. The melody ends on: *do* (1̂)   *re* (2̂)   *mi* (3̂)   *sol* (5̂)

11. The bass ends on: *do* (1̂)   *re* (2̂)   *mi* (3̂)   *sol* (5̂)

12. The final harmony is: I   ii   IV   V

13. The phrase's cadence type is: PAC   IAC   HC

Complete your answers to exercises 14–16 in the workspace.

14. Capture the bass line (bassoon part).

   (a) In the single-line bass staff, notate the bass rhythm. Include the meter signature and bar lines. Beam notes to show beat grouping.

   (b) Beneath each note in the single-line bass staff, write the syllables or numbers of the bassoon's pitches.

   (c) In the five-line bass staff, write the key and meter signatures. Begin with D3 and notate the bass line's pitches and rhythm. Refer to your workspace answers.

15. Capture the essential harmonies.

   (a) Beneath each bass-pitch *do* ($\hat{1}$), write Roman numeral I.

   (b) Beneath bass-pitch *sol* ($\hat{5}$), write V. If a pitch repeats, don't rewrite its Roman numeral.

   (c) For each bass-pitch *sol* ($\hat{5}$), if you hear *fa* ($\hat{4}$) above it, write V7.
       If you hear *sol-fa* ($\hat{5}$–$\hat{4}$), write V8–7.

16. Capture the soprano line (flute part).

   (a) In the single-line treble staff, notate the soprano rhythm. Include the meter signature and bar lines. Beam notes to show beat grouping.

   (b) Beneath each note in the single-line treble staff, write the syllables or numbers of the flute's pitches.

   (c) In the five-line treble staff, write the appropriate key and meter signatures. Begin with A5 and notate the soprano line's pitches and rhythm. Refer to the workspace answers.

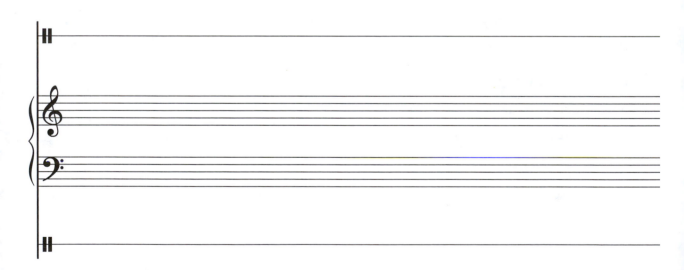

CHAPTER 13

Dominant Sevenths and Predominants

NAME _____

In this chapter you'll learn to:

- Associate bass pitches with chords and chord inversions
- Identify dominant seventh and predominant chords in harmonic progressions
- Identify authentic and half cadences that are prepared with predominant chords

More Tonic-Dominant-Tonic (T–D–T) Progressions

Focusing on bass pitches helps you determine dominant- and tonic-function chords and their Roman-numeral representations.

If the bass pitch is . . .	Write	And listen above the bass for . . .	If present, then write
sol ($\hat{5}$)	V	sol–fa ($\hat{5}$–$\hat{4}$)	V$^{8-7}$
ti ($\hat{7}$)	V^6	fa ($\hat{4}$)	V$^6_5$
re ($\hat{2}$)	V$^4_3$		
fa–mi ($\hat{4}$–$\hat{3}$)	V$^4_2$–I^6		
fa–me ($\hat{4}$–$\flat\hat{3}$)	V$^4_2$–i^6		

Tonic-Chord Listening Strategies

If the bass pitch is . . .	Write
do ($\hat{1}$)	I for major; i for minor
mi ($\hat{3}$) or me ($\flat\hat{3}$)	I^6 or i^6

Try it 1

Look at the given items, then listen to four-part progressions. Sing each part.

- Write the key name and quality: uppercase for major, lowercase for minor (e.g., C or g).
- Notate the pitches and rhythm of the bass and soprano.
- In the blanks beneath the bass pitches, write the Roman numeral and figure (if needed) that represents the harmony.

- Identify the cadence type.
- For an extra challenge, perform and then notate the inner voices.

1. Cadence type: PAC   IAC   HC

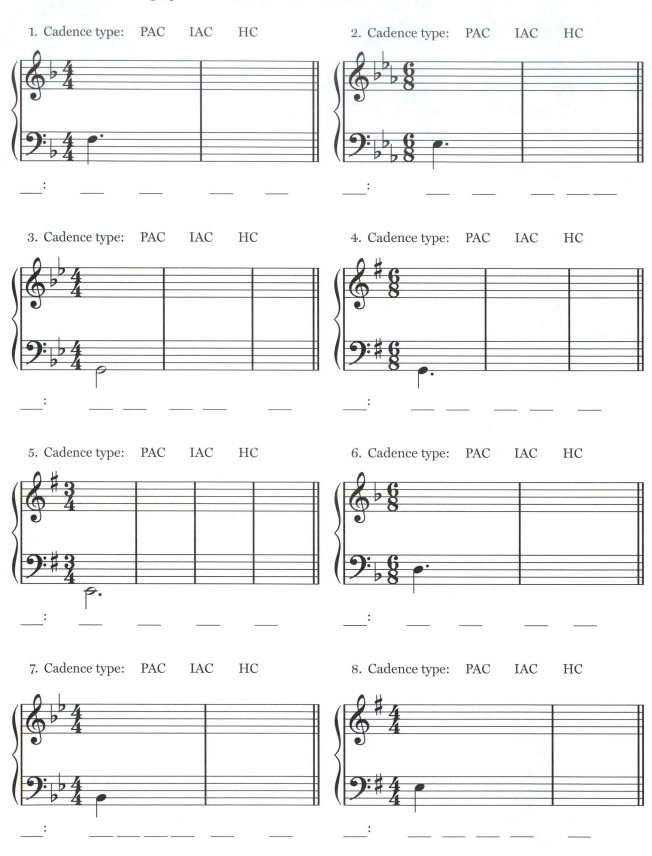

2. Cadence type: PAC   IAC   HC

3. Cadence type: PAC   IAC   HC

4. Cadence type: PAC   IAC   HC

5. Cadence type: PAC   IAC   HC

6. Cadence type: PAC   IAC   HC

7. Cadence type: PAC   IAC   HC

8. Cadence type: PAC   IAC   HC

Contextual Listening 13.1

- Beginning with the given items, capture the excerpt in the workspace.
- Between the treble staves, write harmonic interval numbers.
- In each chord blank specified, write the Roman numeral and figure (if needed) that represents the harmony.
- Hint: If a harmony is sustained, write a figure that matches the chord's lowest-sounding pitch.

1. The phrase ends with which cadence type?   PAC   IAC   HC

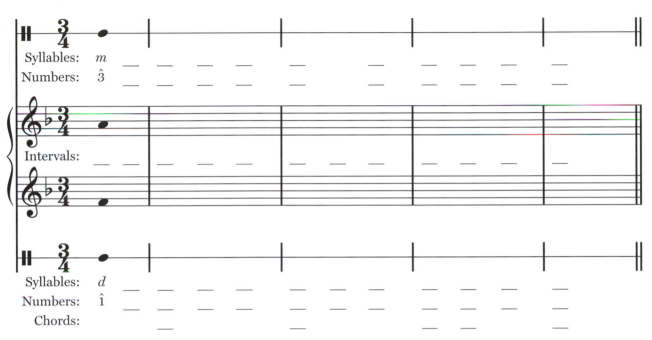

2. The phrase ends with which cadence type?   PAC   IAC   HC

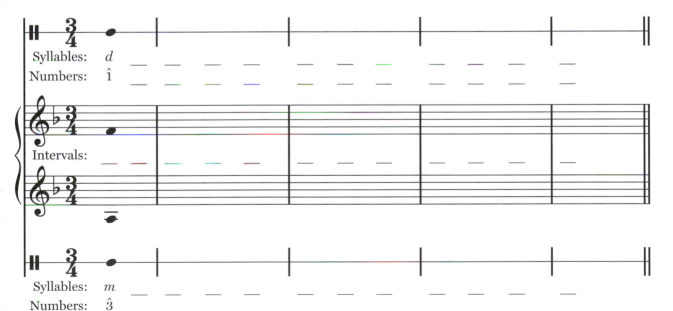

Now, listen to two phrases from a piano sonata and complete the remaining exercises.

3. Beginning with the given items, capture the excerpt in the workspace.

   (a) In the single-line staves, notate the rhythm of the bass and soprano lines.

   (b) Below each note, write the syllables and numbers of the pitches.

   (c) In the grand staff, notate the pitches and rhythm of both parts. Refer to the single-line notation. Check your work at a keyboard.

   (d) In each chord blank, write the Roman numeral and figure (if needed) that represents the harmony.

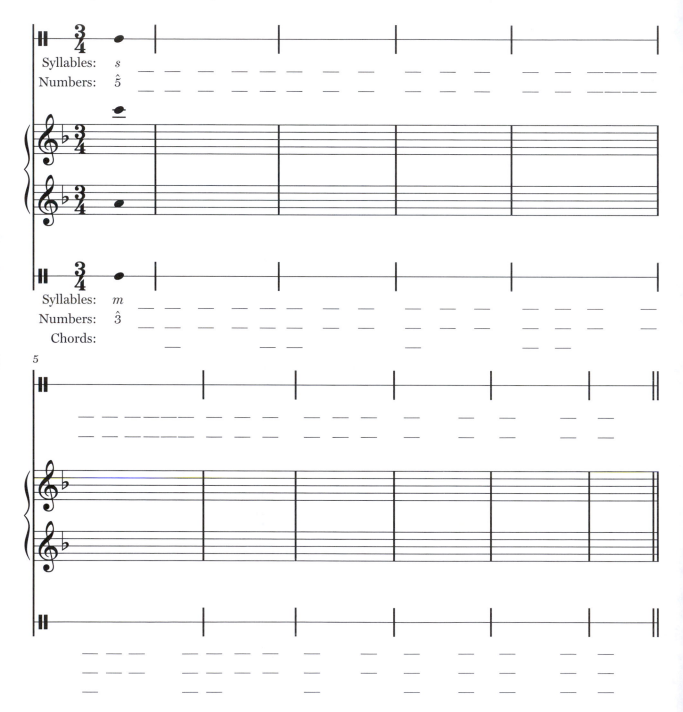

4. At the beginning, the bass and middle pitch form which harmonic interval?

   unison   third   fifth   sixth

5. Phrase 1 ends with which cadence type?   PAC   IAC   HC
   Hint: Listen for cadential pitches in both the bass and the soprano.

6. Phrase 2's first melodic pitch is embellished with an/a:

   upper neighbor   lower neighbor   consonant skip   passing tone

7. Phrase 2 ends with which cadence type?   PAC   IAC   HC

8. Measure 8 sounds final, but the music continues. Measures 9–10 feature which of the following?

   tonic prolongation   cadential extension

   contrary-motion octaves   all of these

Contextual Listening 13.2

Exercises 1–3 each feature a three-chord progression. Focus especially on the bass and soprano and refer to the *Try it* listening strategies.

1. (a) Chords 1 and 3 are: i i^6 V^{8-7} V^6_5 V^4_3 V^4_2

   (b) Chord 2 is: i i^6 V^{8-7} V^6_5 V^4_3 V^4_2

   (c) The progression ends with the cadence type: PAC   IAC   HC

2. (a) Chord 1 is: i i^6 V^{8-7} V^6_5 V^4_3 V^4_2

   (b) Chord 2 is: i i^6 V^{8-7} V^6_5 V^4_3 V^4_2

   (c) Chord 3 is: i i^6 V^{8-7} V^6_5 V^4_3 V^4_2

3. (a) Chord 1 is: i i^6 V^{8-7} V^6_5 V^4_3 V^4_2

   (b) Chord 2 is: i i^6 V^{8-7} V^6_5 V^4_3 V^4_2

   (c) Chord 3 is: i i^6 V^{8-7} V^6_5 V^4_3 V^4_2

Now, listen to a folk song arrangement and complete the remaining exercises.

4. Beginning with the given items, capture the excerpt in the workspace.

   (a) In the single-line staves, notate the rhythm of the bass and soprano lines.

   (b) Below each note, write the syllables and numbers of the pitches.

   (c) In the grand staff, notate the pitches and rhythm of both parts. Refer to the single-line notation. Check your work at a keyboard.

   (d) In each chord blank, write the Roman numeral and figure (if needed) that represents the harmony.

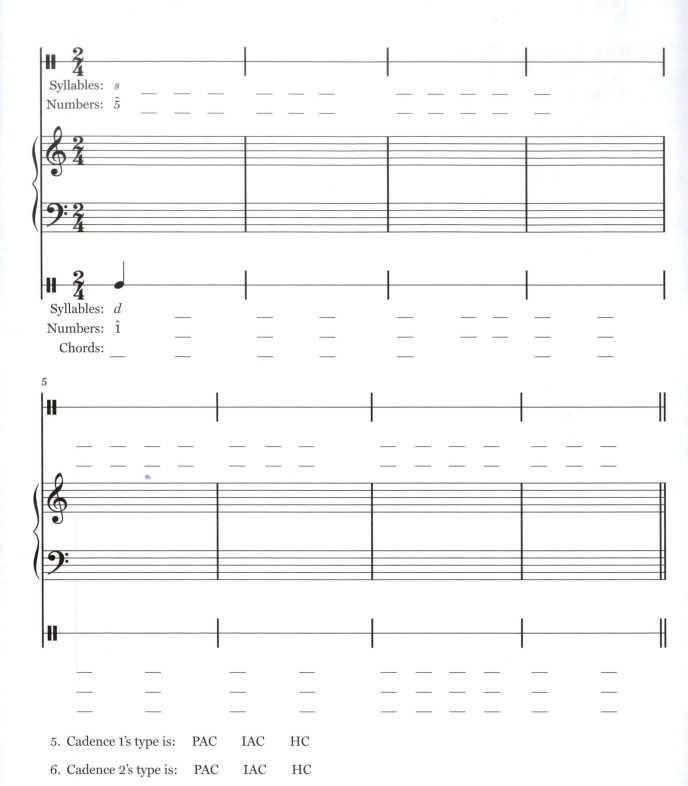

Syllables: *s*

Numbers: $\hat{5}$

Syllables: *d*

Numbers: $\hat{1}$

Chords:

5

5. Cadence 1's type is: PAC   IAC   HC

6. Cadence 2's type is: PAC   IAC   HC

Predominant Chords

When bass pitch *fa* (4̂) rises to *sol* (5̂), the function of the chord above *fa* (4̂) is predominant.
For now, we focus on the most common predominant-function chords: ii⁶, ii⁶₅, and IV.

Above fa (4̂), if you hear . . .	in major write	in minor write	then beneath sol (5̂), write
re (2̂)	ii⁶	ii°⁶	V
re + do (2̂ + 1̂)	ii⁶₅	ii⌀⁶₅	V
only *do* (1̂)	IV	iv	V

Try it 2

1. Cadence type: PAC   IAC   HC

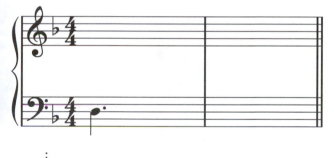

___ : ___   ___   ___   ___

2. Cadence type: PAC   IAC   HC

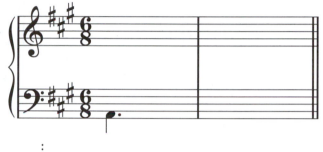

___ : ___   ___   ___   ___

3. Cadence type: PAC   IAC   HC

___ : ___   ___   ___   ___

4. Cadence type: PAC   IAC   HC

___ : ___   ___   ___   ___

5. Cadence type: PAC   IAC   HC

6. Cadence type: PAC   IAC   HC

7. Cadence type: PAC   IAC   HC

8. Cadence type: PAC   IAC   HC

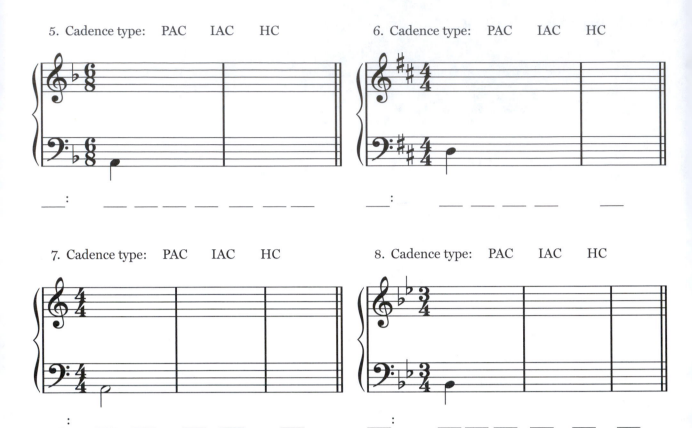

____ : ____ ____ ____ ____

____ : ____ ____ ____ ____

____ : ____ ____ ____ ____

____ : ____ ____ ____ ____

Contextual Listening 13.3

Exercises 1–2 feature short progressions. Focus especially on the bass and soprano and refer to the *Try it* listening strategies.

1. (a) Chords 1 and 4 are: I   V   V8–7   V$^6_5$ V$^4_3$ V$^4_2$

   (b) Chord 2 is: ii^6 ii$^6_5$ IV

   (c) Chord 3 is: I   V   V8–7   V$^6_5$ V$^4_3$ V$^4_2$

   (d) The progression ends with which cadence type?   PAC   IAC   HC

2. (a) Chord 1 is: I   V   V8–7   V$^6_5$ V$^4_3$ V$^4_2$

   (b) Chord 2 is: ii^6 ii$^6_5$ IV

   (c) Chord 3 is: I   V   V8–7   V$^6_5$ V$^4_3$ V$^4_2$

   (d) The progression ends with which cadence type?   PAC   IAC   HC

Now, listen to two phrases from an arrangement of an American spiritual.

3. Beginning with the given items, capture the excerpt in the workspace.

   (a) In the single-line staves, notate the rhythm of the bass and soprano lines.

   (b) Below each note, write the syllables and numbers of the pitches.

   (c) In the grand staff, notate the pitches and rhythm of both parts. Refer to the single-line notation. Check your work at a keyboard.

   (d) In each chord blank, write the Roman numeral and figure (if needed) that represents the harmony.

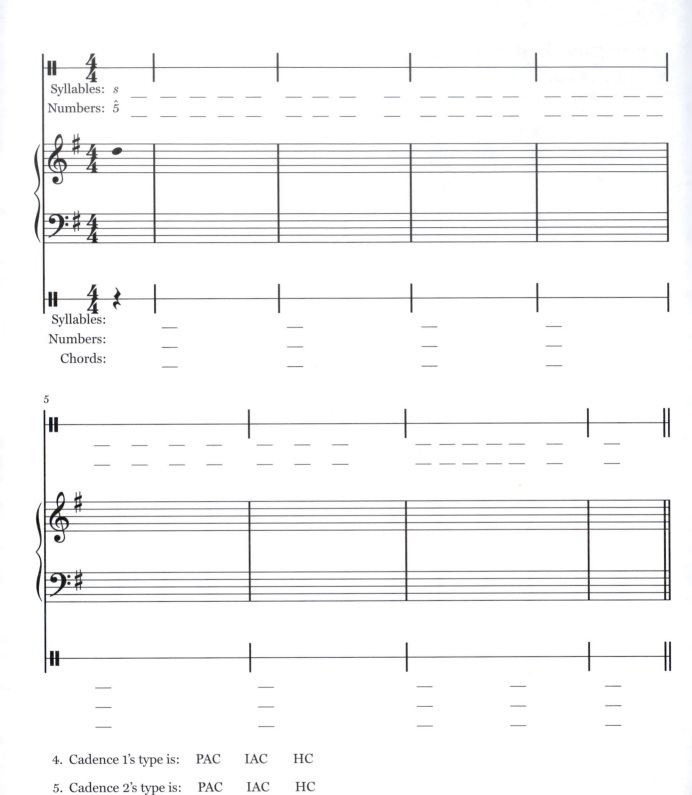

Syllables: *s*

Numbers: $\hat{5}$

Syllables:

Numbers:

Chords:

5

4. Cadence 1's type is: PAC   IAC   HC

5. Cadence 2's type is: PAC   IAC   HC

Contextual Listening 13.4

Exercises 1–2 each consist of one phrase of two-part counterpoint.

1. (a) The beat division is: simple   compound

   (b) Which rhythmic device is featured?   anacrusis   syncopation   triplets

   (c) The predominant chord implied is: ii⁶   ii⁶₅   IV

   (d) The cadence type is: PAC   IAC   HC

2. (a) Chords 1–2 are represented by which pair?

      I–V   V–I   ii⁶–V   IV–V

   (b) The predominant chord implied is: ii⁶   ii⁶₅   IV

   (c) The cadence type is: PAC   IAC   HC

Now, listen to one phrase from a piano sonata and complete the remaining exercises.

3. Beginning with the given items, capture the excerpt in the workspace.

   (a) In the single-line staves, notate the rhythm of the bass and soprano lines.

   (b) Below each note, write the syllables and numbers of the pitches.

   (c) In the grand staff, notate the pitches and rhythm of both parts. Refer to the single-line notation. Check your work at a keyboard.

   (d) In each chord blank, write the Roman numeral and figure (if needed) that represents the harmony.

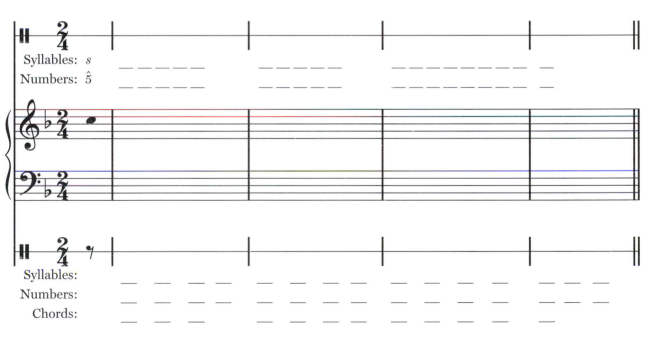

4. The cadence type is: PAC   IAC   HC

CHAPTER 14

Expanding Harmonies with $^6_4$ Chords

NAME _____

In this chapter you'll learn to:

• Identify $^6_4$ harmonies typical of Common Practice compositions

Expanding Harmonies with $^6_4$ Chords

In Common Practice music, $^6_4$ chords appear only in these four ways.

$^6_4$ type	What it does	Listen for . . .
Passing	harmonizes the passing tone in a voice exchange	tonic expansions to feature *do-re-mi* and *mi-re-do* $\hat{1}$-$\hat{2}$-$\hat{3}$ and $\hat{3}$-$\hat{2}$-$\hat{1}$
Neighboring (Pedal)	prolongs a triad's third and fifth with their upper neighbors	*mi-fa-mi* and *sol-la-sol* $\hat{3}$-$\hat{4}$-$\hat{3}$ and $\hat{5}$-$\hat{6}$-$\hat{5}$ over bass pitch *do* ($\hat{1}$)
Cadential	delays the resolution to the third and fifth of the V chord	*mi* → *re* ($\hat{3}$ → $\hat{2}$) *do* → *ti* ($\hat{1}$ → $\hat{7}$) over bass pitch *sol* ($\hat{5}$)
Arpeggiated	describes a moment where a triad's fifth is the lowest pitch	bass arpeggiation of a chord's root, third, fifth

Try it

Listen to four-part progressions. Sing each part aloud. In each exercise, identify beat division, predominant chord, type of $^6_4$ chords used, and cadence type.

1. (a) Beat division: simple   compound

   (b) Predominant: ii6   ii$^6_5$ IV

   (c) First $^6_4$: passing   neighboring   cadential

   (d) Second $^6_4$: passing   neighboring   cadential

   (e) Cadence type: PAC   IAC   HC

2. (a) Beat division: simple   compound

   (b) Predominant: ii^6 ii$^6_5$ IV

   (c) First $^6_4$:   passing   neighboring   cadential

   (d) Second $^6_4$:   passing   neighboring   cadential

   (e) Cadence type: PAC   IAC   HC

3. (a) Beat division: simple   compound

   (b) Predominant: ii^{o6} ii$^6_5$ iv

   (c) First $^6_4$:   passing   neighboring   cadential

   (d) Second $^6_4$:   passing   neighboring   cadential

   (e) Cadence type: PAC   IAC   HC

4. (a) Beat division: simple   compound

   (b) Predominant: ii^{o6} ii$^{\varnothing 6}_5$ iv

   (c) First $^6_4$:   passing   neighboring   cadential

   (d) Second $^6_4$:   passing   neighboring   cadential

   (e) Cadence type: PAC   IAC   HC

5. (a) Beat division: simple   compound

   (b) Predominant: ii^6 ii$^6_5$ IV

   (c) First $^6_4$:   passing   neighboring   cadential

   (d) Second $^6_4$:   passing   neighboring   cadential

   (e) Cadence type: PAC   IAC   HC

6. (a) Beat division: simple   compound

   (b) Predominant: ii^{o6} ii$^{\varnothing 6}_5$ iv

   (c) First $^6_4$:   passing   neighboring   cadential

   (d) Second $^6_4$:   passing   neighboring   cadential

   (e) Cadence type: PAC   IAC   HC

7. (a) Beat division: simple   compound

   (b) Predominant: ii^{o6} ii$^{\varnothing 6}_5$ iv

   (c) First $^6_4$:   passing   neighboring   cadential

   (d) Second $^6_4$:   passing   neighboring   cadential

   (e) Cadence type: PAC   IAC   HC

8. (a) Beat division: simple   compound

   (b) Predominant: ii^6 ii$^6_5$ IV

   (c) First $^6_4$:   passing   neighboring   cadential

   (d) Second $^6_4$:   passing   neighboring   cadential

   (e) Cadence type: PAC   IAC   HC

Contextual Listening 14.1

In exercises 1–3, write the syllables and numbers of the bass part. Beneath them, write the Roman numeral and figure (if needed) that represents the harmony.

1. Bass pitch:	1	2	3	4	5
Syllable:					
Number:					
Roman numeral:					

2. Bass pitch:	1	2	3	4	5
Syllable:					
Number:					
Roman numeral:					

3. Bass pitch:	1	2	3	4	5
Syllable:					
Number:					
Roman numeral:					

Now, listen to one phrase from a piano work and complete the remaining exercises.

4. Beginning with the given items, capture the excerpt in the workspace.

   (a) In the single-line staves, notate the rhythm of the bass and soprano lines.

   (b) Below each note, write the syllables and numbers of the pitches.

   (c) In the grand staff, notate the pitches and rhythm of both parts. Refer to the single-line notation. Check your work at a keyboard.

   (d) Between treble and bass staves, write the harmonic interval numbers.

   (e) In each chord blank, write the Roman numeral and figure (if needed) that represents the harmony.

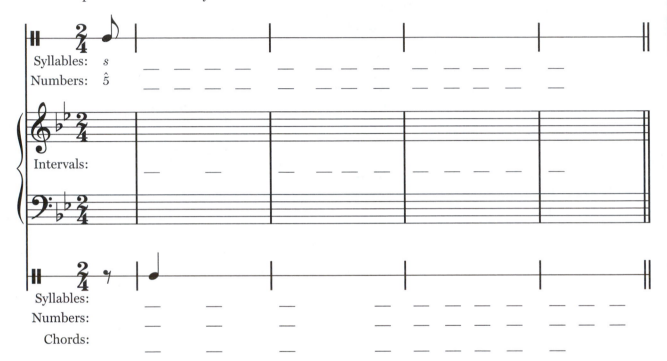

5. The type of $^6_4$ chord is: neighboring   passing   cadential

6. The phrase ends with which cadence type?   PAC   IAC   HC

Contextual Listening 14.2

1. (a) Listen to two measures of music. Identify the bass pitches, harmonies, and $^6_4$ types.

Bass pitch:	1	2	3	4	5
Syllable:					
Number:					
Roman numeral:					

(b) In chords 1–3, the motion between bass and soprano is:

contrary   oblique   similar   parallel

(c) Chord 2's $^6_4$ type is: passing   neighboring   cadential

(d) Chord 4's $^6_4$ type is: passing   neighboring   cadential

(e) The progression ends with which cadence type?   PAC   IAC   HC

2. (a) Listen to two measures of music. Identify the bass pitches, harmonies, and $^6_4$ type.

Bass pitch:	1	2	3	4	5	6
Syllable:						
Number:						
Roman numeral:						

(b) In chords 1–3, the motion between bass and soprano is:

contrary   oblique   similar   parallel

(c) Chord 4's $^6_4$ type is: passing   neighboring   cadential

(d) The progression ends with which cadence type?   PAC   IAC   HC

Now, listen to the first phrase of a piano sonata and complete the remaining exercises.

3. (a) Identify the bass pitches, harmonies, and $^6_4$ type. Ignore chord 5.

Bass pitch:	1	2	3	4	5	6
Syllable:						
Number:						
Roman numeral:						

(b) In chords 2–4, the motion between bass and soprano is:

contrary   oblique   similar   parallel

(c) Chord 3's $^6_4$ type is: passing   neighboring   cadential

(d) The progression ends with which cadence type?   PAC   IAC   HC

Contextual Listening 14.3

1. (a) Listen to two measures of music. Identify bass pitches 1–5, their harmonies, the $^6_4$ type, and the cadence.

Bass pitch:	1	2	3	4	5
Syllable:					
Number:					
Roman numeral:					

   (b) During chords 1–3, the motion between bass and soprano is:

   contrary   oblique   similar   parallel

   (c) Melodic pitches 1–3 feature which embellishment?

   consonant skip   neighboring tone   passing tone

   (d) Chord 2's $^6_4$ type is: passing   neighboring   cadential

   (e) The progression ends with which cadence type?   PAC   IAC   HC

2. (a) Listen to two measures of music. Identify bass pitches 1–5, their harmonies, the $^6_4$ type, and the cadence.

Bass pitch:	1	2	3	4	5
Syllable:					
Number:					
Roman numeral:					

   (b) During chords 1–3, the motion between bass and soprano is:

   contrary   oblique   similar   parallel

   (c) Chord 4's $^6_4$ type is: passing   neighboring   cadential

   (d) The progression ends with which cadence type?   PAC   IAC   HC

Now, listen to one phrase from a chorale and complete the remaining exercises.

3. Beginning with the given items, capture the excerpt in the workspace.

    (a) In the single-line staves, notate the rhythm of the bass and soprano lines.

    (b) Below each note, write the syllables and numbers of the pitches.

    (c) In the grand staff, notate the pitches and rhythm of both parts. Refer to the single-line notation. Check your work at a keyboard.

    (d) Between treble and bass staves, write the harmonic interval numbers that occur on each beat.

    (e) In each chord blank, write the Roman numeral and figure (if needed) that represents the harmony.

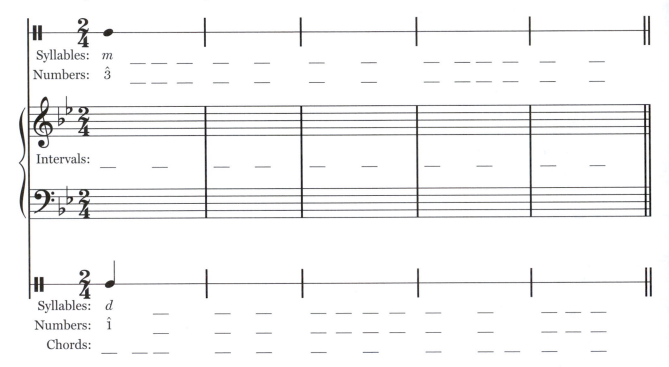

4. The type of $^6_4$ chord heard in the first measure is:

    passing   neighboring   cadential

5. The phrase ends with which cadence type?   PAC   IAC   HC

Contextual Listening 14.4

Exercises 1–2 consist of two measure of music.

1. Listen to two measures of music. Identify the harmonies and $^6_4$ type.

    (a) What is the harmony in measure 1?   I   ii⁶   IV   V⁸⁻⁷   V$^{6-5}_{4-3}$

    (b) In measure 2, which represents the harmony?   I   ii⁶   IV   V⁸⁻⁷   V$^{6-5}_{4-3}$

    (c) The $^6_4$ chord type is: passing   neighboring   cadential

    (d) The progression ends with which cadence type?   PAC   IAC   HC

2. Listen to two measures of music. For bass pitches 1–5, write the syllable and number. Beneath, write the Roman numeral that represents the harmony.

Bass pitch:	1	2	3	4	5
Syllable:					
Number:					
Roman numeral:					

    (a) The $^6_4$ chord type is: passing   neighboring   cadential

    (b) The progression ends with which cadence type?   PAC   IAC   HC

Now, listen to one phrase from a piano sonata and complete the remaining exercises. For ease of dictation, the phrase is notated in the key of C (i.e., the dominant of F major).

3. Beginning with the given items, capture the excerpt in the workspace.

   (a) In the single-line staves, notate the rhythm of the bass and soprano lines.

   (b) Below each note, write the syllables and numbers of the pitches.

   (c) In the grand staff, notate the pitches and rhythm of both parts. Refer to the single-line notation. Check your work at a keyboard.

   (d) In each chord blank, write the Roman numeral and figure (if needed) that represents the harmony.

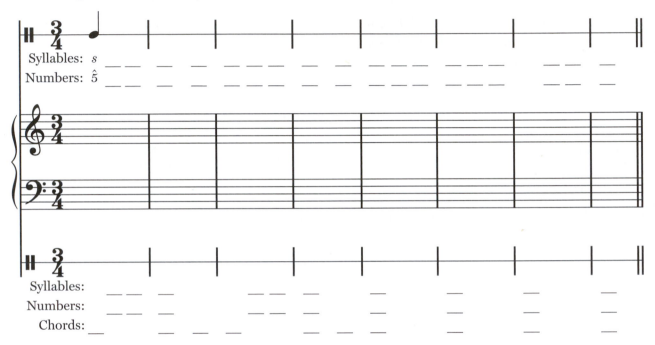

4. The phrase ends with which cadence type?   PAC   IAC   HC

CHAPTER 15

New Cadence Types

NAME _____

In this chapter you'll learn to:

- Recognize Phrygian, deceptive, and plagal cadences and resolutions
- Associate all cadence types with bass lines and their syllables and numbers

Deceptive, Plagal, and Phrygian Cadences and Resolutions

The Phrygian half cadence occurs frequently in minor-key works. Deceptive and plagal cadences are somewhat rare, but deceptive and plagal resolutions are common. Deceptive resolutions occur mid-phrase and delay the arrival of an authentic cadence. Plagal resolutions often extend or prolong an authentic cadence. Cadential bass pitches help you determine these progressions.

If cadential bass pitches are . . .	the cadence or resolution is called . . .
le-sol ($\flat\hat{6}$–$\hat{5}$)	Phrygian (PHC)
sol-la ($\hat{5}$–$\hat{6}$)	deceptive (DC)
fa-do ($\hat{4}$–$\hat{1}$)	plagal (PC)

Try it

Listen to four-part progressions. Sing each part aloud. In each exercise, identify beat division, predominant chord, the type of $^6_4$ chord or V chord specified, and the cadence type.

1. (a) Beat division: simple   compound

   (b) Predominant: ii⁶   ii$^6_5$ IV

   (c) $^6_4$ type: passing   neighboring   cadential

   (d) Cadence type: PAC   IAC   HC   PHC   DC   PC

2. (a) Beat division: simple   compound

   (b) Predominant: ii⁶   ii$^6_5$ IV

   (c) $^6_4$ type: passing   neighboring   cadential

   (d) Cadence type: PAC   IAC   HC   PHC   DC   PC

3. (a) Beat division: simple   compound

   (b) Predominant: ii^{o6} ii$^{\o 6}_5$ iv^6

   (c) $^6_4$ type: passing   neighboring   cadential

   (d) Cadence type: PAC   IAC   HC   PHC   DC   PC

4. (a) Beat division: simple   compound

   (b) Predominant: ii^6 ii$^6_5$ IV

   (c) $^6_4$ type: passing   neighboring   cadential

   (d) Cadence type: PAC   IAC   HC   PHC   DC   PC

5. (a) Beat division: simple   compound

   (b) Predominant: ii^{o6} ii$^{\o 6}_5$ iv

   (c) Chord 2 is: V   V$^6_5$ V$^6_4$ V$^4_3$ V$^4_2$

   (d) $^6_4$ type: passing   neighboring   cadential

   (e) Cadence type: PAC   IAC   HC   PHC   DC   PC

6. (a) Beat division: simple   compound

   (b) Predominant: ii^{o6} ii$^{\o 6}_5$ iv^6

   (c) Chord 2 is: V   V$^6_5$ V$^6_4$ V$^4_3$ V$^4_2$

   (d) Cadence type: PAC   IAC   HC   PHC   DC   PC

7. (a) Beat division: simple   compound

   (b) Predominant: ii^6 ii$^6_5$ IV

   (c) Chord 2 is: V   V$^6_5$ V$^6_4$ V$^4_3$ V$^4_2$

   (d) $^6_4$ type: passing   neighboring   cadential

   (e) Cadence type: PAC   IAC   HC   PHC   DC   PC

8. (a) Beat division: simple   compound

   (b) Predominant: ii^{o6} ii$^{\o 6}_5$ iv^6

   (c) Chord 4 is: V   V$^6_5$ V$^6_4$ V$^4_3$ V$^4_2$

   (d) $^6_4$ type: passing   neighboring   cadential

   (e) Cadence type: PAC   IAC   HC   PHC   DC   PC

Contextual Listening 15.1

Exercises 1–3 feature two-part counterpoint.

1. (a) The parallel harmonic intervals are of which size?   3   5   6   8

   (b) The cadence type is: PAC   IAC   HC   PHC   DC   PC

2. (a) The first harmonic interval is which size?   3   5   6   8

   (b) The recurring suspensions create which interval pattern?

      2-3   4-3   7-6   9-8

   (c) The cadence type is: PAC   IAC   HC   PHC   DC   PC

3. (a) The recurring harmonic intervals are: 3-3   3-4   3-5   3-6

   (b) The cadence type is: PAC   IAC   HC   PHC   DC   PC

Now, listen to four two-measure phrases consisting of the outer parts from a chorale. Then, complete the remaining exercises.

4. Beginning with the given items, capture the excerpt in the workspace.

   (a) In the single-line staves, notate the rhythm of the bass and soprano lines.

   (b) Below each note, write the syllables and numbers of the pitches.

   (c) In the grand staff, notate the pitches and rhythm of both parts. Refer to the single-line notation. Check your work at a keyboard.

   (d) Between the treble and bass staves, write the harmonic interval numbers.

5. Phrase 1's cadence type is: PAC   IAC   HC   PHC   DC   PC

6. Phrase 2's suspensions are: 2-3   4-3   7-6   9-8

7. Phrase 2's cadence type is: PAC   IAC   HC   PHC   DC   PC

8. Phrase 3's cadence type is: PAC   IAC   HC   PHC   DC   PC

9. Phrase 4's cadence type is: PAC   IAC   HC   PHC   DC   PC

10. The final three chords imply which progression?

    I–V–I   I–IV–I   ii6–V–I   IV–V–I

11. Every harmonic interval 4 is a result of which embellishment?

    passing tone   neighboring tone   suspension

Contextual Listening 15.2

Listen to a four-part progression. Sing each part aloud. In each exercise, identify the requested items.

1. Cadence type: PAC   IAC   HC   PHC   DC   PC

2. (a) Predominant: ii°6   iiø$^6_5$ iv6

   (b) $^6_4$ type: passing   neighboring   cadential

   (c) Cadence type: PAC   IAC   HC   PHC   DC   PC

3. (a) Predominant: ii°6   iiø$^6_5$ iv6

   (b) $^6_4$ type: passing   neighboring   cadential

   (c) Cadence type: PAC   IAC   HC   PHC   DC   PC

Now, listen to the first phrase of a Baroque dance.

4. Beginning with the given items, capture the excerpt in the workspace.

    (a) In the single-line staves, notate the rhythm of the bass and soprano lines.

    (b) Below each note, write the syllables and numbers of the pitches.

    (c) In the grand staff, notate the pitches and rhythm of both parts. Refer to the single-line notation. Check your work at a keyboard.

    (d) In each chord blank, write the Roman numeral and figure (if needed) that represents the harmony.

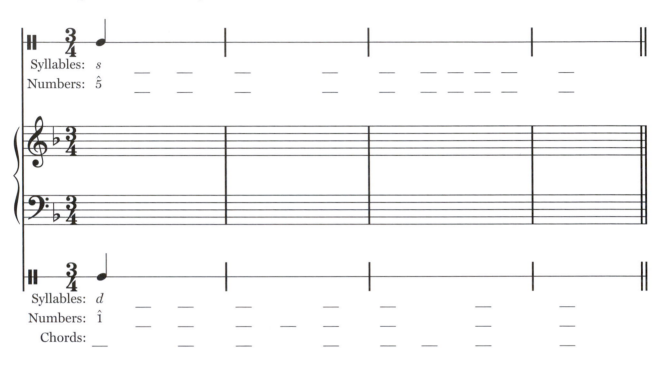

5. Measure 1, beat 3 features which $^6_4$ type?   passing   neighboring   cadential

6. Which of the following occurs on measure 3, beat 1?

    PAC   IAC   HC   PHC   DC   PC

7. Phrase 1's cadence type is:

    PAC   IAC   HC   PHC   DC   PC

Listen to phrase 1 again, now followed by a second phrase.

8. The final cadence type is:

    PAC   IAC   HC   PHC   DC   PC

Contextual Listening 15.3

Listen to a four-part progression. Sing each part aloud. In each exercise, identify the requested items.

1. (a) Chord 2 is: V   V$^6_5$ V$^6_4$ V$^4_3$ V$^4_2$

   (b) Chord 3 is: V   V$^6_5$ V$^6_4$ V$^4_3$ V$^4_2$

   (c) Cadence type: PAC   IAC   HC   PHC   DC   PC

2. (a) Chord 2 is: V   V$^6_5$ V$^6_4$ V$^4_3$ V$^4_2$

   (b) $^6_4$ type: passing   neighboring   cadential

   (c) Cadence type: PAC   IAC   HC   PHC   DC   PC

3. (a) Predominant: ii^6 ii$^6_5$ IV

   (b) $^6_4$ type: passing   neighboring   cadential

   (c) Cadence type: PAC   IAC   HC   PHC   DC   PC

Now, listen to one phrase from a piano sonata and complete the remaining exercises.

4. Beginning with the given items, capture the excerpt in the workspace.

   (a) In the single-line staves, notate the rhythm of the bass and soprano lines.

   (b) Below each note, write the syllables and numbers of the pitches.

   (c) In the grand staff, notate the pitches and rhythm of both parts. Refer to the single-line notation. Check your work at a keyboard.

   (d) In each chord blank, write the Roman numeral and figure (if needed) that represents the harmony.

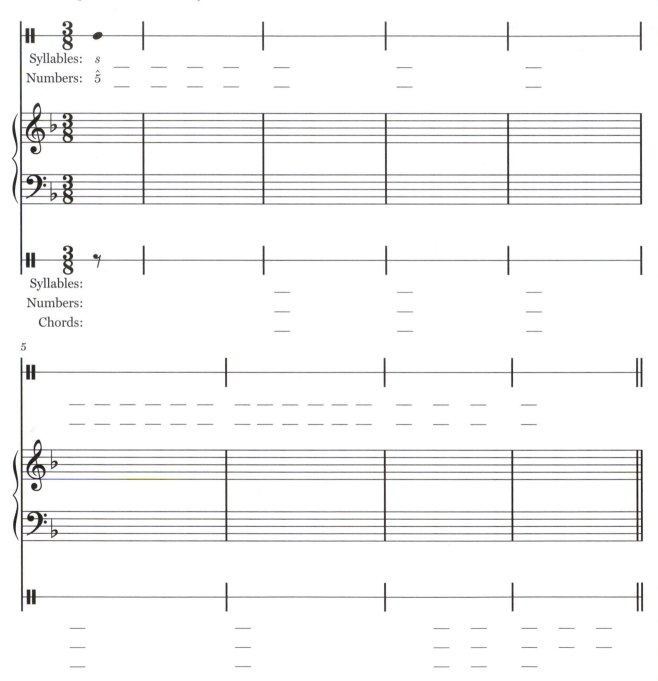

5. In measure 6, the chord's function is: predominant   dominant   tonic

CHAPTER 16

Embellishing Tones

NAME _____

In this chapter you'll learn to:

- Identify the rhythmic displacements anticipations, suspensions, and retardations
- Identify incomplete neighbor tones, pedal points, chromatic and bass-voice passing tones

Rhythmic Displacement, Incomplete Neighbor Tones, and Pedal Points

Some harmonic intervals anticipate or delay resolution to the expected pitch.

Does a pitch . . .		You hear an/a . . .
Anticipate the expected pitch?		Anticipation (A)
Delay the expected pitch? Then, does it . . .	*Fall* to resolve?	Suspension (S)
	Rise to resolve?	Retardation (also S)

Incomplete neighbor tones (N) appear as appoggiaturas or escape tones. Upper parts moving over a stationary bass pitch—usually the dominant or tonic—create a pedal point.

Appoggiatura (N)
Strong-beat neighbor tone
Weak-beat resolution

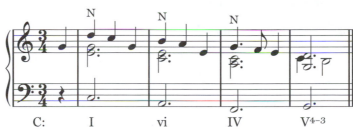

Escape Tone (N)
Strong-beat preparation
Weak-beat neighbor tone
Strong-beat resolution

Try it

Listen to four-part progressions. Sing each part aloud. Identify the items specified.

1. (a) Beat division: simple   compound

   (b) Predominant: ii^6 ii$^6_5$ IV

   (c) Melodic pitches 2 and 4 are: CS   N   P

   (d) Melodic pitch 6 is an/a: anticipation (A)   suspension/retardation (S)

   (e) Cadence type: PAC   IAC   HC   PHC   DC   PC

2. (a) Beat division: simple   compound

   (b) Predominant: ii^{o6} ii$^{\varnothing 6}_5$ iv^6

   (c) Melodic pitch 3 is an/a: anticipation (A)   suspension/retardation (S)
       Choose figure(s):   2-3   4-3   7-6   7-8   9-8

   (d) Cadence type: PAC   IAC   HC   PHC   DC   PC

3. (a) Beat division: simple   compound

   (b) Predominant: ii^{o6} ii$^{\varnothing 6}_5$ iv   iv^6

   (c) The final measure includes an/a: anticipation (A)   suspension/retardation (S)
       Choose figure(s):   2-3   4-3   7-6   7-8   9-8

   (d) $^6_4$ type: passing   neighbor   cadential

   (e) Cadence type: PAC   IAC   HC   PHC   DC   PC

4. (a) Beat division: simple   compound

   (b) Predominant: ii^6 ii$^6_5$ IV

   (c) Melodic pitch 5 is an/a: anticipation (A)   suspension/retardation (S)
       Choose figure(s):   2-3   4-3   7-6   7-8   9-8

   (d) $^6_4$ type: passing   neighbor   cadential

   (e) Cadence type: PAC   IAC   HC   PHC   DC   PC

5. (a) Beat division: simple   compound

   (b) Bass pitch 2 is a: CS   N   P   chromatic P

   (c) Melodic pitch 3 is a: CS   N   P   chromatic P

   (d) The final measure includes an/a: anticipation (A)   suspension/retardation (S)
       Choose figure(s):   2-3   4-3   7-6   7-8   9-8

   (e) Cadence type: PAC   IAC   HC   PHC   DC   PC

Contextual Listening 16.1

Listen to four-part progressions. Sing each part aloud. Identify the items specified.

1. (a) Beat division: simple   compound

   (b) Chord 1 is: V   V7   V$^6_5$ V$^4_3$ V$^4_2$

   (c) Melodic pitches 4, 7, 10 are which type of N: appoggiaturas   escape tones

   (d) $^6_4$ type: passing   neighbor   cadential

   (e) The final measure includes an/a: anticipation (A)   suspension/retardation (S)

   Choose figure(s):   2–3   4–3   7–6   7–8   9–8

   (f) Cadence type: PAC   IAC   HC   PHC   DC   PC

2. (a) Beat division: simple   compound

   (b) $^6_4$ type: passing   neighbor   cadential

   (c) Melodic pitch 6 is an/a: anticipation (A)   suspension/retardation (S)

   (d) Cadence type: PAC   IAC   HC   PHC   DC   PC

Now, listen to one phrase from a choral work and complete the remaining exercises.

3. Beginning with the given items, capture the excerpt in the workspace.

   (a) In the single-line staves, notate the rhythm of the bass and soprano lines.

   (b) Below each note, write the syllables and numbers of the pitches.

   (c) In the grand staff, notate the pitches and rhythm of both parts. Refer to the single-line notation. Sing aloud to check your work.

   (d) In each chord blank, write the Roman numeral and figure (if needed) that represents the harmony.

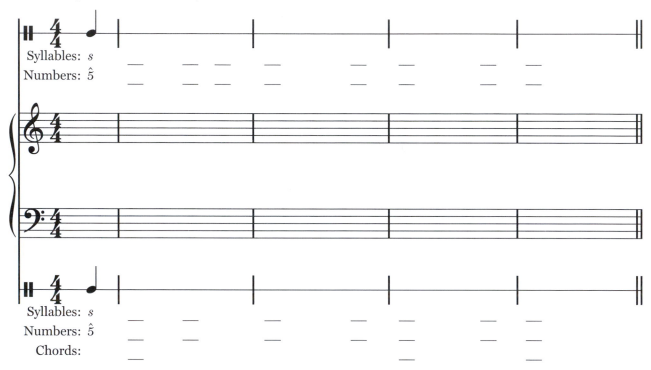

Translation: How hopeful is the world around.

4. Over bass pitch 6, which dissonance occurs?

   anticipation (A)   4–3 suspension (S)

   incomplete neighbor tone (N)   chromatic passing tone (P)

5. The next-to-last melodic pitch is which type of dissonance?

   anticipation (A)   4–3 suspension (S)

   incomplete neighbor tone (N)   chromatic passing tone (P)

6. The cadence type is:

   PAC   IAC   HC   PHC   DC   PC

Contextual Listening 16.2

Listen to two progressions. Sing each part aloud. Identify the items specified.

1. (a) Beat division: simple   compound

   (b) Melodic pitch 1 is embellished with a/an: upper N   lower N   incomplete N

   (c) The bass throughout is a/an: arpeggiating $^6_4$ pedal point   CS

2. (a) Beat division: simple   compound

   (b) Melodic pitches 2 and 5 are which type of N?   appoggiaturas   escape tones

   (c) Chord 2 is: V⁶   V$^6_5$ V$^4_3$ V$^4_2$

   (d) $^6_4$ type: passing   neighbor   cadential

   (e) Cadence type: PAC   IAC   HC   PHC   DC   PC

Now, listen to two, four-measure phrases for piano and complete the remaining exercises.

3. Write syllables and numbers for melodic pitches 1–7.

   m __ __ __ __ __ __

   $\hat{3}$ __ __ __ __ __ __

4. Melodic pitch 1, *mi* ($\hat{3}$), is embellished with an/a:

   upper N   lower N   incomplete N   CS

5. Melodic pitch 5, *re* ($\hat{2}$), is which embellishment?

   upper N   lower N   incomplete N   CS

6. Melodic pitches 6–7 are which embellishment?

   upper N   lower N   incomplete N   CS

7. During most of phrase 1, the bass line's role is:

   tonic pedal point   dominant pedal point

8. Phrase 1's cadence type is: PAC   IAC   HC   PHC   DC   PC

9. Near the end, the $^6_4$ type is: passing   neighbor   cadential

10. The final two chords are: I-V   IV-V   V-I   V7-I

11. Phrase 2's cadence type is: PAC   IAC   HC   PHC

Sketch space

Part II Diatonic Harmony and Tonicization

Contextual Listening 16.3

Listen to three-chord progressions and complete the exercises.

1. (a) The bass-line scale degrees are: $\hat{1}$-$\hat{2}$-$\hat{3}$ $\hat{1}$-$\hat{4}$-$\hat{3}$ $\hat{1}$-$\hat{7}$-$\hat{1}$ $\hat{3}$-$\hat{2}$-$\hat{1}$

   (b) Which of these is present between the bass line and an upper part?

   parallel 6ths   parallel 10ths   a voice exchange   a suspension

   (c) Chord 2 is: V^6_4 V^4_3 $V6$ V^6_5

2. (a) The bass-line scale degrees are: $\hat{1}$-$\hat{2}$-$\hat{3}$ $\hat{1}$-$\hat{4}$-$\hat{3}$ $\hat{1}$-$\hat{7}$-$\hat{1}$ $\hat{3}$-$\hat{2}$-$\hat{1}$

   (b) Which of these is present between the bass line and an upper part?

   parallel 6ths   parallel 10ths   a voice exchange   a suspension

   (c) Chord 2 is: V^6_4 V^4_3 $V6$ V^6_5

3. (a) The bass-line scale degrees are: $\hat{1}$-$\hat{2}$-$\hat{3}$ $\hat{1}$-$\hat{4}$-$\hat{3}$ $\hat{1}$-$\hat{7}$-$\hat{1}$ $\hat{3}$-$\hat{2}$-$\hat{1}$

   (b) Chord 2 is: V^6_4 V^4_3 $V6$ V^6_5

Now, listen to two phrases from a piano work and complete the remaining exercises.

4. Beginning with the given items, capture the excerpt in the workspace.

   (a) In the single-line staves, notate the rhythm of the bass and soprano lines.

   (b) Below each note, write the syllables and numbers of the pitches.

   (c) Write harmonic interval numbers between the treble and bass staves. Identify each dissonant interval number (2, 4, or 7) by writing N for neighbor tone or S for suspension.

   (d) In the grand staff, notate pitches and rhythm of both parts. Refer to the single-line notation. Check your work at a keyboard.

   (e) In the given chord blanks, write the Roman numeral and figure (if needed) that represents the harmony.

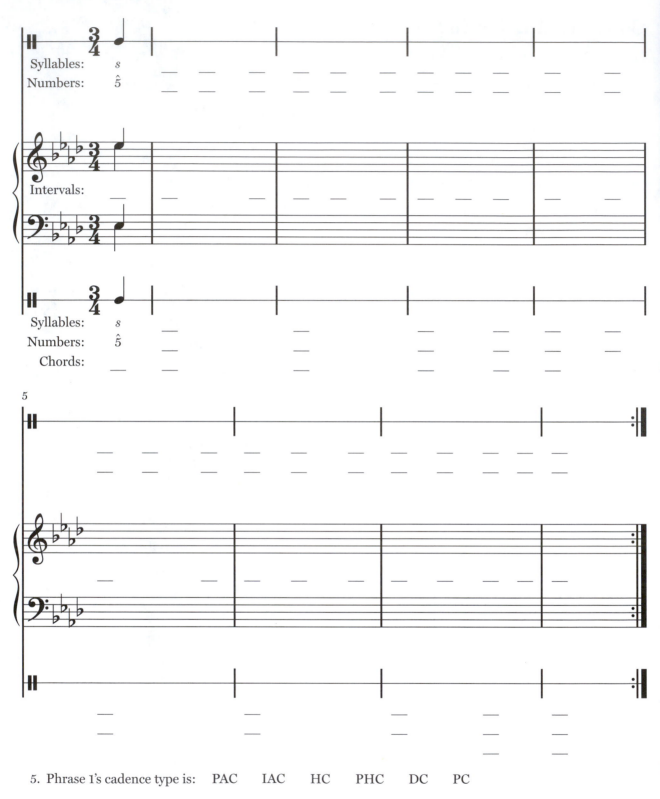

5. Phrase 1's cadence type is: PAC   IAC   HC   PHC   DC   PC

6. The third-to-last melodic pitch is which type of neighbor tone?

   upper   lower   appoggiatura   escape tone

7. Phrase 2's cadence type is: PAC   IAC   HC   PHC   DC   PC

More Dominant-Function Harmonies

CHAPTER 17

NAME _____

In this chapter you'll learn to:

- Distinguish between V^7 and vii^{o7} and their inversions
- Distinguish between vii^{o6} and V^6_4

Dominant-Function Seventh Chords and Their Tonic-Chord Resolutions (D–T)

Dominant-function seventh chords V^7 and vii^{o7} both lead to tonic. Here are four examples of dominant-function seventh chords with their resolutions. The following observations can help you identify these D–T progressions.

- The V^7 and vii^{o7} bass lines in 1–3 are identical: *ti-do* ($\hat{7}$-$\hat{1}$); *fa-me* ($\hat{4}$-$\flat\hat{3}$); and *re-do* ($\hat{2}$-$\hat{1}$).

- Example 4—*sol* ($\hat{5}$) in V^7 or *le* ($\flat\hat{6}$) in vii^{o7}—resolves to *sol* ($\hat{5}$).

- Certain bass-line scale degrees imply specific chords and resolutions: for example, *ti-do* ($\hat{7}$-$\hat{1}$) in the bass implies either V^6_5-i or vii^{o7}-i.

- To hear the voice leading, sing the bass line as a four-part canon.

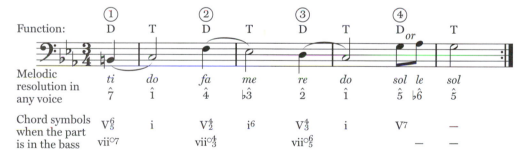

	①		②		③		④		
Function:	D	T	D	T	D	T	D *or*		T
Melodic resolution in any voice	*ti* $\hat{7}$	*do* $\hat{1}$	*fa* $\hat{4}$	*me* $\flat\hat{3}$	*re* $\hat{2}$	*do* $\hat{1}$	*sol* $\hat{5}$	*le* $\flat\hat{6}$	*sol* $\hat{5}$
Chord symbols when the part is in the bass	V^6_5 vii^{o7}	i	V^4_2 vii^{o4}_3	i^6	V^4_3 vii^{o6}_5	i	V^7 —	—	—

- Because V7 and vii°7 share *ti-re-fa* ($\hat{7}$-$\hat{2}$-$\hat{4}$), the differences shown here can help you determine which chord you heard.

Chord	V7	vii°7
Chord quality	dominant	fully diminished
Common tone with i	yes	no
Distinct pitch	*sol* ($\hat{5}$)	*le* ($\flat\hat{6}$)
Tritone(s)	1	2

Try it 1

Use the strategies you just learned to identify V7 and vii°7 in these paired, four-part progressions.

1. (a) Chord 2 is: V^6_5 vii°7
   (b) Chord 4 is: V^4_2 vii°$^4_3$
   (c) Predominant: ii°6   ii$^{ø6}_5$ iv   iv6
   (d) Cadence type: PAC   IAC   HC   PHC

2. (a) Chord 2 is: V^6_5 vii°7
   (b) Chord 4 is: V^4_2 vii°$^4_3$
   (c) Predominant: ii°6   ii$^{ø6}_5$ iv   iv6
   (d) Cadence type: PAC   IAC   HC   PHC

3. (a) Chord 2 is: V^4_3 vii°$^6_5$
   (b) Chord 4 is: V^6_5 vii°7
   (c) Predominant: ii°6   ii$^{ø6}_5$ iv   iv6
   (d) Cadence type: PAC   IAC   HC   PHC

4. (a) Chord 2 is: V^4_3 vii°$^6_5$
   (b) Chord 4 is: V^6_5 vii°7
   (c) Predominant: ii°6   ii$^{ø6}_5$ iv   iv6
   (d) Cadence type: PAC   IAC   HC   PHC

5. (a) Chord 2 is: V^4_2 vii°$^4_3$
   (b) Chord 4 is: V^4_3 vii°$^6_5$
   (c) Predominant: ii°6   ii$^{ø6}_5$ iv   iv6
   (d) Cadence type: PAC   IAC   HC   PHC

6. (a) Chord 2 is: V^4_2 vii°$^4_3$
   (b) Chord 4 is: V^4_3 vii°$^6_5$
   (c) Predominant: ii°6   ii$^{ø6}_5$ iv   iv6
   (d) Cadence type: PAC   IAC   HC   PHC

7. The meter type of exercises 1-6 is: simple   compound

Dominant-Function Triads vii^{o6} and V$^6_4$

Triads vii^{o6} and V$^6_4$ both lead to tonic and often harmonize the passing tone in a voice exchange. Because they share *ti-re* ($\hat{7}$–$\hat{2}$), these differences help you determine which chord you heard.

Chord	V$^6_4$	vii^{o6}
Chord quality	major	diminished
Common tone with i	yes	no
Distinct pitch	*sol* ($\hat{5}$)	*fa* ($\hat{4}$)
Tritone	0	1

Try it 2

Use the strategies you just learned to identify V$^6_4$ and vii^{o6} in these paired, four-part progressions. Near the end, listen for an embellishment.

1. (a) Chord 2 is: V$^6_4$ vii^{o6}

   (b) Predominant: ii^{o6}   ii^{ø6}₅   iv   iv⁶

   (c) Embellishment: CS   N   S   P

   (d) Cadence type: PAC   IAC   HC   PHC

2. (a) Chord 2 is: V$^6_4$ vii^{o6}

   (b) Predominant: ii^{o6}   ii^{ø6}₅   iv   iv⁶

   (c) Embellishment: CS   N   S   P

   (d) Cadence type: PAC   IAC   HC   PHC

3. (a) Chord 2 is: V$^6_4$ vii^{o6}

   (b) Predominant: ii^{o6}   ii^{ø6}₅   iv   iv⁶

   (c) Embellishment: CS   N   S   P

   (d) Cadence type: PAC   IAC   HC   PHC

4. (a) Chord 2 is: V$^6_4$ vii^{o6}

   (b) Predominant: ii^{o6}   ii^{ø6}₅   iv   iv⁶

   (c) Embellishment: CS   N   S   P

   (d) Cadence type: PAC   IAC   HC   PHC

Contextual Listening 17.1

Identify dominant-function chords in these paired, four-part progressions. At the cadence, listen for an embellishment.

1. (a) Chord 2 is: V_4^6 vii^{o6}

   (b) Predominant: ii^{o6} $ii^{\varnothing\frac{4}{3}}$ iv iv^6

   (c) Embellishment: CS   N   S   P

   (d) Cadence type: PAC   IAC   HC   PHC

2. (a) Chord 2 is: V_4^6 vii^{o6}

   (b) Predominant: ii^{o6} $ii^{\varnothing\frac{6}{5}}$ iv iv^6

   (c) Embellishment: CS   N   S   P

   (d) Cadence type: PAC   IAC   HC   PHC

Now, listen to one phrase from a classical piano sonata and complete the remaining exercises.

3. Beginning with the given items, capture the music in the workspace.

   (a) In the single-line staves, notate the rhythm of the bass and soprano lines.

   (b) Below each note, write the syllables and numbers of the pitches.

   (c) In the grand staff, notate pitches and rhythm of both parts. Refer to the single-line notation. Check your work at a keyboard.

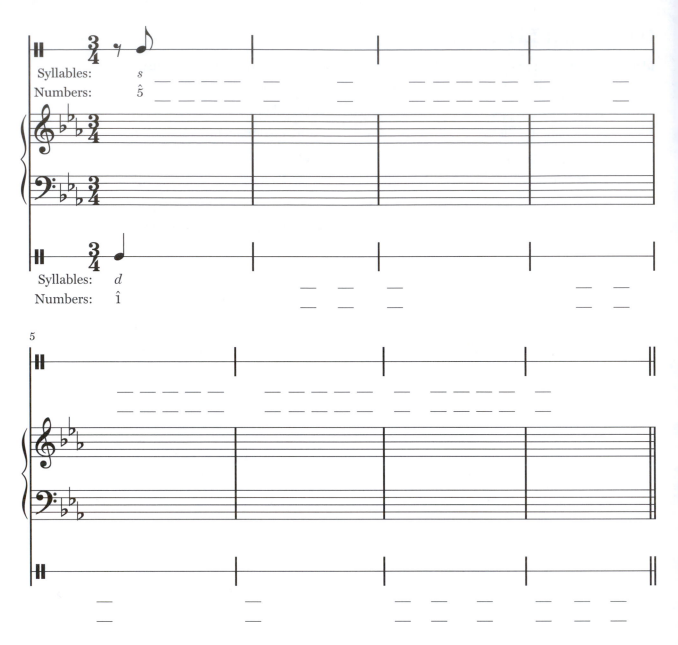

4. The progression in measures 1–4 is:

    i–V7–i⁶   i–ii°–i⁶   i–vii°⁶–i⁶

5. The four chords implied in measures 7–8 are:

    i–v⁶–iv⁶–V   i–VI–iv–V   i⁶–ii°⁶–V–i

Contextual Listening 17.2

Identify dominant-function seventh chords in these four-chord progressions.

1. (a) Chord 2 is: V^4_3 vii°$^6_5$
   (b) Chord 3 is: V^4_2 vii°$^4_3$

2. (a) Chord 2 is: V^4_3 vii°$^6_5$
   (b) Chord 4 is: V^4_3 vii°$^6_5$

Now, listen to one phrase from a classical piano sonata and complete the remaining exercises.

3. Beginning with the given items, capture the music in the workspace.

   (a) In the single-line staves, notate the rhythm of the bass and soprano lines.

   (b) Below each note, write the syllables and numbers of the pitches.

   (c) In the grand staff, notate pitches and rhythm of both parts. Refer to the single-line notation. Sing aloud to check your work.

   (d) Beneath each bass pitch, write the Roman numeral and figure (if needed) that represents the harmony.

4. Near the end, the embellishment is a: CS   N   S   P

5. The cadence type is: PAC   IAC   HC   PHC

Contextual Listening 17.3

Identify dominant-function seventh chords in these four-chord progressions.

1. (a) Predominant: ii°6   ii∅$^4_3$ iv   iv6   2. (a) Chords 1-2 are: i$^5_3$-$^6_4$ i-iv

   (b) Chord 3 is: V$^6_5$ vii°7   (b) Chord 3 is: V$^6_5$ vii°7

Now, listen to an instrumental adaptation of a choral work and complete the remaining exercises.

3. Beginning with the given items, capture the music in the workspace.

   (a) In the single-line staves, notate the rhythm of the bass and soprano lines.

   (b) Below each note, write the syllables and numbers of the pitches.

   (c) In the grand staff, notate pitches and rhythm of both parts. Refer to the single-line notation. Sing aloud to check your work.

   (d) Beneath each bass pitch, write the Roman numeral and figures (if needed) that represents the harmony.

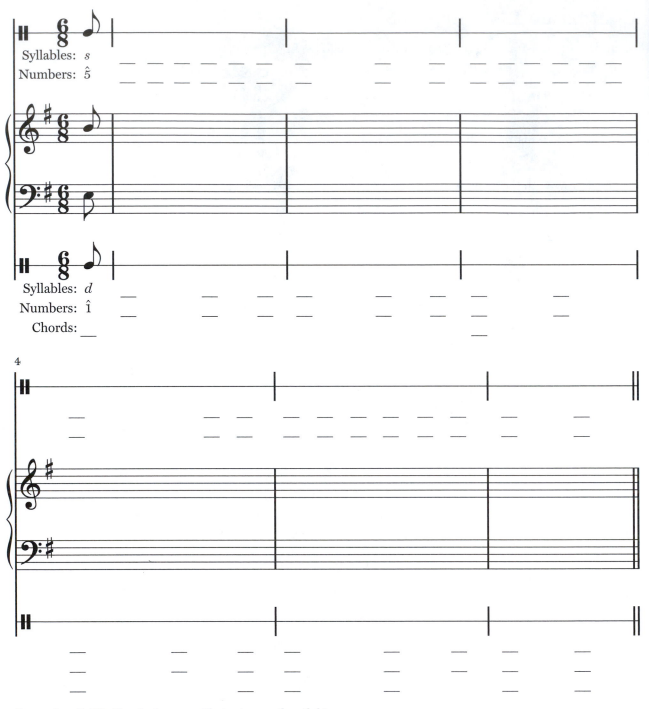

Es rauschen die Wipfel und schauern,
Als machten zu dieser Stund
Um die halbverfallenen Mauern
Die alten Götter die Rund.

The treetops rustle and shiver
as if at this hour
about the half-crumbled walls
the old gods are making their rounds.

CHAPTER 18

Phrase Structure and Motivic Analysis

NAME _____

In this chapter you'll learn to:

- Identify subphrase, motive, sentence, and independent phrase
- Identify parallel and contrasting periods
- Diagram phrase structures

Phrase Subdivisions, Sentence, and Independent Phrase

Phrases can contain smaller units called subphrases, which themselves may consist of or contain a motive.

Phrase:	the smallest complete idea that ends with a cadence
Subphrase:	a cohesive part of a phrase
Motive:	a recurring idea with distinct rhythm and contour

A phrase made from three subphrases with the proportion 1:1:2 is called a sentence.

x^1		x^2		x^3 or y	→		→	cadence
1 ————	+	1 ———	+	2 ————————————				

An isolated phrase that ends with a PAC is called an independent phrase.

Try it 1

Listen to part of a string quartet and complete the following exercises.

1. At the end, the $^6_4$ chord type is: passing   neighboring   cadential

2. The next-to-last melodic pitch is which embellishment?

    consonant skip   passing tone   retardation

3. The excerpt ends with a/an: PAC   IAC   HC

Identify which term or terms apply to the specified portion. More than one answer may apply.

4. Melodic pitches 1–5:

   motive   subphrase   phrase   sentence   independent phrase

5. Melodic pitches 6–10:

   motive   subphrase   phrase   sentence   independent phrase

6. Melodic pitches 11–end:

   motive   subphrase   phrase   sentence   independent phrase

7. The entire excerpt:

   motive   subphrase   phrase   sentence   independent phrase

Periods and Phrase Diagrams

Phrases often group in pairs called a period. Same or similar melodic beginnings receive the same letter name. A contrasting beginning receives a new letter name.

Phrase	Phrase name	Cadence	Melodic beginnings	Letter name	Type of period
1	antecedent	inconclusive, often a HC	initial motive	a	
2	consequent	always a PAC	same/similar to Phrase 1 different from Phrase 1	a or a′ b	parallel contrasting

Phrase diagrams show structural levels, cadences, and unit names.

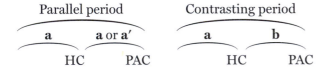

This diagram shows a parallel period comprising two phrases, each a three-subphrase sentence.

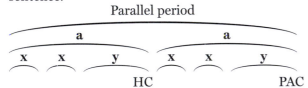

Try it 2

1. Listen to a two-phrase excerpt and complete the exercises.

   (a) Identify which term or terms apply to the specified portion. More than one answer may apply.

   (1) Melodic pitches 1–5:

       motive   subphrase   phrase   sentence   independent phrase

   (2) Melodic pitches 6–10:

       motive   subphrase   phrase   sentence   independent phrase

   (3) Melodic pitches 11–19:

       motive   subphrase   phrase   sentence   independent phrase

   (4) Melodic pitches 1–19:

       motive   subphrase   phrase   sentence   independent phrase

   (b) Phrase 1 ends with a/an: PAC   IAC   HC

   (c) Phrase 2 ends with a/an: PAC   IAC   HC

   (d) Phrases 1–2 complete which pattern?

       motive   subphrase   sentence   period

   (e) Compare phrase 2's beginning with that of phrase 1. Phrase 2 begins:

       the same or similarly (**a** or **a′**)   differently (**b**)

   (f) Which diagram represents the excerpt's structure?

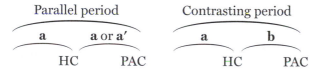

2. Listen to a two-phrase excerpt and complete the exercises.

   (a) Phrase 1 ends with a/an: PAC   IAC   HC

   (b) Phrase 2 ends with a/an: PAC   IAC   HC

   (c) Phrases 1–2 complete which pattern?

       motive   subphrase   sentence   period

   (d) Compare phrase 2's beginning with that of phrase 1. Phrase 2 begins:

       the same or similarly (**a** or **a′**)   differently (**b**)

   (e) Which diagram matches the excerpt's structure?

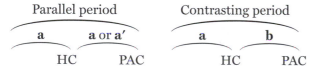

3. Locate and listen online to the initial vocal phrases of Billy Joel's "Piano Man."

   (a) The beat division is: simple   compound

   (b) The lyrics "It's nine o'clock on a Saturday" complete a:

   motive   subphrase   sentence   period

   (c) Compare phrase 2's beginning with that of phrase 1. Phrase 2 begins:

   the same or similarly (**a** or **a′**)   differently (**b**)

   (d) The excerpt's structure is a:

   sentence   parallel period   contrasting period

Contextual Listening 18.1

Listen to an eight-measure excerpt of a keyboard work and complete the following exercises.

1. The beat grouping is: duple   triple   quadruple

2. The beat division is: simple   compound

3. The motive lasts how many measures?   1   2   3   4

4. The excerpt consists of how many subphrases?   1   2   3   4

5. The excerpt ends with which cadence?   PAC   IAC   HC   PHC

6. The excerpt's structure is a/an:

    phrase   sentence   independent phrase   period

Listen to a different eight-measure excerpt of a keyboard work and complete the following exercises.

7. The beat grouping is: duple   triple

8. The beat division is: simple   compound

9. The motive lasts how many measures?   1   2   3   4

10. Phrase 1 ends with a/an: PAC   IAC   HC   PHC

11. Phrase 2 ends with a/an: PAC   IAC   HC   PHC

12. Compare phrase 2's beginning with that of phrase 1. Phrase 2 begins:

    the same or similarly (**a** or **a′**)   differently (**b**)

13. Which diagram matches the excerpt's structure?

Parallel period	Contrasting period
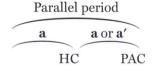	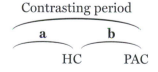

Contextual Listening 18.2

Listen to a two-phrase trumpet melody and complete the following exercises. Recall that melodic pitches can imply harmony.

1. The motive consists of how many pitches?   1   2   3   4   5   6   7   8

2. Phrase 1 ends with a: PAC   IAC   HC   PHC

3. Phrase 1 consists of how many subphrases?   1   2   3   4

4. Phrase 1 is a/an: sentence   period   independent phrase

5. Phrase 2 ends with a/an: PAC   IAC   HC   PHC

6. Which diagram represents the excerpt's structure?

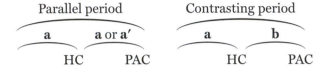

7. Beginning with the given items, capture the melody in the workspace.

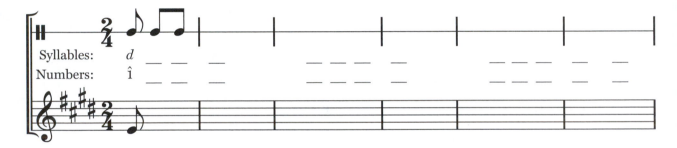

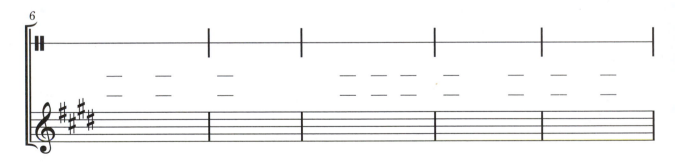

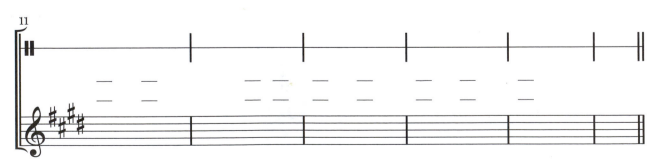

Contextual Listening 18.3

Listen to eight measures from a piano work. Then complete the exercises.

1. The beat grouping is: duple   triple   quadruple

2. The beat division is: simple   compound

3. The motive consists of how many pitches?   1   2   3   4   5   6   7   8

4. In measure 4, beat 1, phrase 1 ends with a: PAC   IAC   HC   PHC

5. Phrase 1 consists of how many subphrases?   1   2   3   4

6. Phrase 1 is a/an: sentence   period   independent phrase

7. Phrase 2 ends with a/an: PAC   IAC   HC   PHC

8. Which diagram represents the excerpt's structure?

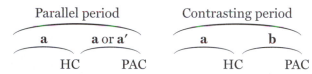

9. Each phrase includes which type of phrase expansion?

   introduction   deceptive resolution   cadential extension

10. Beginning with the given items, capture phrase 1's melody in the workspace. Include key and meter signatures. For help, refer to previous answers.

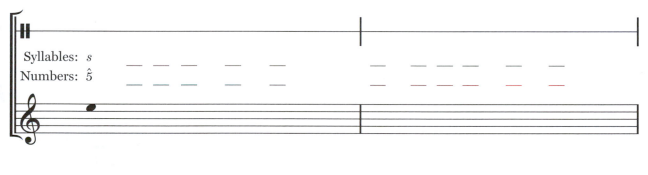

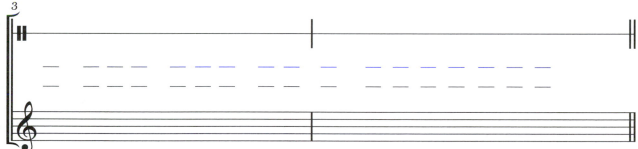

Contextual Listening 18.4

Listen to four measures from a piano work. Then, complete the exercises.

1. The beat division is: simple   compound

2. Phrase 1 ends with a: PAC   IAC   HC   PHC

3. Phrase 1 consists of how many subphrases?   1   2   3   4

4. Phrase 2 ends with a/an: PAC   IAC   HC   PHC

5. The excerpt's structure is a: parallel period   contrasting period

6. Beginning with the given items, capture the melodic and bass lines in the workspace.

   (a) In the single-line staves, notate the rhythm. Below each note, write the syllables and numbers of the pitches.

   (b) In the grand staff, notate the pitches and rhythm of melody and the bass. (There is no need to double the bass one octave lower.)

   (c) In each chord blank, write the Roman numeral and figure (if needed) that represents the harmony.

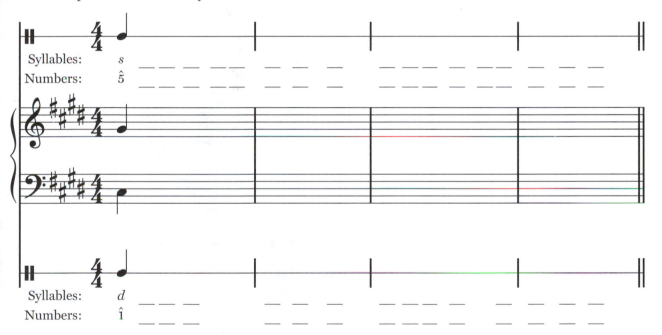

Double Periods

Typically, a double period is a four-phrase period. When the first consequent phrase begins the same or similarly as the first antecedent, the period is parallel. Otherwise, it is contrasting.

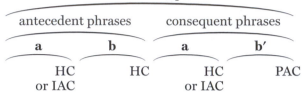

Parallel double period

antecedent phrases		consequent phrases	
a	**b**	**a**	**b′**
HC or IAC	HC	HC or IAC	PAC

Asymmetrical periods have an unequal number of antecedent and consequent phrases.

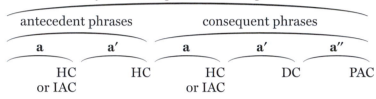

Asymmetrical parallel double period

antecedent phrases		consequent phrases		
a	**a′**	**a**	**a′**	**a″**
HC or IAC	HC	HC or IAC	DC	PAC

Try it 3

1. Listen to a piano work and complete the following exercises.

   (a) The bass rhythm is given. Below each note, write the syllables and numbers of the bass pitch. In each chord blank, write the Roman numeral and figure (if needed).

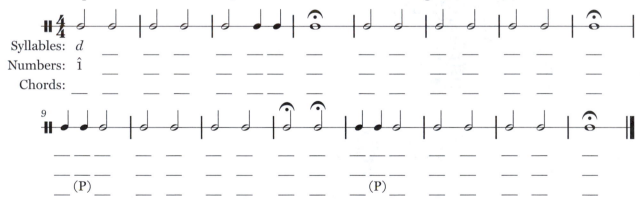

   (b) Diagram the structure. Follow the models given earlier and label each unit.

2. Listen to a different excerpt and diagram the structure. Label each unit.

Contextual Listening 18.5

Listen to a string duo and complete the following exercises.

1. The phrase design letters are: **a a a a**   **a b a a′**   **a b a b′**

2. Phrase 1's melody ends with: *do* (1̂)   *re* (2̂)   *mi* (3̂)   *sol* (5̂)

3. (a) Phrase 2's melody ends with: *do* (1̂)   *re* (2̂)   *mi* (3̂)   *sol* (5̂)

   (b) Phrase 2 has how many subphrases?   1   2   3   4

   (c) Phrase 2's structure is a/an: sentence   independent phrase   period

4. Phrase 3's melody ends with: *do* (1̂)   *re* (2̂)   *mi* (3̂)   *sol* (5̂)

5. Phrase 4's melody ends with: *do* (1̂)   *re* (2̂)   *mi* (3̂)   *sol* (5̂)

6. The cadences occur in which order? Hint: Focus on cadential bass pitches and the answers to exercises 2–5.

   HC–HC–HC–PAC   HC–IAC–HC–PAC

   IAC–HC–IAC–PAC   IAC–IAC–IAC–PAC

7. The excerpt's phrase structure is:

   parallel period   contrasting period

   parallel double period   contrasting double period

8. Draw a diagram of the excerpt's phrase structure. Label cadences, phrase design letters, and the overall structure (the answers to exercises 1, 6, and 7).

CHAPTER 19

Secondary Dominant-Function Chords of V

NAME _____

In this chapter you'll learn to:

- Identify secondary dominant-function chords V^7/V and vii^{o7}/V and their inversions
- Notate music that includes secondary dominant-function chords

Secondary Dominant-Function Chords of V

Sometimes, *fi* (♯$\hat{4}$) is a melodic embellishment, like a chromatic neighbor tone. Other times, it is the leading tone of a dominant-function chord in the key of V. Bracket, slash, and colon notation are three ways to show secondary dominant-function chords.

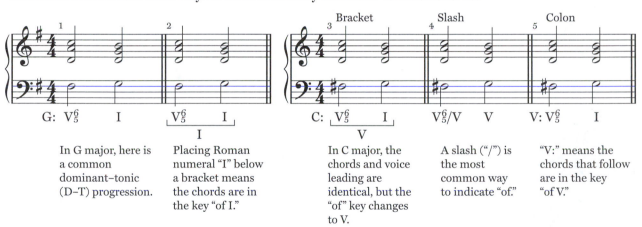

| In G major, here is a common dominant–tonic (D–T) progression. | Placing Roman numeral "I" below a bracket means the chords are in the key "of I." | In C major, the chords and voice leading are identical, but the "of" key changes to V. | A slash ("/") is the most common way to indicate "of." | "V:" means the chords that follow are in the key "of V." |

Try it

Listen to four-part progressions that include dominant-function chords of the tonic (e.g., V^6_5 and vii^{o7}) and of the dominant (e.g., V^6_5/V and vii^{o7}/V) and answer the following.

1. (a) Meter type: simple   compound

   (b) Chord 2 is: V^6_5 vii^{o7} V^4_3 vii^{o6}_5

   (c) Chord 5 is: ii^6 ii^6_5 IV IV^6

   (d) Chord 6 is: V^7/V V^6_5/V V^4_3/V

   (e) Cadence type: PAC   IAC   HC   DC

2. (a) Meter type: simple   compound

   (b) Chord 2 is: V^6_5 vii^{o7} V^4_3 vii^{o6}_5

   (c) Chord 5 is: ii^{o6} $ii^{ø6}_5$ iv iv^6

   (d) Chord 6 is: V^7/V V^6_5/V V^4_3/V

   (e) Cadence type: PAC   IAC   HC   DC

3. (a) Meter type: simple   compound
   (b) Chord 2 is: V_3^4 $vii^{\circ6}_5$ V_2^4 $vii^{\circ4}_3$
   (c) Chord 4 is: V7/V V_5^6/V $vii^{\varnothing}7$/V
   (d) $_4^6$ type: neighboring   passing   cadential
   (e) Cadence type: PAC   IAC   HC   DC

4. (a) Meter type: simple   compound
   (b) Chord 2 is: V_5^6 $vii^{\circ}7$ V_3^4 $vii^{\circ6}_5$
   (c) Chord 4 is: V7/V V_5^6/V $vii^{\circ}7$/V
   (d) $_4^6$ type: neighboring   passing   cadential
   (e) Cadence type: PAC   IAC   HC   DC

5. (a) Meter type: simple   compound
   (b) Chord 4 is: $ii^{\circ6}$ $ii^{\varnothing6}_5$ iv iv^6
   (c) Chord 5 is: V7/V V_5^6/V $vii^{\circ}7$/V
   (d) $_4^6$ type: neighboring   passing   cadential
   (e) Cadence type: PAC   IAC   HC   PHC

6. (a) Meter type: simple   compound
   (b) Chord 4 is: $ii^{\circ6}$ $ii^{\varnothing6}_5$ iv iv^6
   (c) Chord 6 is: V7/V V_5^6/V $vii^{\circ}7$/V
   (d) $_4^6$ type: neighboring   passing   cadential
   (e) Cadence type: PAC   IAC   HC   PHC

7. (a) Meter type: simple   compound
   (b) Chord 2 is: V_3^4 $vii^{\circ6}$ V_2^4 $vii^{\varnothing4}_3$
   (c) Chord 4 is: V7/V V^6/V $vii^{\circ}7$/V
   (d) Cadence type: PAC   IAC   HC   PHC

8. (a) Meter type: simple   compound
   (b) Chord 2 is: V_4^6 $vii^{\circ6}$ V_2^4 $vii^{\circ6}_5$
   (c) Chord 5 is: V7/V V^6/V $vii^{\circ}7$/V
   (d) Cadence type: PAC   IAC   HC   PHC

Contextual Listening 19.1

CL 19.1A Listen to two phrases from a chorale and complete the following exercises.

1. Phrase 1's cadence type is: PAC   IAC   HC   DC

2. Phrase 2's cadence type is: PAC   IAC   HC   DC

3. Diagram the excerpt's structure. Draw curves for phrases. Label each phrase, cadence, and the entire structure.

4. In the top row of blanks, write phrase 2's bass pitches using syllables or numbers.

    ___   ___   ___   ___   ___   ___

    ___   ___   ___   ___   ___

5. Beneath the answers to exercise 4, write the Roman numerals and figures (if needed). Indicate secondary dominant–function chords using bracket, slash, or colon notation.

CL 19.1B Listen to two phrases from a chorale and complete the following exercises.

6. Phrase 1's melody ends with:

    mi-fa ($\hat{3}$-$\hat{4}$)   *fi-sol* ($\sharp\hat{4}$-$\hat{5}$)   *si-la* ($\sharp\hat{5}$-$\hat{6}$)   *ti-do* ($\hat{7}$-$\hat{8}$)

7. Phrase 1's final two chords are: I–V   IV–V   V/V–V   V–I

8. Phrase 2's cadence type is: PAC   IAC   HC   DC

9. In the top row of blanks, write the final three bass pitches with syllables or numbers.

    ___   ___   ___

    ___   ___   ___

10. Beneath the answers to exercise 9, write the Roman numerals and figures (if needed). Indicate secondary dominant–function chords using bracket, slash, or colon notation.

CL 19.1C Listen to one phrase from a chorale and complete the following exercises.

11. The cadence type is: PAC   IAC   HC   DC

12. In the top row of blanks, write the final three bass pitches using syllables or numbers.

    ___   ___   ___

    ___   ___   ___

13. Beneath the answers to exercise 12, write the Roman numerals and figures (if needed). Indicate secondary dominant–function chords using bracket, slash, or colon notation.

Contextual Listening 19.2

CL 19.2A Near the end of CL 19.2A, listen for *fi* ($\sharp\hat{4}$) in the inner voice.

1. The final three bass pitches are:

   re-sol-do ($\hat{2}$-$\hat{5}$-$\hat{1}$)   *mi-sol-do* ($\hat{3}$-$\hat{5}$-$\hat{1}$)   *fa-sol-do* ($\hat{4}$-$\hat{5}$-$\hat{1}$)   *sol-sol-do* ($\hat{5}$-$\hat{5}$-$\hat{1}$)

2. The last three chords are: ii–V–I   IV–V–I   V7/V–V7–I   ii–V$^6_5$–I

CL 19.2B Listen to a phrase from a string quartet. At the end, focus on the bass line.

3. The final three bass pitches are:

   do-mi-sol ($\hat{1}$-$\hat{3}$-$\hat{5}$)   *re-sol-do* ($\hat{2}$-$\hat{5}$-$\hat{1}$)   *fa-fi-sol* ($\hat{4}$-$\sharp\hat{4}$-$\hat{5}$)   *ti-sol-sol* ($\hat{7}$-$\hat{5}$-$\hat{5}$)

4. *Fi* ($\sharp\hat{4}$) is part of which chord? Hint: Listen for the next-to-last melodic pitch.

   I7   ii7   V7/V   vii$^{\varnothing}$7/V

CL 19.2C Listen to a phrase from a song. Focus especially on the bass pitches.

Translation: Beside the brook grow many small flowers, gazing out of bright blue eyes.

5. Chords 1–3 form which progression?

   I–V–I   I–V$^6_4$–I6   I–V$^4_3$–I6   I–ii–I6

6. Bass pitches 4–6 are:

   do-di-re ($\hat{1}$-$\sharp\hat{1}$-$\hat{2}$)   *re-ri-mi* ($\hat{2}$-$\sharp\hat{2}$-$\hat{3}$)   *mi-fa-sol* ($\hat{3}$-$\hat{4}$-$\hat{5}$)   *fa-fi-sol* ($\hat{4}$-$\sharp\hat{4}$-$\hat{5}$)

7. *Fi* ($\sharp\hat{4}$) is harmonized with which chord?   ii7   V7   V$^6_5$/V   vi

Contextual Listening 19.3

Listen to short excerpts and choose the progression played.

1.   I–V7–I   I–V$^6_5$–I   I–V$^4_3$–I^6 I–V$^4_2$–I^6

2.   I–V7–I   I–V$^6_5$–I   I–V$^4_3$–I^6 I–V$^4_2$–I^6

3.   I–V7–I   I–V$^6_5$–I   I–V$^4_3$–I^6 I–V$^4_2$–I^6

Now, listen to two phrases from a piano work and complete the remaining exercises.

4. Which meter signature is most likely? $\frac{3}{4}$ $\frac{6}{8}$ $\frac{9}{8}$

5. Initially, the two lower parts are doubled at which harmonic interval?

    third   fifth   sixth   octave

6. Phrase 1's cadence type is: PAC   IAC   HC   DC

7. Phrase 2's cadence type is: PAC   IAC   HC   DC

8. Diagram the excerpt's structure. Draw curves for phrases. Label each phrase, cadence, and the entire structure.

9. Beginning with the given items, capture the excerpt in the workspace.

   (a) In the single-line staves, notate the rhythm of the melody and bass. Below each note, write the syllables and numbers of the pitches.

   (b) In the grand staff, notate the pitches and rhythm of the melody and bass lines.

   (c) In the chord blanks specified, write the Roman numeral and figure (if needed) that represents the harmony.

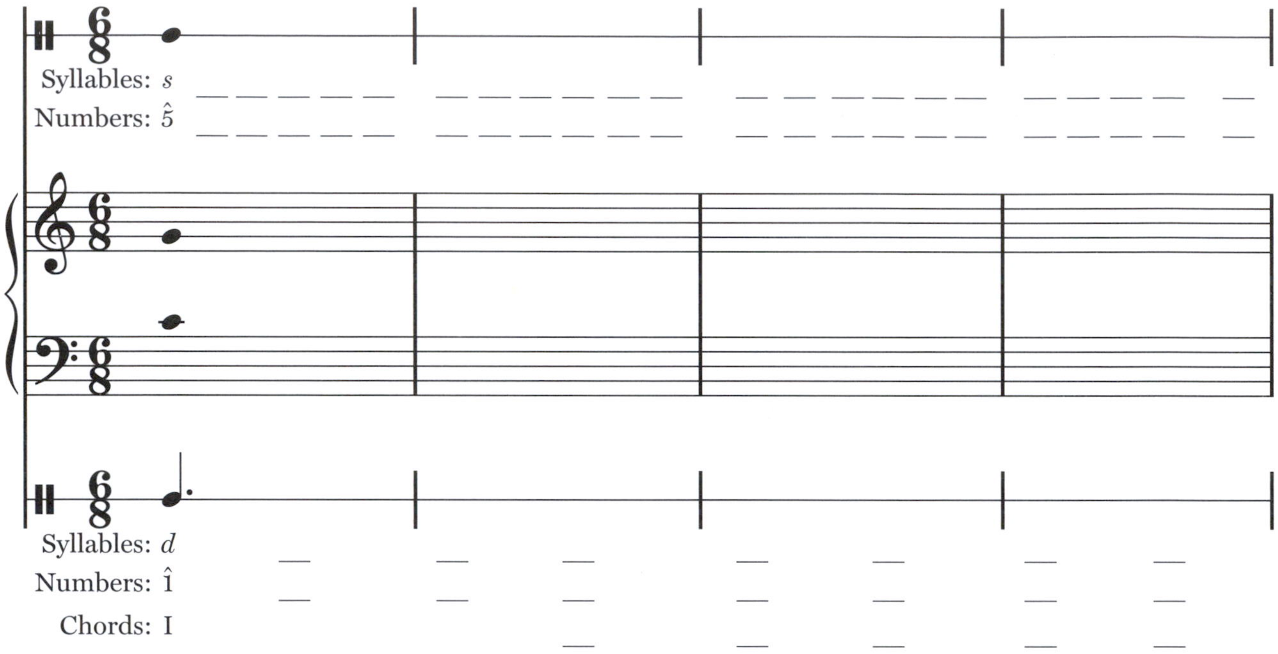

Syllables: *s*

Numbers: $\hat{5}$

Syllables: *d*

Numbers: $\hat{1}$

Chords: I

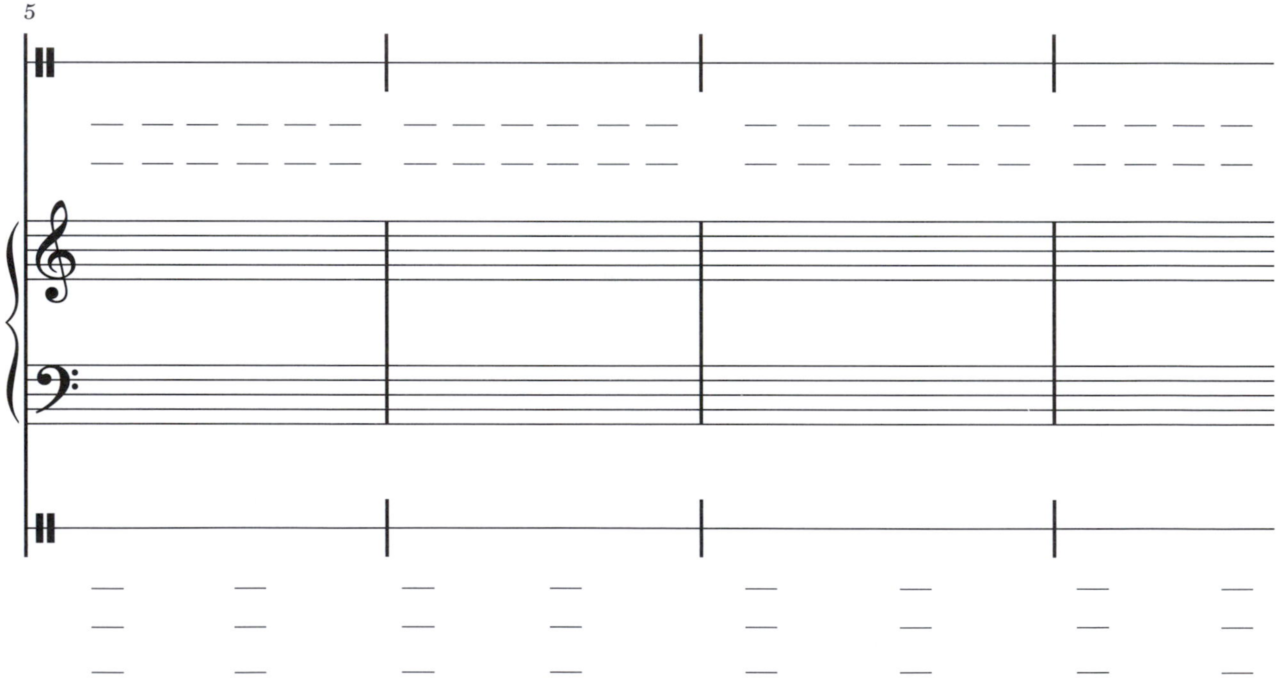

5

Contextual Listening 19.4

Listen to short excerpts and choose the progression played.

1. I–vi–ii^6–V   I–IV–I–V   I–ii^6–I^6–V

2. V–V7–I^6 V–V$^6_5$–I^6 V–V$^4_2$–I^6

3. I–vi–ii^6–V   I–vi–V7/V–V   I–IV–V$^6_5$/V–V

Now, listen to two phrases from a piano work and complete the remaining exercises.

4. Phrase 1's cadence chord is: I   V   vi

5. Phrase 2's cadence chord is: I   V   vi

6. The phrase design letters are: **a a**   **a a′**   **a b**

7. Beginning with the given items, capture the excerpt in the workspace.

  (a) In the single-line staves, notate the rhythm of the melody and bass. Below each note, write the syllables and numbers of the pitches.

  (b) In the grand staff, notate the pitches and rhythm of the melody and bass lines.

  (c) In each chord blank, write the Roman numeral and figure (if needed) that represents the harmony.

Contextual Listening 19.5

A pizzicato-chord accompaniment begins on tonic before changing to a different chord. Focus on the strong-beat bass pitches and choose the correct progression.

1.   i–ii$^{\varnothing 6}_{5}$ i–iv   i–V7   i–V$^4_3$ i–V7/V

2.   i–ii$^{\varnothing 6}_{5}$ i–iv   i–V7   i–V$^4_3$ i–V7/V

3.   i–ii$^{\varnothing 6}_{5}$ i–iv   i–V7   i–V$^4_3$ i–V7/V

4.   i–ii$^{\varnothing 6}_{5}$ i–iv   i–V7   i–V$^4_3$ i–V7/V

Now, listen to an arrangement of a song. After a two-measure introduction, you will hear a melody that consists of four segments.

5. Which meter signature is most likely? $\frac{2}{4}$ $\frac{6}{8}$ $\frac{9}{8}$

6. The melodic design letters are: **a a b a**   **a b a b**   **a b a c**   **a b c d**

7. Beginning with the given items, capture the music in the workspace.

    (a) In the single-line staff, notate the melodic rhythm. Below each note, write the syllables and numbers of the pitches.

    (b) In the treble staff, notate the pitches and rhythm of the melody.

    (c) From the chord choices given, circle the one that represents the implied harmony.

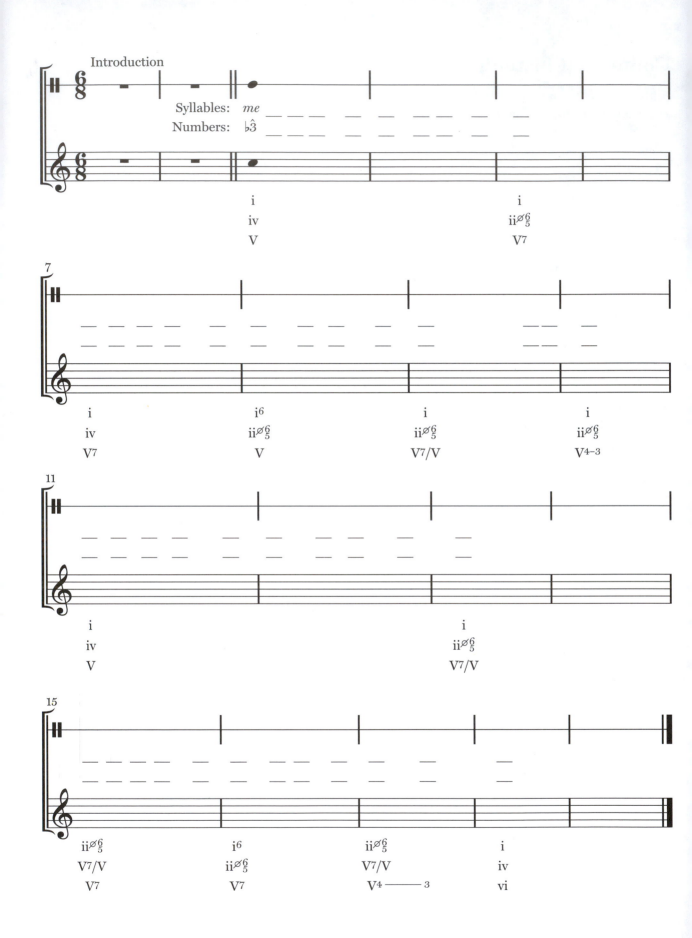

CHAPTER 20

Tonicizing Scale Degrees Other Than $\hat{5}$

NAME _____

In this chapter you'll learn to:

- Identify tonicizations of scale degrees other than $\hat{5}$
- Notate music that includes secondary dominant-function chords and their inversions

Tonicizing Scale Degrees Other Than $\hat{5}$

Any major or minor triad may be tonicized. Here, a dominant-tonic progression is transposed repeatedly, tonicizing chords ii, iii, IV, V, and vi. Each tonicization appears in bracket notation with the D–T progression shown over the Roman numeral of the tonicized chord.

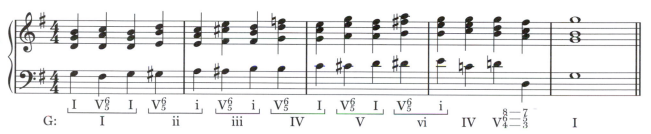

Tonicization can also be shown using slash notation (V^6_5/ii–ii, etc.) or colon notation (ii: V^6_5–ii, etc.).

Listening Strategies

Chromatic pitches often imply tonicization. Raised pitches rise, and can sound like *ti* ($\hat{7}$). Lowered pitches fall, and can sound like *fa* ($\hat{4}$), *le* ($\flat\hat{6}$), or *ra* ($\flat\hat{2}$).

Ti ($\hat{7}$) functions as a diatonic pitch in both major and minor, even though in minor keys it requires an accidental. Canceling *ti* ($\hat{7}$)'s accidental so that it becomes *te* ($\flat\hat{7}$) can signal movement away from tonic.

Major keys *If you hear . . .*	*the chord tonicized is . . .*	Minor keys *If you hear . . .*	*the chord tonicized is . . .*
fi–sol ($\sharp\hat{4}$–$\hat{5}$)	V (most common)	*fi–sol* ($\sharp\hat{4}$–$\hat{5}$)	V or v (very common)
si–la ($\sharp\hat{5}$–$\hat{6}$)	vi (common)	*mi–fa* ($\natural\hat{3}$–$\hat{4}$)	iv (very common)
di–re ($\sharp\hat{1}$–$\hat{2}$)	ii (somewhat common)	*te*, not *ti* ($\flat\hat{7}$, not $\hat{7}$)	III (most common)
ri–mi ($\sharp\hat{2}$–$\hat{3}$)	iii (rare)	*te* and *ra* ($\flat\hat{7}$ and $\flat\hat{2}$)	VI (common)
te–la ($\flat\hat{7}$–$\hat{6}$)	IV (very common)		

Try it

A three-chord progression establishes the key. Chords 4–5 create a tonicization. Identify the initial progression, the chromatic pitch(es), and the tonicized chord. Then, write the tonicization (chords 4–5) using bracket, slash, and colon notation.

1. (a) The initial progression is: I–V7–I   I–V$_5^6$–I   I–V$_3^4$–I^6 I–V$_2^4$–I^6
   (b) The chromatic pitch is: *di* ($\sharp\hat{1}$)   *fi* ($\sharp\hat{4}$)   *si* ($\sharp\hat{5}$)   *te* ($\flat\hat{7}$)
   (c) The tonicized chord is: ii   IV   V   vi
   (d) Write the tonicization (chords 4–5) using bracket, slash, and colon notation.
      Bracket   *Slash*   *Colon*

2. (a) The initial progression is: I–V7–I   I–V$_5^6$–I   I–V$_3^4$–I^6 I–V$_2^4$–I^6
   (b) The chromatic pitch is: *di* ($\sharp\hat{1}$)   *fi* ($\sharp\hat{4}$)   *si* ($\sharp\hat{5}$)   *te* ($\flat\hat{7}$)
   (c) The tonicized chord is: ii   IV   V   vi
   (d) Write the tonicization (chords 4–5) using bracket, slash, and colon notation.
      Bracket   *Slash*   *Colon*

3. (a) The initial progression is: I–V7–I   I–V$_5^6$–I   I–V$_3^4$–I^6 I–V$_2^4$–I^6
   (b) The chromatic pitch is: *di* ($\sharp\hat{1}$)   *fi* ($\sharp\hat{4}$)   *si* ($\sharp\hat{5}$)   *te* ($\flat\hat{7}$)
   (c) The tonicized chord is: ii   IV   V   vi
   (d) Write the tonicization (chords 4–5) using bracket, slash, and colon notation.
      Bracket   *Slash*   *Colon*

4. (a) The initial progression is: I–V–I   I–V$_5^6$–I   I–V$_3^4$–I^6 I–V$_2^4$–I^6

   (b) The chromatic pitch is: *di* (♯$\hat{1}$)   *fi* (♯$\hat{4}$)   *si* (♯$\hat{5}$)   *te* (♭$\hat{7}$)

   (c) The tonicized chord is: ii   IV   V   vi

   (d) Write the tonicization (chords 4–5) using bracket, slash, and colon notation.
       Bracket   *Slash*   *Colon*

5. (a) The initial progression is: i–V7–i   i–V$_5^6$–i   i–V$_3^4$–i^6 i–V$_2^4$–i^6

   (b) The chromatic pitch(es) is (are):   *ra* (♭$\hat{2}$)   *mi* (♮$\hat{3}$)   *fi* (♯$\hat{4}$)   *te* (♭$\hat{7}$)

   (c) The tonicized chord is: III   iv   V or v   VI

   (d) Write the tonicization (chords 4–5) using bracket, slash, and colon notation.
       Bracket   *Slash*   *Colon*

6. (a) The initial progression is: i–V–i   i–V$_5^6$–i   i–V$_3^4$–i^6 i–V$_2^4$–i^6

   (b) The chromatic pitch(es) is (are):   *ra* (♭$\hat{2}$)   *mi* (♮$\hat{3}$)   *fi* (♯$\hat{4}$)   *te* (♭$\hat{7}$)

   (c) The tonicized chord is: III   iv   V or v   VI

   (d) Write the tonicization (chords 4–5) using bracket, slash, and colon notation.
       Bracket   *Slash*   *Colon*

7. (a) The initial progression is: i–vii°7–i   i–vii°$_5^6$–i^6 i–vii°$_3^4$–i^6

   (b) The chromatic pitch(es) is (are):   *ra* (♭$\hat{2}$)   *mi* (♮$\hat{3}$)   *fi* (♯$\hat{4}$)   *te* (♭$\hat{7}$)

   (c) The tonicized chord is: III   iv   V or v   VI

   (d) Write the tonicization (chords 4–5) using bracket, slash, and colon notation.
       Bracket   *Slash*   *Colon*

Contextual Listening 20.1

Listen to three-chord progressions that begin on tonic and complete the exercises.

1. (a) Bass pitches 1–3 are scale degrees:

   ($\hat{1}$-$\hat{5}$-$\hat{1}$)   ($\hat{1}$-$\hat{7}$-$\hat{1}$)   ($\hat{1}$-$\hat{2}$-$\hat{3}$)   ($\hat{1}$-$\hat{4}$-$\hat{3}$)

   (b) Melodic pitches 3 and 6 are which type of embellishment?

   neighbor   consonant skip   passing tone   suspension

   (c) Melodic pitches 4 and 7 are which type of embellishment?

   incomplete neighbor   consonant skip   passing tone   suspension

   (d) The chromatic pitch is: none   *di* (♯$\hat{1}$)   *fi* (♯$\hat{4}$)   *si* (♯$\hat{5}$)   *te* (♭$\hat{7}$)

   (e) The tonicized chord is: only I   ii   IV   V   vi

   (f) Write the progression. If there is a tonicization, use bracket, slash, and colon notation.
   Bracket   *Slash*   *Colon*

2. (a) Bass pitches 1–3 are scale degrees:

   ($\hat{1}$-$\hat{5}$-$\hat{1}$)   ($\hat{1}$-$\hat{7}$-$\hat{6}$)   ($\hat{1}$-$\hat{2}$-$\hat{3}$)   ($\hat{1}$-$\hat{4}$-$\hat{3}$)

   (b) Melodic pitches 3 and 6 are which type of embellishment?

   neighbor   consonant skip   passing tone   suspension

   (c) Melodic pitches 4 and 7 are which type of embellishment?

   incomplete neighbor   consonant skip   passing tone   suspension

   (d) The chromatic pitch is: none   *di* (♯$\hat{1}$)   *fi* (♯$\hat{4}$)   *si* (♯$\hat{5}$)   *te* (♭$\hat{7}$)

   (e) The tonicized chord is: only I   ii   IV   V   vi

   (f) Write the progression. If there is a tonicization, use bracket, slash, and colon notation.
   Bracket   *Slash*   *Colon*

3. (a) The chromatic bass pitch is: none   *di* (♯$\hat{1}$)   *fi* (♯$\hat{4}$)   *si* (♯$\hat{5}$)   *te* (♭$\hat{7}$)

   (b) The tonicized chord is: only I   ii   IV   V   vi

   (c) Write the progression. If there is a tonicization, use bracket, slash, and colon notation.
   Bracket   *Slash*   *Colon*

Now, listen to two phrases from a piano work and complete the remaining exercises.

4. Beginning with the given items, capture only phrase 2 in the workspace.

   (a) In the single-line staves, notate the rhythm of the bass and melody.

   (b) Below each note, write the syllables and numbers of the pitches.

   (c) In the grand staff, notate pitches and rhythm of both parts. Refer to the single-line notation.

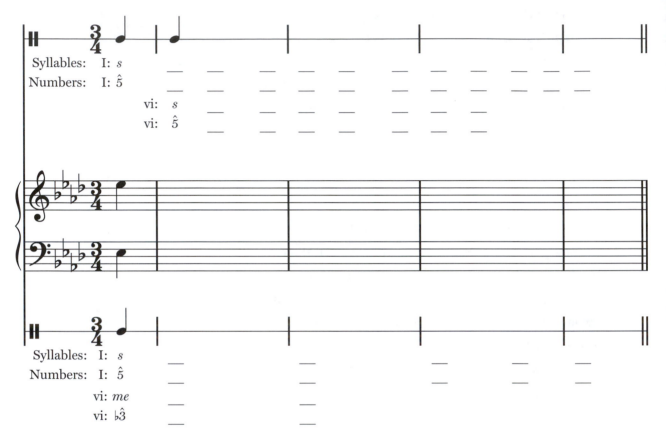

5. Bass pitch 3 supports which type of seventh chord?

   MM7   Mm7   mm7   dm7 ($^{\varnothing}$7)

6. Bass pitches 3–4 create which progression?

   V$^4_3$/vi–vi   vii$^{\circ 6}_5$/vi–vi   V7/V–V   vii$^{\circ}$7/V–V

Contextual Listening 20.2

Listen to short progressions that begin on tonic and complete the exercises.

1. (a) The next-to-last melodic pitch is which embellishment?

   incomplete neighbor   consonant skip   passing tone   suspension

   (b) The chromatic pitch(es) is (are):

   none   *ra* ($\flat\hat{2}$)   *mi* ($\natural\hat{3}$)   *fi* ($\sharp\hat{4}$)   *te* ($\flat\hat{7}$)

   (c) The tonicized chord is: only i   III   iv   V or v   VI

   (d) Write the progression. If there is a tonicization, use bracket, slash, and colon notation.

        Bracket   *Slash*   *Colon*

2. (a) The next-to-last melodic pitch is which type of suspension?

   9–8   7–6   4–3

   (b) The chromatic pitch(es) is (are):

   none   *ra* ($\flat\hat{2}$)   *mi* ($\natural\hat{3}$)   *fi* ($\sharp\hat{4}$)   *te* ($\flat\hat{7}$)

   (c) The tonicized chord is: only i   III   iv   V or v   VI

   (d) Write the progression. If there is a tonicization, use bracket, slash, and colon notation.

        Bracket   *Slash*   *Colon*

3. (a) The next-to-last melodic pitch is which type of suspension?

   9–8   7–6   4–3

   (b) The chromatic pitch(es) is (are):

   none   *ra* ($\flat\hat{2}$)   *mi* ($\natural\hat{3}$)   *fi* ($\sharp\hat{4}$)   *te* ($\flat\hat{7}$)

   (c) The tonicized chord is: only i   III   iv   V or v   VI

   (d) Write the progression. If there is a tonicization, use bracket, slash, and colon notation.

        Bracket   *Slash*   *Colon*

4. (a) The next-to-last melodic pitch is which type of suspension?

   9–8   7–6   4–3

   (b) The chromatic pitch(es) is (are):

   none   *ra* ($\flat\hat{2}$)   *mi* ($\natural\hat{3}$)   *fi* ($\sharp\hat{4}$)   *te* ($\flat\hat{7}$)

   (c) The tonicized chord is: only i   III   iv   V or v   VI

   (d) Write the progression. If there is a tonicization, use bracket, slash, and colon notation.

        Bracket   *Slash*   *Colon*

Now, listen to twelve measures from a piano work and complete the remaining exercises.

5. Phrase 1's cadence type is: PAC   IAC   HC   PHC

6. In the middle, a pedal point occurs on which scale degree?

   tonic   subdominant   dominant

7. The final cadence type is: PAC   IAC   HC   PHC

8. Beginning with the given items, capture the music in the workspace.

   (a) In the single-line staves, notate the rhythm of the bass and soprano lines.

   (b) Below each note, write the syllables and numbers of the pitches.

   (c) In the grand staff, notate pitches and rhythm of both parts. Refer to the single-line notation.

   (d) In each chord blank, write the Roman numeral and figure (if needed) that represents the harmony. Indicate any tonicization with bracket, slash, or colon notation.

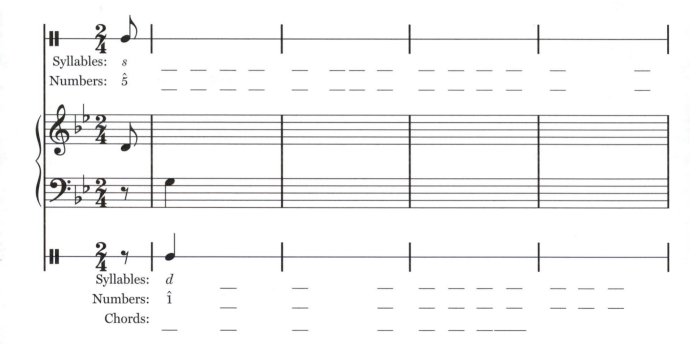

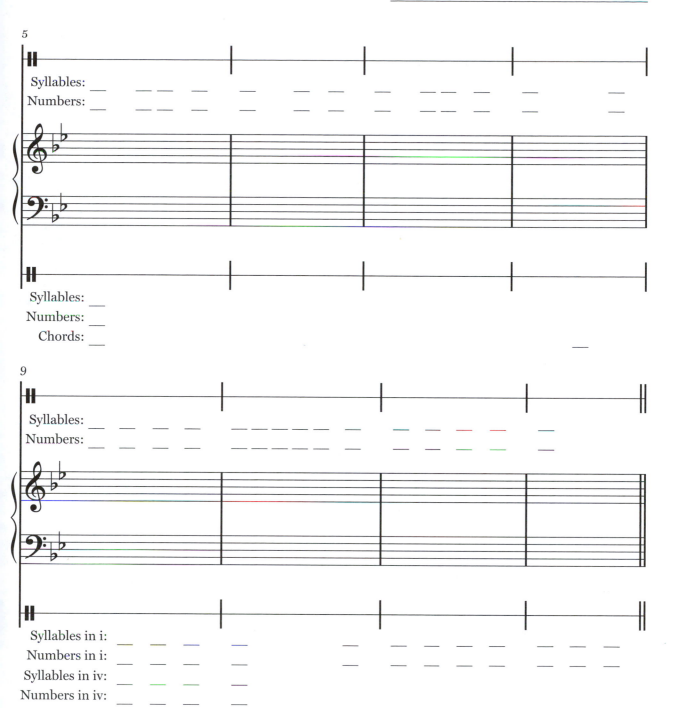

NAME _____

Contextual Listening 20.3

Listen to short progressions that begin on tonic and complete the exercises.

1. (a) Melodic pitch 3 is which embellishment?

   incomplete neighbor consonant skip passing tone suspension

   (b) The chromatic pitch is: *ra* ($\flat\hat{2}$) *mi* ($\natural\hat{3}$) *fi* ($\sharp\hat{4}$) *te* ($\flat\hat{7}$)

   (c) The tonicized chord is: III iv V or v VI

   (d) Write the progression. If there is a tonicization, use bracket, slash, and colon notation.
     Bracket   *Slash*   *Colon*

2. (a) Melodic pitch 3 is which embellishment?

   incomplete neighbor consonant skip passing tone suspension

   (b) The chromatic pitch is: *ra* ($\flat\hat{2}$) *mi* ($\natural\hat{3}$) *fi* ($\sharp\hat{4}$) *te* ($\flat\hat{7}$)

   (c) The tonicized chord is: III iv V or v VI

   (d) Write the progression. If there is a tonicization, use bracket, slash, and colon notation.
     Bracket   *Slash*   *Colon*

3. (a) Melodic pitch 3 is which embellishment?

   incomplete neighbor consonant skip passing tone suspension

   (b) The chromatic pitch is: *ra* ($\flat\hat{2}$) *mi* ($\natural\hat{3}$) *fi* ($\sharp\hat{4}$) *te* ($\flat\hat{7}$)

   (c) The tonicized chord is: III iv V or v VI

   (d) Write the progression. If there is a tonicization, use bracket, slash, and colon notation.
     Bracket   *Slash*   *Colon*

Now, listen to two phrases from a Baroque dance and complete the remaining exercises. First, focus only on phrase 1. During it, a five-pitch melodic motive repeats four times.

4. Melodic pitch 3 is which embellishment?

   incomplete neighbor consonant skip passing tone suspension

5. Phrase 1's cadence type is: PAC IAC HC PHC

6. Phrase 1's next-to-last chord includes which suspension? 9-8 7-6 4-3

7. Beginning with the given items, capture phrase 1 in the workspace.

 (a) In the single-line staves, notate the rhythm of the bass and melody.

 (b) Below each note, write the syllables and numbers of the pitches.

 (c) In the grand staff, notate pitches and rhythm of both parts. Refer to the single-line notation.

 (d) In each chord blank, write the Roman numeral and figure (if needed) that represents the chord. Indicate any tonicization with bracket, slash, or colon notation.

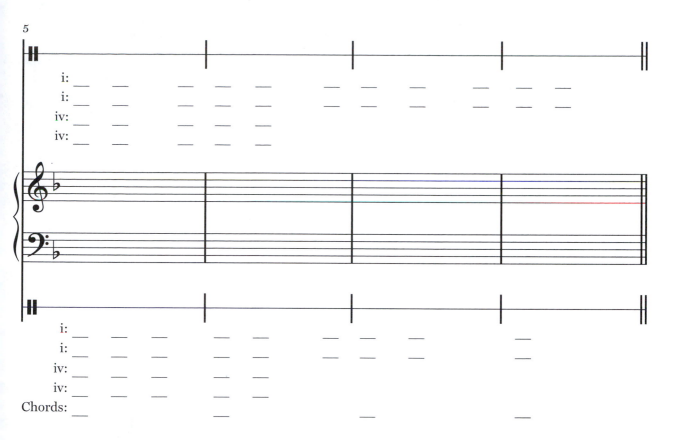

8. Now, listen again to the entire excerpt. Diagram its phrase structure. Draw curves for phrases and label each cadence. Include phrase design letters and the overall structure name.

Contextual Listening 20.4

Listen to three-chord progressions that begin on tonic and complete the exercises.

1. (a) Melodic pitch 2 is which embellishment?

   incomplete neighbor   consonant skip   passing tone   retardation

   (b) The chromatic pitch(es) is (are):

   none   *di* (♯$\hat{1}$)   *fi* (♯$\hat{4}$)   *si* (♯$\hat{5}$)   *te* (♭$\hat{7}$)

   (c) The tonicized chord is: only I   ii   IV   V   vi

   (d) Write the progression. If there is a tonicization, use bracket, slash, and colon notation.
   Bracket   *Slash*   *Colon*

2. (a) The chromatic pitch(es) is (are):

   none   *di* (♯$\hat{1}$)   *fi* (♯$\hat{4}$)   *si* (♯$\hat{5}$)   *te* (♭$\hat{7}$)

   (b) The tonicized chord is: only I   ii   IV   V   vi

   (c) Write the progression. If there is a tonicization, use bracket, slash, and colon notation.
   Bracket   *Slash*   *Colon*

3. (a) The chromatic pitch(es) is (are):

   none   *di* (♯$\hat{1}$)   *fi* (♯$\hat{4}$)   *si* (♯$\hat{5}$)   *te* (♭$\hat{7}$)

   (b) The tonicized chord is: only I   ii   IV   V   vi

   (c) Write the progression. If there is a tonicization, use bracket, slash, and colon notation.
   Bracket   *Slash*   *Colon*

4. (a) The chromatic pitch(es) is (are):

   none   *di* (♯$\hat{1}$)   *fi* (♯$\hat{4}$)   *si* (♯$\hat{5}$)   *te* (♭$\hat{7}$)

   (b) The tonicized chord is: only I   ii   IV   V   vi

   (c) Melodic pitch 5 is which embellishment?

   incomplete neighbor   consonant skip   passing tone   retardation

   (d) Write the progression. If there is a tonicization, use bracket, slash, and colon notation.
   Bracket   *Slash*   *Colon*

Now, listen to eight measures from a piano work and complete the remaining exercises.

5. On beat 2, the $^6_4$ type is:

    cadential   passing   neighboring   arpeggiating

6. Melodic pitch 5 is which embellishment?

    incomplete neighbor   consonant skip   passing tone   retardation

7. The next-to-last melodic pitch is which embellishment?

    incomplete neighbor   consonant skip   passing tone   retardation

8. (a) The next-to-last melodic pitch is: *di* ($\sharp\hat{1}$)   *fi* ($\sharp\hat{4}$)   *si* ($\sharp\hat{5}$)   *te* ($\flat\hat{7}$)

    (b) The tonicized chord is: ii   IV   V   vi

9. Near the end, the $^6_4$ type is:

    cadential   passing   neighboring   arpeggiating

10. Beginning with the given items, capture the music in the workspace.

    (a) In the single-line staves, notate the rhythm of the bass and soprano lines.

    (b) Below each note, write the syllables and numbers of the pitches.

    (c) In the grand staff, notate pitches and rhythm of both parts. Refer to the single-line notation.

    (d) In each chord blank, write the Roman numeral and figure (if needed) that represents the chord. Indicate any tonicization with bracket, slash, or colon notation.

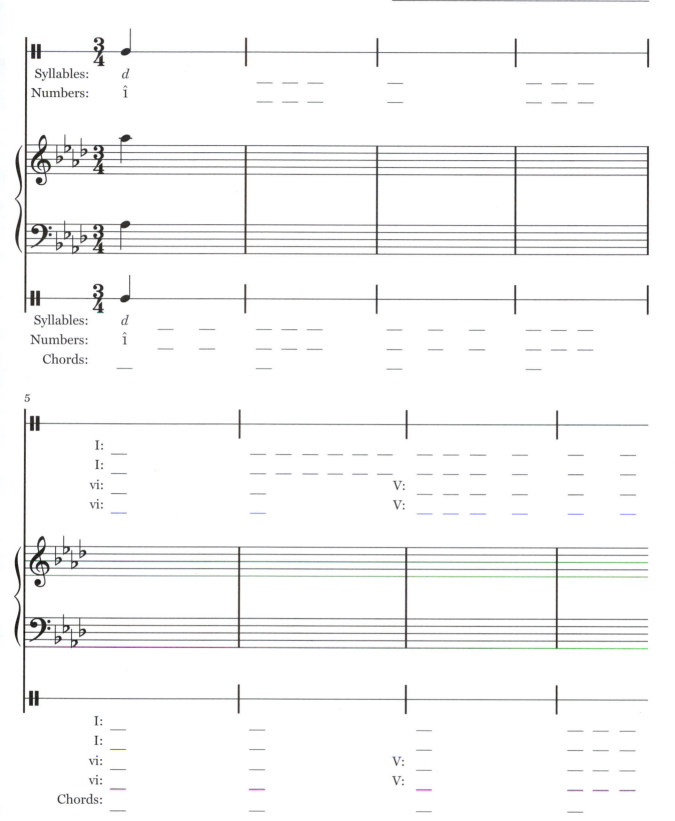

CHAPTER 21

Diatonic Sequences

NAME _____

In this chapter you'll learn to:

- Identify a sequence's attributes and name
- Recognize common melodic and harmonic patterns of diatonic sequences

Sequences

Sequences repeatedly transpose a unit of music down or up by the same interval and always include at least the beginning of a third repetition. A two-repetition unit that ascends is called *monte* and one that descends is called *fonte*.

Sequences can be identified by listening for six attributes: (1) key, (2) unit, (3) direction, (4) interval, (5) number of repetitions (reps), and (6) soprano-bass intervals (linear-intervallic pattern, or LIP).

Identifying a Sequence's Attributes

	What is the ...	Listen for ...	Think or write ...
1	key?	*mi* (3̂) or *me* (♭3̂)	in a major key ... in the key of D minor ... etc.
2	unit?	how much music is transposed	two-chord units ... one-chord units ... etc.
3	direction?	overall contour	descend or ascend
4	interval?	how much lower (higher) unit 2 is than unit 1	by second ... by third ... etc.
5	number of reps?	how many times the unit repeats	in four reps ... in three reps ... etc.
6	LIP?	unit 1's soprano and bass notes e.g., *mi-fa* (3̂-4̂) over *do-fa* (1̂-4̂); *sol-la* (5̂-6̂) over *do-fa* (1̂-4̂)	with a ... 10-8 LIP 5-6 LIP

Use a model sentence to guide your listening. For example, if you hear the following sequence, filling in the model's blanks will describe it.

In the key of C _____ , _____ -chord units _____
         (1) major or minor?   (2) how many?   (3) descend or ascend?

by _____ in _____ reps with a ____-____ LIP.
    (4) interval?   (5) number?   (6) intervals between S and B?

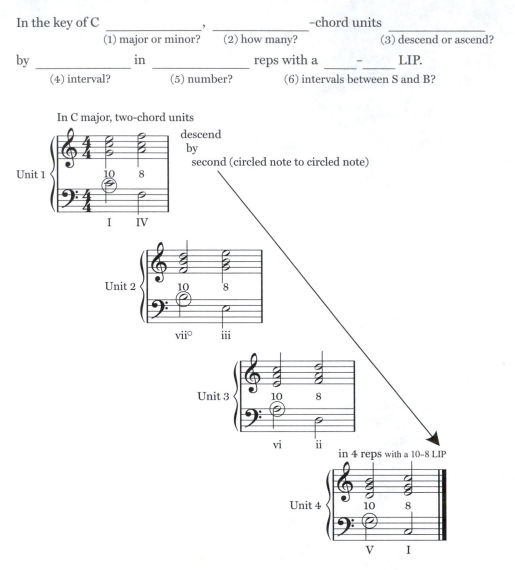

Identifying Common Sequences by Name

Sequence name	Units	Reps	Interval	Common melodies	Chord labels
Descending fifth	2-chord	four	second	*mi-fa* ($\hat{3}$–$\hat{4}$) *re-mi* ($\hat{2}$–$\hat{3}$)… *sol-la* ($\hat{5}$–$\hat{6}$) *fa-sol* ($\hat{4}$–$\hat{5}$)…	I–IV, vii°–iii, vi–ii, V–I
Descending third	2-chord	three	third	*mi-re* ($\hat{3}$–$\hat{2}$) *do-ti* ($\hat{1}$–$\hat{7}$)… *do-ti* ($\hat{1}$–$\hat{7}$) *la-sol* ($\hat{6}$–$\hat{5}$)…	I–IV, vi–iii, IV–I
Parallel $^6_3$	1-chord	varies	second	descending scale… ascending scale…	e.g., i⁵⁻⁶ v⁷⁻⁶ iv⁷⁻⁶… e.g., I⁶ ii⁶ iii⁶ IV⁶…
Ascending 5–6	2-chord	varies	second	*sol-la* ($\hat{5}$–$\hat{6}$) *la-ti* ($\hat{6}$–$\hat{7}$)…	I⁵⁻⁶ ii⁵⁻⁶ iii⁵⁻⁶ IV⁵⁻⁶ or I–vi⁶ ii–vii°⁶ iii–I⁶ IV–ii⁶

Try it

1. Each exercise begins on tonic. Use the tables to identify the sequence's attributes and name.

(a) In a _____ key, _____ –chord units _____ by _____
     major or minor?   how many?   descend or ascend?   interval?

  in _____ reps with a ____ – ____ LIP to create a(n) _____ .
    number?   intervals between S and B?   sequence name?

(b) In a _____ key, _____ –chord units _____ by _____
     major or minor?   how many?   descend or ascend?   interval?

  in _____ reps with a ____ – ____ LIP to create a(n) _____ .
    number?   intervals between S and B?   sequence name?

(c) In a _____ key, _____ –chord units _____ by _____
     major or minor?   how many?   descend or ascend?   interval?

  in _____ reps with a ____ – ____ LIP to create a(n) _____ .
    number?   intervals between S and B?   sequence name?

(d) In a _____ key, _____ –chord units _____ by _____
     major or minor?   how many?   descend or ascend?   interval?

  in _____ reps with a ____ – ____ LIP to create a(n) _____ .
    number?   intervals between S and B?   sequence name?

2. Each exercise begins on tonic and with the given items. Write the key name and quality, notate the bass and soprano, and write Roman numerals and LIP numbers.

(a) Sequence name: _____

  Syllables: __ __ __ __ __ __ __ __
  Numbers: __ __ __ __ __ __ __ __

  LIP: __ __ __ __ __ __

  Syllables: d __ __ __ __ __ __
  Numbers: $\hat{1}$ __ __ __ __ __ __

  _____ : __ __ __ __ __ __

(b) Sequence name: _____

  Syllables: __ __ __ __ __
  Numbers: __ __ __ __ __

  LIP: __ __ __ __ __

  Syllables: d __ __ __ __ __
  Numbers: $\hat{1}$ __ __ __ __ __

  _____ : __ __ __ __ __

(c) Sequence name: _____

    Syllables: __ __ __ __ __ __ __ __

    Numbers: __ __ __ __ __ __ __ __

LIP: __ __ __ __ __ __ __ __

    Syllables: *d* __ __ __ __ __ __ __

    Numbers: $\hat{1}$ __ __ __ __ __ __ __

_____ : __ __ __ __ __ __ __

(d) Sequence name: _____

    Syllables: __ __ __ __ __ __ __

    Numbers: __ __ __ __ __ __ __

LIP: __ __ __ __ __ __

    Syllables: *d* __ __ __

    Numbers: $\hat{1}$ __ __ __

_____ : __ __ __ __

(e) Sequence name: _____

    Syllables: __ __ __ __ __ __ __ __

    Numbers: __ __ __ __ __ __ __ __

LIP: __ __ __ __ __ __ __ __

    Syllables: *d* __ __ __ __

    Numbers: $\hat{1}$ __ __ __ __

_____ : __ __ __ __ __

Contextual Listening 21.1

In exercises 1–3 the initial bass pitch is C4. Identify the sequence's attributes and name.

Hint: On beat 1 of every measure, identify the bass and soprano (violin 1 and cello) using syllables or numbers; for example, if you hear *do-mi* (1̂-3̂), the interval is 10.

1. In the key of C _____ , _____ –chord units _____ by _____
                   major or minor?   how many?   descend or ascend?   interval?

   in _____ reps with a _____ – _____ LIP to create a(n) _____ .
       number?   intervals between S and B?   sequence name?

2. In the key of C _____ , _____ –chord units _____ by _____
                   major or minor?   how many?   descend or ascend?   interval?

   in _____ reps with a _____ – _____ LIP to create a(n) _____ .
       number?   intervals between S and B?   sequence name?

3. In the key of C _____ , _____ –chord units _____ by _____
                   major or minor?   how many?   descend or ascend?   interval?

   in _____ reps with a _____ – _____ LIP to create a(n) _____ .
       number?   intervals between S and B?   sequence name?

Now, listen to one phrase from a string quartet and complete the remaining exercises.

4. In the key of C _____ , _____ –chord units _____ by _____
                   major or minor?   how many?   descend or ascend?   interval?

   in _____ reps with a _____ – _____ LIP to create a(n) _____ .
       number?   intervals between S and B?   sequence name?

5. Beginning with the given items, capture the music in the workspace.

    (a) In the single-line staves, notate the rhythm of the outer voices, cello and violin 1.

    (b) Below each note, write the syllables or numbers of the pitches.

    (c) In the grand staff, notate the pitches and rhythm of the outer voices. Refer to the single-line notation.

    (d) In each chord blank provided, write the Roman numeral and figure (if needed) that represents the harmony.

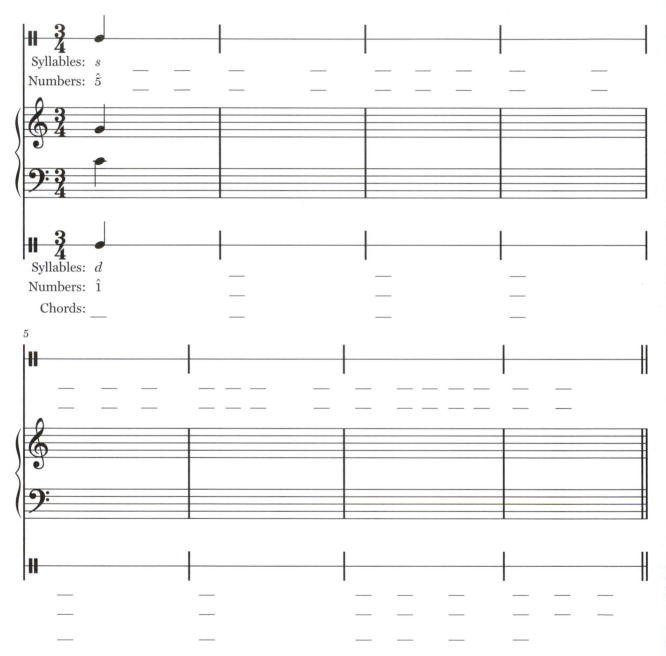

6. Near the end, the ⁶₄ chord type is: cadential   passing   neighbor

7. The next-to-last melodic pitch is which embellishment?

    neighbor tone   consonant skip   passing tone   retardation

8. The cadence type is: PAC   IAC   HC   PHC

Contextual Listening 21.2

In exercises 1–2 the initial bass pitch is G. Identify the sequence's attributes and name.

Hint: At every chord change, identify the outer parts using syllables or numbers; for example, if you hear *do-sol* ($\hat{1}$-$\hat{5}$), the interval is 5.

1. In the key of G _____, _____ –chord units _____ by _____
                      major or minor?   how many?   descend or ascend?   interval?

   in _____ reps with a ____ – ____ LIP to create a(n) _____.
        number?   intervals between S and B?   sequence name?

2. In the key of G _____, _____ –chord units _____ by _____
                      major or minor?   how many?   descend or ascend?   interval?

   in _____ reps with a ____ – ____ LIP to create a(n) _____.
        number?   intervals between S and B?   sequence name?

Now, listen to part of a carol and complete the remaining exercises.

3. Beginning with the given items, capture the music in the workspace.

   (a) In the single-line staves, notate the rhythm of the outer voices, basses and sopranos.

   (b) Below each note, write the syllables or numbers of the pitches.

   (c) In the grand staff, notate the pitches and rhythm of the outer voices parts. Refer to the single-line notation.

   (d) In each chord blank provided, write the Roman numeral and figure (if needed) that represents the harmony.

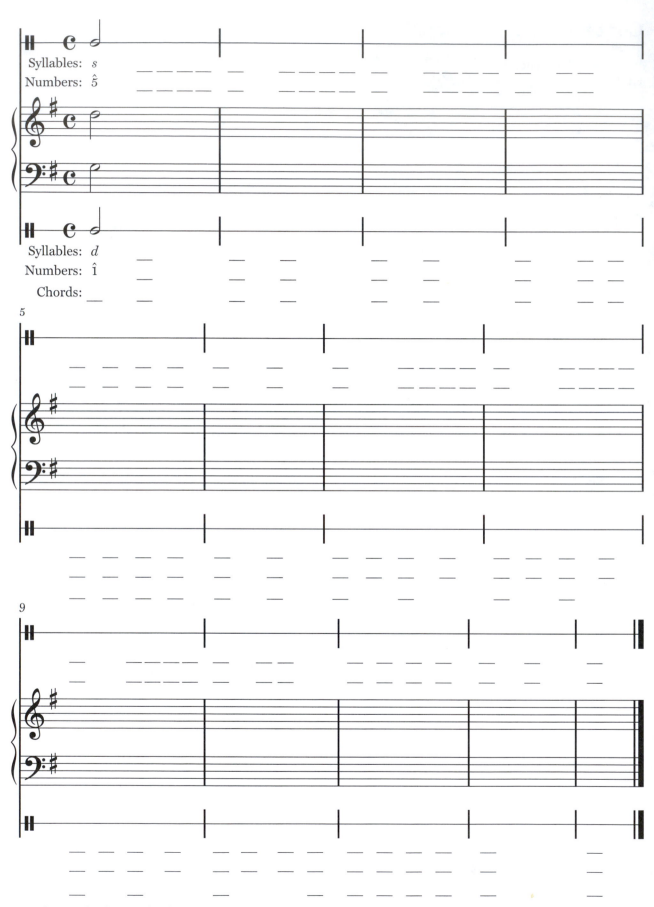

Syllables: *s*
Numbers: $\hat{5}$

Syllables: *d*
Numbers: $\hat{1}$
Chords:

5

9

Translation: Glory be to God in the highest!

Part II Diatonic Harmony and Tonicization

4. Phrase 1's cadence type is: PAC   IAC   HC   PHC

5. Phrase 2's cadence type is: PAC   IAC   HC   PHC

6. Diagram the phrase structure. Draw curves for phrases. Write cadence types, the design letter for each phrase, and the name for the overall structure.

7. During the words "*in excelsis,*" the $^6_4$ chord type is:
   Hint: Listen carefully to the outer voices.

   cadential   passing   neighbor

8. The final cadence features which embellishment?

   consonant skips   double neighbor tones   anticipation   suspension

9. Each time the word "*Deo*" occurs, the $^6_4$ type is:

   cadential   passing   neighbor

10. From phrase 1's end ("*Deo*") to phrase 2's beginning ("*Gloria*"), which error occurs?

   parallel octaves   parallel fifths

   similar motion to an octave   similar motion to a fifth

Contextual Listening 21.3

In exercises 1–3 the initial bass pitch is B♭. Identify the sequence's attributes and name.

Hint: At every chord change, identify the outer parts using syllables or numbers;
for example, if you hear *do-mi* (1̂-3̂), the interval is 10.

1. In the key of B♭ _____ , _____ -chord units _____ by _____

major or minor?   how many?   descend or ascend?   interval?

   in _____ reps with a ____ – ____ LIP to create a(n) _____ .

number?   intervals between S and B?   sequence name?

2. In the key of B♭ _____ , _____ -chord units _____ by _____

major or minor?   how many?   descend or ascend?   interval?

   in _____ reps with a ____ – ____ LIP to create a(n) _____ .

number?   intervals between S and B?   sequence name?

3. In the key of B♭ _____ , _____ -chord units _____ by _____

major or minor?   how many?   descend or ascend?   interval?

   in _____ reps with a ____ – ____ LIP to create a(n) _____ .

number?   intervals between S and B?   sequence name?

Now, listen to part of a carol and complete the remaining exercises.

4. In the key of B♭ _____ , _____ -chord units _____ by _____

major or minor?   how many?   descend or ascend?   interval?

   in _____ reps with a ____ – ____ LIP to create a(n) _____ .

number?   intervals between S and B?   sequence name?

5. Beginning with the given items, capture the music in the workspace.

   (a) In the single-line staves, notate the rhythm of the outer voices, basses and sopranos.

   (b) Below each note, write the syllables or numbers of the pitches.

   (c) In the grand staff, notate the pitches and rhythm of the outer voices parts. Refer
   to the single-line notation.

   (d) In each chord blank provided, write the Roman numeral and figure (if needed)
   that represents the harmony.

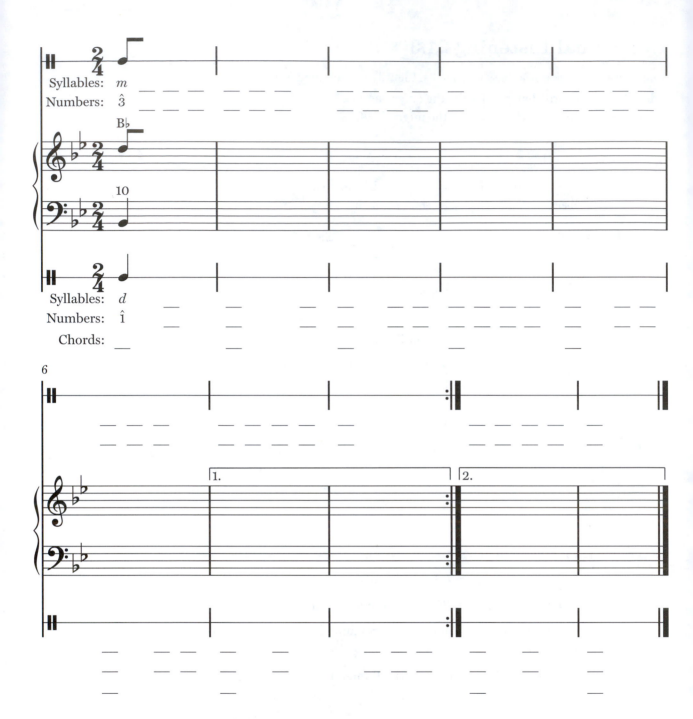

Syllables: *m*
Numbers: $\hat{3}$

B♭

10

Syllables: *d*
Numbers: $\hat{1}$
Chords:

6

1.   2.

6. Bass pitch 4 is which type of chromatic embellishing tone?

   passing   neighbor   appoggiatura   anticipation

7. At each phrase end, the highest parts move in parallel:

   thirds   fourths   fifths   sixths

Contextual Listening 21.4

In exercises 1–3 the initial bass pitch is C. Identify the sequence's attributes and name.

Hint: At every chord change, identify the bass and soprano (violin 1 and cello) using syllables or numbers; for example, if you hear *do-me* (1̂–♭3̂), the interval is 10.

1. In the key of C _____ , _____ -chord units _____ by _____
                 major or minor?   how many?   descend or ascend?   interval?

   in _____ reps with a ____ - ____ LIP to create a(n) _____ .
         number?   intervals between S and B?   sequence name?

2. (a) In the key of C _____ , _____ -chord units _____
                 major or minor?   how many?   descend or ascend?

   by _____ in _____ reps.
        interval?   number?

   (b) At each chord change, record the outer interval. Think syllables or scale degrees.

   ____   ____   ____   ____   ____   ____   ____   ____

   (c) On which chord does the recurring interval pattern begin?

3. In the key of C _____ , _____ -chord units _____ by _____
                 major or minor?   how many?   descend or ascend?   interval?

   in _____ reps with a ____ - ____ LIP to create a(n) _____ .
         number?   intervals between S and B?   sequence name?

Now, listen to one phrase from a chamber-orchestra work and complete the remaining exercises.

4. Beginning with the given items, capture the outer voices in the workspace.

    (a) In the single-line staves, notate the rhythm of the outer voices, cello and violin 1.

    (b) Below each note, write the syllables or numbers of the pitches.

    (c) In the grand staff, notate the pitches and rhythm of the outer voices parts. Refer to the single-line notation.

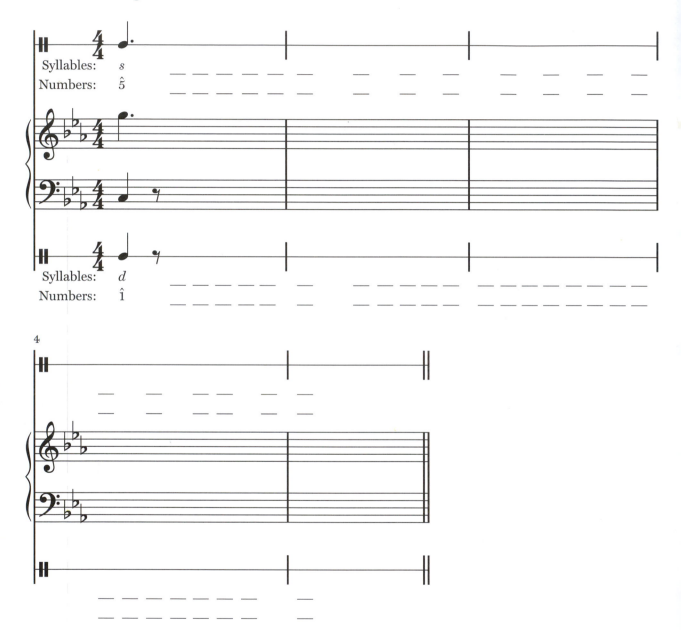

5. During pitches 1–7, which harmonies alternate? Hint: Focus on the bass line.

   i–III   i–iv^6 i–V^6 i–VI

6. Melodic pitch 8 and following feature which rhythmic device?

   syncopation   triplets   hemiola   anacruses

7. From bass pitch 8 to the end, all bass pitches belong to which scale?

   chromatic   major   ascending melodic   descending melodic

Bass pitch 9 begins a sequence.

8. In the key of C _____ , _____ –chord units _____ by _____
                   major or minor?   how many?   descend or ascend?   interval?

   in _____ reps with a _____ – _____ LIP to create a(n) _____ .
         number?   intervals between S and B?   sequence name?

9. The sequence includes which type of embellishment?

   passing tones   suspensions   neighbor tones

10. The concluding bass pitches are:

    do-sol ($\hat{1}$–$\hat{5}$)   re-sol ($\hat{2}$–$\hat{5}$)   le-sol ($\hat{6}$–$\hat{5}$)   sol-do ($\hat{5}$–$\hat{1}$)

11. The cadence type is: PAC   IAC   HC   PHC

PART III

Chromatic Harmony and Form

CHAPTER 22

Modulation

NAME _____

In this chapter you'll learn to:

- Identify and notate phrases and periods that begin in one key and modulate to another
- Identify and notate pivot chords

Modulation

Modulation occurs when music begins in one key and ends in another. Like tonicization, modulation employs secondary-dominant-function harmony. Thus, a chromatic pitch or, in minor keys, the cancelation of *ti* ($\hat{7}$), can signal a modulation.

Major keys *If you hear . . .*	*the modulation is to . . .*	Minor keys *If you hear . . .*	*the modulation is to . . .*
fi–sol ($\sharp\hat{4}$–$\hat{5}$)	V (most common)	*fi–sol* ($\sharp\hat{4}$–$\hat{5}$)	v (very common)
si–la ($\sharp\hat{5}$–$\hat{6}$)	vi (common)	*mi–fa* ($\hat{3}$–$\hat{4}$)	iv (very common)
di–re ($\sharp\hat{1}$–$\hat{2}$)	ii (somewhat common)	*te*, not *ti* ($\flat\hat{7}$, not $\hat{7}$)	III (most common)
ri–mi ($\sharp\hat{2}$–$\hat{3}$)	iii (rare)	*te* and *ra* ($\flat\hat{7}$ and $\flat\hat{2}$)	VI (common)
te–la ($\flat\hat{7}$–$\hat{6}$)	IV (very common)		

Often, composers pivot between the origin and destination keys using a common chord or common tone. Colon notation identifies the keys. A bent bracket shows the pivot chord.

Pivot-chord notation	*Interpretation*
I: I IV V I ⌐	The I chord pivots to become
⌐ V: IV V I	IV in the key of the dominant.

Try it 1

Each exercise begins on tonic and then modulates. The initial questions guide your listening and prepare you to notate the music as follows. Notate the key signature. For bass and soprano parts, write the syllables or numbers as well as pitches and rhythm. Indicate the keys with colon notation and the pivot chord at the bent bracket. Write Roman numerals and figures (if needed) beneath the bass staff. Use exercise 1 as a model for where to place your answers.

1. (a) The initial progression is:

	I–V$^{8-7}$–I	I–ii$^6_5$–V–I	i–V$^{8-7}$–i	i–ii$^{ø6}_5$–V–i
Bass:	*d–s–s–d*	*d–f–s–d*	*d–s–s–d*	*d–f–s–d*
	$\hat{1}$–$\hat{5}$–$\hat{5}$–$\hat{1}$	$\hat{1}$–$\hat{4}$–$\hat{5}$–$\hat{1}$	$\hat{1}$–$\hat{5}$–$\hat{5}$–$\hat{1}$	$\hat{1}$–$\hat{4}$–$\hat{5}$–$\hat{1}$

(b) The chromatic pitch is: *fi* (#$\hat{4}$)   *te* (♭$\hat{7}$)

(c) The exercise modulates to the key of: V   III

(d) The example ends with which progression?

I–V$^{8-7}$–I   I–ii$^6_5$–V–I   i–V$^{8-7}$–i   i–ii$^{ø6}_5$–V–i

2. (a) The initial progression is:

	I–vi–ii$^6_5$–V$^{8-7}$–I	I–ii^6–V$^{8-7}_{6-5}_{4-3}$–I
Bass:	*d – l – f – s – d*	*d – f – s – s – d*
	$\hat{1}$ – $\hat{6}$ – $\hat{4}$ – $\hat{5}$ – $\hat{1}$	$\hat{1}$ – $\hat{4}$ – $\hat{5}$ – $\hat{5}$ – $\hat{1}$

	i–VI–ii$^{ø6}_5$–V$^{8-7}$–i	i–ii^{o6}–V$^{8-7}_{6-5}_{4-3}$–i
Bass:	*d – le – f – s – d*	*d – f – s – s – d*
	$\hat{1}$ – ♭$\hat{6}$ – $\hat{4}$ – $\hat{5}$ – $\hat{1}$	$\hat{1}$ – $\hat{4}$ – $\hat{5}$ – $\hat{5}$ – $\hat{1}$

(b) The chromatic pitch is: *fi* (#$\hat{4}$)   *te* (♭$\hat{7}$)

(c) The exercise modulates to the key of: V   III

(d) The example ends with which progression?

I–vi–ii$^6_5$–V$^{8-7}$–I   I–ii^6–V$^{8-7}_{6-5}_{4-3}$–I   i–VI–ii$^{ø6}_5$–V$^{8-7}$–i   i–ii^{o6}–V$^{8-7}_{6-5}_{4-3}$–i

3. (a) The initial progression is:

$$\text{I–V}^6_5\text{–I–ii}^6\text{–V}^{6-5}_{4-3}\text{–I} \qquad \text{I–V}^4_2\text{–I}^6\text{–ii}^6\text{–V}^{8-7}_{6-3 \atop 4-3}\text{–I}$$

Bass:
$$d-t-d-f-s-s-d \qquad d-f-m-f-s-s-d$$
$$\hat{1}-\hat{7}-\hat{1}-\hat{4}-\hat{5}-\hat{5}-\hat{1} \qquad \hat{1}-\hat{4}-\hat{3}-\hat{4}-\hat{5}-\hat{5}-\hat{1}$$

$$\text{i–V}^6_5\text{–i–ii}^{\circ 6}\text{–V}^{6-5}_{4-3}\text{–i} \qquad \text{i–V}^4_2\text{–i}^6\text{–ii}^{\circ 6}\text{–V}^{8-7}_{4-3}\text{–I}$$

Bass:
$$d-t-d-f-s-s-d \qquad d-f-me-f-s-s-d$$
$$\hat{1}-\hat{7}-\hat{1}-\hat{4}-\hat{5}-\hat{5}-\hat{1} \qquad \hat{1}-\hat{4}-\flat\hat{3}-\hat{4}-\hat{5}-\hat{5}-\hat{1}$$

(b) The chromatic pitch is: $di\,(\sharp\hat{1})$ $fi\,(\sharp\hat{4})$ $si\,(\sharp\hat{5})$ $te\,(\flat\hat{7})$

(c) The exercise modulates to the key of: ii   IV   V   vi

(d) The example ends with which progression?

$$\text{I–V}^6_5\text{–I–ii}^6\text{–V}^{6-5}_{4-3}\text{–I} \qquad \text{I–V}^4_2\text{–I}^6\text{–ii}^6\text{–V}^{8-7}_{6-3 \atop 4-3}\text{–I}$$

$$\text{i–V}^6_5\text{–i–ii}^{\circ 6}\text{–V}^{6-5}_{4-3}\text{–i} \qquad \text{I–V}^4_2\text{–i}^6\text{–ii}^{\circ 6}\text{–V}^{8-7}_{4-3}\text{–I}$$

I: $m\,(\hat{3})$ ___ ___ ___   ___ ___ ___| ___ ___

: ___ ___ ___   ___ ___ ___ ___   ___ ___ ___

$d\,(\hat{1})$ ___ ___ ___   ___ ___ ___

I: I ___ ___ ___   ___ ___ ___|

: ___ ___ ___   ___ ___ ___ ___   ___ ___ ___

4. The initial and concluding bass lines are identical in their respective keys. Focus on the soprano to identify the progression.

(a) The initial progression is:

$$\text{Sop.:} \quad \overset{m-f-s\ldots}{\underset{\hat{3}-\hat{4}-\hat{5}}{\text{I}-\text{V}^4_3-\text{I}6-\text{ii}6-\text{V}^{8-7}_{6-\overset{}{4}-3}-\text{I}}} \qquad \overset{m-r-d\ldots}{\underset{\hat{3}-\hat{2}-\hat{1}}{\text{I}-\text{V}^6_4-\text{I}6-\text{ii}6-\text{V}^{6-5}_{4-3}-\text{I}}}$$

$$\text{Sop.:} \quad \overset{me-f-s\ldots}{\underset{\flat\hat{3}-\hat{4}-\hat{5}}{\text{i}-\text{V}^4_3-\text{i}6-\text{ii}^{o}6-\text{V}^{8-7}_{6-\overset{}{4}-3}-\text{i}}} \qquad \overset{m-r-d\ldots}{\underset{\hat{3}-\hat{2}-\hat{1}}{\text{i}-\text{V}^6_4-\text{i}6-\text{ii}6-\text{V}^{6-5}_{4-3}-\text{i}}}$$

(b) The chromatic pitch is: $di\,(\sharp\hat{1})$ $fi\,(\sharp\hat{4})$ $si\,(\sharp\hat{5})$ $te\,(\flat\hat{7})$

(c) The exercise modulates to the key of: ii   IV   V   vi

(d) The example ends with which progression?

$\text{I}-\text{V}^4_3-\text{I}6-\text{ii}6-\text{V}^{8-7}_{4-3}-\text{I}$ $\text{I}-\text{V}^6_4-\text{I}6-\text{ii}6-\text{V}^{6-5}_{4-3}-\text{I}$

$\text{i}-\text{V}^4_3-\text{i}6-\text{ii}^{o}6-\text{V}^{8-7}_{4-3}-\text{i}$ $\text{i}-\text{V}^6_4-\text{i}6-\text{ii}6-\text{V}^{6-5}_{4-3}-\text{i}$

Contextual Listening 22.1

Exercises 1–2 begin on tonic and then modulate. To identify progressions, focus on the bass.

1. (a) The initial progression is:

          I–V⁸–⁷–I   I–ii$^6_5$–V–I   i–V⁸–⁷–i   i–ii$^{⌀6}_5$–V–i

Bass: d–s–s–d d–f–s–d d–s–s–d d–f–s–d

          $\hat{1}$–$\hat{5}$–$\hat{5}$–$\hat{1}$ $\hat{1}$–$\hat{4}$–$\hat{5}$–$\hat{1}$ $\hat{1}$–$\hat{5}$–$\hat{5}$–$\hat{1}$ $\hat{1}$–$\hat{4}$–$\hat{5}$–$\hat{1}$

(b) The chromatic pitch is: *fi* ($\sharp\hat{4}$)   *te* ($\flat\hat{7}$)

(c) The exercise modulates to the key of: V   III

(d) The example ends with which progression?

   I–V⁸–⁷–I   I–ii$^6_5$–V–I   i–V⁸–⁷–i   i–ii$^{⌀6}_5$–V–i

(e) Notate the key signature, bass, soprano, and Roman numerals. Indicate the keys with colon notation and the pivot chord at the bent bracket.

   I: *m* ($\hat{3}$)

   d ($\hat{1}$)

   I: I

2. (a) The initial progression is:

	I–ii6–V–I	I–V8–7–I	i–ii°6–V–i	i–V8–7–i
Bass:	*d-f-s-d*	*d-s-s-d*	*d-f-s-d*	*d-s-s-d*
	$\hat{1}$-$\hat{4}$-$\hat{5}$-$\hat{1}$	$\hat{1}$-$\hat{5}$-$\hat{5}$-$\hat{1}$	$\hat{1}$-$\hat{4}$-$\hat{5}$-$\hat{1}$	$\hat{1}$-$\hat{5}$-$\hat{5}$-$\hat{1}$

(b) The chromatic pitch is: *di* ($\sharp\hat{1}$)   *fi* ($\sharp\hat{4}$)   *si* ($\sharp\hat{5}$)   *te* ($\flat\hat{7}$)

(c) The exercise modulates to the key of: ii   IV   V   vi

(d) The example ends with which progression?

I–ii6–V–I   I–V8–7–I   i–ii°6–V–i   i–V8–7–i

(e) Notate the key signature, bass, soprano, and Roman numerals. Indicate the keys with colon notation and the pivot chord at the bent bracket.

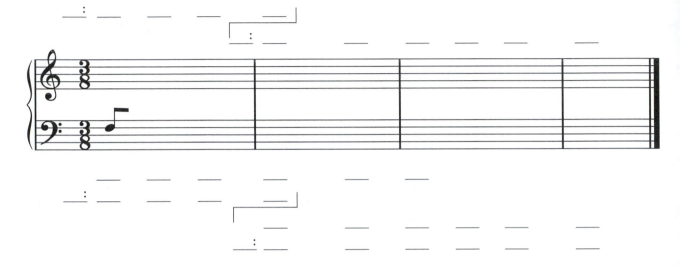

Now, listen to two phrases from a minuet and complete the remaining exercises.

3. Begin with the given items and capture the music in the workspace.

   (a) In the single-line staves, notate the rhythm of the outer parts.

   (b) Below each note, write the syllables or numbers of the pitches.

   (c) In the grand staff, notate the key signature and the pitches and rhythm of the outer parts. Refer to the single-line notation.

   (d) Write the Roman numerals and figures (if needed) that represent the harmony. Indicate the keys with colon notation and the pivot chord with a bent bracket.

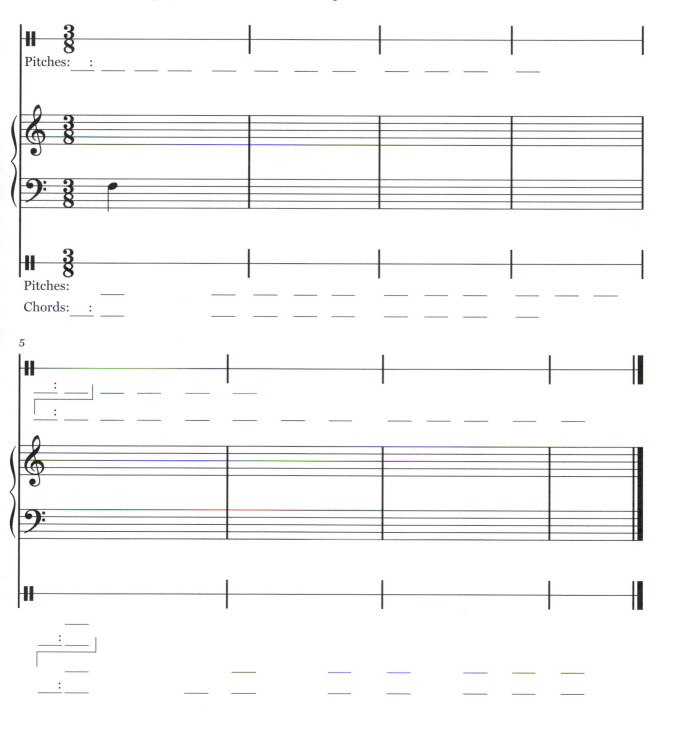

Contextual Listening 22.2

Exercises 1–2 begin on tonic and then modulate.

1. (a) The initial progression is: $I-V^6_4-I^6$ $I-vii^{o6}-I^6$ $i-V^6_4-i^6$ $i-vii^{o6}-i^6$

   Hint: Listen for chord 2's quality.

   (b) The chromatic pitch is: $di\,(\sharp\hat{1})$ $fi\,(\sharp\hat{4})$ $si\,(\sharp\hat{5})$ $te\,(\flat\hat{7})$

   (c) The exercise modulates to the key of: ii   IV   V   vi

   (d) The example ends with which progression? $ii-V^{8-7}-I$ $IV-V^{6-5}_{4-3}-I$ $ii^o-V^{8-7}-i$ $iv-V^{6-5}_{4-3}-i$

   (e) Notate the key signature, bass, soprano, and Roman numerals. Indicate the keys
       with colon notation and the pivot chord at the bent bracket.

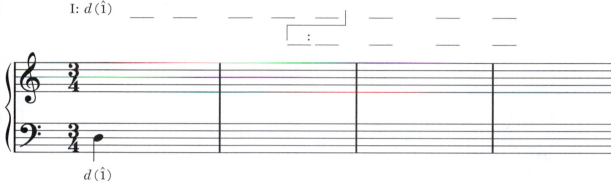

I: $d\,(\hat{1})$ ___ ___   ___ ___ ___| ___   ___   ___

: ___   ___   ___   ___

$d\,(\hat{1})$ ___ ___   ___ ___   ___   ___   ___

I: I   ___   ___   ___   ___|

: ___   ___   ___   ___

2. (a) The initial progression is: I–V$^4_3$–I^6 I–V$^4_2$–I^6 i–V$^4_3$–i^6 i–V$^4_2$–i^6

Hint: Listen for chord 2's bass pitch.

(b) The chromatic pitch is: *di* (#$\hat{1}$)   *fi* (#$\hat{4}$)   *si* (#$\hat{5}$)   *te* ($\flat\hat{7}$)

(c) The exercise modulates to the key of: ii   IV   V   vi

(d) The example ends with which progression? Hint: Listen to the bass.

	I–ii^6–V7–I	I–V$^{6-5}_{4-3}$–I	i–ii$^{\circ 6}$–V7–i	i–V$^{6-5}_{4-3}$–i
Bass:	*d -f- s - d*	*d - s - s - d*	*d - f - s - d*	*d - s - s - d*
	$\hat{1}$-$\hat{4}$-$\hat{5}$-$\hat{1}$	$\hat{1}$-$\hat{5}$-$\hat{5}$-$\hat{1}$	$\hat{1}$-$\hat{4}$-$\hat{5}$-$\hat{1}$	$\hat{1}$-$\hat{5}$-$\hat{5}$-$\hat{1}$

(e) Notate the key signature, bass, soprano, and Roman numerals. Indicate the keys with colon notation and the pivot chord at the bent bracket.

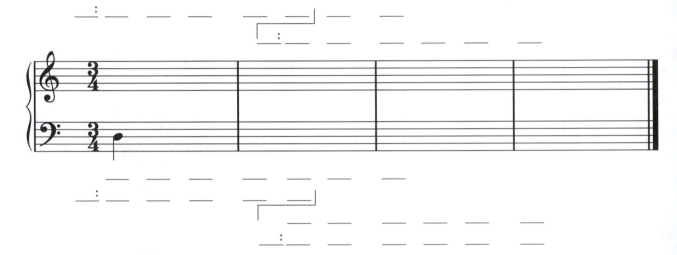

Now, listen to two phrases from a trio and complete the remaining exercises.

3. Begin with the given items and capture the music in the workspace.

(a) In the single-line staves, notate the rhythm of the outer parts.

(b) Below each note, write the syllables or numbers of the pitches.

(c) In the grand staff, notate the key signature and the pitches and rhythm of the outer parts. Refer to the single-line notation.

(d) Write the Roman numerals and figures (if needed) that represent the harmony.

(e) Near the beginning, indicate the tonicization with bracket, slash, or colon notation.

(f) At the modulation, indicate the keys with colon notation and the pivot chord with a bent bracket.

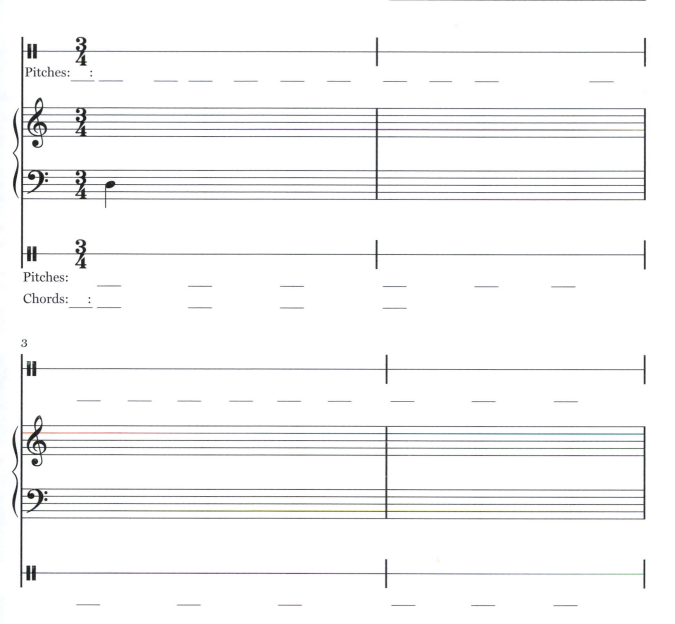

Pitches: ___ : ___ ___ ___ ___ ___ ___ ___ ___ ___

Pitches: ___ ___ ___ ___ ___ ___ ___

Chords: ___ : ___ ___ ___ ___ ___ ___

3

Contextual Listening 22.3

Exercises 1–2 begin on tonic and then modulate.

1. (a) The chromatic pitches is/are: *ra* ($\flat\hat{2}$)   *mi* ($\hat{3}$)   *fi* ($\sharp\hat{4}$)   *te* ($\flat\hat{7}$)

   (b) The exercise modulates to the key of: III   iv   v   VI

   (c) The example ends with which progression?

   I–V⁸⁻⁷–I   I–V$^{6-5}_{4-3}$–I   i–V⁸⁻⁷–i   i–V$^{6-5}_{4-3}$–i

   (d) Notate the key signature, bass, soprano, and Roman numerals. Indicate the keys with colon notation and the pivot chord at the bent bracket.

2. (a) The initial progression is:
   Hint: Listen for chord quality.

   I–V$^{6-5}_{4-3}$–I   i–vii°7–vii°$^6_5$–i

   (b) The chromatic pitch(es) is/are: *ra* ($\flat\hat{2}$)   *mi* ($\hat{3}$)   *fi* ($\sharp\hat{4}$)   *te* ($\flat\hat{7}$)

   (c) The exercise modulates to the key of: III   iv   v   VI

   (d) The example ends with which progression?

   I–V7–I   V$^{6-5}_{4-3}$–I   i–V7–i   V$^{6-5}_{4-3}$–i

   (e) Notate the key signature, bass, soprano, and Roman numerals. Indicate the keys with colon notation and the pivot chord at the bent bracket.

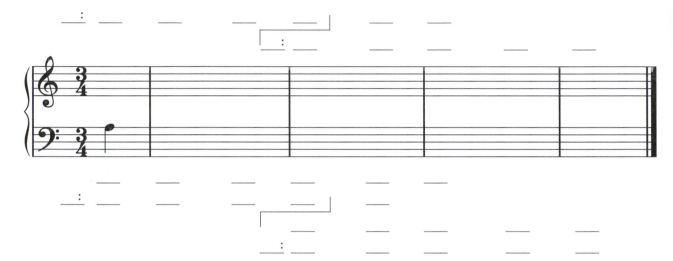

Now, listen to two phrases from a scherzo and complete the remaining exercises.

3. Begin with the given items and capture the music in the workspace.

   (a) In the single-line staves, notate the rhythm of the outer parts.

   (b) Below each note, write the syllables or numbers of the pitches.

   (c) In the grand staff, notate the key signature and the pitches and rhythm of the outer parts. Refer to the single-line notation.

   (d) Write the Roman numerals and figures (if needed) that represent the harmony.

   • At the modulation, indicate the keys with colon notation and the pivot chord with a bent bracket.

   • After the modulation, indicate the tonicization with bracket, slash, or colon notation.

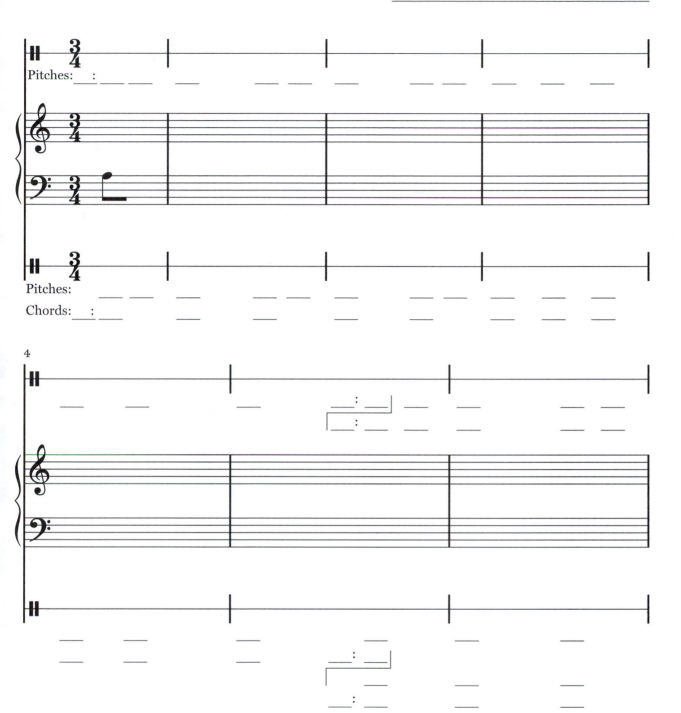

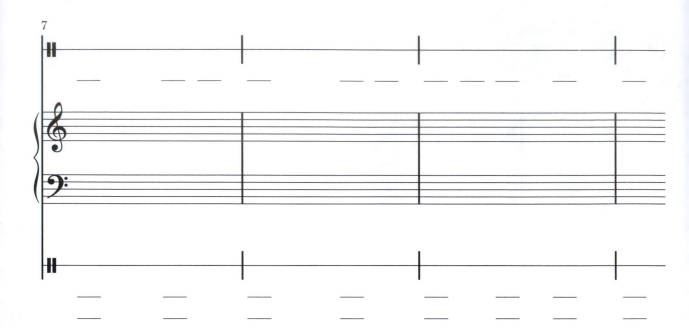

Modulatory Periods

Modulatory periods begin in one key and end in another. Phrase diagrams indicate each cadence's key in parentheses and include the term "modulatory" in the descriptor.

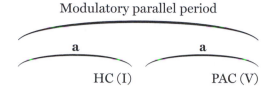

Modulatory parallel period		Modulatory contrasting period	
a	**a**	**a**	**b**
HC (I)	PAC (V)	HC (i)	PAC (III)

Try it 2

Listen and choose the diagram that matches the phrase structure.

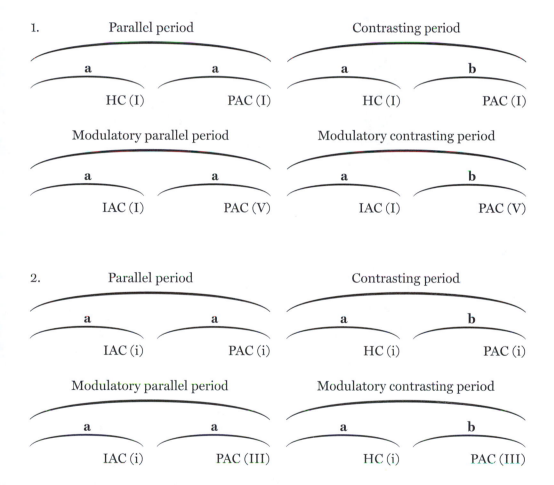

1.

Parallel period		Contrasting period	
a	**a**	**a**	**b**
HC (I)	PAC (I)	HC (I)	PAC (I)

Modulatory parallel period		Modulatory contrasting period	
a	**a**	**a**	**b**
IAC (I)	PAC (V)	IAC (I)	PAC (V)

2.

Parallel period		Contrasting period	
a	**a**	**a**	**b**
IAC (i)	PAC (i)	HC (i)	PAC (i)

Modulatory parallel period		Modulatory contrasting period	
a	**a**	**a**	**b**
IAC (i)	PAC (III)	HC (i)	PAC (III)

Contextual Listening 22.4

Listen to two phrases from a chamber work and complete the exercises.

1. In the space below, diagram the excerpt's phrase structure. Draw curves to represent phrases. Write the cadence type and the key in which it occurs (PAC (V), for example). Include design letters and label the entire structure.

2. Begin with the given items and capture the music in the workspace.

   (a) In the single-line staves, notate the rhythm of the outer parts.

   (b) Below each note, write the syllables or numbers of the pitches.

   (c) In the grand staff, notate the key signature and the pitches and rhythm of the outer parts. Refer to the single-line notation.

   (d) Write the Roman numerals and figures (if needed) that represent the harmony. At the modulation, indicate the keys with colon notation and the pivot chord with a bent bracket.

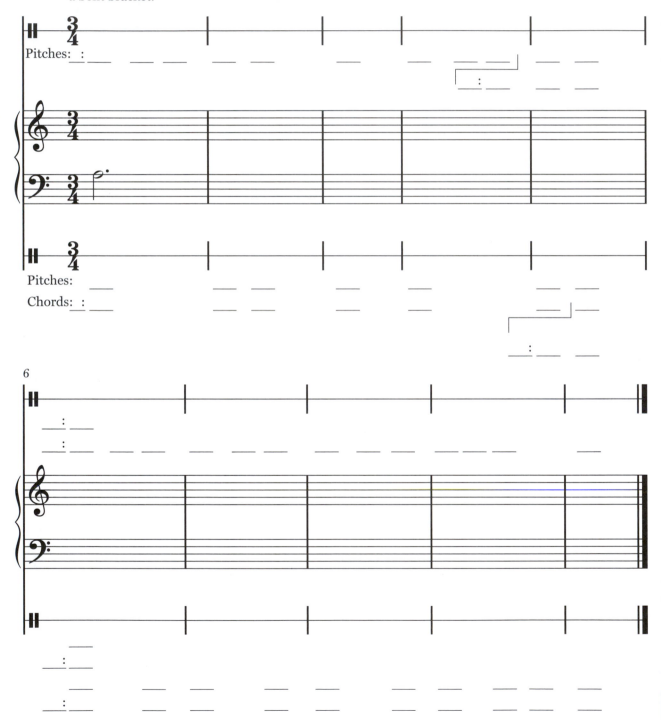

CHAPTER 23

Binary and Ternary Forms

NAME _____

In this chapter you'll learn to:

- Identify binary, ternary, and composite forms

Binary Forms

Form is the product of a piece's harmonic structure and melodic design. Two-part forms are called binary. Each part is a repeatable section. Most binary pieces repeat both sections. Several terms distinguish specific binary-form types.

Is the binary form . . .	Choose option 1 if . . .	Choose option 2 if . . .
(1) rounded or (2) simple?	Section 2 ends with a recapitulation of section 1.	There is no recapitulation of section 1.
(1) sectional or (2) continuous?	Section 1 ends with a PAC in I (or i).	Section 1 ends any other way.
balanced, (1) yes or (2) no?	Both sections conclude similarly.	The sections end differently.

In binary form diagrams, uppercase letters represent section design. Roman numerals show keys. The label may include descriptors, like "simple sectional" or "rounded continuous."

Simple sectional binary

‖: A ‖ B
I —— I :‖‖: V —— I :‖

Rounded continuous binary

‖: A ‖ B   A′
i —— III :‖‖: III — i —— :‖

Bar form binary repeats section 1, but not section 2.

‖: A :‖ B ‖

Try it 1

1. Listen to section 1 of a string quartet movement. Focus first on the phrases, then the section.

   (a) Which diagram represents the phrase structure?

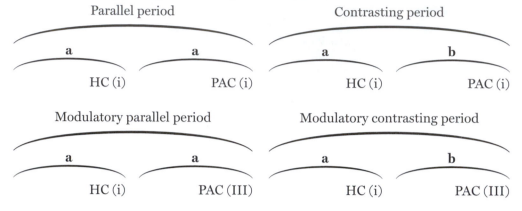

   (b) The excerpt is section 1 of a binary composition. The binary form is:

   sectional   continuous

Exercises 2-4 are complete compositions. Focus first on the phrase structure, then the sections, and finally, the overall form.

2. (a) Which is section 1's phrase diagram?

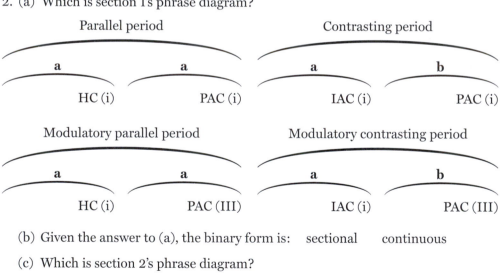

   (b) Given the answer to (a), the binary form is: sectional   continuous

   (c) Which is section 2's phrase diagram?

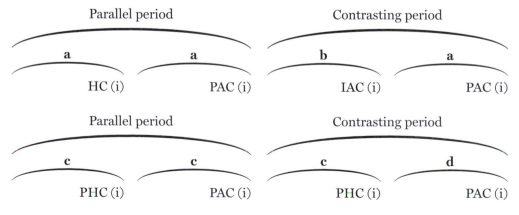

(d) At the end, is there a recapitulation? yes no

(e) Do the sections end with similar melodies? yes no

(f) Which diagram matches the binary form?

Simple sectional binary

Rounded sectional binary

Simple continuous binary   *Rounded continuous binary*

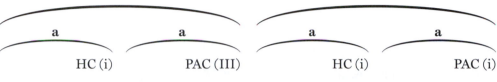

3. (a) Which is section 1's phrase diagram?

Modulatory parallel period   Parallel period

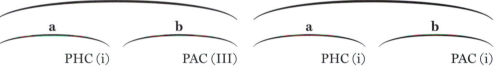

(b) Given the answer to (a), the binary form is: sectional continuous

(c) Which is section 2's phrase diagram?

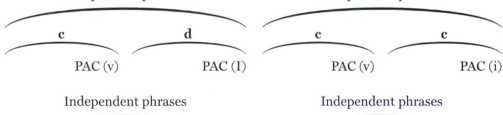

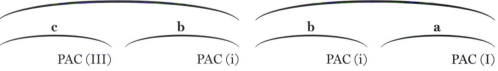

(d) At the end, is there a recapitulation? yes no

(e) Do the sections end with similar melodies? yes no

(f) Which diagram matches the binary form?

Simple sectional binary

$\|{:}\ \text{i} \underline{\hspace{2cm}} \text{i} :\|\|{:}\ \text{III} \underline{\hspace{2cm}} \text{I} :\|$

Rounded sectional binary

A $\quad$ B $\quad$ A′

$\|{:}\ \text{i} \underline{\hspace{2cm}} \text{i} :\|\|{:}\ \text{III} - \text{i} \underline{\hspace{1cm}} :\|$

Simple continuous binary

A $\quad$ B

$\|{:}\ \text{i} \underline{\hspace{2cm}} \text{III} :\|\|{:}\ \text{III} \underline{\hspace{2cm}} \text{I} :\|$

Rounded continuous binary

A $\quad$ B $\quad$ A′

$\|{:}\ \text{i} \underline{\hspace{2cm}} \text{III} :\|\|{:}\ \text{III} - \text{i} \underline{\hspace{1cm}} :\|$

4. (a) Diagram and label section 1's phrases and period:

(b) Given the answer to exercise (a), the binary form is: sectional   continuous

(c) Diagram and label section 2's phrases and period:
Hint: Periods with odd-numbered phrases are "asymmetrical."

(d) At the end, is there a recapitulation?   yes   no

(e) Do the sections end with similar melodies?   yes   no

(f) Incorporating the diagrams from exercises 1 and 3, Diagram and label the form of the entire minuet:

Contextual Listening 23.1

Listen to an entire theme, the beginning of which appeared as Contextual Listening 22.1.

1. Which is section 1's phrase diagram?

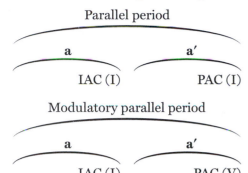

Parallel period

a   a'

IAC (I)   PAC (I)

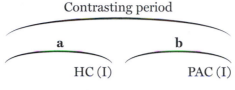

Contrasting period

a   b

HC (I)   PAC (I)

Modulatory parallel period

a   a'

IAC (I)   PAC (V)

Modulatory contrasting period

a   b

HC (I)   PAC (V)

2. Given the answer to exercise 1, the binary form is: sectional   continuous

3. Which is section 2's phrase diagram?

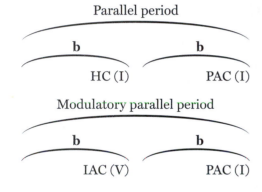

Parallel period

b   b

HC (I)   PAC (I)

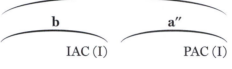

Contrasting period

b   a''

IAC (I)   PAC (I)

Modulatory parallel period

b   b

IAC (V)   PAC (I)

Modulatory contrasting period

b   a''

HC (V)   PAC (I)

4. At the end, is there a recapitulation?   yes   no

5. Do the sections end with similar melodies?   yes   no

6. The $^6_4$ type near each section's end is: passing   neighboring   cadential

7. Which diagram matches the piece's binary form?

Simple sectional balanced binary

A   **B**

‖: I ——— I :‖‖: V ——— I :‖

Rounded sectional binary

A   **B**   **A'**

‖: I ——— I :‖‖: V ——— I :‖

Simple continuous balanced binary

A   **B**

‖: I ——— V :‖‖: V ——— I :‖

Rounded continuous binary

A   **B**   **A'**

‖: I ——— V :‖‖: V ——— I :‖

Contextual Listening 23.2

Listen to a chorale and complete the following exercises. Focus first on phrase 1.

1. Use the workspace to capture phrase 1's outer parts and chords. Begin with the given items.

   (a) In the single-line staves, notate the rhythm of the outer parts.

   (b) Below each note, write the syllables or numbers of the pitches.

   (c) In the grand staff, notate the pitches and rhythm of the outer parts. Refer to the single-line notation.

   (d) Write the Roman numerals and figures (if needed) that represent the harmony.

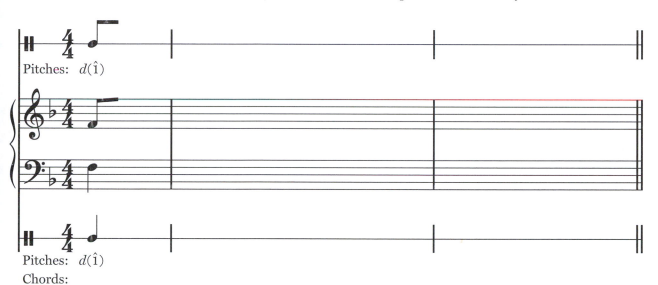

Pitches: $d(\hat{1})$

Pitches: $d(\hat{1})$

Chords:

2. Phrase 1's cadence type is: PAC (I)   IAC (I)   HC (I)   PAC (V)

Listen again and focus on all of section 1.

3. Phrase 2's cadence type is: PAC (I) IAC (I) HC (I) PAC (V)

4. Phrase 3 begins by tonicizing which chord? Hint: Listen to bass pitches 1–2.

              ii   IV   V   vi

Bass: *di-re* ($\sharp\hat{1}$–$\hat{2}$)   *te-la* ($\flat\hat{7}$–$\hat{6}$)   *fi-sol* ($\sharp\hat{4}$–$\hat{5}$)   *si-la* ($\sharp\hat{5}$–$\hat{6}$)

5. Phrase 3's cadence type is: PAC (I) IAC (I) HC (I) PAC (V)

6. Diagram section 1's phrase structure. For help, refer to the answers to questions 2–5.

Listen again, focusing on section 2.

7. Section 2, phrase 1 modulates to which key? Hint: Which chromatic pitch sounds near the cadence?

              Key: ii   IV   V   vi

Chromatic pitch: *di* ($\sharp\hat{1}$)   *te* ($\flat\hat{7}$)   *fi* ($\sharp\hat{4}$)   *si* ($\sharp\hat{5}$)

8. Does section 2 repeat? yes no

Now, listen to the entire piece, focusing on the overall form.

9. Which diagram represents the overall form?

Simple sectional bar form

   A   B

‖: I ——— I :‖ I ——— I ‖

Simple continuous bar form

   A   B

‖: I ——— V :‖ V ——— I ‖

Rounded sectional binary

   A   B   A′

‖: I ——— I :‖: V ——— I :‖

Rounded continuous binary

   A   B   A′

‖: I ——— V :‖: V ——— I :‖

Contextual Listening 23.3

Alberti figures prolong a bass line by embellishing it with consonant skips in smaller note values.

Notate the rhythm of the prolonged bass pitches (as opposed to every pitch). Beneath each note, write its syllable or number. Only once per measure, write the Roman numeral and figure(s) of the implied chord. For trills, write the main note and the symbol *tr*.

1.

2.

Now, listen to a minuet and complete the remaining exercises.

3. Begin with the given items and capture the music in the workspace.

   (a) In the upper single-line staff, notate the rhythm of the melody. Write *tr* for trill. In the lower single-line staff, the rhythm is given.

   (b) Below each note, write the syllables or numbers of the pitches.

   (c) In the grand staff, notate the pitches and rhythm of the outer parts. Refer to the single-line notation.

   (d) Write the Roman numerals and figures (if needed) that represent the harmony. Indicate the keys with colon notation and the pivot chord with a bent bracket.

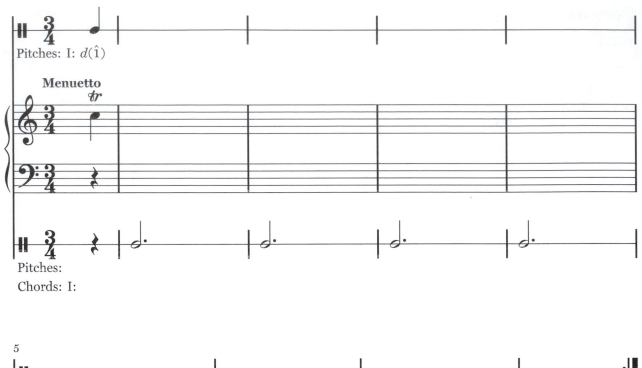

Pitches: I: *d*(î)

Menuetto

Pitches:

Chords: I:

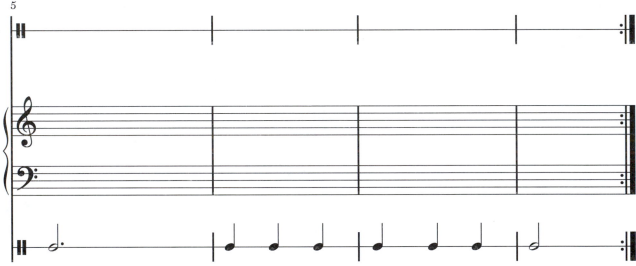

5

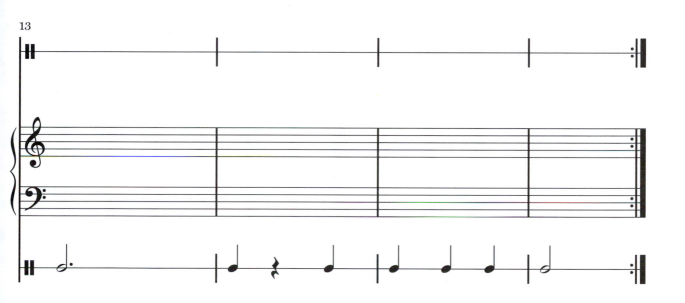

4. Diagram and label section 1's phrases and period:

5. Given the answer to exercise 4, the binary is: sectional   continuous

6. Diagram and label section 2's phrases and period:

7. At the end, is there a recapitulation?   yes   no

8. Do the sections end with similar melodies?   yes   no

9. The $^6_4$ type near each section's end is: passing   neighboring   cadential

10. Incorporating the diagrams from exercises 4 and 6, diagram and label the form of the entire minuet:

Contextual Listening 23.4

Listen to a theme from a piano sonata. Focus first only on phrase 1.

1. Begin with the given items and capture the music in the workspace.

   (a) In the single-line staves, notate the rhythm of the outer parts.

   (b) Below each note, write the syllables or numbers of the pitches.

   (c) In the grand staff, notate the pitches and rhythm of the outer parts. Refer to the single-line notation.

   (d) Write the Roman numerals and figures (if needed) that represent the harmony.

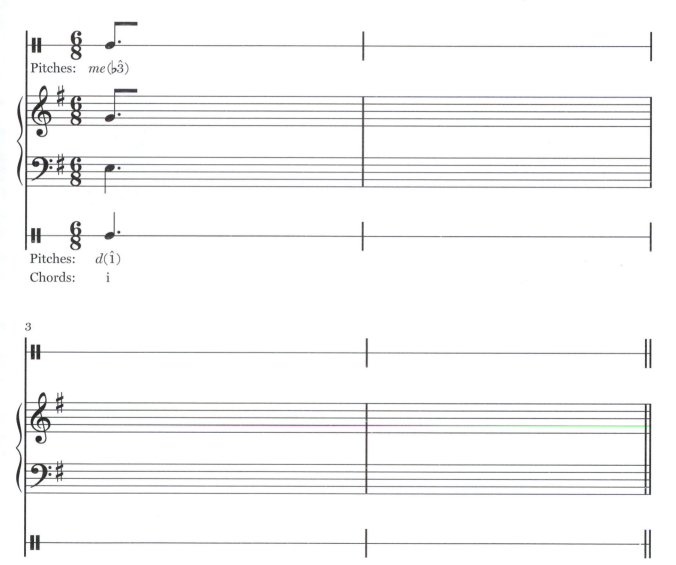

2. Phrase 1's internal organization is a:　motive　segment　sentence　section

3. Phrase 1's cadence type is:　PAC (i)　IAC (i)　HC (i)　PAC (III)

4. Phrase 2, segment 2 tonicizes which chord? What chromatic pitch(es) are used?

	III	iv	v	VI
pitch(es):	*te* ($\flat\hat{7}$)	*mi* ($\hat{3}$)	*fi* ($\sharp\hat{4}$)	*te* ($\flat\hat{7}$) and *ra* ($\flat\hat{2}$)

5. Phrase 2's cadence type is:　PAC (i)　IAC (i)　HC (i)　PAC (III)

6. Phrases 1–2 create which structure?

parallel period　　　　　　　　contrasting period

modulatory parallel period　　modulatory contrasting period

Now, focus on the entire example.

7. Diagram the form of the entire example:

Ternary Form and Composite Form

Ternary is three-part form, exemplified by *da capo* arias and minuet-trio-minuet movements. Often, ternary forms are sectional, meaning each section ends with a PAC in the key of that section. When a ternary form's **B** section ends with anything besides a PAC in its key, the ternary form is continuous.

Composite form is form within form. Traditional dances, like minuets and trios, are themselves binary. When combined into a single three-section movement, they create composite ternary. Often, trios are in key of the subdominant (IV).

Composite Ternary

A Section 1 / Minuet
Rounded continuous binary

B Section 2 / Trio
Simple sectional binary

A Section 3 / Minuet
Rounded continuous binary

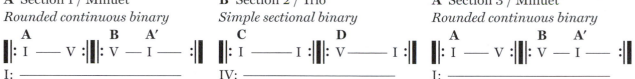

Try it 2

Listen to an entire work and diagram its form. Include descriptors for the overall form—binary, ternary, or composite—and phrase-structure diagrams of each section.

Contextual Listening 23.5

Listen to a ragtime piece and diagram its form. As you work, consider these strategies.

- Label each section with a design letter. Section letters are uppercase.

- If a section immediately repeats, use repeat signs (e.g., write **A A** as written ‖: **A** :‖).

- If previously heard music recurs *after a contrasting section*, label it with its original design letter (e.g., **A B A**).

- A key change indicates a large-scale structural change. The number of key changes equals the number of large sections.

- If any large section is itself a small form, like binary or ternary, the overall form is a composite form.

Invention, Fugue, and Baroque Counterpoint

CHAPTER 24

NAME _____

In this chapter you'll learn to:

- Identify common motivic and thematic transformations
- Hear such transformation in the context of Baroque invention and fugue

Motivic and Thematic Transformations

Counterpoint is the interplay of rhythm, contour, and intervals between melodies. Contrapuntal melodies create polyphony because their rhythms and contours contrast, usually as a result of the transformation of motives and themes. Baroque music is filled with such transformations, like those defined here.

Term	Definition
Motive	A memorable melodic idea with distinct rhythm and contour
Theme	A piece or section's principal melody
Inversion	Mirrored melodic contour (e.g., ∧ becomes ∨)
Retrograde	A musical unit presented backward
Non-retrogradable	Sounding the same forward or backward (palindrome)
Retrograde inversion	A musical unit presented upside down and backward
Head	The onset of a theme
Tail (coda, codetta)	The end of a theme
Fragment	Part of a theme
Truncate	Subtract from either end of a theme, usually by shortening its tail
Augmentation	Same rhythmic proportion, but using larger note values (sounds slower)
Diminution	Same rhythmic proportion, but using smaller note values (sounds faster)
Invertible counterpoint	Melody **a** appears over **b**, then later, **b** appears over **a**
Stretto	Overlapping statements of a theme

Try it 1

A motive is the basis for a number of transformations. Every example is played at the same tempo, and sixteenth notes are the smallest rhythmic value you will hear.

1. (a) Listen to the motive. Begin with the given items and notate its rhythm and pitches.

   (b) What key does the motive imply?   G major   E minor

2. (a) Listen to a transformation of the motive and notate its rhythm and pitches.

   (b) Compared with the original motive, this transformation is an/a:

   augmentation   diminution   inversion   retrograde

   (c) Compared with this transformation, the original motive is an/a:

   augmentation   diminution   inversion   retrograde

3. (a) Listen to a transformation of the motive and notate its rhythm and pitches.

   (b) Compared with the motive, this transformation is an/a:

   augmentation   diminution   inversion   retrograde

The remaining exercises feature two-part counterpoint.

4. (a) Listen to a transformation of the motive and notate the rhythm and pitches of both parts.

   (b) Compared with the original motive, melodic pitches 1–6 are an/a:

   inversion   retrograde   retrograde inversion

   (c) Describe this transformation's sequence.

   In a _____ key, _____ –beat units _____ by _____
       major or minor?   how many?   descend or ascend?   interval?

   in _____ reps with a(n) _____ – _____ LIP to create a(n) _____.
       number?   intervals between S and B?   sequence name?

(d) Compared with the original motive, this transformation ends with which cadence (key)?

PAC (i)   HC (i)   PAC (III)   HC (III)

5. (a) Listen to a transformation of the motive and notate the rhythm and pitches of both parts.

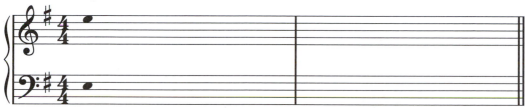

(b) Compared with the original motive, melodic pitches 1–6 are an/a:

augmentation   diminution   inversion   retrograde

(c) Compared with the original motive, the lower part is based on which transformation?

augmentation   diminution   inversion   retrograde

(d) The relationship between the upper and lower parts is:

stretto (overlap)   augmentation   diminution

(e) Describe this transformation's sequence.

In a _____ key, _____ –beat units _____ by _____
   major or minor?   how many?   descend or ascend?   interval?

in _____ reps with a(n) ____ – ____ LIP to create a(n) _____.
   number?   intervals between S and B?   sequence name?

(f) Compared with the motive, this transformation ends with which cadence (key)?

PAC (i)   HC (i)   PAC (III)   HC (III)

6. (a) Listen to a transformation of the motive. From the given items, notate only the first measure of both parts.

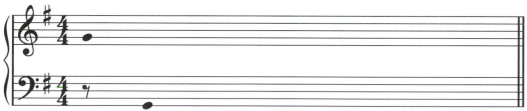

(b) In the upper part, beat 2 of the first four measures relates to the motive's:

head   tail

(c) For several measures, the relationship between the upper and lower parts is:

stretto (overlap)   augmentation   diminution

Imitative Polyphony, Invention, and Fugue

Imitative polyphony features a melody followed by one or more copies of itself.

Term	Definition
Canon	A melody followed by a copy (or copies) of itself at specified time and pitch intervals
Round	A simple canon that features imitation at the unison/octave
Invention	A two-voice contrapuntal work featuring the exposition of a theme that is developed extensively throughout the piece
Sinfonia	A three-voice invention
Fugue	A contrapuntal process that requires at minimum a thematic exposition in at least three voices with imitations in both the tonic and dominant keys
Subject	The theme of a fugue or other contrapuntal work
Answer	A subject transposed to the key of the dominant
Real answer	An exact, interval-by-interval transposition of a subject to the key of the dominant
Tonal answer	Any answer other than an exact transposition of the subject to the dominant key
Countersubject	The recurring counterpoint to the answer
Bridge/Link	A passage that connects the end of one idea with the onset of another, often the end of the answer to the beginning of a subject
Exposition	The initial presentation of a fugue's subject and answer statements, one per voice
Exposition 2, Exposition 3 . . .	A complete subject-answer presentation during the interior of a work
Episode	A passage lacking a complete statement of the theme
Middle entry	A theme statement not part of an exposition

Try it 2

1. Listen to part of a composition and complete the following exercises.

   (a) The excerpt likely belongs to which of these? Why?

      invention   sinfonia   fugue

   (b) For the first several measures, which term describes the imitation? Why?

      canonic   fugal

2. Listen to the beginning of an invention and complete the following exercises.

   (a) At the beginning, the rhythmic relationship between the parts is:

   anacrusis   syncopation   hemiola   diminution

   (b) Compared with the lower part, the higher part is which transformation?

   inversion   retrograde   retrograde inversion

   (c) Compared with the beginning, the excerpt's second half is:

   a varied repetition   in the same key

   invertible counterpoint   all of these

   (d) In the upper part, pitch 3 is: di ($\sharp\hat{1}$) te ($\flat\hat{7}$) fi ($\sharp\hat{4}$) sol ($\hat{5}$)

   (e) Given the response to (d), melodic pitch 3 implies which secondary dominant?

   V7/ii   V7/IV   V7/V   V7/vi

Contextual Listening 24.1

This contextual listening may be assigned in three parts: exercises 1-12, 13-19, and 20-33.

Listen to a keyboard work in its entirety (CL 24.1). Then, listen to parts of it separately as directed.

Exercises 1-12 focus on part 1, which consists of six segments in the higher voice (CL 24.1a).

For exercises 1, 2, and 5, write the segment's syllables or numbers in the blanks beneath the staff. Refer to them when notating the segment's pitches. In other exercises that require notation, imagine the syllable or number when writing the pitches.

1. Notate segment 1 (pitches 1-10). This is called the motive (or theme or subject).

$d(\hat{1})$ ___ ___ ___ ___ ___ ___ ___ ___ ___

2. Notate segment 2 (pitches 11-20).

___ ___ ___ ___ ___ ___ ___ ___ ___ ___

3. Compared with the motive, segment 2 is a:

   melodic inversion   transposition   rhythmic diminution   retrograde

4. Segment 2 implies which secondary dominant chord? Hint: Listen for the chromatic pitch.

	V7/ii	V7/IV	V7/V	V7/vi
Chromatic pitch:	di ($\sharp\hat{1}$)	te ($\flat\hat{7}$)	fi ($\sharp\hat{4}$)	si ($\sharp\hat{5}$)

5. Notate segment 3 (pitches 21-30).

___ ___ ___ ___ ___ ___ ___ ___ ___ ___

6. Compared with the motive, segment 3 is a:

   melodic inversion   transposition   rhythmic diminution   retrograde

7. Notate segment 4 (pitches 31-40).

8. Compared with the motive, segment 4 is a:

   melodic inversion   transposition   rhythmic diminution   retrograde

9. Notate segments 5 and 6 (pitches 41–60).

10. Compared with the motive, both segment 5 and segment 6 are:

   melodic inversions   transpositions   rhythmic diminutions   retrogrades

11. Segments 1–6 outline which harmonic progression?

   tonic-dominant-tonic (T–D–T)   tonic-predominant-dominant (T–PD–D)

   tonic-predominant-tonic (T–PD–T)   dominant-tonic-predominant (D–T–PD)

12. Which term describes *all* of part 1?

   exposition   episode   middle entry   coda

Exercises 13–19 focus on part 2 (CL 24.1b), which begins immediately after segment 6 ends.

Part 2 comprises seven segments, each one six pitches long.

13. Segments 7–11 alternate between the lower and higher voices. Beginning with the given information, notate the pitches and rhythm of segments 7–13.

14. Compared with the motive, segment 7 is:

   a fragmentation of the motive's beginning   a transposition down one octave

   an interval change on pitch 6   all of these

15. Compared with segment 7, segment 8 is:

   a transposition   a melodic inversion

   a rhythmic augmentation   a retrograde

16. Segments 7–13 outline which sequence?

   descending fifth   descending third

   descending parallel $^6_3$ chords   ascending 5–6

17. Part 2 ends with which cadence type?   PAC   IAC   HC   DC

18. Segment 13 features which type of phrase expansion?

 introduction   internal expansion   cadential extension

19. Which term describes *all* of part 2?

 exposition   episode   middle entry   coda

Exercises 20–27 focus on part 3 (CL 24.1c).
Immediately after segment 13, the lower voice descends with a three-pitch arpeggio.

Part 3 begins on the following downbeat and includes twelve segments (14–25), each one ten pitches long.

20. Part 3 begins in the key of: ii   IV   V   vi

21. Part 3 begins with which transformation? (segments 14–19)

 augmentation   invertible counterpoint   diminution   retrograde

22. Part 3 begins with which procedure? (segments 14–19)

 episode   middle entry   exposition 2   coda

23. Segment 21 includes which secondary dominant chord, using which chromatic pitch?

 V7/ii   V7/IV   V7/V   V7/vi
 di ($\sharp\hat{1}$)   *te* ($\flat\hat{7}$)   *fi* ($\sharp\hat{4}$)   *si* ($\sharp\hat{5}$)

24. Segment 23 includes which secondary dominant chord?

	V7/ii	V7/IV	V7/V	V7/vi
chromatic pitch?	*di* ($\sharp\hat{1}$)	*te* ($\flat\hat{7}$)	*fi* ($\sharp\hat{4}$)	*si* ($\sharp\hat{5}$)

25. Segment 25 includes which secondary dominant chord?

	V7/ii	V7/IV	V7/V	V7/vi
chromatic pitch?	*di* ($\sharp\hat{1}$)	*te* ($\flat\hat{7}$)	*fi* ($\sharp\hat{4}$)	*si* ($\sharp\hat{5}$)

26. Compare the answers to exercises 23–25. Which sequence do they imply?

 descending fifth   descending third

 descending parallel $\frac{6}{3}$ chords   ascending 5-6

27. Part 3 ends in the key of ii with which cadence type?   PAC   IAC   HC   PHC

Part 4 begins on C2 with the first of seven variations of the motive (segments 26-32, CL 24.1d).

28. The relationship between the voices may be described by which term?

    stretto (overlap)   canon at two octaves   imitative polyphony   all of these

29. Beginning with C2, notate only the first pitch of segments 26-32.
Four pitches appear in the bass staff and three in the treble.

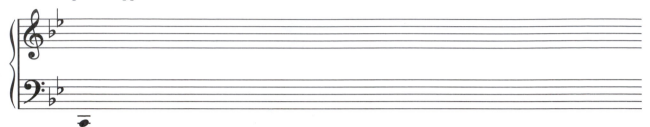

30. In exercise 29, examine only the bass pitches (pitches 1, 3, 5, 7).
Despite their direction, which sequence do they imply?

    descending fifth   descending third

    descending parallel $\frac{6}{3}$ chords   ascending 5-6

At end of part 4, both voices perform rhythmically identical six-pitch segments that lead to an IAC in the tonic key (segments 33-43).

31. Compared with the motive, which describes these six-pitch segments?

    fragmentation of the motive's head   interval change on pitch 6

    alternation between original and inverted forms of the motive

    all of these answers

Part 5 begins immediately after the IAC in the tonic key and continues until the end (segments 44-end, CL 24.1e).

32. At the beginning of part 5, which describes the relationship between the voices?

    stretto (overlap)   canon at the octave

    imitative polyphony   all of these answers

33. The final three bass pitches imply which harmonic progression?

    ii6-V-I   IV-V7-I   V$^{6-5}_{4-3}$-I   V8-7-I

Contextual Listening 24.2

Listen to a three-voice fugue for keyboard, first in its entirety (CL 24.2), then as directed in the exercises that follow.

Exercises 1–4 refer to the exposition.

1. The subject is pitches 1–12. In the blanks, write their syllables or numbers. In the staff, notate the subject's pitches and rhythm. Write *tr* over the trilled pitch.

    Pitches: $d(\hat{1})$ __ __ __ __ __ __ __ __ __ __ __

2. Beneath the staff and in the key of the minor dominant, write the answer's syllables or numbers. In the staff, notate the pitches and rhythm. Hint: The key of v requires accidentals.

    Pitches in v: $d(\hat{1})$ __ __ __ __ __ __ __ __ __ __ __

3. Compare exercises 1 and 2. Is the answer real or tonal? Hint: Real transposition is an exact, interval-by-interval transposition. Tonal is not.

    real   tonal

4. Because the subject doesn't recur until measure 6, measure 5 is:

    a bridge/link to the original key   a sequence   an episode

Exercises 5–8 refer to middle entries, transformations of the theme (subject or answer) outside the exposition.

In the staves provided, notate the music to help identify the transformations.

5. Listen to CL 24.2a. Which transformation occurs?

    augmentation   stretto   retrograde   inversion

6. Listen to CL 24.2b. The end features which transformation?

    augmentation   stretto   retrograde   inversion

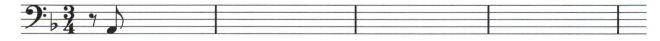

7. Listen to CL 24.2c. Which *two* transformations occur?

augmentation   stretto   retrograde   inversion

8. Listen CL 24.2d. Which *two* transformations occur?

augmentation   stretto   retrograde   inversion

Exercise 9–11 refer to the end of the fugue, CL 24.2e.

9. Listen to CL 24.2e. Initially, which secondary dominant is implied? Using which chromatic pitches?

     V7/iv   V7/v
mi ($\hat{3}$) and *te* ($\flat\hat{7}$)   *fi* ($\sharp\hat{4}$)

10. Listen again to CL 24.2e. Which of these items changes?

tonic quality (Picardy third)   thicker texture (more than three voices)

contrary motion   all of these

11. At the end, which subject transformation(s) occur(s)?

fragmentation (subject pitches 1–6)   original and inversion sound together

doubling in thirds   all of these answers

CHAPTER 25

Variations

NAME _____

In this chapter you'll learn to:

- Identify continuous and sectional variations and techniques used in their realization

Continuous Variations

Continuous variations feature a short, repeated pattern over which melodic variations occur. Historically, these pieces had many names. Today, we use these terms.

Term	What is repeated
Passacaglia, ground bass, or thorough bass	bass line
Chaconne	harmonic progression

Try it 1

Beginning with the given items, notate the passacaglia's bass line and the chords it implies.

1. The lament bass

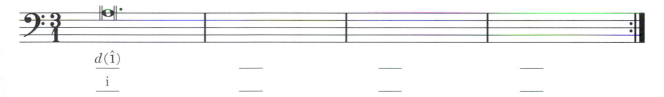

$$\frac{d(\hat{1})}{i} \qquad \underline{} \qquad \underline{} \qquad \underline{}$$

2. The chromatic lament

$$\frac{d(\hat{1})}{i} \qquad \underline{}\ \underline{} \qquad \underline{}\ \underline{} \qquad \underline{}\ \underline{}$$

3. Thirds progression

$d(\hat{1})$

I

Contextual Listening 25.1

Listen to a duet for tenors and basso continuo. Focus initially on the repeated bass line, which may be called a ground bass, thorough bass, or passacaglia.

Translation: Zephyr (the spring wind) returns.

1. The original score features the whole-note beat unit. Begin with the given items and notate the ground bass.

$d(\hat{1})$

2. Transcribe the ground bass into modern notation using a quarter-note beat unit.

$d(\hat{1})$

3. Make a list of how the two vocal parts relate to each other.

4. Make a list of why these variations are continuous.

Sectional Variations (Theme and Variations)

Sectional variations begin with a theme, often a lyrical, binary-form piece. Each variation copies the theme's entire structure and becomes one section of a larger, composite-form movement.

Most sectional variations are figural, each like an étude that explores a particular embellishment (e.g., neighbor tones). Variations include changes in mode, timbre, texture, articulation, register, character, tempo, beat division, dynamics, articulation, and effects such as textural inversion.

Try it 2

Listen to part of a theme followed by a variation. Identify the embellishment type(s).

1. Select the embellishment type(s).

   lower neighbor   appoggiatura   consonant skip   passing tone

2. Select the embellishment type(s).

   lower neighbor   appoggiatura   consonant skip   passing tone

3. Select the embellishment type(s).

   lower neighbor   appoggiatura   consonant skip   passing tone

4. Select the embellishment type(s).

   lower neighbor   appoggiatura   consonant skip   passing tone

Contextual Listening 25.2

Listen to a theme (CL 25.2) and five variations for piano (CL 25.2a–25.2e). This CL divides into two assignments: exercises 1–11 and exercise 12.

Exercises 1–11 refer only to the theme (CL 25.2). Focus on its cadences, phrase and section design, periods, and overall form.

1. Phrase 1's
   (a) cadence type is: PAC (I)   IAC (I)   HC (I)   PAC (V)
   (b) design letter is: **a**   **a′**   **b**

2. Phrase 2's
   (a) cadence type is: PAC (I)   IAC (I)   HC (I)   PAC (V)
   (b) design letter is: **a**   **a′**   **b**

3. Phrase 3's
   (a) cadence type is: PAC (I)   IAC (I)   HC (I)   PAC (V)
   (b) design letter is: **a**   **a′**   **b**   **c**

4. Phrase 4's
   (a) cadence type is: PAC (I)   IAC (I)   HC (I)   PAC (V)
   (b) design letter is: **a**   **a′**   **b**   **c**   **d**

5. Phrases 1–4 create which larger unit(s)?

   two parallel periods   two contrasting periods

   one parallel double period   one contrasting double period

6. Diagram section 1. Label section 1 with an uppercase design letter: **A**.
   Draw phrase curves and incorporate the answers to exercises 1–5.

Focus on the end of the theme, comparing the final two phrases with the **A** section.

7. Diagram the theme's final two phrases. For same or similar music, reuse design letters from the beginning of the theme.

8. Beginning with the given items, capture the pitches and rhythm of the outer parts. Write the Roman numerals and figures (if needed) in the chord blanks.

Pitches: $s(\hat{5})$ $d(\hat{1})$ $d(\hat{1})$ $d(\hat{1})$ $d(\hat{1})$ $d(\hat{1})$

Pitches: $d(\hat{1})$

Chords: ___   ___   ___   ___

___   ___

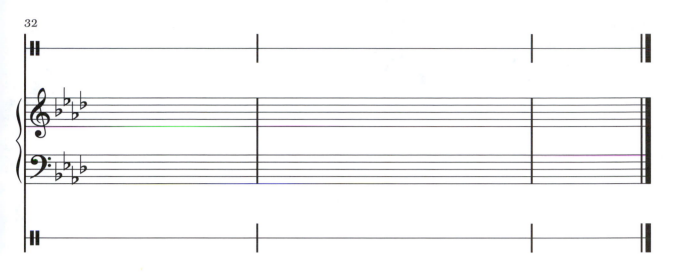

9. In measure 32, beat 1, the implied secondary dominant chord is:

$$V_5^6/\text{ii} \qquad V_5^6/\text{IV} \qquad V_5^6/\text{V} \qquad V_5^6/\text{vi}$$

The chromatic pitch is: $di\,(\sharp\hat{1})$ $te\,(\flat\hat{7})$ $fi\,(\sharp\hat{4})$ $si\,(\sharp\hat{5})$

Listen from the beginning and focus on the **B** section, which begins on phrase 5.

10. Select every true statement. The **B** section:

    begins with a two-step descending pattern called a *fonte*.

    begins with a two-step ascending pattern called a *monte*.

    includes a deceptive resolution.

    cadences with a PAC (V).

11. Which is the theme's overall form? Consider the answer to exercises 1–10.

    simple sectional binary   rounded sectional binary

    simple continuous binary   rounded continuous binary

12. Listen to each variation and compare it with the theme. Record your comparisons.

Compared with the theme, what remains the same?	What changes?
Variation 1 (CL 25.2a)	
Variation 2 (CL 25.2b)	
Variation 3 (CL 25.2c)	
Variation 4 (CL 25.2d)	
Variation 5 (CL 25.2e)	

Contextual Listening 25.3

This work features a theme and five variations (CL 25.3).

Listen to the theme (CL 25.3). Then, focus on the **A** section: phrases 1-2 (CL 25.3a).

1. The violins accompany the clarinet by playing:

   pizzicato   *sol* ($\hat{5}$) *do* ($\hat{1}$)   the V chord   a canon

2. The **A** section's phrase structure is:

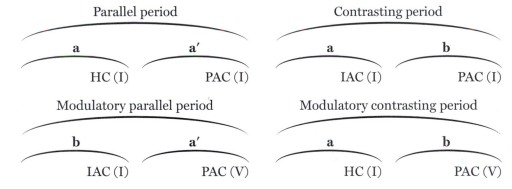

Focus on phrases 3-4 of the theme (0:15-0:27).

3. Begin with the given items and notate phrases 3-4 of the melody (CL 25.3b).

4. The structure of phrases 3–4 is:

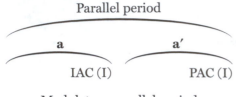

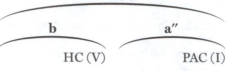

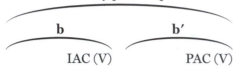

5. The theme's overall form is:

Simple sectional binary
A   **B**
I ——— I   V ——— I

Rounded sectional balanced binary
A   **B**   **A′**
I ——— I   V ——————— I

Simple continuous binary
A   **B**
I ——— V   V ——— I

Rounded continuous balanced binary
A   **B**   **A′**
I ——— V   V ——————— I

After a modulatory interlude, Variation 1 begins with the clarinet in its high register (CL 25.3: 0:32–0:57).

6. Compared with the theme, Variation 1 is transposed:

   up a step   up a third   down a step   down a third

7. Initially, the clarinet melody is doubled by:

   violin   bassoon   flute   piano

Variation 2 includes only part of the theme (CL 25.3: 0:58–1:38).

8. Initially, which of these occurs?

   chromatic descent   figural variations   theme is inverted   piano ostinato

9. Phrase 2 develops the theme in which way?

   inversion   diminution   canon   sequence

10. Variation 2 derives from which phrases of the theme?

   1–2 only   3–4 only   3 only

After a modulatory transition, Variation 3's tempo is faster (CL 25.3: 1:47–2:08).

11. Compared with Variation 2, Variation 3 is transposed:

   up a third   up a fourth   a tritone   down a fourth

12. Variation 3's texture is:

   monophonic   homophonic   heterophonic   polyphonic

13. Variation 3 includes which of the theme's phrases?

   all of them   1–2 only   3–4 only   3 only

Variation 4 is much slower and begins with flute and bassoon (CL 25.3: 2:08–2:23).

14. Which phrase design letters describe the initial music? Refer to exercises 2 and 4.

   The flute plays . . .   *The bassoon plays . . .*

a	**a**
a	**b**
b	**b**
b	**a**

15. The strings' role is to:

   sustain chords   play *pizzicato* chords   play the bass line   rest

16. Variation 4 consists of how many phrases?

   1   2   3   4

17. Variation 4's final harmonic interval is a/an:

   unison/octave   third   fourth   fifth

Variation 5 is louder and slower (CL 25.3: 2:24–2:56).

18. Begin with the given items and notate the pitches and rhythm of the bass line.

   Syllables: *d* __ __ __ __ __ __ __ __ __ __ __ __ __ __ __ __ __
   Numbers: 1̂ __ __ __ __ __ __ __ __ __ __ __ __ __ __ __ __ __

19. Variation 5 consists of which part of the theme?

   all of it   the first half only   the second half only

CHAPTER 26

Modal Mixture

NAME _____

In this chapter you'll learn to:

• Identify chords produced by modal mixture

Modal Mixture

Borrowing chords or pitches from the parallel key is called modal mixture. Often, mixture occurs in major-key works that borrow from the parallel minor. To identify a mixture chord, listen for its root and quality; also include the appropriate inversion symbols.

If the root is . . .	and the quality is . . .	write . . .
re ($\hat{2}$)	d, dm7	ii°, ii°7
me ($\flat\hat{3}$)	M	$\flat$III
fa ($\hat{4}$)	m	iv
sol ($\hat{5}$)	m	v
le ($\flat\hat{6}$)	M	$\flat$VI
te ($\flat\hat{7}$)	M	$\flat$VII
ti ($\hat{7}$)	dd7	vii°7

Try it

Beginning with the given items, notate the outer voices and chord symbols.

1.

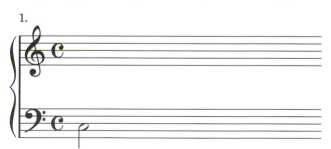

NAME _____

Contextual Listening 26.1

1. Each exercise begins on the tonic and includes modal mixture. Notate the bass pitches. Listen for the chord root and quality to identify chords 2–4.

    (a)

    F: I   ___   ___   ___

    (b)

    F: I7   ___   ___   ___

    (c)

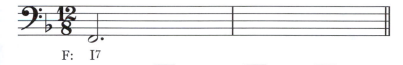

    F: I7   ___   ___   ___

Now, listen to a phrase from a song.

2. Beginning with the given items, capture the outer voices and identify the chords.

    (a) In the upper single-line staff, notate the rhythm of the melody. Beneath each note in both single-line staves, write its syllable or number.

    (b) In the grand staff, notate the pitches and rhythm of the bass and melody. Refer to (a).

    (c) In each chord blank, write the Roman numeral and figure (if needed).
        Circle each chord produced by modal mixture.

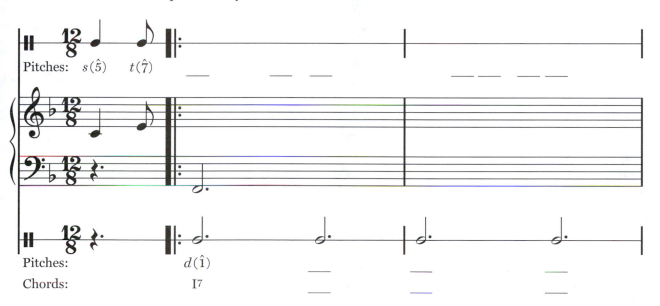

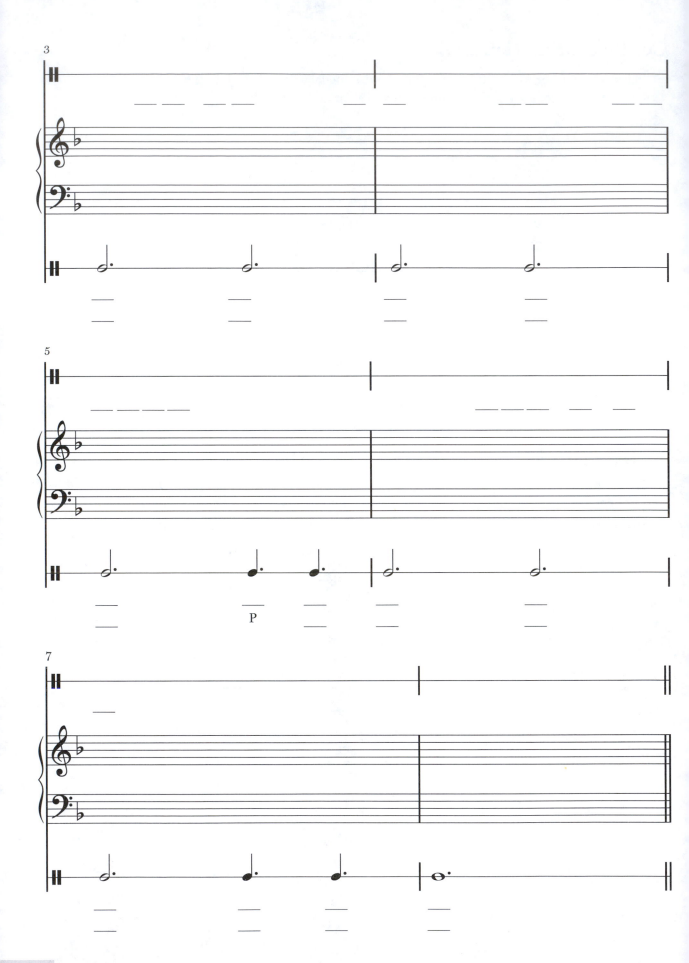

Contextual Listening 26.2

1. Each exercise begins on the tonic and includes modal mixture. Notate the bass pitches. Listen for the chord root and quality to identify chords 2–4. Use these abbreviations to identify the specified melodic embellishment:

Consonant (CS)	Dissonant (SNAP)			
Consonant skip (CS)	Suspension (S) or retardation	Neighbor (N)	Anticipation (A)	Passing (P)

(a)

C: I ___ ___ ___

Melodic pitch 4 is: CS   S   N   A   P

(b)

C: I ___ ___ ___

Melodic pitch 4 is: CS   S   N   A   P
Melodic pitch 10 is: CS   S   N   A   P

(c)

C: I ___ ___ ___

Melodic pitches 1–3 are: CS   S   N   A   P
Melodic pitch 10 is: CS   S   N   A   P

Now, listen part of an iconic American work and complete the remaining exercises.

2. Begin with the given items and capture the outer voices and chords.

   (a) In the single-line staves, notate the rhythm of the bass and melody. Beneath each
       note, write its syllable or number.

   (b) In the grand staff, notate the pitches and rhythm of the bass and melody.
       Both parts are doubled at the octave, but you may notate them in a single register.
       For help, refer to (a).

   (c) In each chord blank, write the Roman numeral and figure (if needed).
       Circle each chord produced by modal mixture.

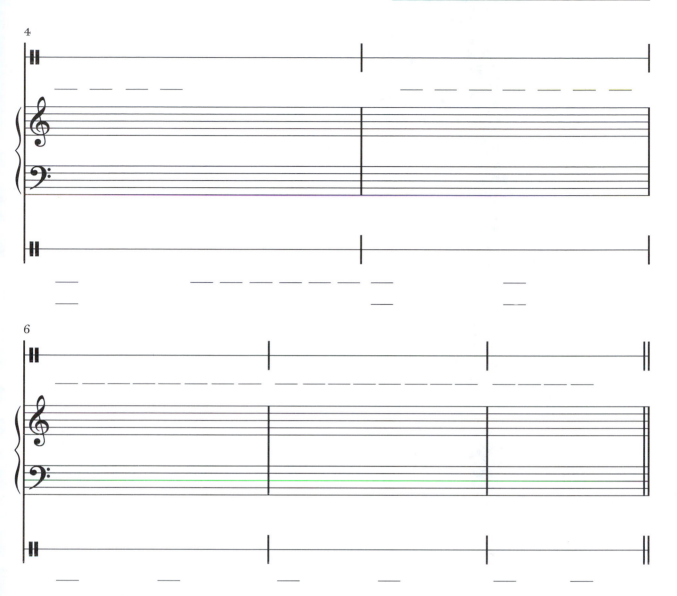

Contextual Listening 26.3

1. In each example, a slow-tempo bass-line melody begins with the given items.

   (a) Write the syllable or number of the bass pitches on each beat. Beneath these, write the Roman numerals and figures (if needed).

Pitches: $d(\hat{1})$ ___ ___ ___ ___ ___ ___

Chords: I ___ ___ ___ _____

   (b) Which of the following describes the bass line?

   basso continuo   pedal point   Alberti bass   walking bass

   (c) Write the syllable or number of the bass pitches on each beat. Beneath these, write the Roman numerals and figures (if needed).

Pitches: $d(\hat{1})$ ___ ___ ___ ___ ___ ___

Chords: I ___ ___ ___ _____

   (d) A bass line embellishes the tonic triad. Notate its pitches and rhythm.
   Hint: Comparing beats 3 and 4 will help you determine beat 4's rhythm.

Now, listen to two phrases from a piano sonata and complete the remaining exercises.

2. Begin with the given items and capture the outer voices and chords.

   (a) In the single-line staves, notate the rhythm of the bass and melody. Beneath each
       note, write its syllable or number.

   (b) In the grand staff, notate the pitches and rhythm of the bass and melody. Refer to (a).

   (c) In each chord blank, write the Roman numeral and figure (if needed). Circle each
       chord produced by modal mixture.

   (d) Compare melodic pitches with the chords. Label each dissonant embellishing
       tone as N (complete neighbor tone), IN (incomplete neighbor tone), or P (passing
       tone).

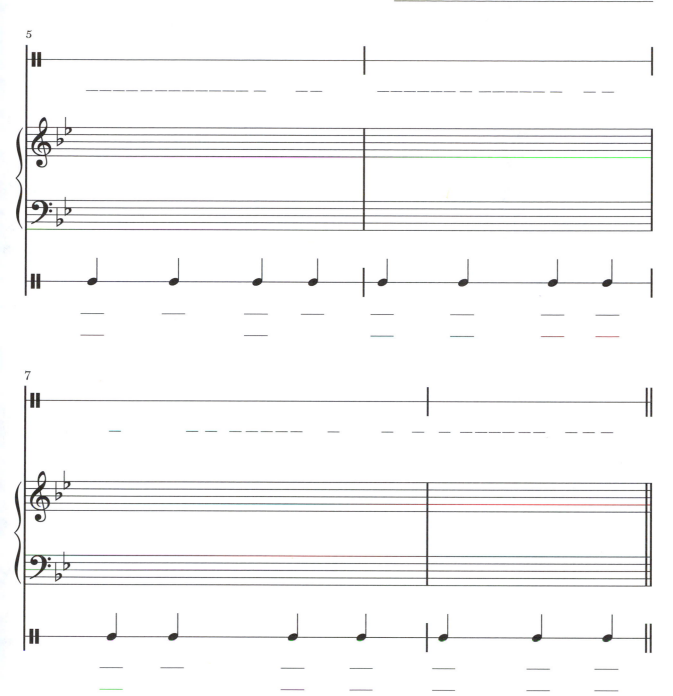

Focus on the highest melodic pitch and the music that follows it.

3. The highest melodic pitch is which of the following?　escape tone　appoggiatura

4. Descending from the high pitch is which scale type?
   major　　　　　　natural (descending melodic) minor
   harmonic minor　　ascending melodic minor

5. Just after the highest pitch, which resolution occurs?
   deceptive　Phrygian　plagal　Picardy

Focus once more on the entire excerpt.

6. Compared with chord 1, the final chord is: I   ♭III   V   ♭VI

7. The phrase structure is:

parallel period   contrasting period

modulatory parallel period   modulatory contrasting period

CHAPTER 27

The Neapolitan Sixth and Augmented-Sixth Chords

NAME _____

In this chapter you'll learn to:

- Identify Neapolitan sixth (N^6) and augmented-sixth (A6) chords

The Neapolitan Sixth (N^6)

Three minor-key predominant triads use identical voice leading but differ by one pitch: *do* ($\hat{1}$), *re* ($\hat{2}$), or *ra* ($\flat\hat{2}$). Because *ra* ($\flat\hat{2}$) is chromatic, the Neapolitan sixth (N^6) is a chromatic predominant (PD).

PD-Triad Listening Strategy: Bass ascends *fa-sol* ($\hat{4}$–$\hat{5}$)

Above fa ($\hat{4}$), *do you hear . . .*	*do* ($\hat{1}$),	*re* ($\hat{2}$),	*ra* ($\flat\hat{2}$)?
The PD triad is . . .	iv	ii°6	N^6

Try it 1

Preparation:

- Perform chord 1.
- Choose and perform a PD chord—2a, b, or c.
- Perform or omit chord 3. Perform either 4a → 4b or just 4b.
- Repeat and perform with part 3 up one octave.

Follow this procedure to create other voicings and progressions. However, avoid N^6 with part 2 in the soprano, because it produces P5-P5.

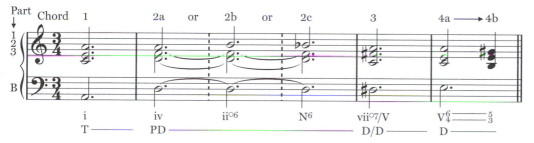

1. Listen to an exercise based on the model provided. Identify its chords and starting pitch.

(a)

Chord 1 is i	The PD chord is	vii°7/V is	The cadence is	The soprano begins on
	iv	played	V^{6-5}_{4-3}	do ($\hat{1}$)
	ii°6	not played	V	me ($\flat\hat{3}$)
	N6			

(b)

Chord 1 is i	The PD chord is	vii°7/V is	The cadence is	The soprano begins on
	iv	played	V^{6-5}_{4-3}	do ($\hat{1}$)
	ii°6	not played	V	me ($\flat\hat{3}$)
	N6			

(c)

Chord 1 is i	The PD chord is	vii°7/V is	The cadence is	The soprano begins on
	iv	played	V^{6-5}_{4-3}	do ($\hat{1}$)
	ii°6	not played	V	me ($\flat\hat{3}$)
	N6			

(d)

Chord 1 is i	The PD chord is	vii°7/V is	The cadence is	The soprano begins on
	iv	played	V^{6-5}_{4-3}	do ($\hat{1}$)
	ii°6	not played	V	me ($\flat\hat{3}$)
	N6			

(e)

Chord 1 is i	The PD chord is	vii°7/V is	The cadence is	The soprano begins on
	iv	played	V^{6-5}_{4-3}	do ($\hat{1}$)
	ii°6	not played	V	me ($\flat\hat{3}$)
	N6			

Contextual Listening 27.1

1. Listen to four measures of accompaniment. Notate the bass pitches and chord symbols.

(a)

g: i   _____   _____   _____

(b)

g: i   _____   _____   _____

(c)

g: i   _____   _____   _____

(d)

g: i   _____   _____   _____

Study the following translation. Then, listen to section one of a German song.

Translation: When a loyal heart perishes from love, the lilies wither in every field; the full moon must hide itself in the clouds, so people won't see its tears; and the angels close their eyes, sob, and sing the soul to peace.

2. Begin with the given items and capture the vocal melody, the piano's bass line, and the chords.

   (a) The rhythm of the piano bass line appears in the lower single-line staff. In the upper single-line staff, notate the rhythm of the vocal melody. Beneath each note in the single-line staves, write the pitch's syllable or number.

   (b) In the bass-clef staff, notate the pitches and rhythm of the piano bass line. If a bass note is doubled at the octave, you may notate it in a single register. For help, refer to (a).

   (c) In each chord blank, fill in the Roman numeral analysis. Indicate tonicization using bracket, slash, or colon notation.

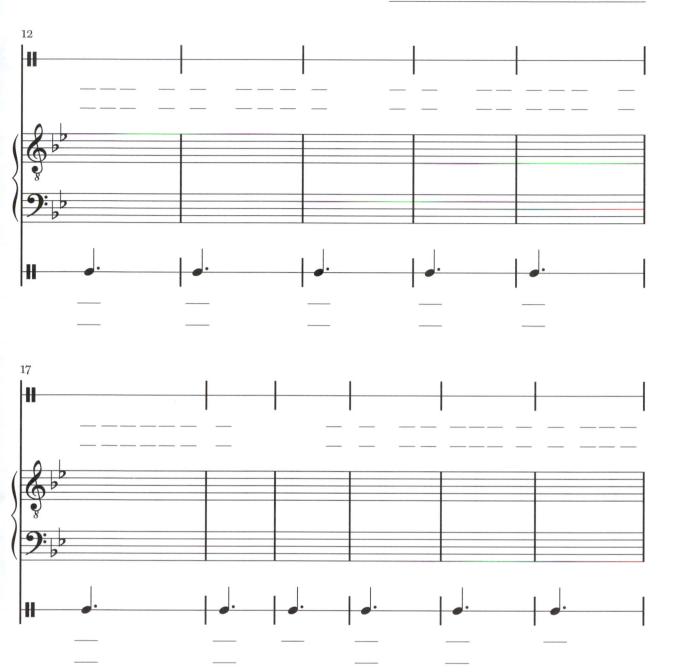

23

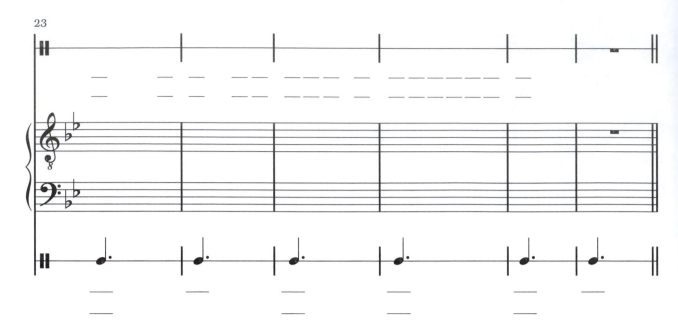

3. Initially, the bass line is a/an:

    tonic pedal point   walking bass   Alberti bass

4. The first melodic skip is a: M3   P4   P5   m6

5. The highest melodic pitch is: *do* (1̂)   *fa* (4̂)   *le* (♭6̂)   *ti* (7̂)

Contextual Listening 27.2

1. For each progression, notate the pitches and rhythm of the melody. Then notate the second bass pitch and its chord symbol. Include the figure for each suspension.

(a)

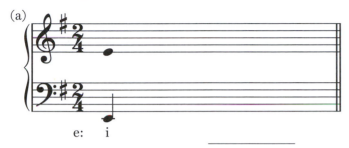

e: i   _____

(b)

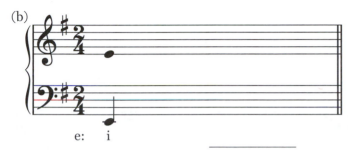

e: i   _____

(c)

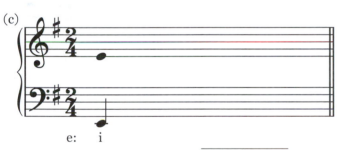

e: i   _____

2. Listen to a passage of music and notate it, beginning with the given items and capturing the melody and the chords.

   (a) In the upper single-line staff, notate the melodic rhythm. Beneath each note, write the syllable or number.

   (b) Refer to (a) to notate the melodic pitches and rhythm in the treble staff.

   (c) In each chord blank, fill in the Roman numeral analysis. Tonicization is indicated for you using bracket notation.

Augmented-Sixth Chords (A6)

Substituting *fi* (#$\hat{4}$) for *fa* ($\hat{4}$) in a Phrygian resolution (iv⁶–V) creates a chromatic predominant called an augmented-sixth chord (A6). The symbols It⁺⁶, Fr⁺⁶, and Gr⁺⁶ represent each of the three types of A6 chords.

To determine the A6 chord type when the bass descends *le-sol* (♭$\hat{6}$–$\hat{5}$):

Above le (♭$\hat{6}$), do you hear fa ($\hat{4}$) . . .	*or fi (#$\hat{4}$)?*			
The diatonic PD triad is iv⁶.	The chromatic PD is an A6.			
	Does the A6 chord include . . .	*doubled do ($\hat{1}$),*	*re ($\hat{2}$), or*	*me (♭$\hat{3}$)?*
	The A6 chord type is . . .	It⁺⁶	Fr⁺⁶	Gr⁺⁶

Try it 2

Preparation:

- Perform chord 1.
- Choose and perform a PD chord: 2a, b, c, or d.
- Perform either 3a → 3b or just 3b.
- Perform again, taking parts 2 or 3 up one octave to become the melody.

Follow this procedure to create other examples. Gr⁺⁶ may resolve to V despite the P5–P5. Mozart wrote these characteristic parallel fifths so often they are called "Mozart fifths."

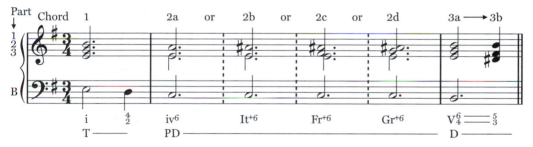

1. Listen to an exercise based on the model above. Identify its chords and starting pitch.

(a)	*Chord 1 is i*	*The PD chord is*	*The cadence is*	*The soprano begins on*
		iv⁶	V⁶⁻⁵₄⁻³	*me (♭$\hat{3}$)*
		It⁺⁶	V	*do ($\hat{1}$)*
		Fr⁺⁶		*sol ($\hat{5}$)*
		Gr⁺⁶		

(b)

Chord 1 is i	The PD chord is	The cadence is	The soprano begins on
	iv^6	V$^{6-5}_{4-3}$	me (♭$\hat{3}$)
	It^{+6}	V	do ($\hat{1}$)
	Fr^{+6}		sol ($\hat{5}$)
	Gr^{+6}		

(c)

Chord 1 is i	The PD chord is	The cadence is	The soprano begins on
	iv^6	V$^{6-5}_{4-3}$	me (♭$\hat{3}$)
	It^{+6}	V	do ($\hat{1}$)
	Fr^{+6}		sol ($\hat{5}$)
	Gr^{+6}		

(d)

Chord 1 is i	The PD chord is	The cadence is	The soprano begins on
	iv^6	V$^{6-5}_{4-3}$	me (♭$\hat{3}$)
	It^{+6}	V	do ($\hat{1}$)
	Fr^{+6}		sol ($\hat{5}$)
	Gr^{+6}		

(e)

Chord 1 is i	The PD chord is	The cadence is	The soprano begins on
	iv^6	V$^{6-5}_{4-3}$	me (♭$\hat{3}$)
	It^{+6}	V	do ($\hat{1}$)
	Fr^{+6}		sol ($\hat{5}$)
	Gr^{+6}		

(f)

Chord 1 is i	The PD chord is	The cadence is	The soprano begins on
	iv^6	V$^{6-5}_{4-3}$	me (♭$\hat{3}$)
	It^{+6}	V	do ($\hat{1}$)
	Fr^{+6}		sol ($\hat{5}$)
	Gr^{+6}		

Contextual Listening 27.3

1. For each progression, notate the pitches and rhythm of the outer parts. Beneath the bass, write the chord symbols.

(a)

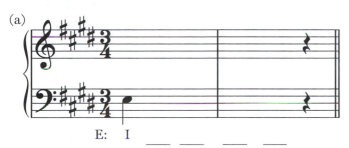

E: I ___ ___ ___ ___

(b)

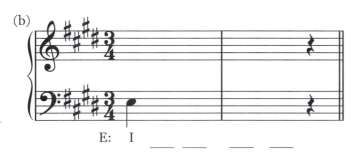

E: I ___ ___ ___ ___

(c)

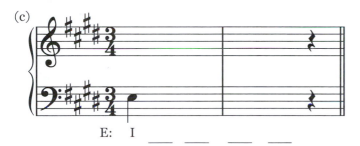

E: I ___ ___ ___ ___

Now, listen to the opening of a symphony movement and complete the remaining exercises.

2. Begin with the given items and capture the outer parts and the chords.

   (a) In the single-line staves, notate the rhythm of the outer parts. Beneath each note, write its syllable or number.

   (b) Refer to (a) to notate the outer-part pitches and rhythm in the grand staff.

   (c) In each chord blank, write the chord symbols.

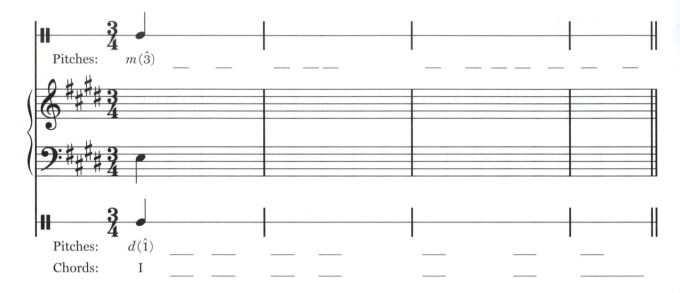

Pitches: $m(\hat{3})$ ___ ___   ___ ___   ___ ___ ___ ___ ___

Pitches: $d(\hat{1})$ ___ ___   ___ ___   ___   ___   ___

Chords: I   ___ ___   ___ ___   ___   ___   _____

Contextual Listening 27.4

1. For each progression, notate the bass pitches and write the chord symbols.

(a)

a: i$^5_3$ ═══ ____   ____   ____

(b)

a: i   ____   ____   ____

(c)

a: i   ____   ____   ____

(d)

a: i   ____   ____   ____

Now, listen to the first section of a chromatic étude (CL 27.4). Focus especially on the bass part and the harmonies. For help, listen to a simplification (CL 27.4a).

2. Begin with the given items and capture the bass part and the indicated chords.

   (a) In the blanks just below the bass staff, write the syllable or number of the bass pitch.

   (b) Refer to (a) to notate each bass pitch as a quarter note. If a bass pitch is doubled at the octave, notate only the higher pitch.

   (c) In each blank in the lower row, enter your Roman numeral analysis. Measures 7-8 include a tonicization. Use bracket notation to indicate the tonicized chord and the chords in the tonicized key.

3. Chord 2 of each phrase is which $^6_4$ type?

   passing   neighboring   cadential   arpeggiated

4. Why is phrase 4 longer than phrases 1, 2, and 3?

   The introduction is larger.   There is a harmonic sequence.

   The phrase beginning repeats.   A deceptive resolution delays its cadence.

5. Diagram the phrase structure of the entire excerpt. Include phrase curves, unit labels, design letters, cadence types, and the key in which each cadence occurs, for example, PAC (V).

CHAPTER 28

Chromatic Sequences and Voice-Leading Chords

NAME _____

In this chapter you'll learn to:

- Identify chromatic variants of common sequences
- Identify common-tone diminished seventh (CT$^{\circ7}$) and augmented-sixth (CT A6) chords

Chromatic Sequences

Chromatic sequences include one or more chromatic pitches or secondary-dominant-function chords. Often, they modulate. Chromaticism can also highlight important moments within sequences.

Modulatory sequences can be identified by listening for seven attributes: (1) key, (2) unit, (3) direction, (4) interval, (5) number of repetitions (reps), (6) soprano-bass intervals (linear-intervallic pattern, or LIP), and (7) destination key. Using these attributes, we can write sentences that describe modulatory sequences, like the one in this example.

Listen for:	key	unit	direction	interval	repetitions	LIP	modulation
Write:	Beginning on I,	2-chord units	descend	by 2nd	in 4 reps	with a 10–8 LIP	and modulate to V.

Try it 1

As you listen, use the model above to write a sentence describing the sequence. Then, beginning on tonic, notate the outer parts and chord symbols. Show tonicization or modulation using bracket, colon, or slash notation. Write the LIP above the soprano.

1.

2.

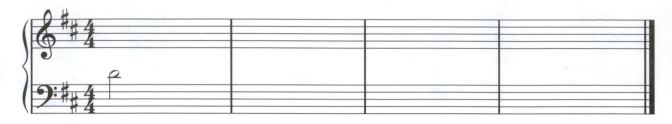

3.

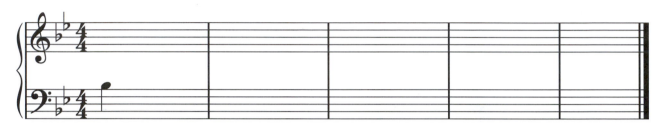

4.

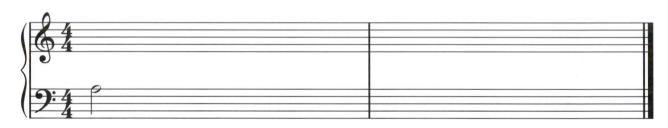

5.

Contextual Listening 28.1

Listen to one phrase from a piano work and complete the exercises.

1. Write a sentence that describes the opening sequential pattern. Hint: Use the highest melodic pitch in each measure to identify the outer-voice intervals.

2. Describe how internal repetition expands the phrase.

3. Begin with the given items and capture the outer parts and the chords.

   (a) In the single-line staves, notate the rhythm of the outer parts. Beneath each note, write its syllable or number.

   (b) In the grand staff, notate the pitches and rhythm of the outer parts. Refer to (a).

   (c) In each chord blank, write the Roman numeral and figure (if needed). Indicate tonicization using bracket, slash, or colon notation.

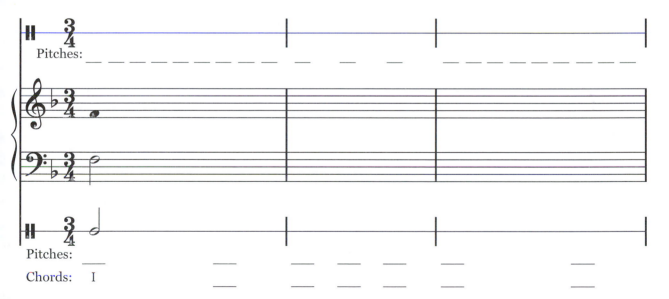

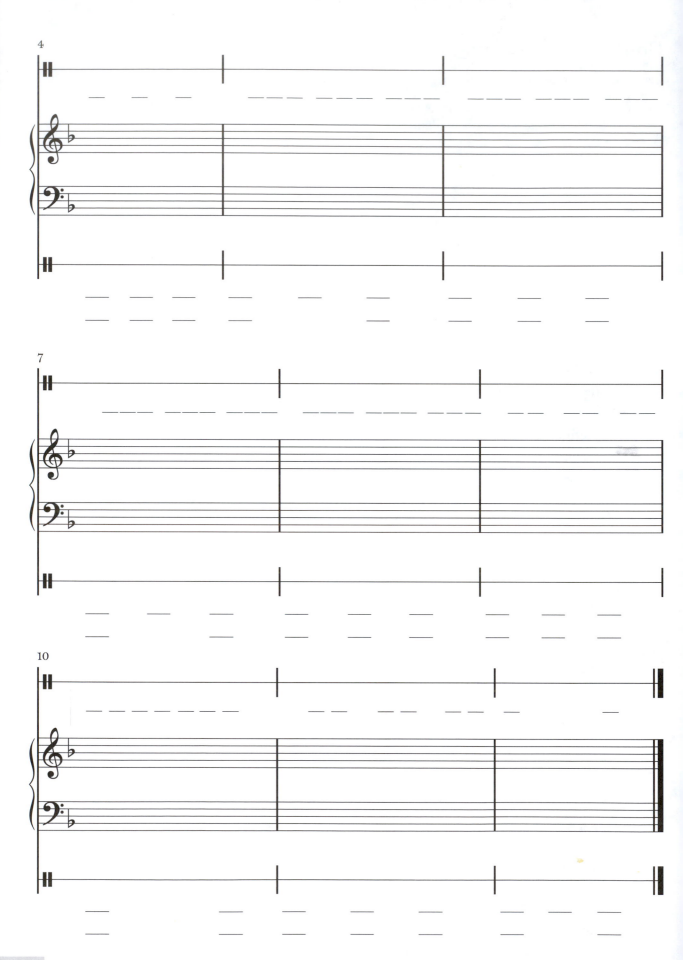

Contextual Listening 28.2

Listen to a phrase from a string quartet that begins with a sequence and complete the exercises.

1. Write a sentence that describes the opening sequence.

2. Diagram the phrase structure using phrase curve(s) and letter(s); indicate the key of the cadence(s) and cadence type(s). Describe how internal repetition expands the phrase.

3. Begin with the given items and capture the outer parts and the chords.

   (a) In the single-line staves, notate the rhythm of the outer parts. Beneath each note, write its syllable or number.

   (b) In the grand staff, notate the pitches and rhythm of the outer parts. Refer to (a).

   (c) In each chord blank, write the Roman numeral and figure (if needed). Indicate tonicization and modulation using bracket, slash, or colon notation.

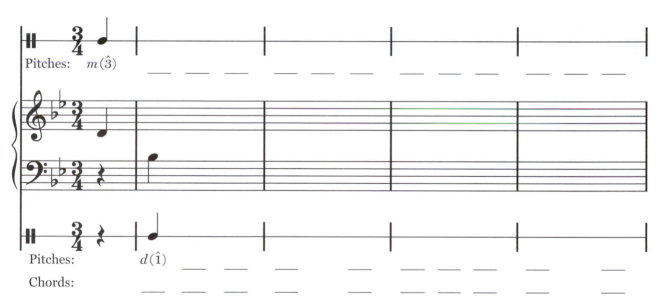

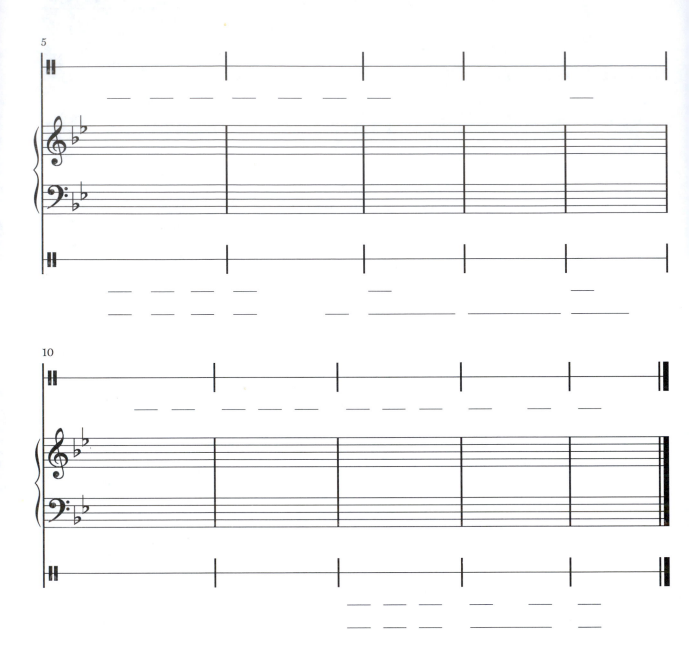

Voice-Leading Chords

Some vertical sonorities look like functional chords but are instead melodic embellishments. For example, embellishing a major triad with chromatic neighbor tones can produce a common-tone diminished seventh (CT°7) or augmented-sixth chord (CT A6).

Try it 2

Listen to sixteen measures of $\frac{3}{4}$ and choose the correct voice-leading chord, CT°7 or CT A6. Hint: CT°7 features lower neighbor tones; CT A6 has both lower and upper neighbor tones.

	m. 1	m. 2	m. 3	m. 4
CT:	°7 A6	°7 A6	°7 A6	
Chord:				

	m. 5	m. 6	m. 7	m. 8
CT:	°7 A6		°7 A6	°7 A6
Chord:				

	m. 9	m. 10	m. 11	m. 12
CT:	°7 A6		°7 A6	
Chord:				

	m. 13	m. 14	m. 15	m. 16
CT:	°7 A6		°7 A6	
Chord:				

Contextual Listening 28.3

Listen to two phrases from a piano work and complete the exercises.

1. Begin with the given items and capture the outer parts and the chords.

   (a) In the single-line staves, notate the rhythm of the outer parts. Beneath each note, write its syllable or number. Indicate tonicizations with colon notation.

   (b) In the grand staff, notate the pitches and rhythm of the outer parts. Refer to (a).

   (c) In each chord blank, write the Roman numeral and figure (if needed). For common-tone chords, write either CT°7 or CT A6. From measure 5 to the end, indicate the modulation using colon or bracket notation.

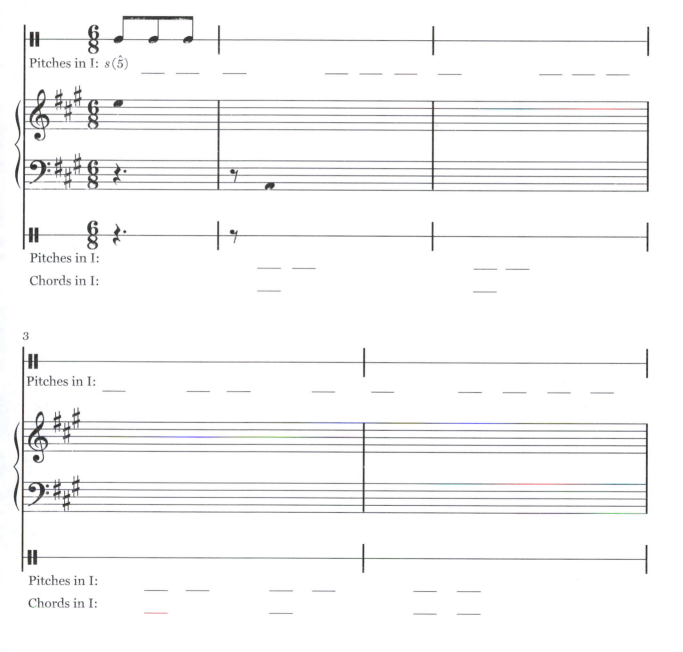

5

Pitches in I: ___   ___ ___ ___   ___   ___ ___ ___

Pitches in I: ___ ___   ___ ___   ___ ___ ___
Pitches in key #2: ___ ___   ___ ___   ___ ___ ___
Chords in key #2: ___   ___   ___ ___

7

Pitches in I: ___   ___ ___   ___ ___   ___
Pitches in new key: ___   ___ ___   ___ ___   ___

Pitches in I: ___   ___   ___
Pitches in new key: ___   ___   ___
Chords in new key: _____   ___

2. Diagram the phrase structure using phrase curves and letters; indicate the key of the cadences and their type.

Contextual Listening 28.4

1. Write a sentence that describes the opening sequence.
   Hint: Use melodic pitches 1 and 5 to figure the outer-voice intervals.

2. Describe the phrase's internal expansion.

3. Begin with the given items and capture the outer parts and the chords.

   (a) In the single-line staves, notate the rhythm of the outer parts. Beneath each note, write its syllable or number.

   (b) In the grand staff, notate the pitches and rhythm of the outer parts. Refer to (a).

   (c) In each chord blank, write the Roman numeral and figure (if needed). Indicate tonicization using bracket, slash, or colon notation.

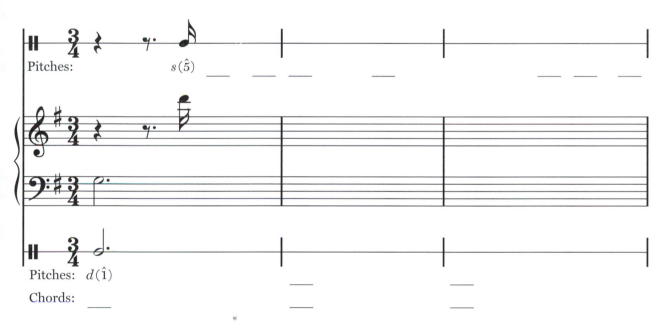

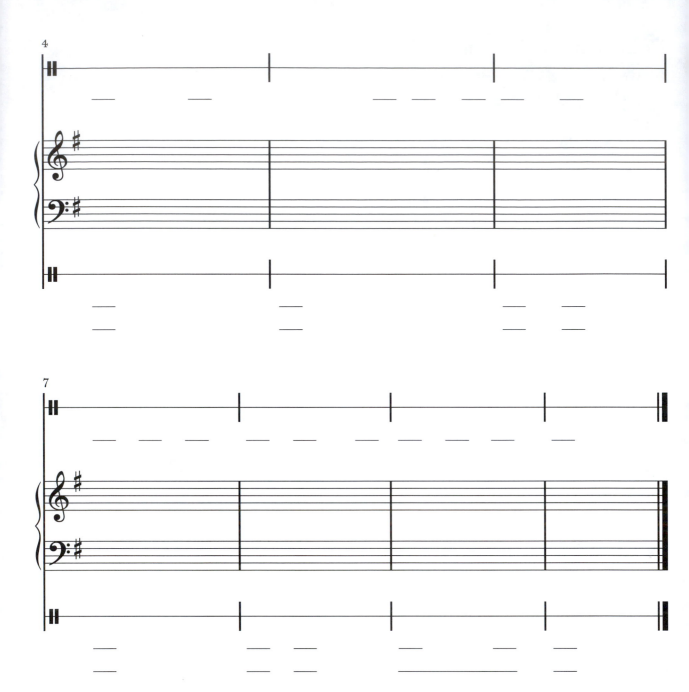

CHAPTER 29

Vocal Forms

NAME _____

In this chapter you'll learn to:

- Use musical analysis to understand text painting in vocal music

Text Painting

Emphasizing the meaning of text when setting it to music is called text painting. For example, a mournful text might be set with sad, slow music, or the word "high" might be sung as a high pitch.

Try it

When painting text, composers often use mixture or chromatic chords. Beginning with the given items, notate the outer voices and chord symbols.

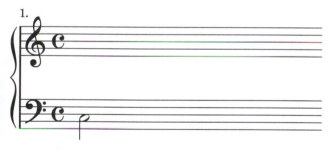

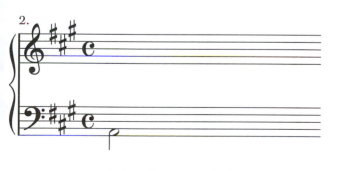

Contextual Listening 29.1

Study the poetry, then listen to an aria and complete the exercises.

Schafe können sicher weiden,	Sheep may safely graze,
wo ein guter Hirte wacht,	where a good shepherd watches over them.
Wo Regenten wohl regieren,	Where rulers govern well,
kann man Ruh und Frieden spüren	one can feel rest and peace
und was Länder glücklich macht.	and that which makes countries content.

Focus first on the four-measure introduction.

1. Initially, the flutes harmonize at which interval?

    third   fifth   sixth   octave

2. Initially, the bass line is:

    a walking bass   a tonic pedal point   an Alberti figure

3. At the end of the introduction, the flutes harmonize at which interval?

    third   fifth   sixth   octave

In the following excerpt, the soprano sings the first couplet of the poem twice.

4. Capture the pitches and rhythm of the vocal melody.

    (a) In the single-line staff, notate the melodic rhythm. Beneath each note, write its syllable or number. Show all solmization in the tonic or change keys to show tonicizations.

    (b) In the treble staff, notate the melodic pitches and rhythm. Refer to (a). Write *tr* over trilled notes.

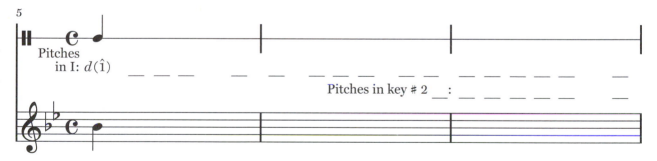

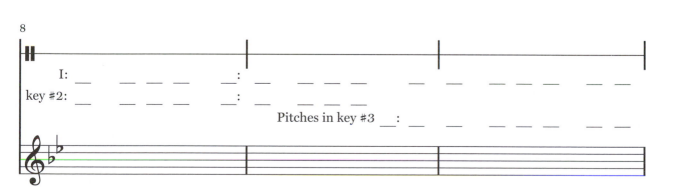

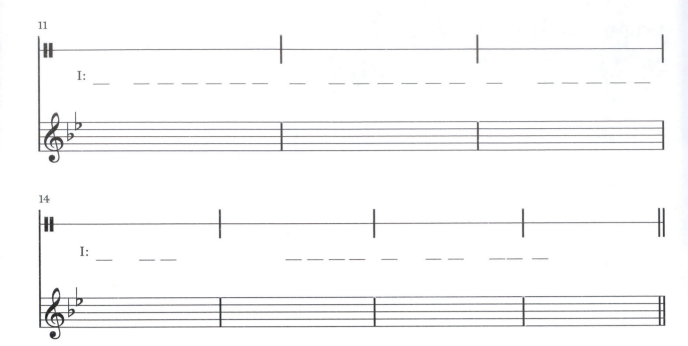

5. After the introduction, Section 1's form is:

   parallel period + codetta   contrasting period + codetta

   parallel double period   contrasting double period

Exercises 6–9 refer to the entire song.

6. Section 2 ends in the key of: I   IV   V   vi

7. The section design of the entire aria is:

   A A   A A′   A B   A B A

8. The form of the entire aria is:

   simple binary   rounded binary   simple ternary

9. This song's text has two meanings. The superficial meaning honors a benevolent ruler. The subtext honors the composer's Christian beliefs. Discuss each meaning and the text painting.

Contextual Listening 29.2

1. Each exercise begins and ends on the tonic. Listen for chord quality to identify chords 2 and 3.

   (a) Chord 2: iv^6 $\flat VI$ $vii^{\circ 4}_3/V$ $vii^{\varnothing 7}/V$

       Chord 3 V^{8-7} V^{6-5}_{4-3} $V^{8-7}_{6-5}{}_{4-3}$

   (b) Chord 2: iv^6 $\flat VI$ $vii^{\circ 4}_3/V$ $vii^{\varnothing 7}/V$

       Chord 3 V^{8-7} V^{6-5}_{4-3} $V^{8-7}_{6-5}{}_{4-3}$

Study the poetry, then listen to the beginning of a song (CL 29.2).

Guten Abend, mein Schatz,	Good evening, my sweetheart,
guten Abend, mein Kind!	good evening, my dear!
Ich komm' aus Lieb' zu dir,	I come out of love for you,
Ach, mach' mir auf die Tür,	Oh, open your door for me,
mach' mir auf die Tür!	open your door for me!

Next, focus on the phrase that sets lines 3–5 of the poem (CL 29.2a).

2. Begin with the given items and capture the outer parts and the chords.

   (a) In the single-line staves, notate the rhythm of the outer parts. Beneath each note, write its syllable or number.

   (b) In the grand staff, notate the pitches and rhythm of the outer parts. Refer to (a).

   (c) In each chord blank, write the Roman numeral and figure (if needed). Indicate tonicization using bracket, slash, or colon notation.

3. How does the music portray the eagerness and frustration of the suitor?

Contextual Listening 29.3

Listen to the beginning of an arrangement that tells the story of a young girl who must follow her husband to a distant land, never to see her mother again.

1. Focus first on the introduction. Begin with the given items and notate the bass line. There is no key signature, so write using accidentals. Beneath each bass pitch, write "m" for minor quality and "M" for major. Indicate any inversion with its figure.

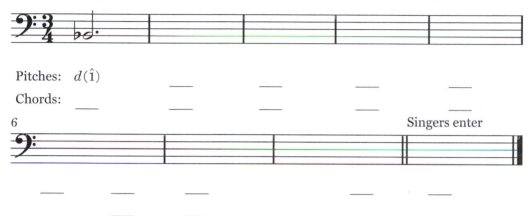

Pitches: $d(\hat{1})$ ___ ___ ___ ___

Chords: ___ ___ ___ ___ ___

6   Singers enter

2. (a) The introduction ends with which cadence?   PAC   IAC   PHC

   (b) What is usual about the use of this cadence?

3. Now, focus on the melody. Beginning with the given items, write the syllables or numbers, then notate the melodic pitches and rhythm.

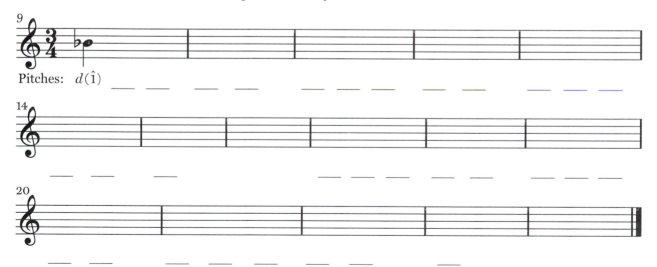

Pitches: $d(\hat{1})$

4. Study the melody by itself. In which key signature could the melody be notated and why?

5. What is the internal structure of each phrase?

6. Does the melodic phrase structure create a period? Why or why not?

7. How does the setting portray the anguish of the separation of a daughter from her mother?

Contextual Listening 29.4

Study the text, then listen to one phrase from a song and complete the exercises.

Ach Veilchen, armes Veilchen,   O violet, poor violet,
wie blühst du aus dem Schnee?   how do you bloom in the snow?
Im kurzen Sonnenweilchen,   In the sun for a brief moment,
dann langem Winterweh, dann langem Winterweh.   then in long winter's pain.

1. Begin with the given items and capture the vocal melody, piano bass, and the chords.

    (a) In the upper single-line staff, notate the rhythm of the vocal line. The bass rhythm appears in the lower single-line staff. Beneath each note in the rhythm staves, write its syllable or number.

    (b) In the grand staff, notate the pitches and rhythm of the outer parts. Refer to (a). The piano bass is doubled at the octave. Notate the higher pitch only.

    (c) In each chord blank, write the Roman numeral and figure (if needed). Indicate tonicization using bracket, slash, or colon notation.

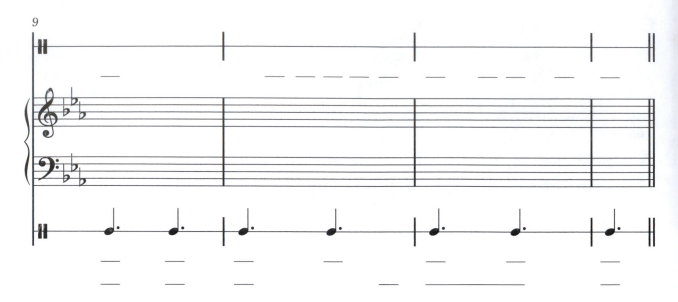

2. How does the composer expand this phrase?

3. Describe the text painting of "*dann langem Winterweh*" ("then in long winter's pain").

4. From measure 4 to the downbeat of measure 5, all of these occur *except*:

chromatic voice exchange common-tone chord

passing $^6_4$ secondary-dominant-function harmony

CHAPTER 30

Sonata Form

In this chapter you'll learn to:

- Recognize the components of sonata form
- Identify these components through guided listening of an entire sonata-form movement

Sonata Form

Compare sonata form with continuous, balanced rounded binary to see that it enlarges the same compositional gestures. A small sonata-form work is called a sonatina.

Continuous Balanced Rounded-Binary Form

‖: **A**   :‖‖: **B**   **A′**   :‖

I: I   V   Digression   HC (I)   I

i: i   III   HC (i)   i

Sonata or Sonatina Form

‖: Exposition   ‖‖: Development   Recapitulation   :‖

   P   TR   S   (C)   DEV   RTR   P   TR   S   (Coda)

I: I   (MC) V   HC (I) I   I

i: i   (MC) III   HC (i) i   i

Abbrev.*	Term	Key
P	primary theme	tonic
TR	transition	begins in tonic; ends in V (major) or III (minor)
	dependent (based on P)	
	independent (not based on P)	
(MC)*	medial caesura (a post-transition pause)	
S	secondary theme	V (major) or III (minor)
(TR²)*	S–C link or transition	V (major) or III (minor)
(C)*	closing theme	V (major) or III (minor)
DEV	development	
RTR	retransition	ends with HC (tonic)
(Coda)*	coda, C or expanded C group	tonic

*Optional components appear in parentheses.

Try it

Sequences often occur during sonata transitions and developments. Beginning with the given items, capture the outer parts and chords. Include the outer-voice intervals (LIP). Show tonicization using bracket, slash, or colon notation.

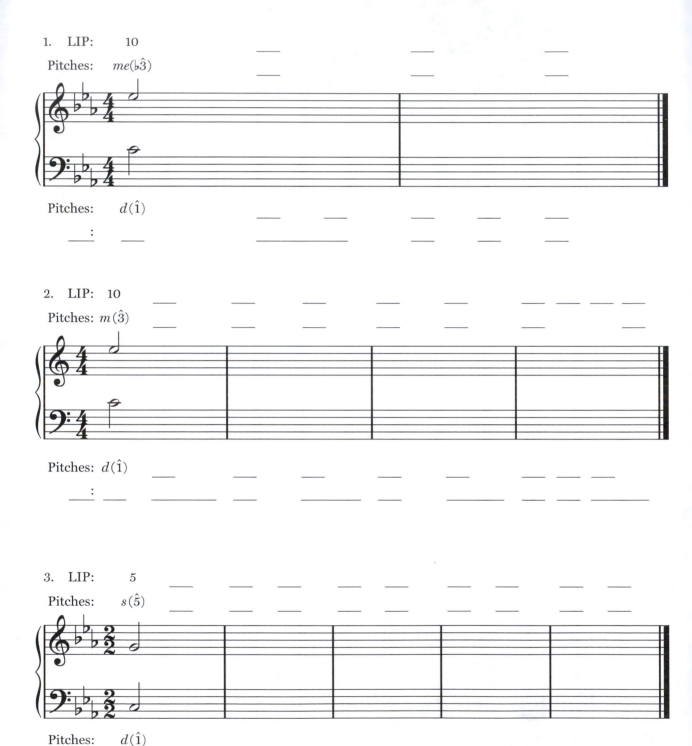

1. LIP: 10   ___   ___   ___
   Pitches: me(♭3̂)

   Pitches: d(1̂)

     ___ :

2. LIP: 10   ___   ___   ___   ___   ___   ___   ___
   Pitches: m(3̂)

   Pitches: d(1̂)

     ___ : ___

3. LIP: 5   ___   ___   ___   ___   ___   ___
   Pitches: s(5̂)

   Pitches: d(1̂)

     ___ :

4. LIP: 10 ___ ___ ___ ___ ___ ___ ___ ___

Pitches: $m(\hat{3})$ ___ ___ ___ ___ ___

Pitches: $d(\hat{1})$ ___ ___ ___ ___ ___ ___ ___ ___

___ : ___ ___ ___ ___ ___ ___ ___

5. LIP: 8 ___ ___ ___ ___ ___ ___ ___ ___ ___

Pitches: $d(\hat{1})$ ___ ___ ___ ___ ___ ___ ___ ___ ___

Pitches: $d(\hat{1})$ ___ ___ ___ ___ ___ ___ ___ ___ ___

___ : ___ ___ ___ ___ ___ ___ ___ ___ ___

Contextual Listening: Sonata Form

All of this chapter's Contextual Listening assignments are based on an entire sonata-form movement. Listen first to the entire movement (CL 30). While listening, sketch the form in the space below. Later, after you have completed the assignments, you can compare your detailed work to these initial ideas.

Contextual Listening 30.1

Listen to an entire sonata-form movement (CL 30.1), then to individual excerpts as specified.

1. Listen to the beginning of the exposition (CL 30.1a), which includes the primary theme (P; CL 30.1b), and transition (TR; CL 30.1c).

Now, focus only on P phrase 1 (CL 30.1d).

2. Begin with the given items and capture phrase 1's melody.

   (a) In the single-line staff, notate the melodic rhythm. Beneath each note, write its syllable or number.

   (b) In the treble staff, notate the pitches and rhythm of the melody. Refer to (a).

   (c) Draw a bracket under pitches 10–16 (m. 5 to the downbeat of m. 7). Label this "motive x."

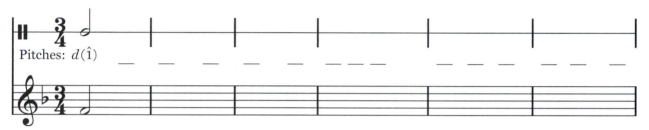

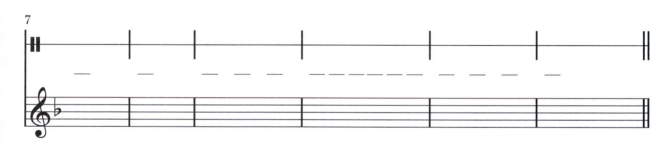

In measure 7 and following (CL 30.1d; starting at 0:08), focus on the bass line.

3. Compared with motive x, the bass line is:

   a rhythmic augmentation   a pedal point

   an imitation of the melody   an Alberti bass

4. Phrase 1 cadences with which progression?

   ii^6–V7–I   IV–IV–I   V$^{6-5}_{4-3}$–I   vi–V$^{8-7}$–I

Focus now on phrases 2–3 (CL 30.1e).

5. Begin with the given items and capture the outer parts and harmonies.

   (a) In the single-line staves, notate the rhythm of the outer parts. Beneath each note, write its syllable or number.

   (b) In the grand staff, notate the pitches and rhythm of the outer parts. Refer to (a).

   (c) Write the Roman numerals and figures (if needed) that represent the harmony.

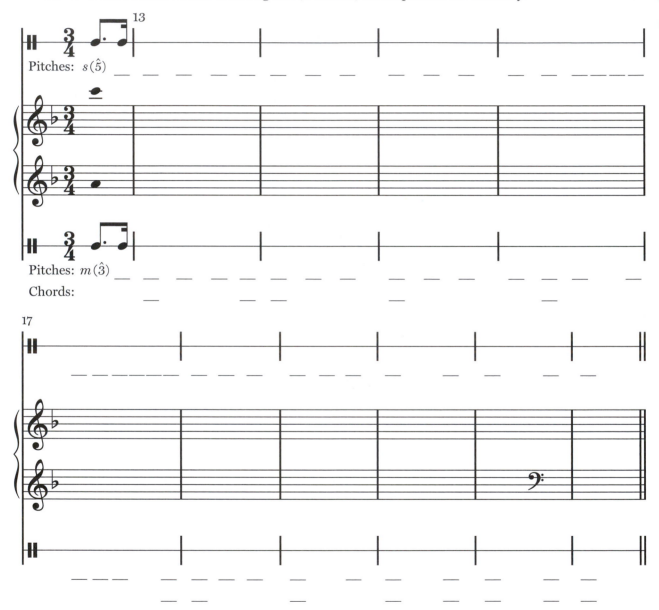

6. Compared with phrase 2, phrase 3 includes which expansion?

   introduction   internal repetition   internal sequence   cadential extension

7. Phrases 2 and 3 create which structure?

   parallel period   contrasting period

   parallel double period   contrasting double period

Exercises 8–13 refer only to the transition (TR; CL 30.1f).

8. The transition begins in which key?   ii   IV   V   vi

9. In the key indicated in exercise 8, the opening chord progression is:

   I–V$^6_4$–I^6 i–vii°$^6_5$–i^6 i–vii°^{6}–i^6 i–V$^4_3$–i^6

10. The transition ends with which cadence (key)?

    HC (I)   PAC (I)   HC (V)   PAC (V)

11. In the key of V, the cadential predominant chord is:

    ii   iv^6 V7/V   A6

12. The transition's cadence is prolonged by which means?

    plagal extension   repeated ii–V progressions   sequence   suspensions

13. The transition's musical material is:

    dependent (based on P)   independent (not based on P)

Contextual Listening 30.2

Listen to an entire sonata-form movement (CL 30.2), then to individual excerpts as specified.

1. Listen to the secondary theme (S; CL 30.2a), which consists of four phrases.

Exercises 2–7 focus only on S phrases 1–2 (CL 30.2b).

2. Begin with the given items and capture the melody of S phrases 1–2.
   Omit the grace notes.

   (a) In the single-line staff, notate the melodic rhythm. Beneath each note, write its syllable or number.

   (b) In the treble staff, notate the melodic pitches and rhythm. Refer to (a).

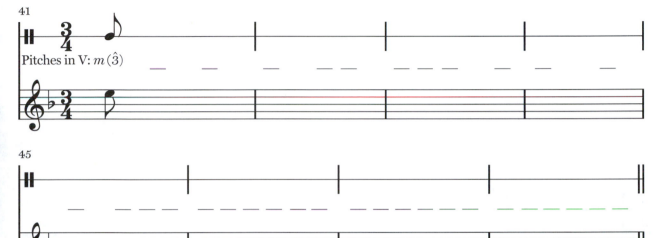

3. Phrase 1's cadence type is: PAC   IAC   HC   PC

4. Phrase 2's cadence type is: PAC   IAC   HC   PC

5. Compared with phrase 1, phrase 3 is a:

   variation, featuring neighbor tones and two-against-three rhythm.

   contrast, featuring different melodic material and harmonies.

6. Phrase 4's cadence type is: PAC   IAC   HC   PC

7. Phrases 1–4 create:

   two parallel periods   two contrasting periods

   one parallel double period   one contrasting double period

Exercises 8–12 refer only to TR², a transition that leads to the closing theme (C; CL 30.2c).

8. Still in the dominant key, TR²'s opening chords are:

   i–ii–V7–I   I–V7–i–V7   I–vi–ii⁶–V   I–vii°7–i–vii°7

9. Which sequence leads to TR²'s cadence? Hint: Focus on the bass pitches.

   descending fifth   descending third   ascending 5–6   ascending fifth

10. The sequence ends with which rhythmic device?

    syncopation   hemiola   rhythmic augmentation of S

11. In Contextual Listening 30.1, you identified motive x. How does TR²'s sequence relate to motive x?

12. In the key of V, TR²'s cadence is extended with which repeating chords?

    iv⁶–V   N⁶–V   V$^6_5$/V–V   vii°7/V–V

Exercises 13–15 refer only to the closing theme (C; CL 30.2d).

13. Begin with the given items and capture the outer parts and chords of C phrase 1.

    (a) In the single-line staves, notate the rhythm of the outer parts. Beneath each note, write its syllable or number.

    (b) In the grand staff, notate the pitches and rhythm of the outer parts. Refer to (a).

    (c) Write the chord symbols below the bass pitches.

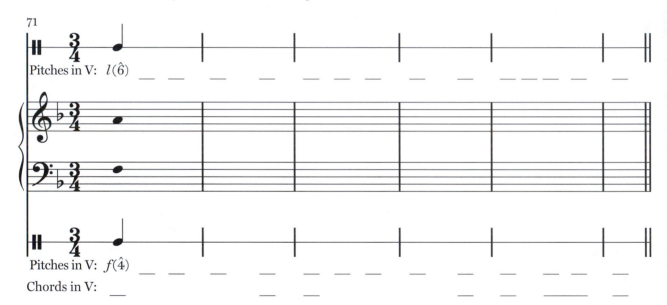

14. Phrase 1's cadence type is: PAC   IAC   HC   PC

15. Compared with C phrase 1, phrase 2 is enlarged. List the ways phrase 2's expansion occurs.

Contextual Listening 30.3

Listen to an entire sonata-form movement (CL 30.3), then to individual excerpts as specified.

1. Listen to the development (CL 30.3a).

Now, focus on phrase 1 (CL 30.3b).

2. Begin with the given items and capture phrase 1's outer parts and chords.

    (a) In the single-line staves, notate the rhythm of the outer parts. Beneath each note, write its syllable or number.

    (b) In the grand staff, notate the pitches and rhythm of the outer parts. Refer to (a).

    (c) Write the chord symbols below the bass pitches.

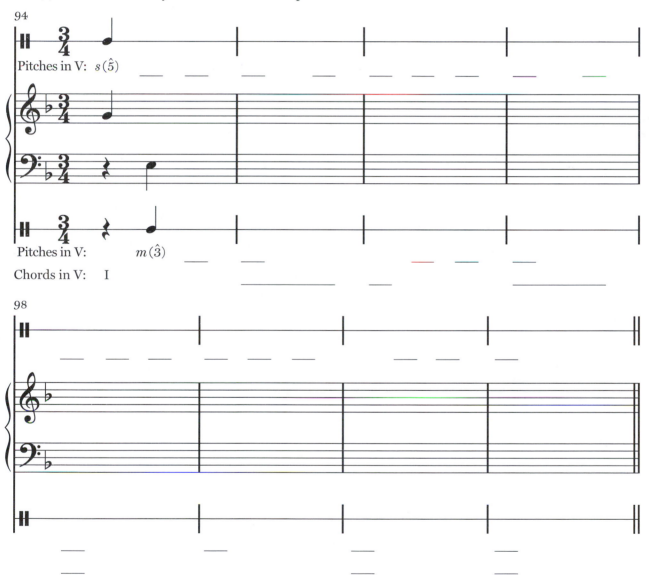

3. Phrase 1's cadence type is: PAC   IAC   HC   DC

4. Compared with phrase 1's melody and harmony,

Phrase 2's melody is:	*Phrase 2's harmony is:*
the same	the same
the same	varied
varied	the same
different	different

The beginning of the retransition elides with the cadence of phrase 2 of the development. Exercises 5–7 refer only to the music of the retransition (RTR; CL 30.3c).

5. The retransition is based on:

   phrase 1 of P (primary theme)   TR (the transition)

   phrase 1 of S (secondary theme)   TR^2 (transition between S and C)

6. Which progression occurs in the key of ii, then again in the key of vi?

   $\text{vii}^{\circ 6}_{5}\text{–i}^6\text{–V}^6_5\text{–i}$ $\text{vii}^{\circ 6}\text{–i}^6\text{–vii}^{\circ 7}\text{–i}$ $\text{V}^6_4\text{–i}^6\text{–vii}^{\circ 7}\text{–i}$ $\text{ii}^{\circ}\text{–i}^6\text{–V}^6\text{–i}$

7. In the key of vi, the retransition's cadence chords are:

   $\text{ii}^6\text{–V}$ $\text{iv}^6\text{–V}$ $\text{It}^{+6}\text{–V}$ $\text{N}^6\text{–V}$

8. (a) Listen again to the exposition (CL 30.3d).

   (b) Then, listen to the recapitulation (CL 30.3e).

9. Compared with P in the exposition, P in the recapitulation:

   is identical.

   begins the same but ends differently.

   begins differently but ends the same.

10. Compared with TR in the exposition, TR in the recapitulation:

    is identical.

    is the same length and cadences on V.

    is longer and cadences on V.

11. Compared with S in the exposition, S in the recapitulation:

    is transposed to the tonic.   is varied at the end.

    is the same length.   includes all of these answers.

Rondo and Related Formal Plans

CHAPTER 31

NAME _____

In this chapter you'll learn to:

- Identify rondo and related formal plans

Rondo and Related Formal Plans

Many compositions are based on *idea-contrast-return*: the **A**–**B**–**A** design of ternary form. Rondo form extends the concept, comprising three or more refrains separated by contrasting episodes. With more sections, it is easy to create composite forms.

Ternary	Five-Part Rondo	Seven-Part Rondo	Arch Rondo (or Composite Ternary)	Sonata-Rondo (a composite form)
A–B–A	A–B–A–C–A	A–B–A–C–A–D–A	**A** – **B** – **A** / A–B–A–C–A–B–A	Expo. Dev. Recap. / ‖: A–B–A :‖‖: C A–B–A :‖

Try it

Often, rondo episodes are in a different key than the refrain, creating additional contrast. Beginning with the given items, capture the outer parts and chords. Indicate the modulation using bracket, slash, or colon notation.

1. Pitches: __ __ __ __ __ __ __

Pitches: $d(\hat{1})$ ___ ___ ___ ___ ___ ___

Chords: ___ ___ ___ ___ ___ ___

2. Pitches: ___ ___ ___ ___ ___ ___ ___ ___

Pitches: $d(\hat{1})$ ___ ___ ___ ___ ___ ___ ___

Chords: ___ ___ ___ ___ ___ ___

3. Pitches: ___ ___ ___ ___ ___ ___ ___ ___

Pitches: $d(\hat{1})$ ___ ___ ___ ___ ___ ___ ___

Chords: ___ ___ ___ ___ ___ ___

4. Pitches: ___ ___ ___ ___ ___ ___ ___ ___

Pitches: $d(\hat{1})$ ___ ___ ___ ___ ___ ___ ___

Chords: ___ ___ ___ ___ ___ ___

5. Pitches: ___ ___ ___ ___ ___ ___ ___ ___

Pitches: $d(\hat{1})$ ___ ___ ___ ___ ___ ___ ___

Chords: ___ ___ ___ ___ ___ ___

Five-Part Rondo Form

Contextual Listening assignments 31.1–31.3 are based on an entire movement from a piano sonata. The first two assignments capture the refrain. The third focuses on the overall form.

Contextual Listening 31.1

CL 31.1 is the **A** section of the binary form that becomes the refrain of the movement's overall form.

First, listen to the entire movement (CL 31.1).

1. Melodic pitches 5-6 create which suspension?　9-8　7-6　4-3

2. The key of phrase 1's cadence is:　I　IV　V　vi

3. Phrase 1's cadence is:　PAC　IAC　HC　PHC

4. What is the term for phrase 1's internal structure? _____

5. Cadence 1's suspension is:　9-8　7-6　4-3

6. The key of phrase 2's cadence is:　I　IV　V　vi

7. Phrase 2's cadence is:　PAC　IAC　HC　PHC

8. Diagram the structure of phrases 1-2.

9. Now, focus only on phrases 1 and 2 (CL 31.1a). Begin with the given items and capture the outer parts and harmonies. Write *tr* for trill.

   (a) In the single-line staves, notate the rhythm of the outer parts. Beneath each note, write its syllable or number. For tonicization or modulation, you may change the solmization to that of the secondary key (e.g., V: $\hat{1}$ $\hat{7}$ $\hat{1}$).

   (b) In the grand staff, notate the pitches and rhythm of the outer parts. Refer to (a).

   (c) Write the chord symbols below the bass pitches. Show tonicization or modulation using bracket, colon, or slash notation.

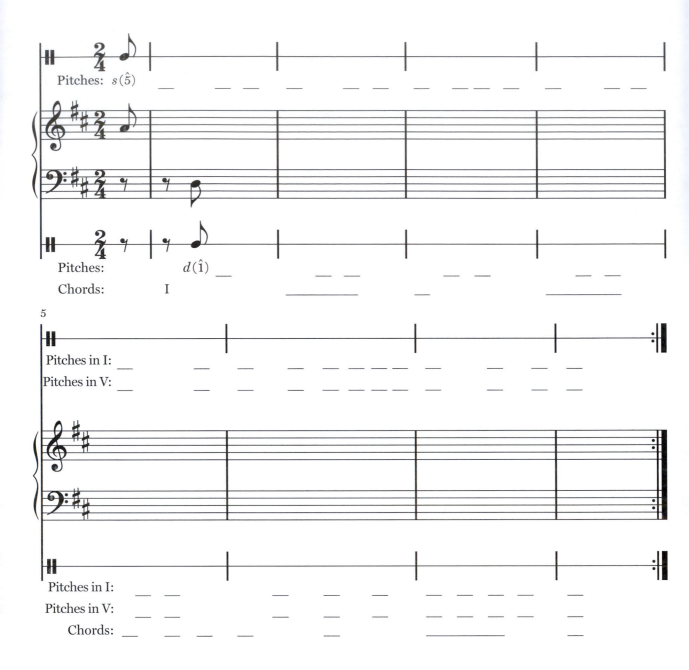

Contextual Listening 31.2

Listen to two phrases from the piano sonata you began studying in Contextual Listening 31.1 and complete the following exercises (CL 31.2). The excerpt ends on the tonic.

1. Begin with the given items and capture the outer parts and harmonies.
   Write *tr* for trill.

   (a) In the single-line staves, notate the rhythm of the outer parts. Beneath each note, write its syllable or number. For tonicization or modulation, you may change the solmization to that of the secondary key (e.g., V: $\hat{1}$ $\hat{7}$ $\hat{1}$).

   (b) In the grand staff, notate the pitches and rhythm of the outer parts. Refer to (a).

   (c) Write the chord symbols below the bass pitches. Show tonicization or modulation using bracket, colon, or slash notation.

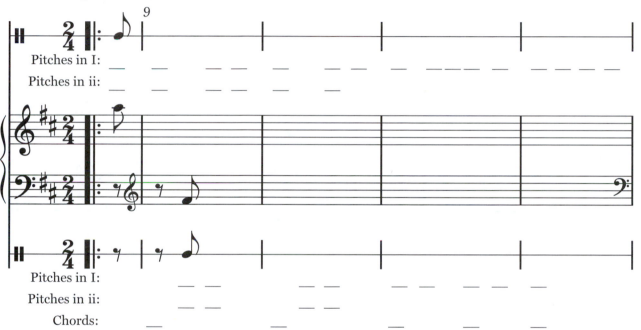

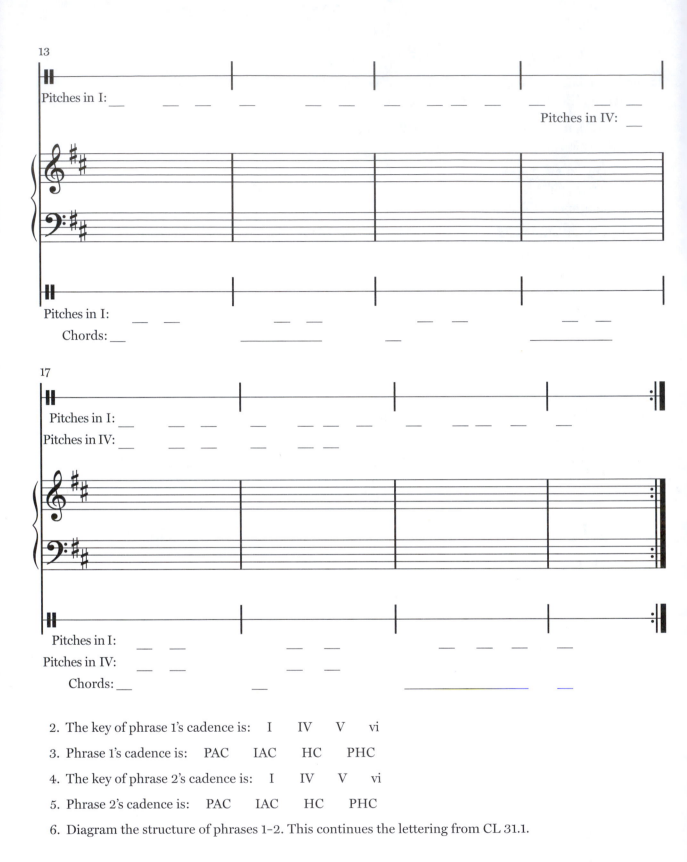

2. The key of phrase 1's cadence is: I   IV   V   vi

3. Phrase 1's cadence is: PAC   IAC   HC   PHC

4. The key of phrase 2's cadence is: I   IV   V   vi

5. Phrase 2's cadence is: PAC   IAC   HC   PHC

6. Diagram the structure of phrases 1–2. This continues the lettering from CL 31.1.

Contextual Listening 31.3

Listen to the entire refrain from the movement studied in Contextual Listening 31.1 and 31.2 and focus on its overall form (CL 31.3).

1. Diagram the refrain's overall form. Incorporate the phrase diagrams from CL 31.1 exercise 9 and CL 31.2 exercise 6.

Now, listen to the entire movement and focus on its overall form (CL 31.3a). Here, Contextual Listening 31.1 and 31.2 combine to become the **A** section refrain of the larger form.

2. The sectional design of the entire movement is:

   ABA   AABA   ABACA   ABACADA

3. Which describes the overall form?

   composite ternary   composite rounded binary

   five-part composite rondo   seven-part composite rondo

Other Rondo Forms

There are rondo forms other than the five-part rondo. For example, some rondo forms are expanded to include more than three occurrences of the refrain; and some rondo forms contain one episode that is repeated, rather than two different episodes.

Contextual Listening 31.4

Listen to the first four phrases from a piano work (CL 31.4) and complete the exercises.

1. Begin with the given items and capture the outer parts and harmonies.

    (a) The essential bass rhythm appears in the lower single-line staff. In the upper single-line staff, notate the rhythm of the melody. Beneath each note, write its syllable or number. For tonicization or modulation, you may change the solmization to that of the secondary key (e.g., V: $\hat{1}$ $\hat{7}$ $\hat{1}$).

    (b) In the grand staff, notate the pitches and rhythm of the outer parts. Refer to (a).

    (c) Write the chord symbols below the specified bass pitches. Show tonicization or modulation using bracket, colon, or slash notation.

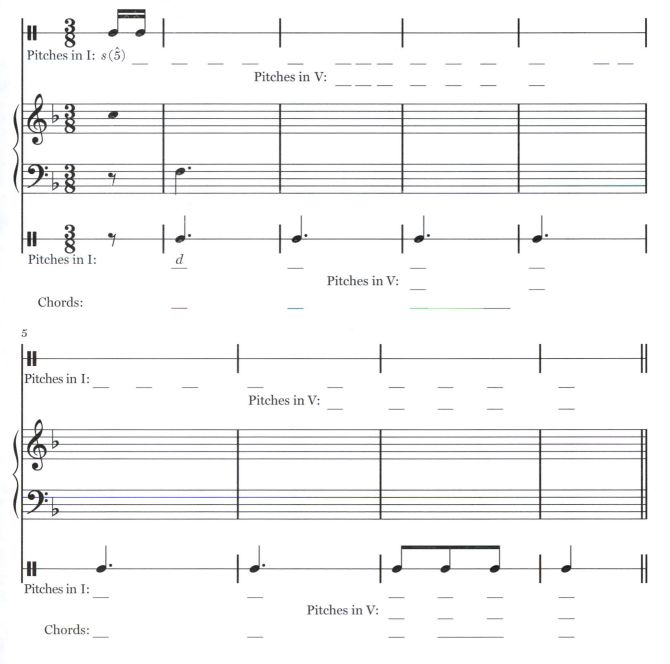

2. Phrase 1's cadence and key is: PAC (I)   HC (I)   PAC (V)   HC (V)

3. Phrase 2's cadence and key is: PAC (I)   HC (I)   PAC (V)   HC (V)

4. Phrase 3's cadence and key is: PAC (I)   HC (I)   PAC (V)   HC (V)

5. Phrase 4's cadence and key is: PAC (I)   HC (I)   PAC (V)   HC (V)

6. Diagram the structure of phrases 1–4.

Now, listen to the entire work, which begins with the refrain (CL 31.4a).

7. How many times does the refrain occur?   1   2   3   4

8. Which is the key of the one contrasting episode?   ii   IV   vi

9. Which describes the overall form?

   five-part rondo   seven-part rondo   ternary   rounded binary

10. Is there a codetta?   yes   no

Contextual Listening 31.5

1. Each exercise begins on tonic and modulates. Focus on bass pitches and chord quality.

(a)

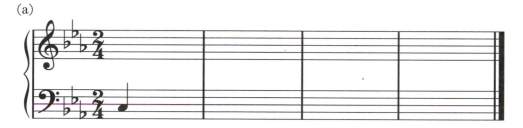

Chord 2 is: V_5^6 $vii^{o}7$ V_2^4 $vii^{o}{}_3^4$

Modulates to: III   iv   V   VI

Cadence type: PAC   IAC   HC

(b)

Chord 2 is: V_5^6 $vii^{o}7$ V_2^4 $vii^{o}{}_3^4$

Modulates to: III   iv   V   VI

In the modulation key, the predominant is: ii ii_5^6 IV

Cadence type: PAC   IAC   HC

Now, listen to an entire work for piano (CL 31.5).

Exercises 2–4 focus only on the **A** section, which consists of phrases 1–2 (CL 31.5a).

2. Begin with the given items and capture the outer parts and harmonies of phrases 1–2.

    (a) The bass rhythm appears in the lower single-line staff. In the upper single-line staff, notate the melodic rhythm. Beneath each note, write its syllable or number. For tonicization or modulation, you may change the solmization to that of the secondary key (e.g., V: î 7̂ î).

    (b) In the grand staff, notate the pitches and rhythm of the outer parts. Refer to (a).

    (c) Write the chord symbols below the bass pitches. Show tonicization or modulation using bracket, colon, or slash notation.

3. The accompaniment rhythm is:

4. Diagram the **A** section's phrase structure.

Exercises 5–6 refer only to section 2, the music immediately following the **A** section.

5. Diagram section 2, phrase 1's internal structure. Label each subphrase with a letter and, if present, any type of phrase expansion.

6. As you listen to section 2, conduct each measure as if it were a single beat. Group these *hyperbeats* into strong-weak units called *hypermeasures* to listen for *hypermeter*.

   (a) The phrase rhythm is: regular   irregular

   (b) If your answer was irregular, why do you think so?

Exercises 7-9 refer only to part 3.

7. Compared with the piece's first phrase, part 3's first phrase is:

   identical.   an exact transposition.

   the same contour with different pitches.   the same rhythm with different pitches.

8. Part 3 concludes on which chord?   i   iv   V   VI

9. As you listen to the conclusion of part 3, conduct the hypermeter.

   (a) The phrase rhythm is: regular   irregular

   (b) If your answer was irregular, describe the phrase expansion.

Exercises 10-13 refer to the piece's overall form.

10. Listen again to the entire piece. As you listen, diagram the sectional form. Label each section with a unique uppercase letter. Back-to-back repetition is considered one section ‖: A :‖ as opposed to **A A**. Contrasting sections feature a change of key, and/or a change of the thematic idea.

11. The piece divides into how many sections?   3   4   5   7

12. The piece's section design is:

    A B A′   A A′ B A′   A B A′ C A″   A B A′ C A″ B A‴

13. Is there a coda?   yes   no

CHAPTER 32

Lead-Sheet Notation, Jazz, and Blues

NAME _____

In this chapter you'll learn to:

- Interpret and write chord symbols using lead-sheet notation
- Identify and notate swing rhythms
- Recognize twelve-bar blues, the blues scale, and melodic riffs

Lead-Sheet Notation and Swing Rhythm

Lead sheets feature a treble-clef melody. Chord symbols appear above and lyrics below.

Lead-sheet chords indicate root and quality. A slash (/) means to play a chord over a specific bass pitch. The chart shows examples of how to realize lead-sheet chords.

When you see this chord symbol . . .	play a . . .
C or Cma or CM	C major triad
Cmaj7 or Cma7 or CM7	C major triad plus a M7 (B)
dm or Dmi or d	D minor triad
Dm7 or Dmi7	D minor triad plus a m7 (C)
Dm7/G	Dm7 chord over bass pitch G
Bø7	B half-diminished seventh chord
B°7	B fully diminished seventh chord
G7	G dominant seventh chord
G7 (♭9)	G7 plus a lowered 9th (A♭)
G7 (+11)	G7 plus a raised eleventh (C♯)

Swing rhythm is notated with simple beat divisions, but performed with long-short compound divisions, stressing the weakest divisions (shown with tenuto marks).

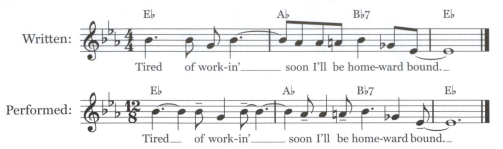

Written:

Tired   of work-in'_____ soon I'll be home-ward bound._

Performed:

Tired__ of work-in'_____ soon I'll be home-ward bound._

Try it 1

Beginning with the given items, notate the remaining bass pitches and the melodic swing rhythm. Listen for chord quality and write the lead-sheet chord symbols.

1. Chords: ____   ____   ____   ____

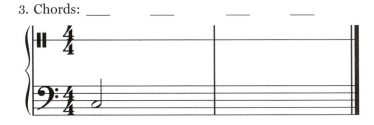

2. Chords: ____   ____   ____   ____

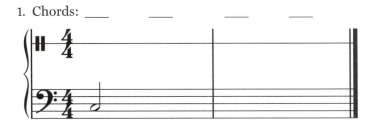

3. Chords: ____   ____   ____   ____

4. Chords: ____   ____   ____   ____

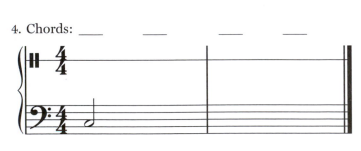

Contextual Listening 32.1

1. Each phrase begins on the tonic. Notate the bass line and melodic rhythm, which is swung. Write lead-sheet chords above. Complete the sentence to describe the phrase's sequence.

   (a) Chords:

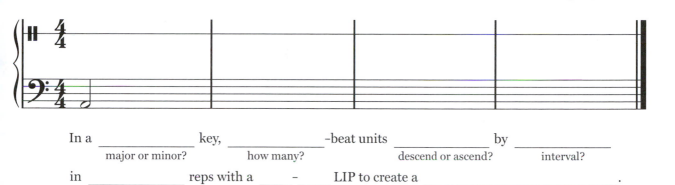

   In a _____ key, _____ –beat units _____ by _____
       major or minor?   how many?   descend or ascend?   interval?

   in _____ reps with a ____–____ LIP to create a _____.
       number?   intervals between S and B?   sequence name?

   (b) Chords:

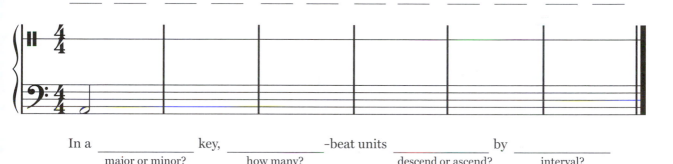

   In a _____ key, _____ –beat units _____ by _____
       major or minor?   how many?   descend or ascend?   interval?

   in _____ reps with a ____–____ LIP to create a _____.
       number?   intervals between S and B?   sequence name?

Now, listen to one phrase from a jazz standard and complete the remaining exercises.

2. Begin with the given items and capture the outer parts and chords.

   (a) In the single-line staves, notate the rhythm of the outer parts. The melody uses swing rhythm. Beneath each pitch, write its syllable or number.

   (b) In the grand staff, notate the pitches and rhythm of the melody and bass. Refer to (a).

   (c) Above each treble-clef measure, write the lead-sheet chord symbol.

   (d) Beneath the bass staff in the specified chord blanks, write the Roman numerals and figures.

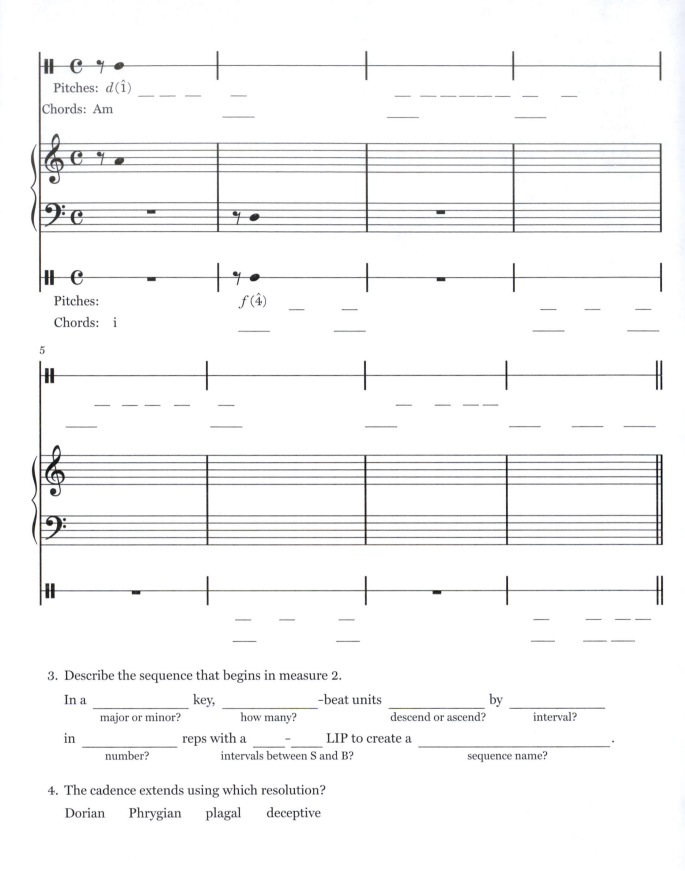

Pitches: d(1̂) _ _ _ _

Chords: Am

Pitches: f(4̂) _ _ _ _ _

Chords: i

5

3. Describe the sequence that begins in measure 2.

In a _____ key, _____-beat units _____ by _____
      major or minor?   how many?   descend or ascend?   interval?

in _____ reps with a ____ - ____ LIP to create a _____.
    number?   intervals between S and B?   sequence name?

4. The cadence extends using which resolution?

   Dorian   Phrygian   plagal   deceptive

Contextual Listening 32.2

1. Capture the bass pitches. Listen for chord quality, then write lead-sheet chord symbols.

    (a) Chords: ___ ___ ___ ___

    (b) Chords: ___ ___ ___ ___

    (c) Chords: ___ ___ ___ ___

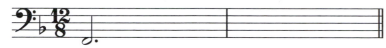

Now, listen to a phrase from a song.

2. Beginning with the given items, capture the outer voices and identify the chords.

    (a) In the single-line staves, notate the rhythm of the bass and melody. Beneath each note, write its syllable or number.

    (b) In the grand staff, notate the pitches and rhythm of the bass and melody. Refer to (a).

    (c) Above the treble staff in the blanks provided, write the lead-sheet chord symbols.

    (d) In each chord blank, write the Roman numeral and figure (if needed). Circle each chord produced by modal mixture.

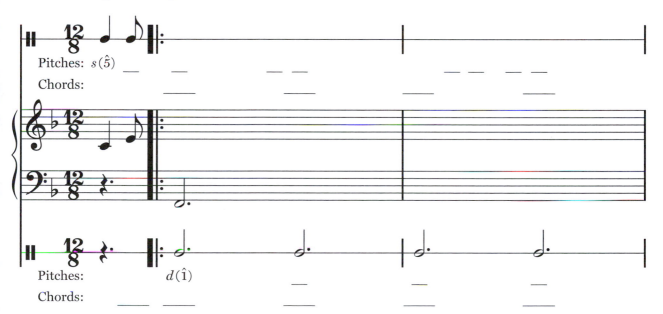

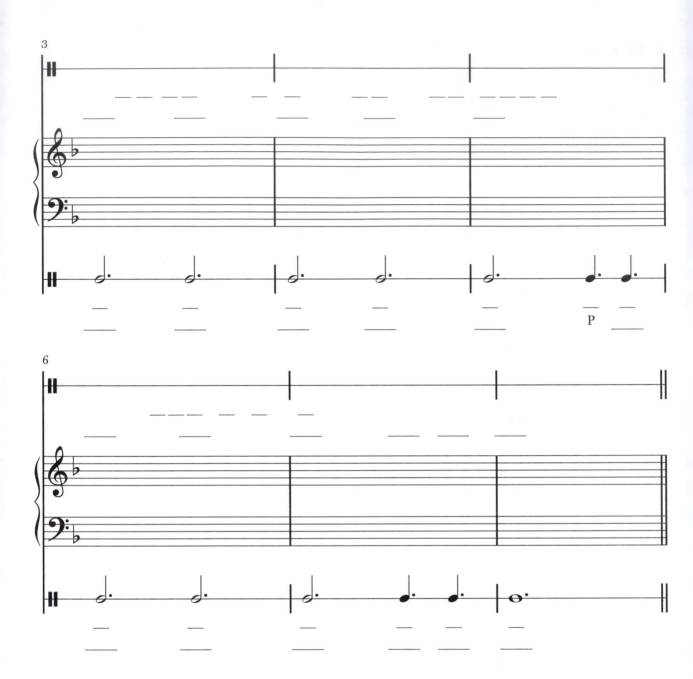

Blues

Adding *fi/se* (♯4̂/♭5̂) to a minor pentatonic scale produces the blues scale. Blues uses the major-key signature and requires accidentals on the modal inflections, which are called blue notes.

do	me	fa	fi	sol	te	do	do	te	sol	se	fa	me	do
1̂	♭3̂	4̂	♯4̂	5̂	♭7̂	1̂	1̂	♭7̂	5̂	♭5̂	4̂	♭3̂	1̂

Blues motives are called riffs. The most common blues form is twelve-bar blues. One pass through the twelve-bar blues pattern is called a chorus.

Try it 2

1. Each exercise features one blues chorus. A slash (/) within the staff represents one beat of chord prolongation. Expect embellishments but capture only the basic chords in the lead-sheet notation.

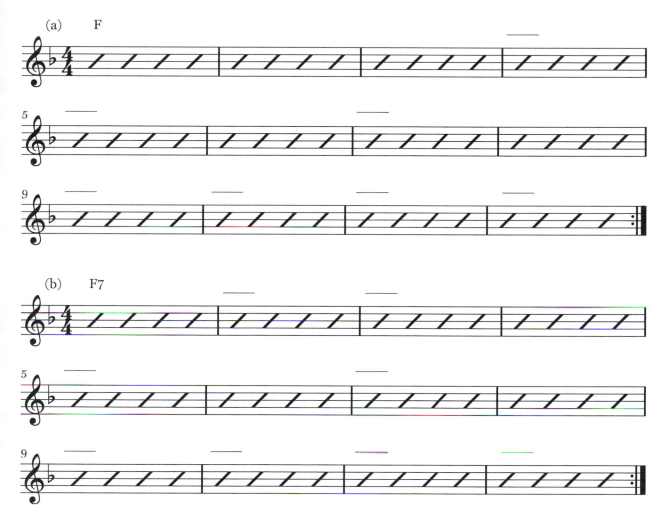

2. In the following exercises, a two-measure riff repeats three times over a blues progression. Capture the riff's pitches and swing rhythm.

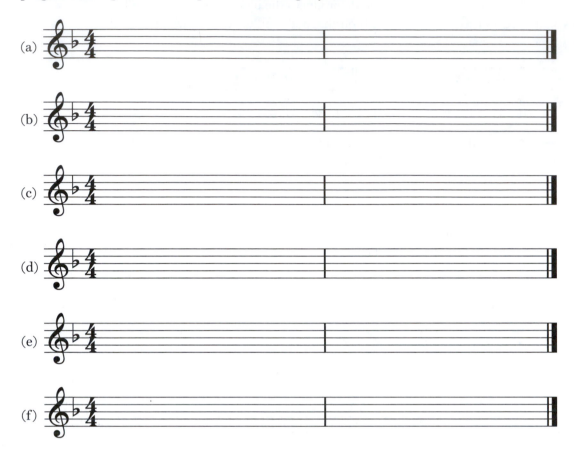

Part III Chromatic Harmony and Form

Contextual Listening 32.3

Listen to the beginning of a blues composition and focus on the music after the introduction.

1. Begin with the given items and capture the pitches and swing rhythm of the opening melody.

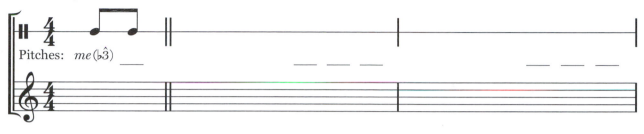

Pitches: *me* (♭3̂) ___

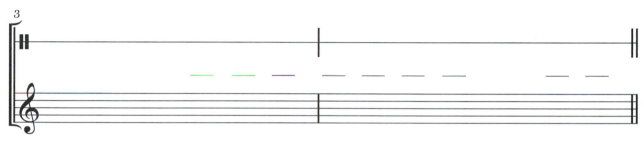

2. The melody in exercise 1 uses five of the six blues-scale pitches. Circle the "missing" blue note.

do	me	fa	fi	sol	te	do
1̂	♭3̂	4̂	♯4̂	5̂	♭7̂	1̂

3. Exercise 1 appears in concert pitch. Transpose the melody up a M2 for B♭ trumpet. Write the appropriate clef and key signature, and include all necessary accidentals.

4. Refer to exercise 1 again to transpose the melody up a M6 for E♭ alto saxophone. Write the appropriate clef and key signature, and include all necessary accidentals.

5. Which is the texture during the second chorus? Select one.

monophony (single-line melody)

melody and accompaniment (single line over an accompaniment)

chordal homophony (multiple parts moving in the same rhythm)

imitative polyphony (call and response)

CHAPTER 33

Popular Song

NAME _____

In this chapter you'll learn to:

• Identify components typical of verse-chorus songs

Verse-Chorus Songs

Many popular songs alternate between verse and chorus and may include other optional items, shown in parentheses. A hook is the most memorable part of a song, usually a catchy motive-lyric combination.

(Intro)	Establishes the song's vibe
Verse	Tells the story of a song
(Prechorus)	Builds toward the chorus
Chorus	Encapsulates the song's sentiment
(Postchorus)	Chorus extension that leads to a new verse
(Bridge)	Contrast to both verse and chorus
(Outro)	Song's codetta

Try it

1. Listen to a rock-ballad progression and complete the exercises.

   (a) The beginning is derived from which sequence?

   descending third   descending fifth   ascending 5–6

   (b) The underlying rhythmic grouping is:

   2 + 3 + 3   3 + 2 + 3   3 + 3 + 2

   (c) Begin with the given items and notate the remaining bass pitches. In the blanks, write the lead-sheet chord symbols.

Chords: ____   ____   ____   ____   ____   ____   ____

2. Listen to a looped Latin-beat chord progression. Beginning with the given items, notate the remaining bass pitches and the lead-sheet chord symbols.

Chords: _____   _____   _____   _____

3. Listen to a folk-song progression. Begin with the given items and notate the remaining bass pitches and all the lead-sheet chord symbols.

Chords: ____   ____   ____   ____   ____   ____   ____   ____

Contextual Listening 33.1

Listen to Billy Joel's song "She's Always a Woman," which appears at his official VEVO webpage. The lyrics appear on numerous online sites.

1. The beat division is: simple compound

2. The opening chord progression is: I–IV–I I–V–I I–vi–I

3. The opening lyric features which rhythmic device?

    anacrusis hemiola two-against-three (2:3)

4. (a) As you listen to the opening lyric, sketch the beat grouping. What is unusual about it?

    (b) How does the beat grouping paint the text?

5. What changes in instrumentation distinguish verse 2 from verse 1?

6. This work is a "list song" that describes the singer's beloved. What concept unifies the singer's list?

7. Listen to a sequence that begins with the given items (CL 33.1a).

   (a) Capture the remaining pitches of the outer voices.

   (b) Above the treble staff, write lead-sheet chords and the outer-voice intervals (LIP).

   (c) Beneath the bass staff, write the remaining Roman numerals and figures (if needed). Show tonicization using slash, bracket, or colon notation.

Chords: ____ ____   ____ ____   ____ ____   ____

   LIP: ____ ____   ____ ____   ____ ____   ____

E♭ RNs: vi   ____   ____   ____   ____   ____   ____

8. Describe how the song's sequence differs from that in exercise 7.

9. Listen to a second sequence that begins with the given items (CL 33.1b)

   (a) Capture the remaining pitches of the outer voices.

   (b) Above the treble staff, write lead-sheet chords and the outer-voice intervals (LIP).

   (c) Beneath the bass staff, provide a Roman numeral analysis.

Chords: ____ ____   ____ ____   ____ ____   ____

   LIP: ____ ____   ____ ____   ____ ____   ____

B♭ (V) RNs: iv   ____   ____ ____   ____ ____   ____

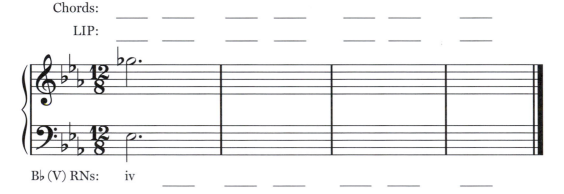

10. Complete the sentence to describe sequence 2.

In the dominant key, _____ –chord units _____ by _____

                     how many?   descend or ascend?   interval?

in _____ reps with a ____ – ____ LIP to create a _____ .

    number?   intervals between S and B?   sequence name?

11. Describe how the end of the chorus paints the text.

12. Often, lyrical ambiguities invite listeners to identify with the song. This song celebrates the composer's then-spouse and business manager. As a manager, she was a shrewd businessperson, but with the composer, a loving partner. How does knowing this change how you relate to the lyrics?

Contextual Listening 33.2

Listen to an indie rock song (CL 33.2) and complete the exercises.

1. The initial chord is: A   C♯m   E7   F♯m7

2. Behind verse 1, the accompanying rhythm is: _____

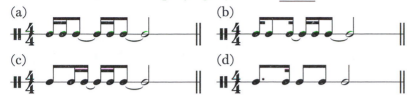

3. Behind verse 1, the guitar melody descends using which pattern?

   chromatic scale   natural minor   major scale   pentatonic scale

4. To which part of the song do the lyrics "You feel yourself slipping away . . ." belong?

   verse   prechorus   chorus   bridge

The following exercises refer only to the chorus.

5. Beginning with the given items, capture the melodic rhythm and pitches. Focus only on the first half of the chorus.

   (a) In the single-line staff, notate the melodic rhythm. Keep in mind that lead sheets often simplify the rhythm, which allows performers freedom to interpret the song. Beneath each note, write its syllable or number.

   (b) In the treble staff, notate the melodic pitches and rhythm. Refer to (a).

Pitches: *m* (3̂)

6. The chorus begins with which chords?

   A–C♯7–D   A–Dmaj7–Bm   A–E7–F♯m   A–F♯m7–G

7. During the chorus lyric "sleeping tonight," the $^6_4$ chord type is:

   passing   cadential   neighboring

8. Following the second chorus (2:21) is a/an:

   verse   prechorus   bridge   outro

9. During the segment identified in exercise 8, the meter signature is: $\frac{3}{8}$ $\frac{6}{8}$ $\frac{5}{8}$ $\frac{7}{8}$

10. The song ends with which texture?

   monophony   homophony   imitative polyphony   non-imitative polyphony

Contextual Listening 33.3

Listen to a contemporary folk-rock song (CL 33.3) and complete the exercises.

1. How does the music paint the word "broken"?

2. Begin with the given items and capture the initial melodic rhythm and pitches.

   (a) In the single-line staff, notate the melodic rhythm. Beneath each pitch write its syllable or number.

   (b) In the treble staff, notate the rhythm and pitches of the melody. Refer to (a).

   (c) Above the treble staff, notate the lead-sheet chord symbols. "NC" indicates "no chord." Listen especially to the bass and chord quality.

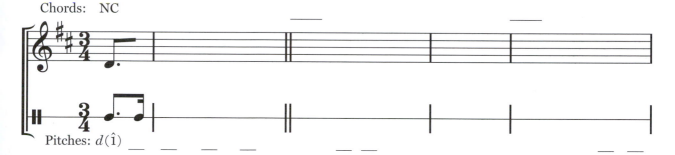

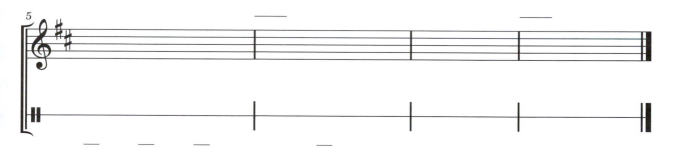

3. Each chorus begins with which four-pitch pattern?

   d–m–d–r   *d–f–r–m*   *d–s–r–f*   *d–l–m–s*
   $\hat{1}$–$\hat{3}$–$\hat{1}$–$\hat{2}$ $\hat{1}$–$\hat{4}$–$\hat{2}$–$\hat{3}$ $\hat{1}$–$\hat{5}$–$\hat{2}$–$\hat{4}$ $\hat{1}$–$\hat{6}$–$\hat{3}$–$\hat{5}$

4. The chorus features which rhythmic device?

   2:3 rhythm   3:4 rhythm   rhythmic diminution   rhythmic augmentation

5. How do you interpret the lyrics as a story?

6. The lyrics were originally written about a friend's loss but came to reflect the agony of withdrawal from the prescribed use of topical steroid medication. How does knowing this change the way you understand the lyrics?

7. In the space provided, diagram the formal segments of the entire song.

The Twentieth Century and Beyond

PART IV

CHAPTER 34

Tetrachords, Pentatonic Scales, and Modes

NAME _____

In this chapter you'll learn to:

- Identify major, minor, Phrygian, harmonic, and whole-tone tetrachords in the context of twentieth-century literature
- Notate melodies based on the major pentatonic scale, the minor pentatonic scale, and modes

Try it

1. **Tetrachords**: Look at the whole- and half-step construction of the five tetrachords. Then, listen to short melodies. In the blank for each exercise, write the name of the tetrachord the melody is based on.

Major	Minor	Phrygian	Harmonic	Whole-Tone
W–W–H	W–H–W	H–W–W	H–³⁄₂–H	W–W–W

(a) _____

(b) _____

(c) _____

(d) _____

(e) _____

2. **Major and minor pentatonic scales**: Look at the construction of the two pentatonic scales. Then, listen to short melodies that begin on the tonic pitch. In the blank for each exercise, write the name of the pentatonic scale the melody is based on.

Major Pentatonic   **Minor Pentatonic**

do	re	mi	sol	la	do	do	me	fa	sol	te	do
$\hat{1}$	$\hat{2}$	$\hat{3}$	$\hat{5}$	$\hat{6}$	$\hat{1}$	$\hat{1}$	$\flat\hat{3}$	$\hat{4}$	$\hat{5}$	$\flat\hat{7}$	$\hat{1}$

(a) _____

(b) _____

(c) _____

3. **Modes**: Study the upper and lower tetrachord construction of the six modes. Then, listen to short melodies. In the blanks for each exercise, write the mode the melody is based on.

Ionian	Dorian	Phrygian	Lydian	Mixolydian	Aeolian
major	minor	Phrygian	whole-tone	major	minor
+	+	+	+	+	+
major	minor	Phrygian	major	minor	Phrygian

(a) _____

(b) _____

(c) _____

(d) _____

(e) _____

(f) _____

Contextual Listening 34.1

In exercises 1–3, a two-beat count-off precedes a short melody.

1. (a) Circle the correct meter type: simple   compound

   (b) The final interval is: m3   M3   P4   P5

   (c) Pitches 1–4 create which tetrachord?

      major   minor   Phrygian   harmonic

   (d) The last four pitches create which tetrachord?

      major   minor   Phrygian   harmonic

   (e) Which is the scale or mode of the melody?

      major pentatonic   minor pentatonic   Dorian   Mixolydian

2. (a) Circle the correct meter type: simple   compound

   (b) Pitches 1–4 create which tetrachord?

      major   minor   Phrygian   harmonic

   (c) The last four pitches create which tetrachord?

      major   minor   Phrygian   harmonic

   (d) Which is the scale or mode of the melody?

      major pentatonic   minor pentatonic   Dorian   Mixolydian

3. (a) Circle the correct meter type: simple   compound

   (b) The only skip in the melody is a: m3   M3   P4   P5

   (c) Which is the scale or mode of the melody?

      major pentatonic   minor pentatonic   Dorian   Mixolydian

Now listen to the beginning of a piano work (CL 34.1) and complete the following exercises.

4. Circle the correct meter type: simple   compound

5. The first melodic skip creates the interval: m3   M3   P4   P5

6. Melodic pitches 1–7 create which tetrachord?

   major   minor   Phrygian   harmonic

7. The last four melodic pitches create which tetrachord?

   major   minor   Phrygian   harmonic

8. Which is the scale or mode of the melody?

   major pentatonic   minor pentatonic   Dorian   Mixolydian

9. Begin with the given items and capture the melodic rhythm and pitches.

   (a) In the single-line staff, notate the melodic rhythm. Beneath each pitch, write its syllable or number.

   (b) In the bass staff, notate the melodic pitches and rhythm. Refer to (a). The melody is tripled; notate it only in the middle octave.

Pitches: $d(\hat{1})$

Contextual Listening 34.2

In exercises 1–3, a two-beat count-off precedes a short melody that begins on the tonic pitch.

1. (a) Circle the correct meter type: simple   compound

    (b) Pitches 1–4 create which tetrachord?

        major   minor   Phrygian   harmonic

    (c) Which is the scale or mode of the melody?

        major pentatonic   major scale   Dorian   Mixolydian

2. (a) Circle the correct meter type: simple   compound

    (b) Pitches 1–4 create which tetrachord?

        major   minor   Phrygian   harmonic

    (c) Which is the scale or mode of the melody?

        major pentatonic   major scale   Dorian   Mixolydian

3. (a) Circle the correct meter type: simple   compound

    (b) If pitch 1's value is a quarter, which is the meter signature? $\frac{4}{4}$ $\frac{3}{4}$ $\frac{2}{4}$

    (c) The first melodic skip forms which interval? m3   M3   P4   P5

    (d) The final two pitches form which interval? m3   M3   P4   P5

    (e) Which is the scale or mode of the melody?

        major pentatonic   major scale   Dorian   Mixolydian

Now listen to an excerpt from an orchestral suite (CL 34.2) and complete the remaining exercises.

4. Circle the correct meter type: simple   compound

5. The first melodic skip forms which interval: m3   M3   P4   P5

6. Pitches 1–6 belong to which tetrachord?

    major   minor   Phrygian   harmonic

7. The last five pitches belong to which tetrachord?

    major   minor   Phrygian   harmonic

8. Which is the scale or mode of the melody?

    major pentatonic   minor pentatonic   Dorian   Mixolydian

9. Begin with the given items and capture the melodic rhythm and pitches.

   (a) In the single-line staff, notate the melodic rhythm. Beneath each pitch, write its syllable or number.

   (b) In the treble staff, notate the melodic pitches and rhythm. Refer to (a).

Pitches: $d(\hat{1})$ ___ ___ ___ ___ ___ ___ ___

Contextual Listening 34.3

In exercises 1–4, a two-beat count-off precedes a short melody.

1. (a) Circle the correct meter type: simple   compound

   (b) The opening interval is: m3   M3   P4   P5

   (c) All melodic pitches complete which scale or mode?
       major pentatonic   minor pentatonic   Dorian   Mixolydian

2. (a) Circle the correct meter type: simple   compound

   (b) All melodic pitches complete which scale or mode?
       major pentatonic   minor pentatonic   Dorian   Mixolydian

3. (a) Circle the correct meter type: simple   compound

   (b) All melodic pitches complete which scale or mode?
       major pentatonic   minor pentatonic   Dorian   Mixolydian

4. (a) Circle the correct meter type: simple   compound

   (b) All melodic pitches complete which scale or mode?
       major pentatonic   minor pentatonic   Dorian   Mixolydian

Now listen to a melody from an Impressionist piano work (CL 34.3) and complete the remaining exercises.

5. Circle the correct meter type: simple   compound

6. Which best represents the meter signature? $\frac{2}{4}$ $\frac{3}{4}$ $\frac{6}{8}$ $\frac{9}{8}$

7. At the beginning, the melodic pitches complete which scale or mode?
       major pentatonic   minor pentatonic   Dorian   Mixolydian

8. Begin with the given items and capture the melodic rhythm and pitches.

   (a) In the single-line staff, notate the melodic rhythm. Beneath each pitch, write its syllable or number.

   (b) In the bass staff, notate the melodic rhythm and pitches. Refer to (a). To determine the last melodic pitch, follow the next-to-last pitch's tendency to resolve.

Pitches: $d(\hat{1})$ __   __ __ __ __ __ __

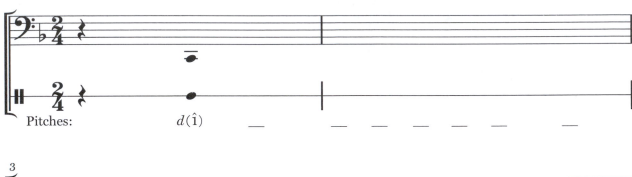

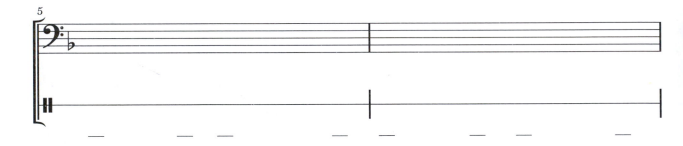

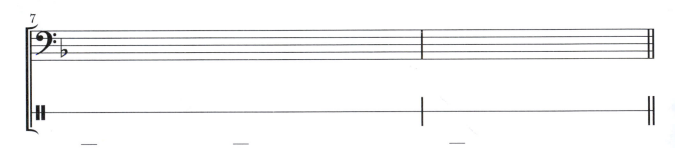

CHAPTER 35

Asymmetric Meter, Changing Meter, and Polymeter

NAME _____

In this chapter you'll learn to:

- Identify asymmetric and changing meter in both traditional and popular music
- Identify polymeter

Asymmetric and Changing Meter

Much new music emphasizes asymmetric and changing meters, but as we have seen, these rhythmic practices have precedents in traditional music.

Try it 1

1. Listen to four complete measures of a traditional melody. Write the meter signature. Then, begin with the given items and notate the melody.

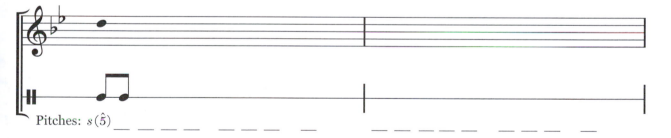

Pitches: $s(\hat{5})$ __ __ __ __ __ __ __ __ __ __ __ __

2. Listen to seven complete measures of a traditional song. Write the meter signature. Then, begin with the given items and notate only measures 1–2 of the melody.

Pitches: *s* ($\hat{5}$) _ _ _ _ _ _   _ _ _ _ _ _

In exercises 3–4, begin with the given items and notate the remaining rhythm and pitches. Include the meter signature(s). Beam simple divisions of beats in twos and compound divisions of beats in threes.

3. Each melody consists of two complete measures of asymmetric meter.

(a)

(b)

(c)

(d)

(e)

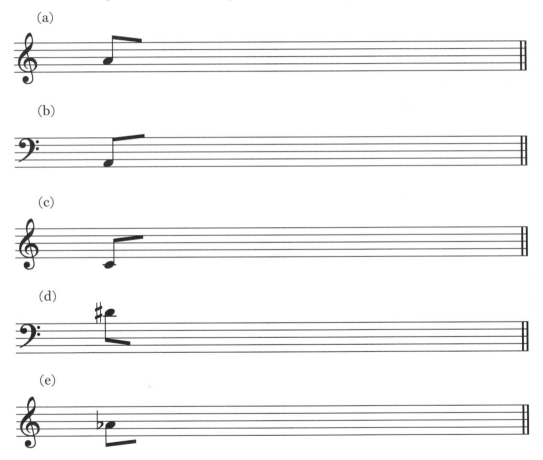

4. Each melody consists of two complete measures of changing meter.

(a)

(b)

(c)

(d)

(e)

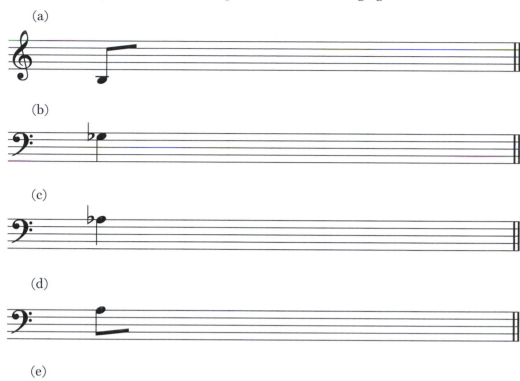

Contextual Listening 35.1

Exercises 1–4 are based on Paul Simon's "Have a Good Time," which appears on his official website.

The first two exercises refer only to the music of the verse (0:08).

1. (a) Assume the beat unit to be a quarter note. In which meter signatures might the music be notated?

   (b) Which choice do you prefer and why?

2. Focus on the bass and chord quality. Chords 1–4 are:

   B♭–Cm7–B♭–F7   B♭–E♭–Cm7–F7   B♭7–E♭7–B♭7–F7   B♭7–E♭7–F7–B♭7

The next exercises refer to the chorus, which begins with the song's title (0:40).

3. The meter signature of the chorus is: $\frac{3}{4}$ $\frac{4}{4}$ $\frac{5}{4}$ $\frac{7}{4}$

4. How do meter and lyrics portray the personality of the song's protagonist?

Exercises 5–7 are based on Pink Floyd's "Money," which appears on the band's official website.

5. If the song were notated using a single meter signature, which would it be?

$\frac{3}{4}$ $\frac{4}{4}$ $\frac{5}{4}$ $\frac{7}{4}$

The cash-register noises were recorded on tape, which was looped and played throughout the song. After the cash-register noises, the bass enters.

6. Using the meter signature from exercise 5, notate one measure of the bass rhythm and pitches, which sound one octave lower than notated.

Pitches: $d(\hat{1})$ __ __ __ __ __ __ __

7. How do elements of the song portray an unhealthy relationship with money?

Exercises 8–10 are based on Sting's "Saint Augustine in Hell," which appears on his official website.

8. If the song is notated using a single meter signature, which would it be?

$\frac{5}{4}$ $\frac{7}{4}$ $\frac{9}{4}$ $\frac{11}{4}$

9. Within each measure, how do the beats group (2 + 3, 2 + 3 + 2, 3 + 2 + 2 + 2, etc.)?

10. Diagram the song's structure. For comparison with your peers, include timings.

Polymeter

Polymeter features two or more meters at the same time. A simple example uses the same beat unit, but a different beat grouping.

More sophisticated examples feature different beat units and grouping simultaneously.

Try it 2

This song's lyrics are provocative, but we will focus primarily on the rhythm and meter.

Listen to "5/4" by Gorillaz, which appears on the band's website. The introduction consists of eight complete measures.

1. Assume the initial note value to be an eighth. The opening meter signature is:

   $\frac{3}{8}$ $\frac{4}{8}$ $\frac{5}{8}$ $\frac{7}{8}$

2. Within each measure, how do the beats group (2 + 3, 2 + 3 + 2, 3 + 2 + 2 + 2, etc.)?

3. The intro repeats which four-pitch pattern?

   C–E♭–C–D   C–F–C–E♭   C–G–C–E♭   C–G–C–F

Both singer and drums enter in measure 9.

4. Focus only on the drums. Assume the initial drum value to be a quarter note. The drums group in measures of how many beats?   2   3   5

5. Use the answers to exercises 1, 2, and 4 to notate the rhythm of the guitar and drums on the staves provided. For each instrument, notate a distinct meter signature and bar lines. On the guitar staff, beam eighth notes to show beat grouping.

Guitar

Drums

Contextual Listening 35.2

Listen to the beginning of Maria Schneider's "Hang Gliding," which appears on her official website.

1. Devise several strategies for how the meter might be notated. List the pros and cons for each.

Strategy	Pros	Cons

Listen to System of a Down's "Question!" which appears on SOAD's official website.

2. Listen to the first introduction (0:21) several times until you memorize the solo guitar's recurring pattern. Slow it in your imagination until you can tap the pattern. Devise several strategies for how the meter might be notated. List the pros and cons for each.

Strategy	Pros	Cons

3. Listen to the second introduction (0:37), which features the full ensemble. In what meter(s) might this be notated?

4. Listen to the onset of the verse (0:53). In what meter might it be notated?

5. Lyrics "Are you . . ." (0:59) and "Are you dreaming" (1:07) foreshadow the meter of the chorus. In which meter signature might these segments and the first chorus be notated?

6. The meter of chorus 3 differs from that of chorus 1 and 2. Which is the meter signature of chorus 3?

7. Diagram the structure of the song. Include timings to facilitate discussion with others. In which meter signature(s) might each segment be notated?

8. How does SOAD's Armenian heritage influence the rhythm and meter found in their music?

Contextual Listening 35.3

Before listening to an art song, study a translation of the lyrics.

Translation: Ah, and you, my cool water! Ah, and you, my red little rose!
How can you bloom for me so early? I have no one for whom to pick you!

Exercises 1–3 focus only on the piano introduction.

1. Begin with the given items and notate the introductory piano melody.

   (a) In the single-line staff, notate the rhythm of the two-measure piano melody. Include the meter signature. Beneath each note, write its syllable or number.

   (b) In the treble staff, notate the pitches and rhythm of the piano melody. Refer to (a).

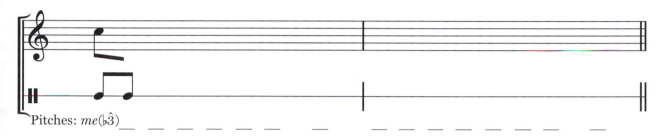

Pitches: *me*(♭3̂) __ __ __ __ __ __ __   __ __ __ __ __ __ __

2. Initially, the piano melody is doubled at which interval?

   third   fifth   sixth   octave

3. Initially, the piano melody and its accompaniment feature which rhythmic relationship?

   2:3   3:2   3:4   4:3

Exercises 4–7 focus on the four-measure vocal melody.

4. Begin with the given items and notate the four-measure vocal melody.

   (a) In the single-line staff, notate the rhythm of the four-measure vocal melody. Include the meter signature. Beneath each note, write its syllable or number.

   (b) In the treble staff, notate the pitches and rhythm of the vocal melody. Refer to (a).

Pitches: $f(\hat{4})$ — — — — — — — — — —

— — — — — — — — — — — —

5. Vocal phrase 1 ends with which $^6_4$ chord type (on "*Wasser*")?

   neighbor (pedal)   cadential   passing   arpeggiated

6. What is the vocal melody's scale?

   ascending melodic   harmonic minor   natural minor   Dorian mode

7. Vocal phrases 1–4 create which structure(s)?

   a phrase group   a parallel double period

   two simple periods   a contrasting double period

NAME _____

Contextual Listening 35.4

Listen to part of a composition for wind instruments and complete the exercises.

The excerpt begins with a seven-measure trumpet theme.

1. Begin with the given items and notate the trumpet theme.

    (a) In the single-line staff, notate the rhythm, including any meter change. Beneath each note, write its syllable or number.

    (b) In the treble staff, notate the pitches and rhythm of the trumpet theme. Refer to (a).

Pitches: $d(\hat{1})$

2. Compared with the theme's second statement, the third statement:

    follows it in canon.   is a melodic inversion.

    is a rhythmic augmentation.   is a rhythmic diminution.

3. How does theme statement 4 develop the theme? (Choose all that apply.)

    The initial pitch intervals are larger.   Only the initial portion is performed.

    It is sequenced down by step.   It is now in compound meter.

4. This composition imitates which earlier period?

    Renaissance   Baroque   Classical   Romantic

CHAPTER 36

PCsets as Motive

NAME _____

In this chapter you'll learn to:

- Identify motivic pcsets and calculate their ic vectors
- Compare equivalent sets for transposition and inversion

PCsets as Motive

Pitch-class sets are among many items that are considered motivic. Segmenting the following melody into trichords can reveal aspects of the melody's internal organization.

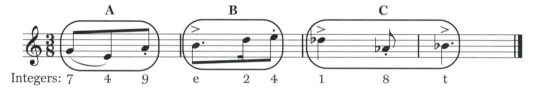

Integers: 7   4   9   e   2   4   1   8   t

1. Place each set's pcs in ascending numerical order.

2. Calculate the interval classes (ics).

   1 or e = ic1   4 or 8 = ic4
   2 or t = ic2   5 or 7 = ic5
   3 or 9 = ic3   6 = ic6

3. Create an ic vector by tallying how many of each ic appear in the set.

A: 479	B: 24e	C: 18t
9 − 7 = 2 ic2 9 − 4 = 5 ic5 7 − 4 = 3 ic3	e − 4 = 7 ic5 e − 2 = 9 ic3 4 − 2 = 2 ic2	t − 8 = 2 ic2 t − 1 = 9 ic3 8 − 1 = 7 ic5
ic123456 [011010]	ic123456 [011010]	ic123456 [011010]

4. Find the normal order {smallest, most compact span} by rotating the three elements XYZ, YZX, and ZXY.

5. Sets with the same ic content are typically transpositions or inversions of one another. Use the normal order to calculate the relationship.

XYZ	A {479}	B 24e	C 18t
YZX	794	4e2	{8t1}
ZXY	947	{e24}	t18

Transposition B = T₇A

B	{e24}	Place the elements of set B in normal order.
− A	{479}	From B, subtract A's elements in normal order. (For 2 − 7, use mod 12: 12 + 2 − 7 = 7)
T =	777	T, the number of semitones of transposition, is revealed by subtracting the elements.

Inversion C = T₅I A

C	{8t1}	Place the elements of set C in *ascending* normal order.
+ A	{974}	Place the elements of set A in *descending* normal order. (For 8 + 9 − 17, use mod 12: 17 − 12 = 5)
T =	555	The index number T is revealed by adding the elements.

Note that when combined, sets A and B complete the E minor pentatonic scale.

Try it

1. Beginning with the given items, notate the remaining pitches. Write the pc integers and letter names. Calculate and write the set's normal order and ic vector.

Set   Notation

Normal order and ic vector

A

Integers: _____ _____ _____

Letters: _____ _____ _____

normal order {____ ____ ____}

ic vector [____ ____ ____ ____ ____ ____]

B

Integers: _____ _____ _____

Letters: _____ _____ _____

normal order {____ ____ ____}

ic vector [____ ____ ____ ____ ____ ____]

C

Integers: _____ _____ _____

Letters: _____ _____ _____

normal order {____ ____ ____}

ic vector [____ ____ ____ ____ ____ ____]

D

Integers: _____ _____ _____

Letters: _____ _____ _____

normal order {____ ____ ____}

ic vector [____ ____ ____ ____ ____ ____]

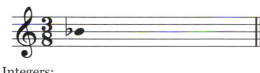

E

normal order {___ ___ ___}

ic vector [___ ___ ___ ___ ___ ___]

Integers: _____ _____ _____

Letters: _____ _____ _____

F

normal order {___ ___ ___}

ic vector [___ ___ ___ ___ ___ ___]

Integers: _____ _____ _____

Letters: _____ _____ _____

G

normal order {___ ___ ___}

ic vector [___ ___ ___ ___ ___ ___]

Integers: _____ _____ _____

Letters: _____ _____ _____

H

normal order {___ ___ ___}

ic vector [___ ___ ___ ___ ___ ___]

Integers: _____ _____ _____

Letters: _____ _____ _____

2. Compare the specified sets from exercise 1. Complete the one equation that shows their relationship. Show the steps you took to determine the relationship.

(a) B = T___ A *or* B = T___ I A

(b) D = T___ C *or* D = T___ I C

(c) F = T___ E *or* F = T___ I

(d) H = T___ G *or* H = T___ I G

Contextual Listening 36.1

Thinking in terms of pcsets and scales can provide insight into any musical genre. Listen to Stevie Wonder's "Higher Ground," which can be found on the composer's official webpage.

Focus first on the opening bass line, played on a keyboard called a clavinet.

1. Begin with the given items and notate the bass-line rhythm and pitches.

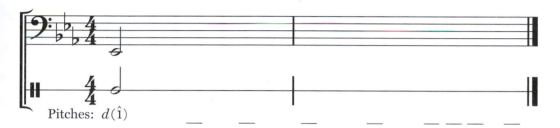

Pitches: $d(\hat{1})$ ___ ___ ___ ___ ___ ___ ___

2. (a) Set A is bass pitches 1–3. Find and write the normal order of set A. _____

   (b) Calculate the interval classes between set A's pitches. Which is set A's ic vector?

   [020100]   [011010]   [010101]   [010020]

3. (a) Set B is the opening vocal motive (syllables 1–6). Compare set B with set A. Describe how the two sets are related.

   (b) Write the equation to show their relationship. _____

4. The melodic pitches derive from which of these collections?

   E♭ major scale   E♭ ascending melodic minor scale

   E♭ minor pentatonic   E♭ Lydian mode

5. Describe how set A relates to the answer to exercise 4.

6. Diagram the song's structure. Include timings to facilitate group discussion.

7. Describe how this funk song might be understood as an adaptation or derivation of the blues.

8. How do the music and lyrics paint the song's subject of reincarnation?

9. Wonder composed and recorded this song by playing and singing every part himself. How is this similar to what Romantic-era composers were able to? How is it different?

Contextual Listening 36.2

Listen to the beginning of an *a cappella* choral work and complete the exercises.

1. Begin with the given items and capture the soprano and bass parts.

    (a) In the single-line staves, notate the rhythm. Beneath each note, write its pc integer and letter name.

    (b) In the grand staves, notate the pitches and rhythm of the soprano and bass. Refer to (a).

2. Set A comprises soprano pitches 1–9. Find and notate set A's normal order.

3. Initially, the voices double at which interval?

Diatonic:	M3	P4	P5	M6
Semitones:	4	5	7	8

4. The women sing "and the bridesmaids all wore" to which parallel harmonic intervals?

    all thirds   3-3-3-6-6-6   6-6-6-3-3-3   all sixths

5. The men begin singing "bridesmaids all wore" to which chord quality?

    major triad   minor triad   MM7   mm7

6. When the men sing "green, green," the chord qualities alternate between:

    minor triad and Mm7   minor triad and mm7

    major triad and MM7   major triad and mm7

7. (a) Set B is the final three unique bass pitches. Find and notate the normal order of B.

    (b) Compare B with A. Write the equation to show their relationship. Show the steps you took to determine the relationship.

8. (a) From the men's entrance until the end, all choral pitches belong to which mode?

    Dorian   Phrygian   Lydian   Mixolydian

    (b) If the answer to 8(a) were different, would the pcset class differ? Why or why not?

Contextual Listening 36.3

Listen to the beginning of a piano piece and complete the exercises.

1. Begin with the given items and capture the melodic rhythm and pitches.

   (a) In the single-line staff, notate the melodic rhythm. Beneath each pitch, write its pitch-class integer number and letter name.

   (b) In the treble staff, notate the melodic pitches and rhythm. Refer to (a). Since the melody is doubled at the octave, notate only the higher pitches.

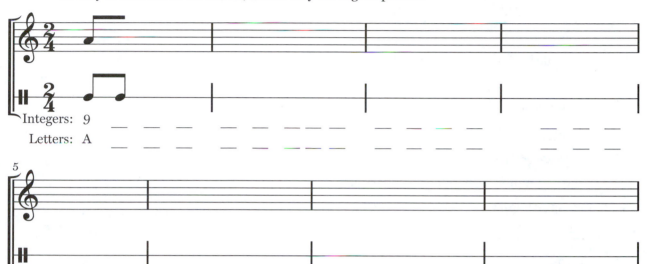

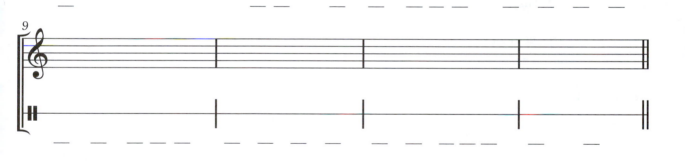

2. Consider set A to be melodic pitches 1–6. Find and write set A's normal order.

   _____

3. Consider set B to be melodic pitches 10–13 (all of measure 3).
   Find and write set B's normal order. _____

Focus only on the first half of the excerpt to discover the collection to which all the pitches belong.

4. (a) Notate the letter name of each unique pitch class in the melody. Include the pcs of the bass pitches in the punctuating chord.

_____ _____ _____ _____ _____ _____ _____

(b) Rearrange these pcs into a scale that ascends from B3.

5. (a) The scale begins with which traditional tetrachord?

major   minor   harmonic   Phrygian

(b) Call tetrachord 1 set E. Find and write the normal order of set E.

_____

6. (a) The scale ends with which traditional tetrachord?

major   minor   harmonic   Phrygian

(b) Call tetrachord 2 set F. Find and write the normal order of set F.

_____

Focus on the final four bass pitches. Call these pitch classes set C.

7. Write the letter names of set C.   _____ _____ _____ _____

8. As an *ordered* segment, set C implies which traditional cadence?

PAC   IAC   HC   PHC

9. Now consider set C to be an *unordered* pcset. Find and notate its normal order.

_____

10. Compare set C with set B. Write the equation to show their relationship, showing the steps you took to determine the relationship.

CHAPTER 37

Set Classes

NAME _____

In this chapter you'll learn to:

- Identify set classes, prime form, modes of limited transposition, and complements of pcsets

Set Classes, Prime Form, Modes of Limited Transposition, and Complementation

A set class includes all transpositions and inversions of a pcset. Set classes are represented by a prime form, a normal-order set that begins on pc0. Another naming method uses a Forte set-class number. SC 3-4, for example, is trichord 4 on Allen Forte's set list. The appendix includes a set-class table.

Some collections map onto themselves. Olivier Messiaen identified seven of these as "modes of limited transposition," which include the whole-tone and octatonic scales.

Two sets that combine to produce twelve distinct pcs without duplication (i.e., the twelve-tone chromatic, aggregate, or universal set) are literal complements. Complementary sets may also be transposed or inverted.

Try it

Beginning with the given items, notate the remaining pitches. Write all pc integers. Then, calculate and write each set's normal order, prime form, and Forte SC number.

1. (a) Set A comprises pcs 1–6 and set B pcs 7–12.

Integers: __ __ __ __ __ __   __ __ __ __ __ __

Set A (pcs 1–6)

normal order { _____ }

prime form   [_____]

Forte SC   6-_____

Set B (pcs 7–12)

normal order { _____ }

prime form   [_____]

Forte SC   6-_____

(b) Write an equation that shows how sets B and A are related. Show the steps you took to determine the relationship. There are multiple correct possibilities.

(c) In what other ways can the combination of sets A and B be described?

2. (a) Set C comprises pcs 1–4, D pcs 5–8, E pcs 1–8, and F pcs 9–12.

Integers: __ __ __ __ __ __ __ __ __ __ __ __

Set C (pcs 1–4)
normal order { _____ }
prime form   [_____]
Forte SC   4– _____

Set D (pcs 5–8)
normal order { _____ }
prime form   [_____]
Forte SC   4– _____

Set E (pcs 1–8)
normal order { _____ }
prime form   { _____ }
Forte SC   8– _____

Set F (pcs 9–12)
normal order { _____ }
prime form   [_____]
Forte SC   4– _____

(b) Write an equation that shows how sets D and C are related. Show the steps you took to determine the relationship. There are two correct possibilities.

(c) The pcs of set E complete which scale?

octatonic   whole-tone   Lydian   chromatic

(d) How are sets E and F related?

Contextual Listening 37.1

Read the translation before listening to the beginning of an art song.

Translation: Twilight floats above the night and valley.

1. Which notation represents the opening piano pitches?

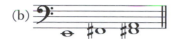

(a)   (b)

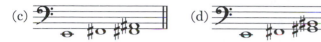
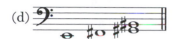

(c)   (d)

2. Begin with the given items and capture the vocal melody.

   (a) In the single-line staff, notate the vocal rhythm. Beneath each note, write its pc integer and letter name. Enharmonic equivalents are permissible.

   (b) In the treble staff, notate the pitches and rhythm of the vocal melody. Refer to (a).

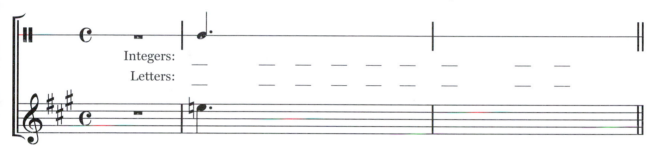

Integers: ___   ___ ___ ___ ___ ___ ___   ___ ___
Letters: ___   ___ ___ ___ ___ ___ ___   ___ ___

Exercises 3–9 focus on set A, which consists of vocal pitches 1–6.

3. Vocal pitches 1–3 and 4–6 complete triads of which quality?

   major   minor   diminished   augmented

4. Vocal pitches 1–6 complete which scale?

   major   octatonic   whole-tone   Lydian

5. (a) Vocal pitches 1–6 belong to a set class represented by which prime form?

   [013579]   [02468t]   [013467]

   (b) Locate the prime form in the set-class table, which appears in the appendix.
       Set A's Forte set-class number is 6-_____.

6. Write the normal order of set A. {_____}

7. Write the literal complement of set A. {_____}

8. Together set A and its literal complement complete which pattern?

   aggregate   chromatic   universal set   all of these answers

9. Why is set A called a "mode of limited transposition"?

10. How does the music paint the text?

Contextual Listening 37.2

Listen to the beginning of a piece for viola and piano and complete the exercises.

1. Begin with the given items and capture only the first half of the viola melody.

   (a) In the single-line staff, notate the melodic rhythm. Beneath each note, write its pc integer and letter name.

   (b) In the five-line staff, draw an appropriate clef. Beginning with the pitch A4, notate the viola's pitches and rhythm. Refer to (a).

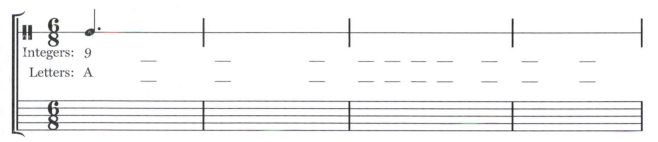

2. In measures 1–4, all melodic and harmonic pitches belong to which scale?

   pentatonic   octatonic   whole-tone   Phrygian

3. Transpose exercise 1 up a M6 for alto saxophone. Write the appropriate clef and accidentals.

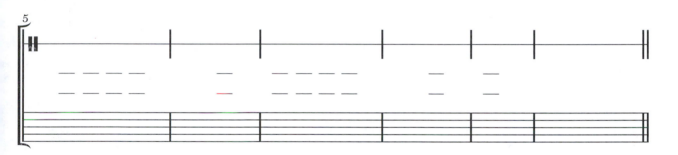

4. (a) In measure 1, notate set A, an ordered segment comprising viola pitches 1–4. Beneath each pitch, write its pc integer.

   (b) In measure 2, rearrange set A from lowest-numbered pc to the highest.

   A ordered segment   A ascending unordered pcset

Integers: __   __   __   __   __   __   __   __

5. (a) Find the pc intervals between each pc in set A and arrange them as an ic vector.

The ic vector of set A is [_____].

(b) What is remarkable about this tetrachord's interval content?

6. (a) Play and notate the four rotations of unordered pcset A.

(b) Write set A's normal order. { _____ }

7. During measures 9–10, the viola sustains a cadential pitch over:

a major triad   an augmented triad

a major seventh chord   a minor seventh chord

After its cadential pitch, the viola begins a new phrase. Exercises 8–10 focus on the beginning of the new phrase.

8. (a) In measure 1, notate set B, an ordered segment comprising viola pitches 1–4. Beneath each pitch, write its pc integer.

(b) In measure 2, rearrange set B from lowest-numbered pc to the highest.

B ordered segment   **B** ascending unordered pcset

Integers: __   __   __   __   __   __   __   __

9. (a) Find the pc intervals between each pc in set B and arrange them as an ic vector.

The ic vector of set B is [_____].

(b) What is remarkable about this tetrachord's interval content?

10. (a) Play and notate the four rotations of unordered pcset B.

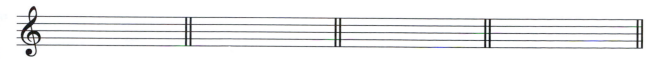

    (b) Write set B's normal order. { _____ }

11. Compare set B with set A. Complete the equation that shows their relationship. Show how you determined their relationship.

    B = t____ A *or* B = t____ I A

12. (a) Calculate set A's prime form.

    A { _____ } ← Write the normal order of set A.

    – _____ ← Subtract its first element from every element . . .

    [_____] ← . . . to reveal the prime form of the set class to which A belongs.

    (b) Look in the appendix to find the set-class table. In the list, locate the prime form. Write its Forte set-class number: 4–Z_____

    (c) Check the table to see whether the ic vector matches your previous answers.

    (d) Find the other tetrachord with a "Z" in its Forte set-class name. 4–Z_____
What is notable about its ic vector?

Contextual Listening 37.3

Listen to the beginning of a traditional Japanese folk song and complete the exercises.

1. Begin with the given items and capture the melody.

   (a) In the single-line staff, notate the melodic rhythm. Beneath each note, write its syllable or scale-degree number and its pc integer.

   (b) In the treble staff, notate the pitches and rhythm of the melody. Refer to (a).

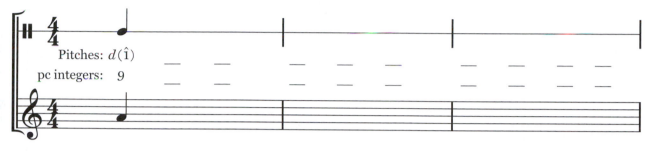

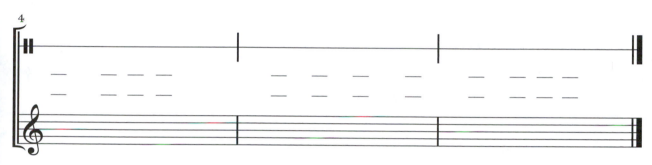

Set A comprises all melodic pitches. Determine A's normal order, prime form, and Forte set-class number.

2. (a) In measure 1, begin with A's lowest pc integer and write the set in ascending order.

   (b) In measures 2–5, write A's remaining rotations.

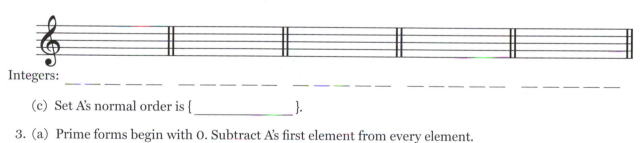

Integers: ___ ___ ___ ___   ___ ___ ___ ___   ___ ___ ___ ___   ___ ___ ___ ___

   (c) Set A's normal order is { _____ }.

3. (a) Prime forms begin with 0. Subtract A's first element from every element.

   { _____ }

   (b) Why doesn't this transposition of A appear in the list of prime forms?

4. (a) Invert set A. Call A's highest pitch 0 and count down in semitones.

   { _____ }

   (b) What is set A's Forte SC number? 5-_____

Now, listen to *"Aynih"* ("Your Eye"), which is found on Aster Aweke's official website. The lyrics express the singer's infatuation with her beloved, who is both idealized and distant.

The following exercises focus on the instrumental melody found at 1:28–1:45.

5. Begin with the given items and capture the instrumental melody.

   (a) In the single-line staff, write the melodic rhythm. Beneath each note, write its syllable or scale-degree number and its pc integer.

   (b) In the treble staff, write the pitches and rhythm of the instrumental melody. Refer to (a).

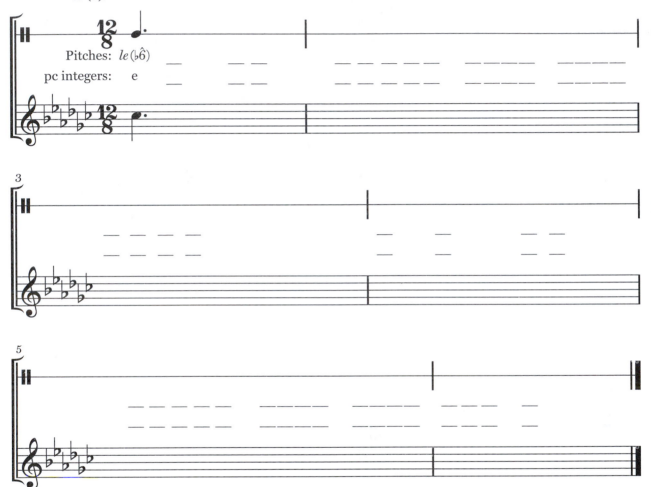

Set B comprises the instrumental melodic pitches. Find set B's normal order, prime form, and Forte set-class number.

6. (a) In measure 1, begin with B's lowest pc integer and write the set in ascending order.

   (b) In measures 2–5, write B's remaining rotations.

   Integers: ___ ___ ___ ___   ___ ___ ___ ___   ___ ___ ___ ___   ___ ___ ___ ___   ___ ___ ___ ___

   (c) Set B's normal order is { _____ }.

7. (a) Prime forms begin with 0. Subtract B's first element from every element.

   { _____ }

   (b) Why doesn't this transposition of B appear in the list of prime forms?

8. (a) Invert set B. Call B's highest pitch 0 and count down in semitones.

   { _____ }

(b) What is set B's Forte SC number? 5-_____

9. Compare set B with set A. Complete the one equation that shows their relationship. Show the steps you took to determine the relationship.

   B = t___ A *or* B = t___ I A

Ordered Segments and Serialism

CHAPTER 38

NAME _____

In this chapter you'll learn to:

- Identify ordered segments using ordered pitch intervals and pc interval sequences
- Identify and compare twelve-tone row forms

Ordered Segments and Ordered Pitch Intervals

Some chromatic themes are ordered successions with distinct rhythms and contour. One way to identify them uses ordered pitch intervals, which record the direction (+ for up and – for down) and number of semitones between adjacent pitches.

To identify relationships between ordered segments, use these strategies.

Compared with P, if the ordered pitch intervals are . . .	then the segment's form is . . .
identical	P
the same, but have opposite signs	I
identical, but in reverse order	RI
in reverse order *and* have opposite signs	R

For example, an identical succession with opposite signs means set I is an inversion of set P.

Arnold Schoenberg, *Variations for Orchestra*, Op. 31, beginning of tone row

Set R's succession is reversed and the signs are opposite, so R is a retrograde of P.
Set RI's succession is reversed, meaning RI is the retrograde of P's inversion.

419

Try it 1

1. Listen to ordered segment P. Begin with the given items and notate the remaining pitches. Write pc integers and the ordered pitch intervals.

   Form: P

   pcs: ___ ___ ___

   ordered pitch intervals: ___ ___

2. Listen to ordered segment P. Each subsequent segment relates to P. Notate the pitches, pcs, and ordered pitch intervals. Use the strategies you just learned to identify the segment's form as I, R, or RI.

   (a) Form: ____

   pcs: ___ ___ ___

   ordered pitch intervals: ___ ___

   (b) Form: ____

   pcs: ___ ___ ___

   ordered pitch intervals: ___ ___

   (c) Form: ____

   pcs: ___ ___ ___

   ordered pitch intervals: ___ ___

   (d) Form: ____

   pcs: ___ ___ ___

   ordered pitch intervals: ___ ___

Contextual Listening 38.1

Listen to an entire piano work and complete the exercises.

Exercises 1–4 focus only on the theme, which comprises pitches 1–10 of the higher part. The theme consists of two segments.

1. (a) Begin with the given items and notate the pitches and rhythm of the theme

   (b) Beneath each note, write its pc integer.

   (c) Above the staff, draw two brackets labeled segment 1 (pcs 1–4) and segment 2 (pcs 5–10). Other exercises will refer to these segments.

   (d) Write the ordered pitch interval numbers. Between each pair of pcs, write + for up and – for down and the interval in semitones (e.g., < +1 –4, etc. >). Pitch intervals help you identify thematic changes like inversion.

pc integers: ___ __ __ __ __   __ __ __ __ __

intervals: < __   __ __ __   __   __ __ __   __ >

2. Consider segment 1 to be an unordered pcset. Find its normal order and prime form. Then, look up its Forte SC number in the appendix.

   normal order { _____ } prime form [_____] Forte SC 4-_____

3. (a) Notate every distinct trichord subset of segment 1.

   (b) Find the prime form and Forte SC for these subsets.

      prime form [_____] Forte SC 3-_____

4. Consider segment 2 to be an unordered pcset. Find its normal order and prime form. Then, look up its Forte SC number in the appendix.

   normal order { _____ } prime form [_____] Forte SC 4-_____

Contextual Listening 38.2

Contextual Listening 38.1 focused on the first statement of the theme from a piano piece. Listen to the entire work again to discover how this theme develops.

Exercises 1–5 compare statements 2–9 of the theme with its first appearance (pitches 1–10 of the higher part).

1. Compared with statement 1 of the theme, which part of statement 2 differs?

   segment 1's pitch   segment 2's pitch

   segment 1's rhythm   segment 2's rhythm

2. Compared with statement 1, statement 3:

   transposes up by tritone   features triplet rhythms

   inverts the melodic contour   augments the rhythm values

3. Compared with statement 1, statements 4–9 employ which motivic development?

   fragmentation   melodic inversion   rhythmic diminution   parallel chords

4. (a) In statements 4–9, the theme descends from the piece's highest pitch, B♭5. Notate only the first pitch of each statement.

   (b) These initial pitches complete which scale?

   pentatonic   whole-tone   harmonic minor   octatonic

5. In the higher part, the final statement of the theme includes which of these?

   inversion   rhythmic augmentation

   segments 1–2 in reverse order   retrograde

Listen to the entire piece again, focusing on the lower part and how it relates to the theme.

6. Compared with the theme, the lower part's first statement is a/an:

   augmentation   diminution   imitation   inversion

7. Compared with the higher part, entrance 2 of the lower part is a/an:

   inversion   imitation   augmentation   fragmentation

8. Entrance 3 of the lower part is a/an:

   imitation   inversion   diminution   fragmentation

Ordered Succession of Pitch Classes and PC Intervals

Tone rows are ordered successions of pitch *classes*. A pc interval (pci) records the smallest positive (clockwise) span between successive pitch classes. Recording and comparing pci sequences allows identification of P (row transpositions), I (row inversions), and the retrogrades of P and I.

To identify relationships between row forms, use these strategies.

Compared with row P, if the pcis are . . .	then the row form is . . .
identical	P
the mod 12 inverse	I
identical, but in reverse order	RI
in reverse order *and* are the mod 12 inverse	R (or RP)

Arnold Schoenberg, *Variations for Orchestra*, Op. 31, entire tone row

P_{10} (row transposition beginning with pc 10)

pcs:	t	4	6	3	5	9	2	1	7	8	e	0
pcis:	6	2	9	2	4	5	e	6	1	3	1	

Compare the pcis of each row form with that of P to see how to apply the strategies.

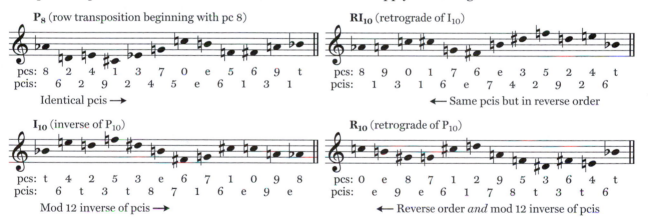

P_8 (row transposition beginning with pc 8)

pcs:	8	2	4	1	3	7	0	e	5	6	9	t
pcis:	6	2	9	2	4	5	e	6	1	3	1	

Identical pcis →

RI_{10} (retrograde of I_{10})

pcs:	8	9	0	1	7	6	e	3	5	2	4	t
pcis:	1	3	1	6	e	7	4	2	9	2	6	

← Same pcis but in reverse order

I_{10} (inverse of P_{10})

pcs:	t	4	2	5	3	e	6	7	1	0	9	8
pcis:	6	t	3	t	8	7	1	6	e	9	e	

Mod 12 inverse of pcis →

R_{10} (retrograde of P_{10})

pcs:	0	e	8	7	1	2	9	5	3	6	4	t
pcis:	e	9	e	6	1	7	8	t	3	t	6	

← Reverse order *and* mod 12 inverse of pcis

Try it 2

1. Listen to just the beginning of row P. Begin with the given items and notate the remaining pitches. Write the pc integers and pitch class intervals (pcis).

Row form: _____

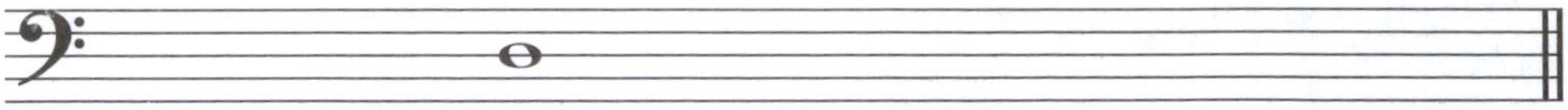

pcs: ___   ___   ___

pcis: ___   ___

2. Listen to the beginning of row P. Each subsequent segment relates to P. Notate the pitches, pcs, and pcis. Use the strategies you just learned to identify the row segment's form as P, I, R, or RI, and include its naming pc, for example, P_2.

(a) Row form: _____

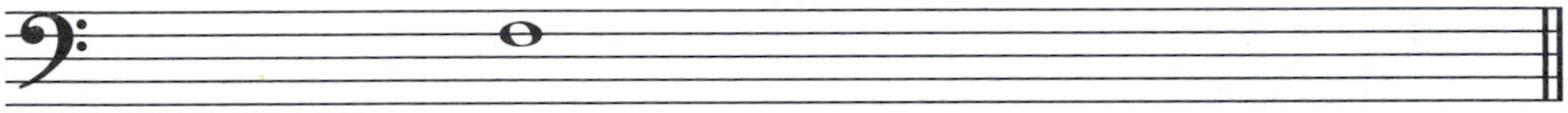

pcs: ___   ___   ___

pcis: ___   ___

(b) Row form: _____

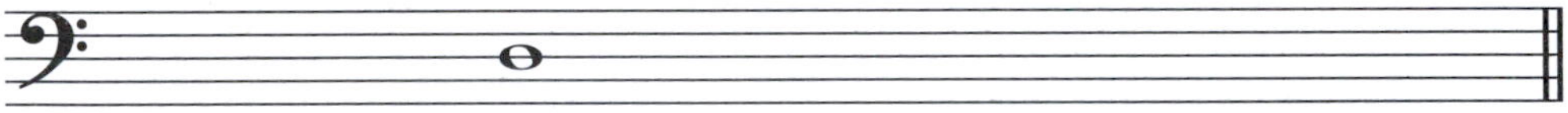

pcs: ___   ___   ___

pcis: ___   ___

(c) Row form: _____

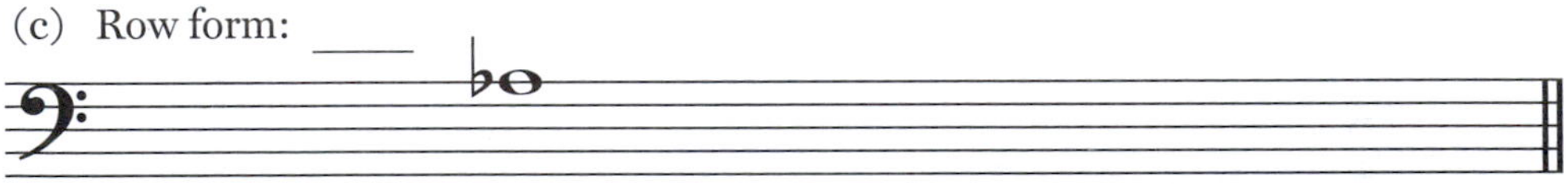

pcs: ___   ___   ___

pcis: ___   ___

(d) Row form: _____

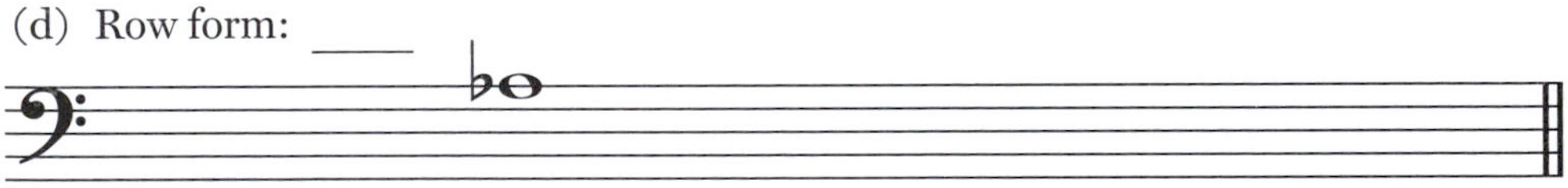

pcs: ___   ___   ___

pcis: ___   ___

Contextual Listening 38.3

Study the poetry before listening to the beginning of a twelve-tone choral work. The excerpt includes only the alto and soprano parts.

The dove descending breaks the air with flame of incandescent terror,
of which the tongues declare the one discharge from sin and error.

1. Begin with the given items and notate the pitches and rhythm of both parts. For an audio hint, listen to a piano reduction (CL 38.3a).

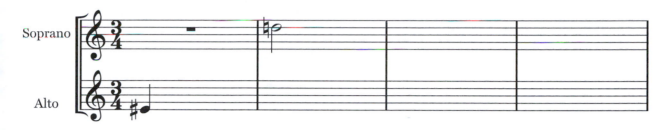

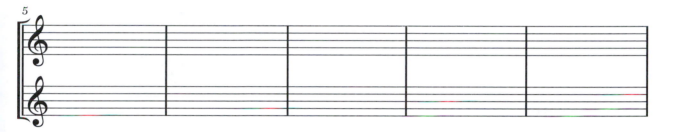

2. Composers choose from P, I, R, and RI row forms. Knowing these possibilities, study your notation and write a paragraph that describes how the composer deploys the row.

Contextual Listening 38.4

Listen again to the work you began in Contextual Listening 38.3. For an audio hint, listen to a piano reduction (CL 38.3a).

1. (a) Begin with E♯4 and notate the alto row, which comprises its first 12 *unique* pitches, sung to the words "The dove descending breaks the air." This row is called P_5.

   (b) Beneath each pitch, write its pc integer.

   (c) Between each adjacent pair of pcs, write the pc interval number (pci). The pci helps you compare this initial statement of the row with other statements.

   (d) Above each pitch, write its row order number, 1–12.

mm. 1–4
order no.: __ __ __ __ __ __ __ __ __ __ __ __

pcs: __ __ __ __ __ __ __ __ __ __ __ __
pcis: __ __ __ __ __ __ __ __ __ __ __

Now, focus on the soprano part at the beginning.

2. (a) Notate the first 12 unique pitches of the soprano, sung to the words, "The dove . . . terror."

   (b) Follow the steps in exercises 1b–d and write the soprano-row pcs, pci, and row numbers.

mm. 2–8
order no.: __ __ __ __ __ __ __ __ __ __ __ __

pcs: __ __ __ __ __ __ __ __ __ __ __ __
pcis: __ __ __ __ __ __ __ __ __ __ __

3. How does the soprano row relate to P_5, the alto's original row?

Exercises 4–5 refer to the music immediately after that analyzed in exercises 2–3.

4. (a) Notate the soprano part's final twelve distinct pitches, sung to "Of which . . . error."

   (b) Follow the steps in exercises 1b–d and write the soprano-row pcs, pci, and row numbers.

mm. 9–14
order no.: ___ ___ ___ ___ ___ ___ ___ ___ ___ ___ ___ ___

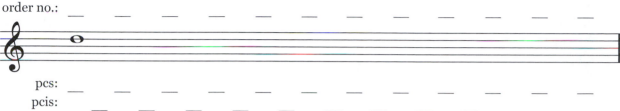

pcs: ___ ___ ___ ___ ___ ___ ___ ___ ___ ___ ___ ___
pcis: ___ ___ ___ ___ ___ ___ ___ ___ ___ ___ ___

5. How does this soprano row relate to P_5, the original row?

Exercises 6–9 focus on the final pitches in the alto part, sung to "Of which . . . error."
Note that there are only eleven unique pitches.

6. (a) Notate the end of the alto part. Include only the unique pitches.

   (b) Follow the steps in exercises 1b–d and write the alto-row pcs, pci, and row numbers.

mm. 9–13
order no.: ___ ___ ___ ___ ___ ___ ___ ___ ___ ___ ___

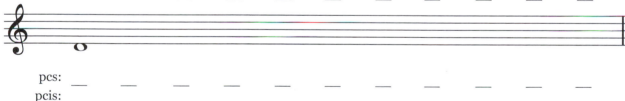

pcs: ___ ___ ___ ___ ___ ___ ___ ___ ___ ___ ___
pcis: ___ ___ ___ ___ ___ ___ ___ ___ ___ ___

7. How does this row relate to P_5, the original row?

8. The music continues beyond this excerpt and the altos sing the next pitch. With which pc would the altos begin their next phrase? Why?

9. Focus on the alto pcs midway through the excerpt. The row begins in the middle of the pitches sung to "air."

   (a) To which row form do they belong?

   (b) Compare your answer with that of exercises 1–5. How are the first two row statements in the alto part linked?

Exercises 10–14 show you how to create and read a 12 × 12 matrix based on the row.

10. Find P_0.

    (a) Copy P_5 here and subtract 5 from each of its elements.

    $P_5 \rightarrow$ 5 __ __ __ __ __ __ __ __ __ __ __ __
    $- $ 5 5 5 5 5 5 5 5 5 5 5 5
    $P_0 \rightarrow$ 0 __ __ __ __ __ __ __ __ __ __ __ __

    (b) Write P_0 from left to right in the top line of the matrix.

11. Write P_0's inversion, I_0, down the matrix's leftmost column.
    Note: Each element of I is the mod 12 inverse of the corresponding element of P_0.

12. Fill in the matrix.

    (a) Consider each pc in the left column to be the first pc of a new row transposition.

    (b) Add that element to every element in P_0, mod 12.

13. Check your work.

    (a) The diagonal from top left to bottom right should contain only zeros.

    (b) Each row and column includes one each of the twelve pc integers. No pc may be duplicated.

14. Read the matrix.

    (a) P forms read from left to right, and R of P (R), from right to left.

    (b) I forms read from top to bottom, and R of I (RI), from bottom to top.

Recent Trends in Rhythm and Meter

CHAPTER 39

NAME _____

In this chapter you'll learn to:

- Identify processes used to organize new works in a variety of genres
- Identify and notate indeterminate rhythms

Processes and Indeterminacy

Musical works may rely on processes to organize aspects such as rhythm, meter, and chords.

Canon	Follower (*comes*) imitates a leader (*dux*) at a specific time and pitch interval
Isorhythm	Rhythm pattern called a *talea* repeats throughout a work
Phrasing	Patterns organized to drift in and out of synchrony
Loop	Repeating pattern of three or more chords
Shuttle	Oscillation between two chords

In some works, the patterns of accents or rests can obscure the actual meter. In other works, meter is absent entirely. In such ametric music, performers may read pitches, but freely interpret their placement in time. Such indeterminacies require new methods of notation, like time lines, graphics, and textual description.

Try it

1. Listen to Radiohead's "Pyramid Song" on the band's official webpage.

   (a) (1) Begin with the given item and write the lead-sheet chords for unique bass pitches 1–3.

   F♯ _____ _____ _____

   (2) The looped progression most resembles which traditional resolution?

   authentic   deceptive   plagal   Phrygian

   (b) Initially, the meter is obscured. Can you detect any pattern(s)? If this were your composition, how could you convey the meter and rhythm to your performers?

(c) After an interlude (ca. 1:56), the drum set enters (2:05). By 2:14 the drums play a steady swing rhythm.

   (1) Use this clear reference to notate the repeating two-measure rhythmic pattern.

   (2) What is remarkable about this rhythm?

   (3) How might the rhythm and the chord loop paint the text of the song title?

2. Listen to a piece for percussion ensemble. After a two-measure introduction, there is an eight-measure motive.

   (a) Begin with the given items and notate the motive's rhythm.

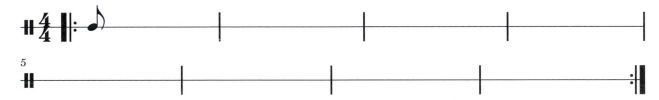

   (b) After the motive's first entrance, it is (circle all that apply):

   repeated   rhythmically augmented   doubled   imitated canonically

   (c) After the second entrance, the motive is (circle all that apply):

   repeated   rhythmically augmented   doubled   imitated canonically

   (d) As the piece continues, describe its organizing principle(s).

3. Listen to a repeated eight-measure excerpt from a stylized Mexican folk dance.

   (a) Describe the piece's metric organization. Hint: Listen to the recurring pattern of accents.

   (b) Begin with the given root and write the lead-sheet chord symbols.

   C_____ _____ _____ _____ _____ _____ _____ _____

Contextual Listening 39.1

Listen to "Oceania" by Icelandic artists Björk Guðmundsdóttir and Sigurjón Birgir Sigurðsson on Björk's official webpage.

1. At the beginning, focus on the choral vocals. How might such music be notated? Use the staff to illustrate your idea(s).

2. The soloist's melodic pitches belong to which F-centric scale or mode?

   major   ascending melodic minor   harmonic minor   Aeolian

At about 1:48, the chorus sings a melody with distinct rhythm and pitches.

3. (a) Begin with the given items and notate the melodic rhythm.

   (b) Beneath each note, write its syllable or scale-degree number.

Pitches: $s(\hat{5})$ __ __   __ __ __   __   __ __ __ __ __

A four-chord loop recurs during much of the work. It is easiest to hear at 3:02.

4. (a) Begin with the given items and notate the bass pitches with whole notes. Beneath each pitch, write its syllable or scale-degree number.

   (b) Listen for chord quality. Above each measure, write a lead-sheet chord symbol.

   Chords: ____   ____   ____   ____

   Pitches: $le\,(\flat 6)$ __   __   __

   (c) Chords 1–2 relate to which traditional resolution?

   Phrygian   plagal   deceptive   authentic

5. (a) Sketch the overall form of the piece. Include phrase- and cadence-level structures.

 (b) How might its structures be viewed as analogous to those in nineteenth-century art song?

6. List examples of text painting.

7. List several items that contribute to this work's eclecticism.

Contextual Listening 39.2

Virtuoso Vache Hovsepyan's performance of a traditional Armenian folk melody called "*Hovern Enkan*" ("A Cool Breeze Is Blowing") is available online from Parseghian Records. Hovsepyan performs the melody on a double-reed instrument called a *duduk*.

Listen to an adaptation of "*Hovern Enkan*" and complete the exercises. Consider the initial pitch to be the work's pitch center.

1. Two instruments sound. Describe the role of the first one you hear.

2. (a) Capture the unique melodic pitches. Begin with the given items and arrange these unique pitches as an ascending scale.

pcs: __   __   __   __   __   __   __   __

   (b) These pitches are a rotation of which traditional scale?

   major   melodic minor   harmonic minor

Segment A comprises pitches 1–4 and segment B, pitches 5–8.

   (c) Segment A completes which traditional tetrachord?

   major   minor   harmonic   Phrygian

   (d) Segment B completes which traditional tetrachord?

   major   minor   harmonic   Phrygian

Consider both A and B to be unordered pcsets. For each, write the normal order and prime form.

   (e) Set A: normal order { _____ } prime form [_____]

   (f) Set B: normal order { _____ } prime form [_____]

3. On your own paper, experiment with several methods of notating the melody. Then, copy your preferred rendition to the staves provided. As you work, consider the following:

(a) *Meter:* The piece is ametric. Develop a method that allows a performer to interpret and perform the melody in a manner consistent with the recording.

(b) *Pitch:* Include dynamics and articulations. Use special symbols to indicate melodic nuances.

Here are some ideas, but you can create your own, too.

- Nonstandard key signature: Write only the sharps and flats the scale requires.
- Pitch bend: draw a line before (or after) the note modified
- Turn ∾: begin with a tone, then perform both its neighbor tones
- Senza vibrato → vibrato: straight line evolves into wavy line
- Sustained pitch: line indicates relative duration

Contextual Listening 39.3

Study the poetry, then listen to a song for soprano and two clarinets.

Laß deinen süßen Rubinenmund	Let not your sweet ruby mouth
Zudringlichkeiten nicht verfluchen;	Condemn me for being so importunate;
Was hat Liebesschmerz andern Grund,	What other reason does heartache have
Als seine Heilung zu suchen?	Than to look for its own healing?

1. Capture the original row, P$_4$.

   (a) Begin with the given items and notate voice pitches 2–12, sung to "*Laß deinen süßen Rubinenmund.*"

   (b) Beneath each pitch, write its pc integer.

   (c) Between each adjacent pair of pc integers, write the pc interval number.

   (d) Above each pitch, write its row order number, 1–12.

Row form: P$_4$
mm. 2–5

The first clarinet that plays is a B♭ clarinet. CL 39.3a is the excerpted clarinet part.

2. Capture the row played by the B♭ clarinet.

   (a) Begin with the given items and notate B♭ clarinet pitches 2–12 at concert pitch.

   (b) Write the pc integers, pcis, and row order numbers.

Row form: ____
mm. 2–5

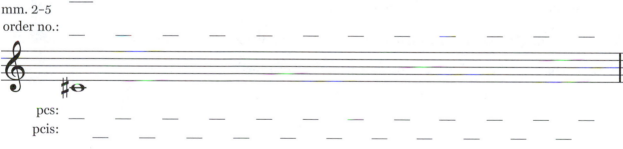

   (c) Compare this row with the original row, P$_4$. This row form is called:

   P____   I____   R____   RI____

   (d) What is the rationale for your answer to (c)?

3. Transpose exercise 2 to create a B♭ clarinet part. Hint: Add 2 to every pc integer.

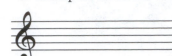

Exercise 4 focuses only on the final 12 pcs of the B♭ clarinet, which begin immediately after those in exercise 2.

4. Begin with the given items and notate the final twelve pitches of the B♭ clarinet.

(a) Write the pc integers, pcis, and row order numbers.

Row form: ____
mm. 12–19
order no.: __   __   __   __   __   __   __   __   __   __   __   __

pcs: __   __   __   __   __   __   __   __   __   __   __   __
pcis: __   __   __   __   __   __   __   __   __   __   __

(b) Compare this row with the original row, P_4. This row form is called:

P____   I____   R____   RI____

(c) What is the rationale for your answer to (b)?

At the beginning, focus on the rhythmic relationship between the voice and the first clarinet entrance.

5. Compared with the voice's rhythm, the B♭ clarinet rhythm is:

a diminution   identical   an augmentation

Focus on the end of the clarinet part and compare its rhythm with the initial voice rhythm.

6. Compared with the beginning of the voice part, the B♭ clarinet's final rhythm is:

a diminution   identical   an augmentation

Contextual Listening 39.4

Contextual Listening 39.4 revisits a work you studied previously.

Create a 12 × 12 matrix based on the work's original row, P_4, voice pitches 1–12.

1. Find P_0.

    (a) Write P_4 here and subtract 4 from each of its elements.

    $$P_4 \rightarrow \quad 4 \quad \underline{\quad} \ \underline{\quad} \ \underline{\quad} \ \underline{\quad} \ \underline{\quad} \ \underline{\quad} \ \underline{\quad} \ \underline{\quad} \ \underline{\quad} \ \underline{\quad} \ \underline{\quad}$$
    $$- \quad \underline{4} \ \ \underline{4} \ \ \underline{4} \ \ \underline{4} \ \ \underline{4} \ \ \underline{4} \ \ \underline{4} \ \ \underline{4} \ \ \underline{4} \ \ \underline{4} \ \ \underline{4} \ \ \underline{4}$$
    $$P_0 \rightarrow \quad 0 \quad \underline{\quad} \ \underline{\quad} \ \underline{\quad} \ \underline{\quad} \ \underline{\quad} \ \underline{\quad} \ \underline{\quad} \ \underline{\quad} \ \underline{\quad} \ \underline{\quad} \ \underline{\quad}$$

    (b) Write P_0 from left to right in the top line of the matrix.

2. Write P_0's inversion, I_0, down the matrix's leftmost column. Each element of I is the mod 12 inverse of the corresponding element of P_0.

3. Fill in the matrix.

    (a) Consider each pc in the left column to be the first pc of a new row transposition.

    (b) Add that element to every element in P_0, mod 12.

4. Check your work.

    (a) The diagonal from top left to bottom right should contain only zeros.

    (b) Each row and column includes one each of the twelve pc integers. No pc may be duplicated.

5. Read the matrix.

    (a) P forms read from left to right, and R of P (R), from right to left.

    (b) I forms read from top to bottom, and R of I (RI), from bottom to top.

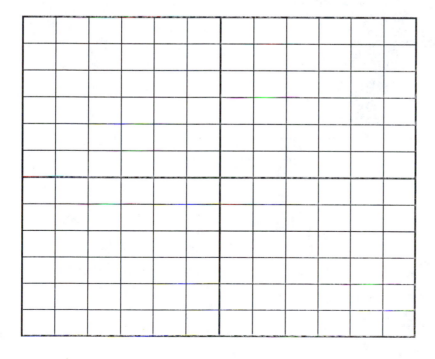

Refer to the matrix to complete the remaining exercises.

6. (a) Begin with the given items and notate the voice pitches sung to "*Zudringlichkeiten nicht verfluchen.*" This music begins immediately after the opening row, P$_4$, voice pitches 1–12.

 (b) Write the pc integer beneath each pitch.

Row form: ____
mm. 6–9
order no.: __ __ __ __ __ __ __ __ __ __ __ __

pcs: __ __ __ __ __ __ __ __ __ __ __ __

 (c) There are only eleven pcs. Which pc is "missing"? pc ____

 (d) Compare this row with the original row, P$_4$. This row form is called:

 P____   I____   R____   RI____

 (e) What is the rationale for your answer to (d)?

 (f) While listening to the voice and clarinet, follow your notation or the row form in the matrix. How does the composer account for the pc "missing" from the voice row?

7. (a) Begin with the given items and notate the voice pitches sung to "*Was hat Liebesschmerz andern Grund*" (ca. 0:24).

 (b) Beneath each pc, write the pc integer.

Row form: ____
mm. 12–15
order no.: __ __ __ __ __ __ __ __ __ __ __ __

pcs: __ __ __ __ __ __ __ __ __ __ __ __

 (c) Compare this melody's contour and intervals with those of the opening voice melody. Compared with P$_4$, describe this row's contour and intervals:

 identical   opposite contour, same intervals   different contour and intervals

 (d) Look at the matrix to confirm what you heard. The row form is: ____

8. (a) Begin with the given items and notate the final pitches of the voice, sung to "*Als seine Heilung zu suchen, zu suchen?*" (ca. 0:35). There are only eleven pitches.

   (b) Write the pc integer beneath each pitch.

Row form: ____
mm. 16–19
order no.: __   __   __   __   __   __   __   __   __   __   __

pcs: __   __   __   __   __   __   __   __   __   __   __

   (c) Compare this row with the original row, P_4. This row form is called:

   P____   I____   R____   RI____

   (d) What is the rationale for your answer to (c)?

   (e) Which pc is missing? pc ____

   (f) While listening to the voice and lower-sounding clarinet, follow the notation or the matrix. How does the composer account for the pc "missing" from the voice row?

9. (a) While the singer holds the last syllable of "*verfluchen*" (ca. 0:18), the E♭ clarinet enters for the first time. Begin with the given items and notate E♭ clarinet pitches 2-12.

   (b) Write the pc integer beneath each pitch.

Row form: ____
mm. 10–13
order no.: __ __ __ __ __ __ __ __ __ __ __ __

pcs: __ __ __ __ __ __ __ __ __ __ __ __

   (c) Compare this melody's contour and intervals with those of the opening voice melody. Compared with P_4, describe this row's contour and intervals:

   identical   opposite contour, same intervals   different contour and intervals

   (d) Look at the matrix to confirm what you heard. The row form is: ____

   (e) Transpose the concert pitches up three semitones to create an E♭ clarinet part.

The E♭ clarinet's second row begins immediately after its first, coinciding with the singer's syllable "*-schmerz*"). For an audio hint, listen to CL 39.4a.

10. (a) Begin with the given items and notate the remaining pitches of the E♭ clarinet melody. There are only eleven pitches.

   (b) Beneath each pitch, write its pc integer.

Row form: ____
mm. 14–18
order no.: __ __ __ __ __ __ __ __ __ __ __

pcs: __ __ __ __ __ __ __ __ __ __ __

   (c) Refer to your matrix and compare this row with the original row, P_4. This row form is called:

   P____   I____   R____   RI____

   (d) Which pc is missing? pc ____

   (e) While listening to the voice and higher-sounding clarinet, follow the notation or the matrix. How does the composer account for the pc "missing" from the voice row?

CHAPTER 40

Borrowing from the Past

NAME _____

In this chapter you'll learn to:

- Identify examples of appropriation and intertextuality

Appropriation and Intertextuality

Artists borrow from existing works, including their own, to make new works. Such appropriation is quite common, especially in popular culture. Also common is intertextuality, which relies on the audience to recognize the influence of an external reference on the present work.

Try it

Terms that apply to these practices include the following.

allusion	An indirect reference to another work (e.g., Radiohead's "Paranoid Android" refers to a character in Douglas Adams's *Hitchhiker's Guide to the Galaxy*)
parody	Originally, merely borrowing (e.g., Dufay's *Missa L'homme armé*), but today, borrowing for humorous purposes (e.g., Weird Al's "Tacky")
pastiche	An affectionate or respectful reference to an earlier work or style (e.g., Stravinsky's *Octet for Wind Instruments*)
quodlibet	A work that juxtaposes two or more existing works (e.g., Roy Kerr's "A Stroke of Genie-us," a bootleg remix of The Strokes' "Hard to Explain" with Christina Aguilera's "Genie in a Bottle")
mashup	A quodlibet or a medley (e.g., Sir Mashalot's "Mind-Blowing Six-Song Country Mashup")
quotation	Inserting part of one work into another (e.g., Puccini's quotation of "The Star-Spangled Banner" in *Madama Butterfly*, to signify Lt. Pinkerton's American origin)

1. Use a web browser to find each example mentioned in the chart. Listen to the example to understand how the work exemplifies the term.

2. Browse again to locate a new example for each term. Without revealing the term you believe applies to a particular example, share it with a peer, who listens and decides independently which term applies. After both have listened to each other's examples, discuss your choice of terms and the rationale for their selection.

Term	Example
allusion	
parody	
pastiche	
quodlibet	
mashup	
quotation	

Contextual Listening 40.1

Listen to Al Jarreau's cover of "Blue Rondo à la Turk" by Dave Brubeck on Jarreau's official website. The lyrics appear in numerous online sources.

1. Assume a single meter signature rather than changing meter. The most likely meter signature is:

$\frac{5}{8}$　$\frac{7}{8}$　$\frac{8}{8}$　$\frac{9}{8}$

Phrase 1 comprises four measures followed immediately by a repetition of the same music.

2. Capture the rhythm and pitches of phrase 1.

   (a) Insert the meter signature from exercise 1.

   (b) Begin with the given items and notate phrase 1's rhythm in the single-line staff. Beneath each note, write its syllable or number.

   (c) In the five-line staff, notate the melody. Refer to (b).

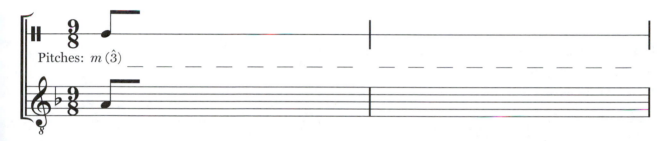

Pitches: *m* ($\hat{3}$)

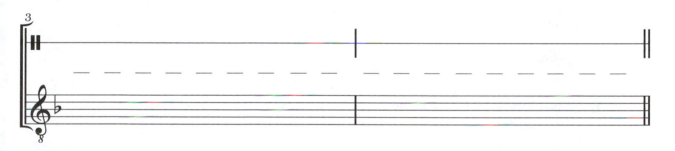

Phrase 2 is a repetition of phrase 1. Focus now on phrase 3.

3. Capture the rhythm and pitches of phrase 3.

    (a) Insert the meter signature from exercise 1.

    (b) Begin with the given items and notate phrase 3's rhythm in the single-line staff. Beneath each note, write its syllable or number.

    (c) In the five-line staff, notate the melody. Refer to (b).

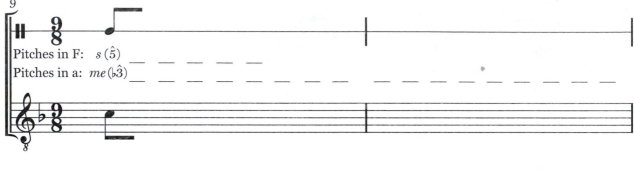

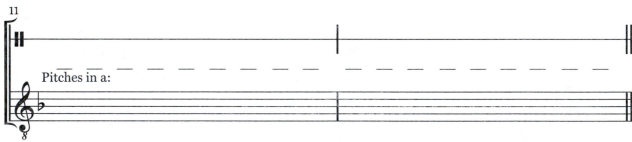

4. Phrase 3 tonicizes which key?

    iii   IV   V   vi

Listen again to the entire piece and focus on the overall form.

5. (a) Diagram the work's overall form. Include sections, but not the phrase-level details.

    (b) Describe your rationale.

6. How do the lyrics change what was originally an instrumental work into a love song? Describe how the text paints a relationship using familiar musical terms.

Contextual Listening 40.2

Listen to part of a work for chorus and orchestra that consists of eight melodic segments. Then, focus on segments 1–4, which contain 8, 8, 8, and 10 pitches, respectively.

1. Segment 1's rhythmic notation is: ____

2. Beginning with the given items, notate the melody of segments 1–4. Include the meter signature from exercise 1. (After segment 4, segment 1 recurs.)

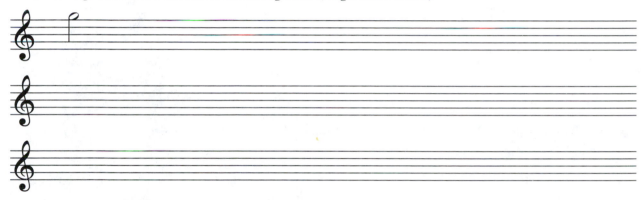

3. The design of segments 1–4 is:

   a a a a   a a a′ b   a b a b   a b a c

4. Call melodic pitches 1–3 unordered pcset A. Use the workspace to identify set A's normal order, prime form, and Forte set-class number.

   A normal order { _____ }   prime form [_____]   Forte SC 3-____

5. Call melodic pitches 4–6 unordered pcset B. Use the workspace to identify set B's normal order, prime form, and Forte set-class number.

   B normal order { _____ }   prime form [_____]   Forte SC 3-____

6. Call melodic pitches 1–6 unordered pcset C. Use the workspace to identify set C's normal order, prime form, and Forte set-class number.

C normal order { _____ }   prime form [_____]   Forte SC 5-____

7. Call segment 3's pcs unordered pcset D. Use the workspace to identify set D's normal order, prime form, and Forte set-class number.

D normal order { _____ }   prime form [_____]   Forte SC 3-____

8. (a) Melodic segment 4's pentachords are which quality?

   major   minor   harmonic   Phrygian

   (b) Melodic segment 4's pentachords belong to which set class?

   [01357]   [01457]   [02357]   [02468]

Contextual Listening 40.3

Listen to an excerpt from an art song, and complete the following exercises.

1. Notate the pitches of the alto flute from the beginning until the soprano enters. Begin on Bb4. Write the appropriate clef and accidentals. Call the four distinct pitch classes set A. For an audio hint, listen to CL 40.3a.

2. Notate the pitches of the alto flute as flutists would read them. The alto flute sounds a P4 below its written pitches.

3. Find the intervals between each pc in set A. Use this information to create its interval-class vector. Perform the intervals between the pcs, or realize set A as pitches on the following staff to help you visualize the process.

   The interval-class vector for set A is [___ ___ ___ ___ ___ ___].

4. What is another name for set A?

   whole-tone tetrachord   Phrygian tetrachord

   all-interval tetrachord   octatonic tetrachord

5. Play the rotations of set A at the keyboard or notate them on the following staff. Find the normal order and prime form. To which set class does this tetrachord belong?

6. The soprano sings the opening motive four times. Which is the interval in semitones? (The third and fourth occurrences are easiest to hear.)

   1   2   3   4

7. After the soprano's first entrance, the flute plays again, adding one pitch to set A. Call set A plus this new pitch set B. Realize set B as pitches and play its rotations at the keyboard, or notate them on the following staves. What is the normal order for set B? To which set class does B belong? For an audio hint, listen to CL 40.3b.

8. After the flute performs set B, the antique cymbals repeat the first interval of the composition, to which one new pitch is added in the glockenspiel. Call this trichord set C. Realize the set as pitches and play its rotations at the keyboard, or notate them on the following staves. What is the normal order for set C? To which set class does C belong?

9. Notate the five distinct pitches of the soprano part on the staff provided. Begin on D5. Write the appropriate clef and accidentals. Call these pcs set D. Realize the set as pitches and play its rotations at the keyboard, or notate them on the following staves. What is the normal order for set D? To which set class does D belong? For an audio hint, listen to CL 40.3c.

10. Realize the pcs of sets B, C, and D as pitches in the order in which they appear. What is the musical significance of the soprano's last pitch?

_____
_____
_____
_____
_____

11. Listen to the soprano's last pitch several times. The percussion adds three pitches to the soprano part to create a tetrachord. Call this tetrachord set E. While the soprano sustains the last pitch, the flute adds three pitches to create a different tetrachord. Call this tetrachord set F. For an audio hint, listen to CL 40.3d.

    Realize each set as pitches and play the rotations at the keyboard, or notate them on the following staves. What are the normal orders for sets E and F? To which set classes do E and F belong?

_____
_____
_____
_____
_____

_____
_____
_____
_____
_____

12. How is set E related to set C?

13. How is set F related to set A?

Try it Answers

Chapter 1 *Try it*

1. (a)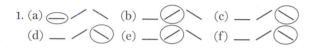

2. (a)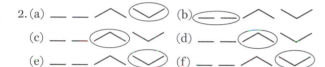

3.

4. (a)

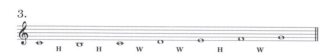

Chapter 2 *Try it*

1. (a) 3, 1   (b) 5, 4   (c) 6, 2   (d) 8, 7

2. (a) 2, 5   (b) 3, 4   (c) 7, 1   (d) 6, 8

3. (a) 2, 1   (b) 3, 2   (c) 4, 1   (d) 2, 3

4. (a)

   (b)

   (c)

   (d)

   (e)

   (f)

Chapter 3 *Try it*

Chapter 4 *Try it*

1.

2. (a) 2, 1   (b) 3, 2   (c) 3, 4   (d) 2, 3

3. (a)

(b)

(c)

(d)

(e)

(f)

(e)

(f)

(g)

(h)

Chapter 5 *Try it*

1. (a) harmonic   simple
   (b) natural   simple
   (c) ascending melodic   compound
   (d) harmonic   compound
   (e) ascending melodic   simple
   (f) natural   compound

2. (a) Dorian   simple
   (b) Phrygian   compound
   (c) Mixolydian   simple
   (d) Dorian   compound
   (e) Lydian   compound
   (f) Phrygian   simple

3. (a)

   (b)

   (c)

   (d)

Chapter 6 *Try it*

1. Division: simple
   Pitches 1-2 form: P5 *do-sol* (1̂-5̂)
   Key: major
   Patterns: | 2 6 | 4 1 ||

2. Division: compound
   Pitches 1-2 form: M3 *do-mi* (1̂-3̂)
   Key: major
   Patterns: | 2 3 | 4 1 ||

3. Division: simple
   Pitches 1-2 form: m3 *do-me* (1̂-♭3̂)
   Key: minor
   Patterns: | 2 6 | 4 1 ||

4. Division: simple
   Pitches 1-2 form: M3 *sol-me* (5̂-♭3̂)
   Key: minor
   Patterns: | 4 2 | 8 1 ||

5. Division: compound
   Pitches 1-2 form: m6 *sol-me* (5̂-♭3̂)
   Key: minor
   Patterns: | 3 3 | 2 1 ||

6. Division: simple
   Pitches 4-5 form: d5 *ti-fa* (7̂-4̂)
   Key: major
   Patterns: | 4 8 | 2 1 ||

7. Division: simple
   Pitches 1-2 form: M6 *sol-mi* (5̂-3̂)
   Key: major
   Patterns: ♪| 2 5 | 7 1 ||

8. Division: compound
   Pitches 1-2 form: P5 *sol-do* (5̂-1̂)
   Key: minor
   Patterns: ♪| 3 5 | 4 1 ||

Chapter 7 *Try it*

1. (a) Triad quality: major
   Last 2 pitches form: P5 *do-sol* ($\hat{1}$-$\hat{5}$)
   Simple or compound: simple
   | 2 6 | 4 1 ||

   (b) Triad quality: major
   Last 2 pitches form: M3 *mi-do* ($\hat{3}$-$\hat{1}$)
   Simple or compound: compound
   | 2 3 | 4 1 ||

   (c) Triad quality: minor
   Last 2 pitches form: m3 *do-me* ($\hat{1}$-$\flat\hat{3}$)
   Simple or compound: simple
   | 2 6 | 4 1 ||

   (d) Triad quality: minor
   Last 2 pitches form: M3 *me-sol* ($\flat\hat{3}$-$\hat{5}$)
   Simple or compound: simple
   | 4 2 | 8 1 ||

   (e) Triad quality: augmented
   Last 2 pitches form: m2 *ti-do* ($\hat{7}$-$\hat{1}$)
   Simple or compound: compound
   | 3 3 | 2 1 ||

   (f) Triad quality: diminished
   Last 2 pitches form: M3 *do-mi* ($\hat{1}$-$\hat{3}$)
   Simple or compound: simple
   | 4 8 | 2 1 ||

   (g) Triad quality: major
   Last 2 pitches form: M6 *do-la* ($\hat{1}$-$\hat{6}$)
   Simple or compound: simple
   ♪ | 2 5 | 7 1 ||

   (h) Triad quality: minor
   Last 2 pitches form: m3 *me-do* ($\flat\hat{3}$-$\hat{1}$)
   Simple or compound: simple
   ♪ | 3 5 | 4 1 ||

2. (a) Chord 1: M Chord 2: M
   (b) Chord 1: m Chord 2: M
   (c) Chord 1: M Chord 2: d
   (d) Chord 1: M Chord 2: m
   (e) Chord 1: m Chord 2: M
   (f) Chord 1: M Chord 2: M
   (g) Chord 1: M Chord 2: M
   (h) Chord 1: m Chord 2: d
   (i) Chord 1: M Chord 2: A
   (j) Chord 1: M Chord 2: M

3. (a) Chord 1: M Chord 2: m Chord 3: M Chord 4: M
   (b) Chord 1: m Chord 2: d Chord 3: M Chord 4: m
   (c) Chord 1: M Chord 2: m Chord 3: m Chord 4: M
   (d) Chord 1: M Chord 2: M Chord 3: m Chord 4: M

Chapter 8 *Try it*

1. (a) MM7   (b) Mm7   (c) mm7   (d) MM7
   (e) mm7   (f) dm7   (g) °7   (h) min7
   (i) 7   (j) 7

2. (a) Chord 1: MM7   Chord 2: dm7
   (b) Chord 1: dm7   Chord 2: Mm7
   (c) Chord 1: mm7   Chord 2: MM7
   (d) Chord 1: min7   Chord 2: min7
   (e) Chord 1: ⌀7   Chord 2: °7

3. (a)

Chord:	1	2	3	4
Quality:	M	mm7	mm7	Mm7

   (b)

Chord:	1	2	3	4
Quality:	m	MM7	mm7	Mm7

   (c)

Chord:	1	2	3
Quality:	dd7	m	M

   (d)

Chord:	1	2	3
Quality:	dm7	Mm7	mm7

   (e)

Chord:	1	2	3	4
Quality:	mm7	mm7	Mm7	MM7
Chord:	5	6	7	8
Quality:	MM7	dm7	Mm7	mm7

4. (a)

Chord:	1	2	3	4
Symbol:	Cmaj	Amin7	Dmin7	G7

   (b)

Chord:	1	2	3	4
Symbol:	Cmin	A♭maj7	Fmin7	G7

   (c)

Chord:	1	2	3
Symbol:	C♯dim7	Dmin	Amaj

   (d)

Chord:	1	2	3
Symbol:	F♯⌀7	B7	Emin7

   (e)

Chord:	1	2	3	4
Symbol:	Amin7	Dmin7	G7	Cmaj7
Chord:	5	6	7	8
Symbol:	Fmaj7	B⌀7	E7	Amin7

Chapter 9 *Try it*

1.

Syllables:	*d*	*r*	*m*	*m*	*r*	*d*
Numbers:	$\hat{1}$	$\hat{2}$	$\hat{3}$	$\hat{3}$	$\hat{2}$	$\hat{1}$

Syllables:	*d*	*t*	*d*	*d*	*t*	*d*
Numbers:	$\hat{1}$	$\hat{7}$	$\hat{1}$	$\hat{1}$	$\hat{7}$	$\hat{1}$
Intervals:	U	3	3	3	3	U
Motion:		contrary	parallel	none	parallel	contrary

2.

Syllables:	*d*	*r*	*m*	*m*	*r*	*d*
Numbers:	$\hat{1}$	$\hat{2}$	$\hat{3}$	$\hat{3}$	$\hat{2}$	$\hat{1}$

Syllables:	*d*	*t*	*l*	*l*	*t*	*d*
Numbers:	$\hat{1}$	$\hat{7}$	$\hat{6}$	$\hat{6}$	$\hat{7}$	$\hat{1}$
Intervals:	U	3	5	5	3	U
Motion:		contrary	contrary	none	contrary	contrary

3.

Syllables:	d	m	r	r	m	d
Numbers:	$\hat{1}$	$\hat{3}$	$\hat{2}$	$\hat{2}$	$\hat{3}$	$\hat{1}$

Syllables:	d	s	t	t	s	d
Numbers:	$\hat{1}$	$\hat{5}$	$\hat{7}$	$\hat{7}$	$\hat{5}$	$\hat{1}$
Intervals:	U	6	3	3	6	U
Motion:		contrary	contrary	none	contrary	contrary

4.

Syllables:	d	f	m	m	f	d
Numbers:	$\hat{1}$	$\hat{4}$	$\hat{3}$	$\hat{3}$	$\hat{4}$	$\hat{1}$

Syllables:	d	l	d	d	l	d
Numbers:	$\hat{1}$	$\hat{6}$	$\hat{1}$	$\hat{1}$	$\hat{6}$	$\hat{1}$
Intervals:	U	6	3	3	6	U
Motion:		contrary	contrary	none	contrary	contrary

5.

Syllables:	d	t	d	d	t	d
Numbers:	$\hat{1}$	$\hat{7}$	$\hat{1}$	$\hat{1}$	$\hat{7}$	$\hat{1}$

Syllables:	d	r	m	m	r	d
Numbers:	$\hat{1}$	$\hat{2}$	$\hat{3}$	$\hat{3}$	$\hat{2}$	$\hat{1}$
Intervals:	8	6	6	6	6	8
Motion:		contrary	parallel	none	parallel	contrary

6.

Syllables:	d	t	d	d	t	d
Numbers:	$\hat{1}$	$\hat{7}$	$\hat{1}$	$\hat{1}$	$\hat{7}$	$\hat{1}$

Syllables:	d	r	me	me	r	d
Numbers:	$\hat{1}$	$\hat{2}$	$\flat\hat{3}$	$\flat\hat{3}$	$\hat{2}$	$\hat{1}$
Intervals:	8	6	6	6	6	8
Motion:		contrary	parallel	none	parallel	contrary

7.

Syllables:	d	r	me	f	s	f	r	d
Numbers:	$\hat{1}$	$\hat{2}$	$\flat\hat{3}$	$\hat{4}$	$\hat{5}$	$\hat{4}$	$\hat{2}$	$\hat{1}$

Syllables:	d	t	d	le	s	l	t	d
Numbers:	$\hat{1}$	$\hat{7}$	$\hat{1}$	$\flat\hat{6}$	$\hat{5}$	$\hat{6}$	$\hat{7}$	$\hat{1}$
Intervals:	U	3	3	6	8	6	3	U
Motion:	contrary	parallel	contrary	contrary	contrary	contrary	contrary

8.

Syllables:	d	te	le	s	s	l	t	d
Numbers:	$\hat{1}$	$\flat\hat{7}$	$\flat\hat{6}$	$\hat{5}$	$\hat{5}$	$\hat{6}$	$\hat{7}$	$\hat{1}$

Syllables:	d	r	d	t	t	d	r	d
Numbers:	$\hat{1}$	$\hat{2}$	$\hat{1}$	$\hat{7}$	$\hat{7}$	$\hat{1}$	$\hat{2}$	$\hat{1}$
Intervals:	8	6	6	6	6	6	6	8
Motion:	contrary	parallel	parallel	none	parallel	parallel	contrary

Chapter 10 *Try it*

1. (a) parallel (b) thirds (c) unison
2. (a) lower (b) consonant skip
3. (a) higher (b) neighbor tone
4. (a) higher (b) suspension
5. (a) lower (b) suspension
6. (a) both (b) consonant skip
7. (a) lower (b) passing tone
8. (a) consonant skip (b) neighbor tone
9. (a) parallel (b) sixths (c) octave
10. (a) higher (b) suspension

11. (a) higher (b) incomplete neighbor
12. (a) both (b) voice exchange

Chapter 11 *Try it*

1. The cadence is: conclusive

2. The cadence is: conclusive

3. The cadence is: less conclusive

4. The cadence is: less conclusive

5. The cadence is: less conclusive

6. The cadence is: less conclusive

7. The cadence is: less conclusive

8. The cadence is: less conclusive

9. The cadence is: conclusive

10. The cadence is: conclusive

Chapter 12 *Try it*

1. Cadence type: PAC

2. Cadence type: IAC

3. Cadence type: PAC

4. Cadence type: HC

5. Cadence type: IAC

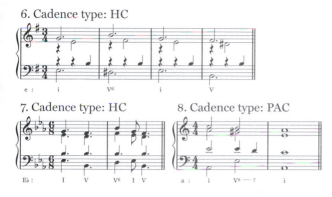

6. Cadence type: HC

e : i   V6   i   V

7. Cadence type: HC

8. Cadence type: PAC

E♭ :   I   V   V6   I V

a :   i   V8 — 7   i

5. Cadence type: PAC

6. Cadence type: PAC

F :   I6   V4/3   I   ii6   V7   V7   I

D :   I   IV   I   V8-7   I

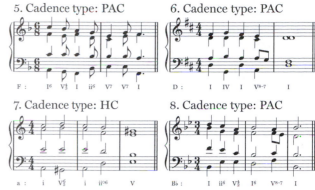

7. Cadence type: HC

8. Cadence type: PAC

a :   i   V6/5   i   ii°6   V

B♭ :   I   ii6   V4/2   I6   V8-7   I

Chapter 13 *Try it 1*

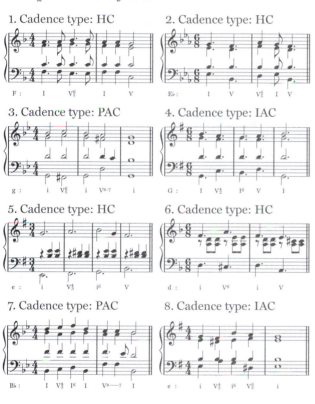

1. Cadence type: HC

2. Cadence type: HC

F :   I   V6/5   I   V

E♭ :   I   V   V6/5   I   V

3. Cadence type: PAC

4. Cadence type: IAC

g :   i   V6/5   i   V8-7   i

G :   I   V4/2   I6   V   I

5. Cadence type: HC

6. Cadence type: HC

e :   i   V4/3   i6   V

d :   i   V6   i   V

7. Cadence type: PAC

8. Cadence type: IAC

B♭ :   I   V4/3   I6   I   V8—7   I

e :   i   V4/2   i6   V6/5   i

Chapter 13 *Try it 2*

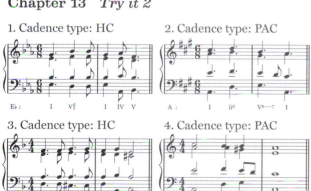

1. Cadence type: HC

2. Cadence type: PAC

E♭ :   I   V6/5   I   IV   V

A :   I   ii6   V8—7   I

3. Cadence type: HC

4. Cadence type: PAC

d :   i   V6/5   i   iv   V

a :   i   ii°6/5   V8-7   i

Chapter 14 *Try it*

1. (a) Beat division: compound
   (b) Predominant: ii6
   (c) First 6/4: neighboring
   (d) Second 6/4: cadential
   (e) Cadence type: HC

2. (a) Beat division: simple
   (b) Predominant: IV
   (c) First 6/4: cadential
   (d) Second 6/4: neighboring
   (e) Cadence type: PAC

3. (a) Beat division: compound
   (b) Predominant: ii°6
   (c) First 6/4: passing
   (d) Second 6/4: cadential
   (e) Cadence type: PAC

4. (a) Beat division: simple
   (b) Predominant: iv
   (c) First 6/4: cadential
   (d) Second 6/4: neighboring
   (e) Cadence type: IAC

5. (a) Beat division: simple
   (b) Predominant: ii6
   (c) First 6/4: neighboring
   (d) Second 6/4: cadential
   (e) Cadence type: HC

6. (a) Beat division: compound
   (b) Predominant: ii∅6/5
   (c) First 6/4: passing
   (d) Second 6/4: cadential
   (e) Cadence type: PAC

7. (a) Beat division: simple
   (b) Predominant: $ii^{\varnothing\frac{6}{5}}$
   (c) First $\frac{6}{4}$: passing
   (d) Second $\frac{6}{4}$: neighboring
   (e) Cadence type: PAC

8. (a) Beat division: compound
   (b) Predominant: $ii^{\frac{6}{5}}$
   (c) First $\frac{6}{4}$: neighboring
   (d) Second $\frac{6}{4}$: cadential
   (e) Cadence type: HC

Chapter 15 *Try it*

1. (a) Beat division: compound
   (b) Predominant: ii^6
   (c) $\frac{6}{4}$ type: neighboring
   (d) Cadence type: DC

2. (a) Beat division: simple
   (b) Predominant: IV
   (c) $\frac{6}{4}$ type: cadential
   (d) Cadence type: DC

3. (a) Beat division: compound
   (b) Predominant: iv^6
   (c) $\frac{6}{4}$ type: passing
   (d) Cadence type: PHC

4. (a) Beat division: simple
   (b) Predominant: IV
   (c) $\frac{6}{4}$ type: neighboring
   (d) Cadence type: PAC

5. (a) Beat division: simple
   (b) Predominant: iv
   (c) Chord 2 is: $V^{\frac{6}{5}}$
   (d) $\frac{6}{4}$ type: passing
   (e) Cadence type: PC

6. (a) Beat division: simple
   (b) Predominant: iv^6
   (c) Chord 2 is: $V^{\frac{4}{3}}$
   (d) Cadence type: PHC

7. (a) Beat division: compound
   (b) Predominant: ii^6
   (c) Chord 2 is: $V^{\frac{6}{5}}$
   (d) $\frac{6}{4}$ type: passing
   (e) Cadence type: DC

8. (a) Beat division: simple
   (b) Predominant: iv^6
   (c) Chord 4 is: $V^{\frac{4}{2}}$
   (d) $\frac{6}{4}$ type: neighboring
   (e) Cadence type: PHC

Chapter 16 *Try it*

1. (a) Beat division: simple
   (b) Predominant: ii^6
   (c) Melodic pitches 2 and 4 are: N
   (d) Melodic pitch 6 is an/a: anticipation (A)
   (e) Cadence type: PAC

2. (a) Beat division: simple
   (b) Predominant: iv^6
   (c) Melodic pitch 3 is an/a: suspension/retardation (S)
   Choose figure(s): 7-6
   (d) Cadence type: PHC

3. (a) Beat division: simple
   (b) Predominant: iv
   (c) The final measure includes an/a: suspension/retardation (S)
   Choose figure(s): 4-3
   (d) $\frac{6}{4}$ type: passing
   (e) Cadence type: PC

4. (a) Beat division: compound
   (b) Predominant: ii^6
   (c) Melodic pitch 5 is an/a: suspension/retardation (S)
   Choose figure(s): 4-3, 7-8, 9-8
   (d) $\frac{6}{4}$ type: cadential
   (e) Cadence type: PAC

5. (a) Beat division: simple
   (b) Bass pitch 2 is a: P
   (c) Melodic pitch 3 is a: chromatic P
   (d) The final measure includes an/a: suspension/retardation (S)
   Choose figure(s): 4-3
   (e) Cadence type: PHC

Chapter 17 *Try it 1*

1. (a) Chord 2 is: $vii^{\circ 7}$
   (b) Chord 4 is: $V^{\frac{4}{2}}$
   (c) Predominant: iv
   (d) Cadence type: HC

2. (a) Chord is: $V^{\frac{6}{5}}$
   (b) Chord 4 is: $vii^{\circ\frac{4}{3}}$
   (c) Predominant: $ii^{\varnothing\frac{6}{5}}$
   (d) Cadence type: HC

3. (a) Chord 2 is: vii°⁶₅   4. (a) Chord is: V⁴₃

(b) Chord 4 is: vii°⁷   (b) Chord 4 is: V⁶₅

(c) Predominant: iv⁶   (c) Predominant: iv

(d) Cadence type: PHC   (d) Cadence type: HC

5. (a) Chord 2 is: vii°⁴₃   6. (a) Chord is: V⁴₂

(b) Chord 4 is: vii°⁶₅   (b) Chord 4 is: V⁴₃

(c) Predominant: iv   (c) Predominant: iv⁶

(d) Cadence type: HC   (d) Cadence type: PHC

7. The meter type of exercises 1–6 is: compound

Chapter 17   *Try it 2*

1. (a) Chord 2 is: V⁶₄   2. (a) Chord 2 is: vii°⁶

(b) Predominant: iv⁶   (b) Predominant: ii°⁶

(c) Embellishment: S   (c) Embellishment: CS

(d) Cadence type: PHC   (d) Cadence type: HC

3. (a) Chord 2 is: vii°⁶   4. (a) Chord 2 is: V⁶₄

(b) Predominant: iv⁶   (b) Predominant: iv

(c) Embellishment: N   (c) Embellishment: S

(d) Cadence type: PHC   (d) Cadence type: HC

Chapter 18   *Try it 1*

1. At the end, the ⁶₄ chord type is: cadential

2. The next-to-last melodic pitch is which embellishment? retardation

3. The excerpt ends with a/an: PAC

4. Melodic pitches 1–5:   motive, subphrase

5. Melodic pitches 6–10:   motive, subphrase

6. Melodic pitches 11–end: motive, subphrase

7. The entire excerpt: phrase, sentence, independent phrase

Chapter 18   *Try it 2*

1. (a) (1) Melodic pitches 1–5:   motive, subphrase

      (2) Melodic pitches 6–10:   motive, subphrase

      (3) Melodic pitches 11–19: motive, subphrase

      (4) Melodic pitches 1–19:   phrase, sentence

(b) Phrase 1 ends with a/an: HC

(c) Phrase 2 ends with a/an: PAC

(d) Phrases 1–2 compete which pattern? period

(e) Compare phrase 2's beginning with that of phrase 1. Phrase 2 begins: the same or similarly (**a** or **a′**)

(f) Which diagram represents the excerpt's structure?

Parallel period

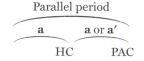

       a   a or a′

     HC   PAC

2. (a) Phrase 1 ends with a/an: HC

(b) Phrase 2 ends with a/an: PAC

(c) Phrases 1–2 compete which pattern? period

(d) Compare phrase 2's beginning with that of phrase 1. Phrase 2 begins: differently (**b**)

(e) Which diagram represents the excerpt's structure?

Contrasting period

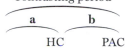

       a   **b**

    HC   PAC

3. (a) The beat division is: compound

(b) The lyrics "It's nine o'clock on a Saturday" complete a: motive, subphrase

(c) Compare phrase 2's beginning with that of phrase 1. Phrase 2 begins: the same or similarly (**a** or **a′**)

(d) The excerpt's structure is a: parallel period

Chapter 18   *Try it 3*

1. (a)

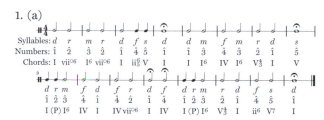

(b)   Parallel double period

antecedent phrases		consequent phrases	
a	b	a′	a′
IAC	HC	IAC	PAC

2.   Asymmetrical parallel double period

antecedent phrases		consequent phrases		
a	a′	a	a′	a″
HC	HC	HC	DC	PAC

Chapter 19   *Try it*

1. (a) Meter type: simple

(b) Chord 2 is: V⁴₃

(c) Chord 5 is: ii⁶₅

(d) Chord 6 is: V⁶₅/V

(e) Cadence type: HC

2. (a) Meter type: compound

(b) Chord 2 is: V⁶₅

(c) Chord 5 is: ii⌀⁶₅

(d) Chord 6 is: V⁶₅/V

(e) Cadence type: HC

3. (a) Meter type: simple
   (b) Chord 2 is: V^4_2
   (c) Chord 4 is: vii^{ø7}/V
   (d) $^6_4$ type: cadential
   (e) Cadence type: PAC

4. (a) Meter type: compound
   (b) Chord 2 is: vii^{o7}
   (c) Chord 4 is: vii^{o7}/V
   (d) $^6_4$ type: cadential
   (e) Cadence type: DC

5. (a) Meter type: compound
   (b) Chord 4 is: ii^{o6}
   (c) Chord 5 is: vii^{o7}/V
   (d) $^6_4$ type: passing
   (e) Cadence type: PAC

6. (a) Meter type: simple
   (b) Chord 4 is: iv^6
   (c) Chord 6 is: vii^{o7}/V
   (d) $^6_4$ type: neighboring
   (e) Cadence type: PHC

7. (a) Meter type: simple
   (b) Chord 2 is: V^4_2
   (c) Chord 4 is: V7/V
   (d) Cadence type: IAC

8. (a) Meter type: simple
   (b) Chord 2 is: V^6_4
   (c) Chord 5 is: V^6/V
   (d) Cadence type: HC

Chapter 20 *Try it*

1. (a) The initial progression is: I-V^6_5-I
   (b) The chromatic pitch is: *si* (♯$\hat{5}$)
   (c) The tonicized chord is: vi
   (d) Tonicization (chords 4-5):

Bracket	*Slash*	*Colon*
V^6_5 i ⌐	V^6_5/vi-vi	vi: V^6_5-i
ii		

2. (a) The initial progression is: I-V^6_5-I
   (b) The chromatic pitch is: *di* (♯$\hat{1}$)
   (c) The tonicized chord is: ii
   (d) Tonicization (chords 4-5):

Bracket	*Slash*	*Colon*
V^6_5 i ⌐	V^6_5/ii-ii	ii: V^6_5-i
ii		

3. (a) The initial progression is: I-V^4_2-I^6
   (b) The chromatic pitch is: *di* (♯$\hat{1}$)
   (c) The tonicized chord is: ii
   (d) Tonicization (chords 4-5):

Bracket	*Slash*	*Colon*
V^4_2 i^6 ⌐	V^4_2/ii-ii^6	ii: V^4_2-i^6
ii		

4. (a) The initial progression is: I-V^6_5-I
   (b) The chromatic pitch is: *te* (♭$\hat{7}$)
   (c) The tonicized chord is: IV
   (d) Tonicization (chords 4-5):

Bracket	*Slash*	*Colon*
V^6_5 I ⌐	V^6_5/IV-IV	IV: V^6_5-I
IV		

5. (a) The initial progression is: i-V^6_5-i
   (b) The chromatic pitch(es) is (are): *ra* (♭$\hat{2}$), *te* (♭$\hat{7}$)
   (c) The tonicized chord is: VI
   (d) Tonicization (chords 4-5):

Bracket	*Slash*	*Colon*
V^6_5 I ⌐	V^6_5/VI-VI	VI: V^6_5-I
VI		

6. (a) The initial progression is: i-V-i
   (b) The chromatic pitch(es) is (are): *te* (♭$\hat{7}$)
   (c) The tonicized chord is: III
   (d) Tonicization (chords 4-5):

Bracket	*Slash*	*Colon*
V I ⌐	V/III-III	III: V-I
III		

7. (a) The initial progression is: i-vii$^{o6}_5$-i^6
   (b) The chromatic pitch(es) is (are): *ra* (♭$\hat{2}$), *mi* (♮$\hat{3}$)
   (c) The tonicized chord is: iv
   (d) Tonicization (chords 4-5):

Bracket	*Slash*	*Colon*
vii$^{o6}_5$ i^6 ⌐	vii$^{o6}_5$/iv-iv^6	iv: vii$^{o6}_5$-i^6
iv		

Chapter 21 *Try it*

1. (a) In a **major** key, two-chord units **ascend** by **second** in **four** reps with a **5-6** LIP to create a(n) **ascending 5-6 sequence**.

   (b) In a **minor** key, two-chord units **descend** by **second** in **four** reps with a **10-6** LIP to create a(n) **descending-fifth sequence**.

   (c) In a **major** key, two-chord units **descend** by **second** in **four** reps with a **10-8** LIP to create a(n) **descending-fifth sequence**.

(d) In a **minor** key, **two**-chord units **descend** by **third** in **three** reps with a **10-5 LIP** to create a(n) **descending-third sequence**.

2. (a) Sequence name: descending fifth

Syllables:	m	f	r	m	d	r	t	d
Numbers:	$\hat{3}$	$\hat{4}$	$\hat{2}$	$\hat{3}$	$\hat{1}$	$\hat{2}$	$\hat{7}$	$\hat{1}$

LIP: 10 – 8   10 – 8   10 – 8   10 – 8

Syllables:	d	f	t	m	l	r	s	d
Numbers:	$\hat{1}$	$\hat{4}$	$\hat{7}$	$\hat{3}$	$\hat{6}$	$\hat{2}$	$\hat{5}$	$\hat{1}$
B♭ major:	I	IV	vii°	iii	vi	ii	V	I

(b) Sequence name: descending third

Syllables:	m	r	d	t	l	s
Numbers:	$\hat{3}$	$\hat{2}$	$\hat{1}$	$\hat{7}$	$\hat{6}$	$\hat{5}$

LIP: 10 – 5   10 – 5   10 – 5

Syllables:	d	s	l	m	f	d
Numbers:	$\hat{1}$	$\hat{5}$	$\hat{6}$	$\hat{3}$	$\hat{4}$	$\hat{1}$
D major:	I	V	vi	iii	IV	I

(c) Sequence name: descending fifth

Syllables:	s	le	f	s	me	f	r	me
Numbers:	$\hat{5}$	♭$\hat{6}$	$\hat{4}$	$\hat{5}$	♭$\hat{3}$	$\hat{4}$	$\hat{2}$	♭$\hat{3}$

LIP: 5 – 10   5 – 10   5 – 10   5 – 10

Syllables:	d	f	te	me	le	r	s	d
Numbers:	$\hat{1}$	$\hat{4}$	♭$\hat{7}$	♭$\hat{3}$	♭$\hat{6}$	$\hat{2}$	$\hat{5}$	$\hat{1}$
A minor:	i	iv	VII	III	VI	ii°	V	i

(d) Sequence name: parallel $^6_3$

Syllables:	s	le	le	s	s	f	s
Numbers:	$\hat{5}$	♭$\hat{6}$	♭$\hat{6}$	$\hat{5}$	$\hat{5}$	$\hat{4}$	$\hat{5}$

LIP: 5 – 6   7 – 6   7 – 6   8

Syllables:	d		te		le		s
Numbers:	$\hat{1}$		♭$\hat{7}$		♭$\hat{6}$		$\hat{5}$
E minor:	i5–6		v7–6		iv7–6		V

(e) Sequence name: ascending 5-6

Syllables:	s	l	l	t	t	d	d	r	r
Numbers:	$\hat{5}$	$\hat{6}$	$\hat{6}$	$\hat{7}$	$\hat{7}$	$\hat{1}$	$\hat{1}$	$\hat{2}$	$\hat{2}$

LIP: 5 – 6   5 – 6   5 – 6   5 – 6   5

Syllables:	d		r		m		f		s
Numbers:	$\hat{1}$		$\hat{2}$		$\hat{3}$		$\hat{4}$		$\hat{5}$
E♭ major:	i5–6		ii5–6		iii5–6		IV5–6		V

Chapter 22   *Try it 1*

1. (a) The initial progression is: I-V$^{8\text{-}7}$-I
   Bass: *d-s-s-d* / $\hat{1}$-$\hat{5}$-$\hat{5}$-$\hat{1}$

   (b) The chromatic pitch is: *fi* (♯$\hat{4}$)

   (c) The exercise modulates to the key of: V

   (d) The example ends with which progression?
   I-ii$^6_5$-V-I

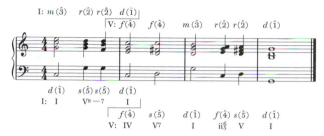

I: m ($\hat{3}$)   r ($\hat{2}$) r ($\hat{2}$)   d ($\hat{1}$) |
　　　　V: f ($\hat{4}$)   f ($\hat{4}$)   m ($\hat{3}$)   r ($\hat{2}$) r ($\hat{2}$)   d ($\hat{1}$)

d ($\hat{1}$)   s ($\hat{5}$) s ($\hat{5}$)   d ($\hat{1}$)
I: I   V$^{8-7}$ I |
　　f ($\hat{4}$)   s ($\hat{5}$)   d ($\hat{1}$)   f ($\hat{4}$) s ($\hat{5}$)   d ($\hat{1}$)
V: IV   V7   I   ii$^6_5$ V   I

2. (a) The initial progression is: i-ii°6-V$^{8\text{-}7}_{6\text{-}5}_{4\text{-}3}$-i
   Bass: *d-f-s-s-d* / $\hat{1}$-$\hat{4}$-$\hat{5}$-$\hat{5}$-$\hat{1}$

   (b) The chromatic pitch is: *te* (♭$\hat{7}$)

   (c) The exercise modulates to the key of: III

   (d) The example ends with which progression?
   I-vi-ii$^6_5$-V$^{8\text{-}7}$-I

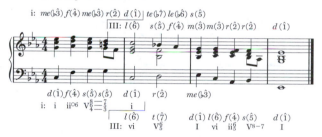

i: me (♭$\hat{3}$) f ($\hat{4}$) me (♭$\hat{3}$) r ($\hat{2}$)   d ($\hat{1}$) | te (♭$\hat{7}$) le (♭$\hat{6}$)   s ($\hat{5}$)
　　　　III: l ($\hat{6}$)   s ($\hat{5}$) f ($\hat{4}$)   m ($\hat{3}$) m ($\hat{3}$) r ($\hat{2}$) r ($\hat{2}$)   d ($\hat{1}$)

d ($\hat{1}$) f ($\hat{4}$)   s ($\hat{5}$) s ($\hat{5}$)   d ($\hat{1}$)   r ($\hat{2}$)   me (♭$\hat{3}$)
i: i   ii°6   V$^{8-7}_{4-3}$ i |
　　　　　　　l ($\hat{6}$)   t ($\hat{7}$)   d ($\hat{1}$) l ($\hat{6}$) f ($\hat{4}$) s ($\hat{5}$)   d ($\hat{1}$)
III: vi   V$^6_5$ I   vi   ii$^6_5$ V$^{8-7}$ I

3. (a) The initial progression is: I-V$^6_5$-I-ii6-V$^{6-5}_{4-3}$-I
   Bass: *d-t-d-f-s-s-d* / $\hat{1}$-$\hat{7}$-$\hat{1}$-$\hat{4}$-$\hat{5}$-$\hat{5}$-$\hat{1}$

   (b) The chromatic pitch is: *si* (♯$\hat{5}$)

   (c) The exercise modulates to the key of: vi

   (d) The example ends with which progression?
   i-V$^6_5$-i-ii°6-V$^{6-5}_{4-3}$-i

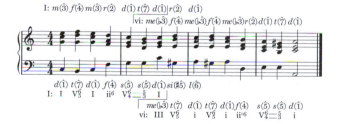

I: m ($\hat{3}$) f ($\hat{4}$) m ($\hat{3}$) r ($\hat{2}$)   d ($\hat{1}$) t ($\hat{7}$) d ($\hat{1}$) | r ($\hat{2}$)   d ($\hat{1}$)
　　　　vi: me (♭$\hat{3}$) f ($\hat{4}$) me (♭$\hat{3}$) f ($\hat{4}$) me (♭$\hat{3}$) r ($\hat{2}$) d ($\hat{1}$) t ($\hat{7}$) d ($\hat{1}$)

d ($\hat{1}$) t ($\hat{7}$)   d ($\hat{1}$) f ($\hat{4}$)   s ($\hat{5}$)   s ($\hat{5}$) d ($\hat{1}$) si (♯$\hat{5}$)   l ($\hat{6}$)
I: I   V$^6_5$ I   ii6   V$^{6-5}_{4-3}$ I |
　　　　me (♭$\hat{3}$) t ($\hat{7}$)   d ($\hat{1}$) t ($\hat{7}$)   d ($\hat{1}$) f ($\hat{4}$)   s ($\hat{5}$) s ($\hat{5}$) d ($\hat{1}$)
vi: III   V$^6_5$ i   V$^6_5$ i   ii°6   V$^{6-5}_{4-3}$ i

4. (a) The initial progression is: I–V$_4^6$–I^6–ii^6–V$_{4-3}^{6-5}$–I
    Soprano: m-r-d . . . / $\hat{3}$-$\hat{2}$-$\hat{1}$

   (b) The chromatic pitch is: te ($\flat\hat{7}$)

   (c) The exercise modulates to the key of: IV

   (d) The example ends with which progression?
    I–V$_3^4$–I^6–ii^6–V$_{4-3}^{8-7}$–I

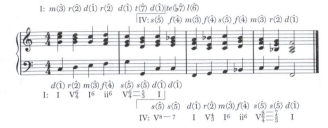

Chapter 22   *Try it 2*

1.   Modulatory contrasting period

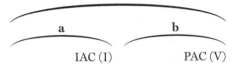

     a   b
   IAC (I)   PAC (V)

2.   Modulatory parallel period

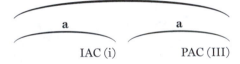

     a   a
   IAC (i)   PAC (III)

Chapter 23   *Try it 1*

1. (a)   Modulatory parallel period

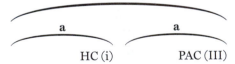

     a   a
   HC (i)   PAC (III)

   (b) The excerpt is section 1 of a binary composition.
    The binary form is: continuous

2. (a) Modulatory contrasting period

     a   b
   IAC (i)   PAC (III)

   (b) Given the answer to (a), the binary form is:
    continuous

   (c)   Contrasting period

     c   d
   PHC (i)   PAC (i)

   (d) At the end, is there a recapitulation? no

   (e) Do the sections end with similar melodies? no

   (f) *Simple continuous binary*

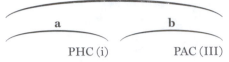

3. (a)   Modulatory contrasting period

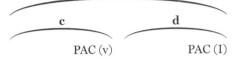

     a   b
   PHC (i)   PAC (III)

   (b) Given the answer to (a), the binary form is:
    continuous

   (c)   Independent phrases

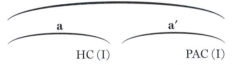

     c   d
   PAC (v)   PAC (I)

   (d) At the end, is there a recapitulation? no

   (e) Do the sections end with similar melodies? no

   (f) *Simple continuous binary*

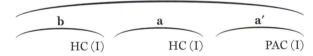

4. (a)   Parallel period

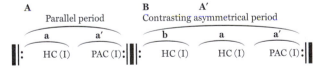

     a   a′
   HC (I)   PAC (I)

   (b) Given the answer to (a), the binary form is:
    sectional

   (c)   Contrasting asymmetrical period

     b   a   a′
  HC (I)   HC (I)   PAC (I)

   (d) At the end, is there a recapitulation? yes

   (e) Do the sections end with similar melodies? yes

   (f) *Sectional rounded binary*

Chapter 23   *Try it 2*

A Section 1 / Minuet
Rounded continuous binary

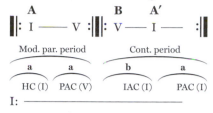

B Section 2 / Trio
Simple sectional binary

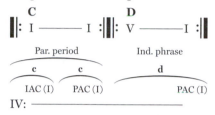

A Section 1 / Minuet
Rounded continuous binary

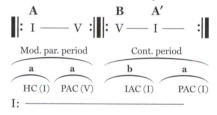

Chapter 24   *Try it 1*

1. (a)

   (b) What key does the motive imply? E minor

2. (a)

   (b) Compared with the original motive, this transformation is an/a: augmentation

   (c) Compared with this transformation, the original motive is an/a: diminution

3. (a)

   (b) Compared with the motive, this transformation is an/a: retrograde

4. (a)

   (b) Compared with the original motive, melodic pitches 1-6 are an/a: retrograde inversion

   (c) In a **major** key, **two**-beat units **descend** by **third** in **3** reps with a(n) **10-10** LIP to create a(n) **descending-third sequence**.

   (d) Compared with the original motive, this transformation ends with which cadence (key)? PAC (III)

5. (a)

   (b) Compared with the original motive, melodic pitches 1-6 are an/a: inversion

   (c) Compared with the original motive, the lower part is based on which transformation? inversion

   (d) The relationship between the upper and lower parts is: stretto (overlap)

   (e) In a **minor** key, **two**-beat units **descend** by **second** in **3.5** reps with a(n) **8-8** LIP to create a(n) **descending-fifth sequence**.

   (f) Compared with the motive, this transformation ends with which cadence (key)? PAC (i)

6. (a)

   (b) In the upper part, beat 2 of the first four measures relates to the motive's: tail

   (c) For several measures, the relationship between the upper and lower parts is: stretto (overlap)

Chapter 24 *Try it 2*

1. (a) The excerpt likely belongs to which of these? Why?
   Invention. Inventions are two-voice works.
   Sinfonias and fugues are three-voice works.

   (b) For the first several measures, which term describes
   the imitation? Why? Canonic. Two-voice music
   suggests an invention. Fugues feature at least three
   parts. The lower part is a copy of the upper, a canon
   at the octave offset by one eighth note.

2. (a) At the beginning, the rhythmic relationship
   between the parts is: syncopation

   (b) Compared with the lower part, the higher part is
   which transformation? inversion

   (c) Compared with the beginning, the excerpt's second
   half is: all of these

   (d) In the upper part, pitch 3 is: *te* ($\flat\hat{7}$)

   (e) Given the response to (d), melodic pitch 3 implies
   which secondary dominant? V7/IV

Chapter 25 *Try it 1*

1. The lament bass

$$d(\hat{1}) \qquad te(\flat\hat{7}) \qquad le(\flat\hat{6}) \qquad s(\hat{5})$$
$$\text{i} \qquad\qquad \text{v}^6 \qquad\qquad \text{iv}^6 \qquad\quad \text{V}$$

2. The chromatic lament

$$d(\hat{1}) \quad t(\hat{7}) \quad te(\flat\hat{7}) \quad l(\hat{6}) \quad le(\flat\hat{6}) \quad s(\hat{5}) \quad le(\flat\hat{6})\, f(\hat{4})\, s(\hat{5})\, d(\hat{1})$$
$$\text{i} \qquad \text{V}^6 \quad\ \text{v}^6 \quad\ \text{IV}^6 \quad\ \text{iv}^6 \quad \text{V} \qquad \text{VI} \ \ \text{ii}^{\circ 6} \ \ \text{V} \quad \text{i}$$

3. Thirds progression

$$d(\hat{1}) \qquad s(\hat{5}) \qquad l(\hat{6}) \qquad m(\hat{3}) \qquad f(\hat{4}) \qquad s(\hat{5})$$
$$\text{I} \qquad\quad \text{V} \qquad\quad \text{vi} \qquad\quad \text{iii} \qquad\quad \text{IV} \qquad\quad \text{V}$$

Chapter 25 *Try it 2*

1. Select the embellishment type(s):
   lower neighbor

2. Select the embellishment type(s):
   appoggiatura

3. Select the embellishment type(s):
   consonant skip

4. Select the embellishment type(s):
   lower neighbor   appoggiatura
   consonant skip   passing tone

Chapter 26 *Try it*

Chapter 27 *Try it 1*

1. (a) *Chord 1 is* i
The PD chord is:	ii$^{\circ 6}$
vii$^{\circ}$7/V is:	played
The cadence is:	V$^{6-5}_{4-3}$
The soprano begins on:	*do* ($\hat{1}$)

   (b) *Chord 1 is* i
The PD chord is:	iv
vii$^{\circ}$7/V is:	played
The cadence is:	V
The soprano begins on:	*do* ($\hat{1}$)

   (c) *Chord 1 is* i
The PD chord is:	N^6
vii$^{\circ}$7/V is:	played
The cadence is:	V$^{6-5}_{4-3}$
The soprano begins on:	*do* ($\hat{1}$)

   (d) *Chord 1 is* i
The PD chord is:	N^6
vii$^{\circ}$7/V is:	played
The cadence is:	V
The soprano begins on:	*me* ($\flat\hat{3}$)

   (e) *Chord 1 is* i
The PD chord is:	N^6
vii$^{\circ}$7/V is:	not played
The cadence is:	V$^{6-5}_{4-3}$
The soprano begins on:	*do* ($\hat{1}$)

Chapter 27 Try it 2

1. (a) *Chord 1 is* i

    The PD chord is: iv^6

    The cadence is: V$^{6-5}_{4-3}$

    The soprano begins on: *sol* ($\hat{5}$)

(b) *Chord 1 is* i

    The PD chord is: It^{+6}

    The cadence is: V$^{6-5}_{4-3}$

    The soprano begins on: *sol* ($\hat{5}$)

(c) *Chord 1 is* i

    The PD chord is: Gr^{+6}

    The cadence is: V

    The soprano begins on: *sol* ($\hat{5}$)

(d) *Chord 1 is* i

    The PD chord is: Fr^{+6}

    The cadence is: V

    The soprano begins on: *sol* ($\hat{5}$)

(e) *Chord 1 is* i

    The PD chord is: Fr^{+6}

    The cadence is: V$^{6-5}_{4-3}$

    The soprano begins on: *do* ($\hat{1}$)

(f) *Chord 1 is* i

    The PD chord is: Fr^{+6}

    The cadence is: V

    The soprano begins on: *me* ($\flat\hat{3}$)

Chapter 28 Try it 1

1. Beginning on I, 2-chord units descend by 2nd in 3.5 reps with a 10-8 LIP and modulate to V.

2. Beginning on I, 2-chord units descend by 3rd in 3.5 reps with a 10-5 LIP.

3. Beginning on I, 2-chord units descend by 2nd in 3.5 reps with a 10-6(-5) LIP and modulate to V. [Beats 2 and 4 are passing tones but can figure in the LIP.]

4. Beginning on i with a 5-6 technique, 2-chord units descend chromatically by 2nd in 2 reps with a 7-6 LIP. You may also say "series of 7-6 suspensions" and identify the cadence as chromaticized Phrygian (A6-V).

5. Beginning on I, 2-chord units ascend by 2nd in 5.5 reps with a 5-6 LIP and modulate to vi.

Chapter 28 Try it 2

	m. 1	m. 2	m. 3	m. 4	m. 5	m. 6	m. 7	m. 8
CT:	°7	A6	A6		°7		°7	A6
Chord:	I				IV		I	

	m. 9	m. 10	m. 11	m. 12	m. 13	m. 14	m. 15	m. 16
CT:	°7		A6		°7		°7	
Chord:	V		I		V/V		V	

Chapter 29 Try it

Chapter 30 *Try it*

1.

2.

3.

4.

5.

Chapter 31 *Try it*

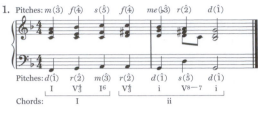

1.

2.

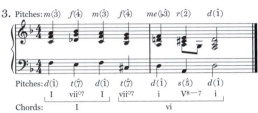

3.

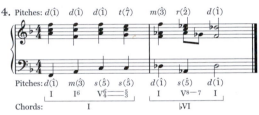

4.

5.

Chapter 32 *Try it 1*

1. Chords: C   Am7   Dm7   G7

2. Chords: C   Eb°7   Dm7   G7

3. Chords: Cmaj7   Dm7   D#°7   Em7

4. Chords: Cmaj7   Bø7   E7   Am7

Chapter 32 *Try it 2*

1. (a)

(b)

2. (a)

(b)

(c)

(d)

(e)

(f)

Chapter 33 *Try it*

1. (a) The beginning is derived from which sequence?
descending fifth

(b) The underlying rhythmic grouping is:
3 + 3 + 2

(c)

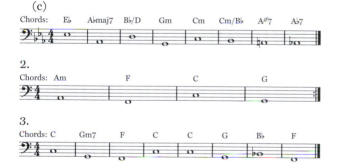

2.

3.

Chapter 34 *Try it*

1. (a) minor   (b) whole-tone   (c) major
   (d) harmonic   (e) Phrygian

2. (a) minor pentatonic   (b) major pentatonic
   (c) major pentatonic

3. (a) Lydian   (b) Phrygian   (c) Dorian
   (d) Mixolydian   (e) Aeolian   (f) Ionian

Chapter 35 *Try it 1*

1.

2.

3. (a) normal order {3 4 7 9}; prime form [0 1 4 6];
   Forte SC 4-Z15; ic vector [111111]

(b) normal order {9 e 0 2}; prime form [0 2 3 5];
   Forte SC 4-10; ic vector [122010]

(c) normal order {e 0 2 3}; prime form [0 1 3 4];
   Forte SC 4-3; ic vector [212100]

(d) normal order {3 4 7 e}; prime form [0 1 4 8];
   Forte SC 4-19; ic vector [101310]

(e) normal order {8 t 0 2}; prime form [0 2 4 6];
   Forte SC 4-21; ic vector [030201]

4. (a) normal order {e 1 2 5 7}; prime form [0 2 3 6 8];
   Forte SC 5-28; ic vector [122212]

(b) normal order {6 8 t 1 3}; prime form [0 2 4 7 9];
   Forte SC 5-35; ic vector [032140]

(c) normal order {2 3 8 9}; prime form [0 1 6 7];
   Forte SC 4-9; ic vector [200022] normal order
   {8 9 2 3}

(d) normal order {9 t 0 1 4 5}; prime form [0 1 3 4 7 8];
Forte SC 6-Z19; ic vector [313431]

(e) normal order {0 1 4 6 7}; prime form [0 1 3 6 7];
Forte SC 5-19; ic vector [212122]

Chapter 35 *Try it 2*

1. Assume the initial note value to be an eighth. The
opening meter signature is: $\frac{5}{8}$

2. Within each measure, how do the beats group
(2 + 3, 2 + 3 + 2, 3 + 2 + 2 + 2, etc.)? 2 + 3

3. The intro repeats which four-pitch pattern?
C-F-C-E♭

4. Focus only on the drums. Assume the initial drum
value to be a quarter note. The drums group in
measures of how many beats? 2

5.
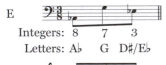

Chapter 36 *Try it*

1.

Set	Notation	Normal order and ic vector
A	 Integers: 7 8 e Letters: G G♯/A♭ B	normal order {78e} ic vector [101100]
B	Integers: e 3 0 Letters: B D♯/E♭ C	normal order {e03} ic vector [101100]
C	Integers: 1 2 7 Letters: C♯ D G	normal order {127} ic vector [100011]
D	Integers: t 9 4 Letters: B♭ A E	normal order {49t} ic vector [100011]
E	Integers: 8 7 3 Letters: A♭ G D♯/E♭	normal order {378} ic vector [100110]
F	Integers: 6 t 5 Letters: G♭ B♭/A♯ F	normal order {56t} ic vector [100110]

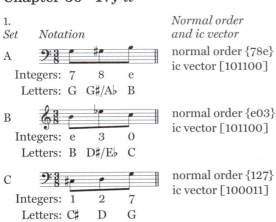

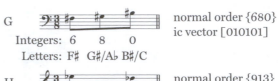

G	Integers: 6 8 0 Letters: F♯ G♯/A♭ B♯/C	normal order {680} ic vector [010101]
H	Integers: 3 9 1 Letters: E♭ A D♭/C♯	normal order {913} ic vector [010101]

2. (a) B = T₄A

B {e03} Place the elements of set B in
normal order.

− A {78e} From B, subtract A's elements in
normal order.

T = 444 T, the number of semitones of
transposition, is revealed by
subtracting the elements.

(b) D = T_eI C Also acceptable D = T₁₁I C

D {49t} Place the elements of set D in
ascending normal order.

+ C {721} Place the elements of set C in
descending normal order.

T = eee The index number is revealed by
adding the elements.

(c) F = T₁I

F {56t} Place the elements of set F in
ascending normal order.

+ E {873} Place the elements of set E in
descending normal order.

T = 111 The index number is revealed by
adding the elements.

(d) H = T₉I G

H {913} Place the elements of set H in
ascending normal order.

+ G {086} Place the elements of set G in
descending normal order.

T = 999 The index number is revealed by
adding the elements.

Chapter 37 *Try it*

1. (a)

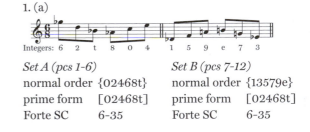

Integers: 6 2 t 8 0 4   1 5 9 e 7 3

Set A (pcs 1–6)	Set B (pcs 7–12)
normal order {02468t}	normal order {13579e}
prime form [02468t]	prime form [02468t]
Forte SC 6-35	Forte SC 6-35

(b) **B = T₁A** Because the sets are whole tone, t3, t5,
                  t7, t9, and te are also correct.

      B {13579e} Place the elements of set B in
                       normal order.

  – A {02468t} From B, subtract A's elements in
                       normal order.

  t = 111111 t in semitones is revealed by
                       subtracting the elements.

B = TₑI A Because the sets are whole tone, t9I,
                  t7I, etc., are also correct.

      B {13579e} Place the elements of set B in
                       ascending normal order.

  + A {t86420} Place the elements of set A in
                       descending normal order.

  t = eeeee The index number is revealed by
                       adding the elements.

(c) Sets A and B complete the aggregate, thus are
    literal complements. Each is also a "mode of limited
    transposition."

2. (a)

Integers: 9 7 0 t   3 1 6 4   5 2 8 e

Set C (pcs 1-4)	*Set D (pcs 5-8)*
normal order {79t0}	normal order {1346}
prime form [0235]	prime form [0235]
Forte SC 4-10	Forte SC 4-10

Set E (pcs 1-8)	*Set F (pcs 9-12)*
normal order {0134679t}	normal order {258e}
prime form [0134679t]	prime form [0369]
Forte SC 8-28	Forte SC 4-28

(b) **D = t₆C**

    D {1346} Place the elements of set D in
                  normal order.

  – C {79t0} From D, subtract C's elements in
                  normal order.

  t = 6666 t in semitones is revealed by
                  subtracting the elements.

D = t₁I C

    D {1346} Place the elements of set D in
                  ascending normal order.

  + C {0t97} Place the elements of set C in
                  descending normal order.

  t = 1111 The index number is revealed by
                  adding the elements.

(c) The pcs of set E complete which scale? octatonic

(d) Sets E and F complete the aggregate, and thus are
    literal complements.

Chapter 38 *Try it 1*

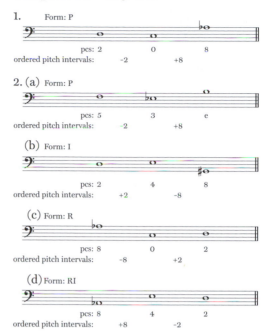

1.   Form: P
      pcs: 2   0   8
  ordered pitch intervals: –2   +8

2. (a) Form: P
      pcs: 5   3   e
  ordered pitch intervals: –2   +8

  (b) Form: I
      pcs: 2   4   8
  ordered pitch intervals: +2   –8

  (c) Form: R
      pcs: 8   0   2
  ordered pitch intervals: –8   +2

  (d) Form: RI
      pcs: 8   4   2
  ordered pitch intervals: +8   –2

Chapter 38 *Try it 2*

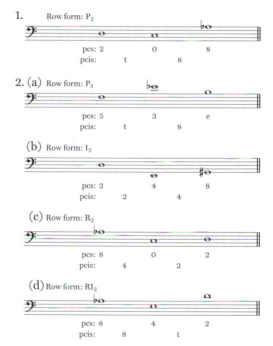

1.   Row form: P₂
      pcs: 2   0   8
      pcis: t   8

2. (a) Row form: P₅
      pcs: 5   3   e
      pcis: t   8

  (b) Row form: I₂
      pcs: 2   4   8
      pcis: 2   4

  (c) Row form: R₂
      pcs: 8   0   2
      pcis: 4   2

  (d) Row form: RI₂
      pcs: 8   4   2
      pcis: 8   t

Chapter 39 *Try it*

1. (a) (1) Begin with the given item and write the lead-
         sheet chords for unique bass pitches 1-3.
         F♯maj   Gmaj7   Amaj⁽ᵃᵈᵈ⁶⁾

      (2) The looped progression most resembles which
         traditional resolution?   Phrygian

  (b) Answers will vary. Discuss the merits of each.
      Try to group patterns and conduct.

(c) (1)

(2) The pattern is non-retrogradable (a palindrome) and resembles the *talea* of an isorhythm.

(3) Pyramids are balanced structures with symmetrical sides. The rhythm pattern is symmetrical around the "axis" of the tied quarter notes; the chord loop is made up of four chords, matching the four sides of a pyramid with a square base.

2. (a)

(b) After the motive's first entrance, it is (circle all that apply):   repeated / doubled

(c) After the second entrance, the motive is (circle all that apply):   repeated / imitated canonically

(d) Each new entrance follows the motive in canon one beat later. While the motive remains constant, with each repetition other entrances drift by one more beat until the motive sounds in all instruments on every beat. This "drifting" may be viewed as one type of phasing. The original motive is the *talea* of an isorhythm, repeating throughout in the same instrument.

3. (a) Changing meter, $\frac{6}{8}$ + $\frac{3}{4}$, or a single meter, either $\frac{6}{8}$ or $\frac{3}{4}$, with accents used to obscure the meter.

(b) Cmaj Fmaj7 Cmaj G7 Cmin Dmaj D♭maj/F Cmaj

Chapter 40   *Try it*

1. Answers will vary. Share one example from each pair with the entire class and discuss.

2. Answers will vary. Share one example from each pair with the entire class and discuss.

Set-Class Table

NAME	PCS	IC VECTOR		NAME	PCS	IC VECTOR
3-1(12)	0,1,2	210000		9-1	0,1,2,3,4,5,6,7,8	876663
3-2	0,1,3	111000		9-2	0,1,2,3,4,5,6,7,9	777663
3-3	0,1,4	101100		9-3	0,1,2,3,4,5,6,8,9	767763
3-4	0,1,5	100110		9-4	0,1,2,3,4,5,7,8,9	766773
3-5	0,1,6	100011		9-5	0,1,2,3,4,6,7,8,9	766674
3-6(12)	0,2,4	020100		9-6	0,1,2,3,4,5,6,8,t	686763
3-7	0,2,5	011010		9-7	0,1,2,3,4,5,7,8,t	677673
3-8	0,2,6	010101		9-8	0,1,2,3,4,6,7,8,t	676764
3-9(12)	0,2,7	010020		9-9	0,1,2,3,5,6,7,8,t	676683
3-10(12)	0,3,6	002001		9-10	0,1,2,3,4,6,7,9,t	668664
3-11	0,3,7	001110		9-11	0,1,2,3,5,6,7,9,t	667773
3-12(4)	0,4,8	000300		9-12	0,1,2,4,5,6,8,9,t	666963
4-1(12)	0,1,2,3	321000		8-1	0,1,2,3,4,5,6,7	765442
4-2	0,1,2,4	221100		8-2	0,1,2,3,4,5,6,8	665542
4-3(12)	0,1,3,4	212100		8-3	0,1,2,3,4,5,6,9	656542
4-4	0,1,2,5	211110		8-4	0,1,2,3,4,5,7,8	655552
4-5	01,2,6	210111		8-5	0,1,2,3,4,6,7,8	654553
4-6(12)	0,1,2,7	210021		8-6	0,1,2,3,5,6,7,8	654463
4-7(12)	0,1,4,5	201210		8-7	0,1,2,3,4,5,8,9	645652
4-8(12)	0,1,5,6	200121		8-8	0,1,2,3,4,7,8,9	644563
4-9(6)	0,1,6,7	200022		8-9	0,1,2,3,6,7,8,9	644464
4-10(12)	0,2,3,5	122010		8-10	0,2,3,4,5,6,7,9	566452
4-11	0,1,3,5	121110		8-11	0,1,2,3,4,5,7,9	565552
4-12	0,2,3,6	112101		8-12	0,1,3,4,5,6,7,9	556543
4-13	0,1,3,6	112011		8-13	0,1,2,3,4,6,7,9	556453
4-14	0,2,3,7	111120		8-14	0,1,2,4,5,6,7,9	555562
4-Z15	0,1,4,6	111111		8-Z15	0,1,2,3,4,6,8,9	555553
4-16	0,1,5,7	110121		8-16	0,1,2,3,5,7,8,9	554563
4-17(12)	0,3,4,7	102210		8-17	0,1,3,4,5,6,8,9	546652
4-18	0,1,4,7	102111		8-18	0,1,2,3,5,6,8,9	546553
4-19	0,1,4,8	101310		8-19	0,1,2,4,5,6,8,9	545752
4-20(12)	0,1,5,8	101220		8-20	0,1,2,4,5,7,8,9	545662
4-21(12)	0,2,4,6	030201		8-21	0,1,2,3,4,6,8,t	474643
4-22	0,2,4,7	021120		8-22	0,1,2,3,5,6,8,t	465562
4-23(12)	0,2,5,7	021030		8-23	0,1,2,3,5,7,8,t	465472
4-24(12)	0,2,4,8	020301		8-24	0,1,2,4,5,6,8,t	464743
4-25(6)	0,2,6,8	020202		8-25	0,1,2,4,6,7,8,t	464644
4-26(12)	0,3,5,8	012120		8-26	0,1,2,4,5,7,9,t	456562

NOTE: Numbers in parentheses show the number of distinct sets in the set class if other than 24.
All brackets are eliminated here for ease of reading.

NAME	PCS	IC VECTOR		NAME	PCS	IC VECTOR
4-27	0,2,5,8	012111		8-27	0,1,2,4,5,7,8,t	456553
4-28(3)	0,3,6,9	004002		8-28	0,1,3,4,6,7,9,t	448444
4-Z29	0,1,3,7	111111		8-Z29	0,1,2,3,5,6,7,9	555553
5-1(12)	0,1,2,3,4	432100		7-1	0,1,2,3,4,5,6	654321
5-2	0,1,2,3,5	332110		7-2	0,1,2,3,4,5,7	554331
5-3	0,1,2,4,5	322210		7-3	0,1,2,3,4,5,8	544431
5-4	0,1,2,3,6	322111		7-4	0,1,2,3,4,6,7	544332
5-5	0,1,2,3,7	321121		7-5	0,1,2,3,5,6,7	543342
5-6	0,1,2,5,6	311221		7-6	0,1,2,3,4,7,8	533442
5-7	0,1,2,6,7	310132		7-7	0,1,2,3,6,7,8	532353
5-8(12)	0,2,3,4,6	232201		7-8	0,2,3,4,5,6,8	454422
5-9	0,1,2,4,6	231211		7-9	0,1,2,3,4,6,8	453432
5-10	0,1,3,4,6	223111		7-10	0,1,2,3,4,6,9	445332
5-11	0,2,3,4,7	222220		7-11	0,1,3,4,5,6,8	444441
5-Z12(12)	0,1,3,5,6	222121		7-Z12	0,1,2,3,4,7,9	444342
5-13	0,1,2,4,8	221311		7-13	0,1,2,4,5,6,8	443532
5-14	0,1,2,5,7	221131		7-14	0,1,2,3,5,7,8	443352
5-15(12)	0,1,2,6,8	220222		7-15	0,1,2,4,6,7,8	442443
5-16	0,1,3,4,7	213211		7-16	0,1,2,3,5,6,9	435432
5-Z17(12)	0,1,3,4,8	212320		7-Z17	0,1,2,4,5,6,9	434541
5-Z18	0,1,4,5,7	212221		7-Z18	0,1,2,3,5,8,9	434442
5-19	0,1,3,6,7	212122		7-19	0,1,2,3,6,7,9	434343
5-20	0,1,3,7,8	211231		7-20	0,1,2,4,7,8,9	433452
5-21	0,1,4,5,8	202420		7-21	0,1,2,4,5,8,9	424641
5-22(12)	0,1,4,7,8	202321		7-22	0,1,2,5,6,8,9	424542
5-23	0,2,3,5,7	132130		7-23	0,2,3,4,5,7,9	354351
5-24	0,1,3,5,7	131221		7-24	0,1,2,3,5,7,9	353442
5-25	0,2,3,5,8	123121		7-25	0,2,3,4,6,7,9	345342
5-26	0,2,4,5,8	122311		7-26	0,1,3,4,5,7,9	344532
5-27	0,1,3,5,8	122230		7-27	0,1,2,4,5,7,9	344451
5-28	0,2,3,6,8	122212		7-28	0,1,3,5,6,7,9	344433
5-29	0,1,3,6,8	122131		7-29	0,1,2,4,6,7,9	344352
5-30	0,1,4,6,8	121321		7-30	0,1,2,4,6,8,9	343542
5-31	0,1,3,6,9	114112		7-31	0,1,3,4,6,7,9	336333
5-32	0,1,4,6,9	113221		7-32	0,1,3,4,6,8,9	335442
5-33(12)	0,2,4,6,8	040402		7-33	0,1,2,4,6,8,t	262623
5-34(12)	0,2,4,6,9	032221		7-34	0,1,3,4,6,8,t	254442
5-35(12)	0,2,4,7,9	032140		7-35	0,1,3,5,6,8,t	254361
5-Z36	0,1,2,4,7	222121		7-Z36	0,1,2,3,5,6,8	444342
5-Z37(12)	0,3,4,5,8	212320		7-Z37	0,1,3,4,5,7,8	434541
5-Z38	0,1,2,5,8	212221		7-Z38	0,1,2,4,5,7,8	434442
6-1(12)	0,1,2,3,4,5	543210				
6-2	0,1,2,3,4,6	443211				
6-Z3	0,1,2,3,5,6	433221				
6-Z4(12)	0,1,2,4,5,6	432321				
6-5	0,1,2,3,6,7	422232		6-Z36	0,1,2,3,4,7	*
6-Z6(12)	0,1,2,5,6,7	421242		6-Z37(12)	0,1,2,3,4,8	
6-7(6)	0,1,2,6,7,8	420243				
6-8(12)	0,2,3,4,5,7	343230		6-Z38(12)	0,1,2,3,7,8	
6-9	0,1,2,3,5,7	342231				
6-Z10	0,1,3,4,5,7	333321		6-Z39	0,2,3,4,5,8	
6-Z11	0,1,2,4,5,7	333231		6-Z40	0,1,2,3,5,8	

*Z-related hexachords share the same ic vector; use vector in the third column

NAME	PCS	IC VECTOR		NAME	PCS	IC VECTOR
6-Z12	0,1,2,4,6,7	332232		6-Z41	0,1,2,3,6,8	
6-Z13(12)	0,1,3,4,6,7	324222		6-Z42(12)	0,1,2,3,6,9	
6-14	0,1,3,4,5,8	323430				
6-15	0,1,2,4,5,8	323421				
6-16	0,1,4,5,6,8	322431				
6-Z17	0,1,2,4,7,8	322332		6-Z43	0,1,2,5,6,8	
6-18	0,1,2,5,7,8	322242				
6-Z19	0,1,3,4,7,8	313431		6-Z44	0,1,2,5,6,9	
6-20(4)	0,1,4,5,8,9	303630				
6-21	0,2,3,4,6,8	242412				
6-22	0,1,2,4,6,8	241422				
6-Z23(12)	0,2,3,5,6,8	234222		6-Z45(12)	0,2,3,4,6,9	
6-Z24	0,1,3,4,6,8	233331		6-Z46	0,1,2,4,6,9	
6-Z25	0,1,3,5,6,8	233241		6-Z47	0,1,2,4,7,9	
6-Z26(12)	0,1,3,5,7,8	232341		6-Z48(12)	0,1,2,5,7,9	
6-27	0,1,3,4,6,9	225222				
6-Z28(12)	0,1,3,5,6,9	224322		6-Z49(12)	0,1,3,4,7,9	
6-Z29(12)	0,1,3,6,8,9	224232		6-Z50(12)	0,1,4,6,7,9	
6-30(12)	0,1,3,6,7,9	224223				
6-31	0,1,3,5,8,9	223431				
6-32(12)	0,2,4,5,7,9	143250				
6-33	0,2,3,5,7,9	143241				
6-34	0,1,3,5,7,9	142422				
6-35(2)	0,2,4,6,8,t	060603				

SOURCE: Allen Forte, *The Structure of Atonal Music* (New Haven: Yale University Press, 1973) (adapted)